CHANGING SUBURBS:
Foundation, Form and Function

STUDIES IN HISTORY, PLANNING AND THE ENVIRONMENT
Series editor   Professor Anthony Sutcliffe

CHANGING SUBURBS:

Foundation, Form and Function

edited by
RICHARD HARRIS and
PETER J. LARKHAM

First published 1999 by E & FN Spon,
11 New Fetter Lane,
London EC4P 4EE

Simultaneously published in the USA and Canada
by Routledge
29 West 35th Street, New York, NY 10001

E & FN Spon is an imprint of the Taylor & Francis Group

© 1999 Selection and editorial matter: Richard Harris and
Peter Larkham; individual chapters, the contributors

Typeset in Times by Keystroke, Jacaranda Lodge, Wolverhampton
Printed and bound in Great Britain by Biddles Ltd, Guildford and King's Lynn

This book was commissioned and edited by Alexandrine Press, Oxford

British Library Cataloguing in Publication Data
A catalogue record for this book is available from the British Library

Library of Congress Cataloging in Publication Data
Changing suburbs : foundation, form and function / edited by Richard
    Harris and Peter Larkham.
        p.   cm. — (Studies in history, planning, and the environment)
    Includes bibliographical references and index.
    1. Suburbs—History—19th century. 2. Suburbs—History—20th
century. I. Harris, Richard, 1952– . II. Larkham, P. J. (Peter
J.), 1960 . III. Series.
HT351.C48   1999
307.74—dc21   99-12105
                                                                          CIP

ISBN 0–419–22050–X

Contents

Part one: early twentieth-century suburbs

Part two: later twentieth-century suburbs

The Contributors

David Ames is Professor of Urban Affairs and Public Policy and Geography, and Director of the Center for Historic Architecture and Design at the University of Delaware, USA. He has written widely on historic preservation and planning topics.

Christine M.H. Carr worked as a Research Associate at the University of Birmingham on a Leverhulme Trust funded research project on inter-war suburbs, and based her PhD thesis on related research. She is currently working as a Research Assistant at the Institute of Urban Planning, University of Nottingham, UK.

Tony Dingle is an Associate Professor of Economic History in the Faculty of Business and Economics at Monash University, Australia. His interests are in post-war suburbia, and especially housing; and he has recently edited *The Cream Brick Frontier: Histories of Australian Suburbia*.

Isabel Dyck is an Associate Professor in the School of Rehabilitation Sciences, University of British Columbia, Canada. She is a social and feminist geographer and has written on women's domestic labour in Canadian contemporary suburbs, geographies of disability, and qualitative methodology.

Kim England is Associate Professor in the Department of Geography and Programme in Planning at the University of Toronto, Canada. Her research interests include local labour markets and women's paid employment; geographies of families, child care and working mothers; and urban spaces and social identities.

Richard Harris is Professor of Geography at McMaster University, Hamilton, Ontario, Canada. He has published chiefly on the subjects of residential segregation, home ownership, owner-building and suburban development, especially on the first half of this century. He is currently the editor of the *Urban History Review*, and his most recent book is *Unplanned Suburbs: Toronto's American Tragedy, 1900–1950*.

Louise Johnson is a feminist geographer and Associate Professor, presently heading the School of Contemporary Art at Deakin University, Australia. She has researched and published widely on gendered spaces, especially workplaces (manufacturing and service), regional shopping centres, houses and neighbourhoods. Her most recent work is on the colonial and gender relations of Australian domestic gardens, postmodern and postcolonial Australian cities, and *Placebound*, an undergraduate feminist geography textbook.

Andrew Jonas is Lecturer in Geography at the University of Hull, UK and Adjunct Professor at the University of California, Riverside, USA. He is interested in urban politics, local environmental policy and the politics of geographic scale. Most of his research is based in the USA and he has just completed a two-year project on habitat conservation planning and suburban development in Southern California. He is co-editing a book on *The Urban Growth Machine: Critical Perspectives Two Years Later*.

Peter J. Larkham is Reader in Planning and Conservation in the Birmingham School of Planning, University of Central England, UK. He has written widely on urban form, planning and conservation; he edits the International Planning History Society's journal *Planning History*. His most recent book is *Conservation and the City*.

Robert Lewis is an Assistant Professor in the Department of Geography and Programme in Planning, University of Toronto, Canada. He has written on the social and economic geography of North American cities. His most recent work is on the manufacturing districts of Montréal, 1850–1920, and he is preparing a book on the industrial suburbs of Chicago between 1880 and 1950.

Larry McCann teaches courses in urban geography and the development of planning thought at the University of Victoria, Australia. He is associated with the Canadian Families Project and is currently researching the links between town planning, families, and the shaping of the suburban landscape in early twentieth-century Canadian cities.

Peter Newby's research interests focus on the creation and consumption of culture. His experience is rooted in urban geography and urban conservation. His work increasingly encompasses leisure shopping, and retailing and tourism. His collaboration with Mark Turner in this volume is an attempt to build a link between historical and cultural analytic perspectives on consumption. He is Head of the Centre for Higher Education Research at Middlesex University, UK.

Veronica Strong-Boag is Professor of Women's Studies and Educational Studies at the University of British Columbia, Canada. Specializing in the history of Canadian women, she has published many books and articles, including *The New Day Recalled: Lives of Girls and Women in English Canada, 1919–39* (1988), which won the Canadian Historical Association for the best book in Canadian history that year.

Richard Turkington is Director of Research in the School of Housing, University of Central England, UK. An urban sociologist, he has a particular interest in the social history of housing and town planning. He recently co-authored, with Alison Ravetz, *The Place of Home: English Domestic Environments 1919–2000*.

Mark Turner is Curator of the Silver Studio at Middlesex University, UK. He has an international reputation in the field of wall paper design and has mounted exhibitions based on the Silver Studio collection in the UK, USA and Australia. Most recently he has been concerned with developing the Silver Studio as the basis for a museum for domestic design at Middlesex University, UK.

J.W.R. Whitehand is Professor at the School of Geography and Environmental Sciences, University of Birmingham, UK. His previous publications include *The Changing Face of Cities* and *The Making of the Urban Landscape*. He is a former Editor of *Area* and is currently Editor of *Urban Morphology*.

Preface

The Preface has, traditionally, been the place where the author provides a personal context to his or her work. Lately, it has become fashionable to introduce such elements into the text itself, as a way of making explicit the author's own biases or, in the current jargon, 'positionalities'. To retain their more personal character, prefaces have then become increasingly confessional – one example being the preface to a recent collection on suburbs (Silverstone, 1997). Taken too far, this practice ceases to add anything useful to the reader's appreciation of the text, and becomes mere display. Readers need to know something about authors, but only in so far as it adds to their understanding of the text before them.

We are both children of English suburbs, and in different ways this has shaped our interest in, and perspective on, the subject. In this context, we offer the following comments on how each of us came to be interested in suburbs and, more particularly, on how we came to assemble the papers that are published here.

Peter Larkham writes

> I have a long-standing interest in urban form, and suburban form has become a focus of concern for we urban morphologists only very recently (cf Whitehand and Carr, this volume, reporting a project which I helped to set up but did not participate in because of a career change). But some of this interest was spurred from youth; from the location and histories of my parents' and grandparents' houses. My paternal grandparents lived in a standard speculative semi from its construction in 1937 until the early 1990s. It was built on a spoil heap of a local colliery, which had closed: the garden soil was poor and stony, and the house raised from the street. The chimney was crooked and had been from construction, but (until the house was sold) no one minded. My parents bought a new version of the semi, differing largely in its integral garage, on a new estate in the late 1950s. Here was a sense of new community, newly-married couples starting new families. We were at the very edge of the town, with the administrative boundary running along our back fence, and rough fields beyond (in which we children spent much time). And this estate – as its name showed – was built on the 'park farm' of a large Georgian estate, the house surviving as a hotel. So, for me, the suburbs did mean the edge of town – but also community, with others of my age; history, with the evidence of the previous landscape; and familiarity, with my grandparents' house.
>
> Searching for a way to express these ideas – what Hayden (1995) memorably calls 'the power of place', but which is more the 'sense of place' – led me to historical geography, urban geography, and finally urban morphology. It is in this academic sub-discipline that I have freedom to bring together ideas of history, form, culture, production, consumption and so on. And, perhaps inevitably, I have returned to my suburban roots – living now in a 1937 semi, close to the country's first conservation area of such houses, and only a few yards away from a row of listed post-war prefabs.

Richard Harris writes

> I have a love-hate relationship with the suburbs. I grew up in a post-war middle-class suburb of Birmingham which, from my teens onwards, I rejected. Like many others of my generation, I reacted against the newness, and the apparent sameness, of the streets; the social conservatism; and, although I was conscious of the fact at the time, I reacted against them as a way of defining my own journey into adulthood, simply because they were there. And so it was that, after emigrating to Canada, marrying, and eventually being in a position to buy a house, I was certain that I did not want to settle in the 'burbs. I was in for a surprise.
>
> In 1984 my wife and I bought a house in Toronto. At the time, I was teaching at one of the suburban campuses of the University of Toronto but, since we did not yet have children, we both wanted to live downtown, within walking distance of libraries, cheap ethnic restaurants, and other amenities of the big city. On a limited budget, we bought a nineteenth-century, gabled, semi-detached house on a 17-foot lot in an immigrant area. We had been reassured by signs of incipient gentrification and, in time, became inured to gridlock on the major streets that bounded our block. Then one day I received a call from a BBC reporter, fresh from London. She had been assigned to prepare a radio documentary on expatriate Brits who had settled in Canada. A mutual friend had given her my name. Could she stop by with a tape recorder? We agreed on a time, and in due course she arrived on the doorstep. I showed her into the front room. After some pleasantries and a sound test, she flicked a switch and asked brightly 'well, and how does it feel to be in the suburbs?'. I was dumbfounded. The suburbs? I thought I had escaped them! The interviewer's question – and my visceral response – taught me as much about the difficulties of defining 'suburbs' as all the texts I had ever read (and that was quite a lot). It struck me that although historical developments over the previous century had extended the urban fringe many miles outwards, the dwelling in which the interview was taking place itself was largely unaltered. The interviewer had instinctively recognized that we were sitting in what was still, recognizably, a front parlour. And as I began to grope for a reply – and prayed that a recording engineer at Broadcasting House would edit away the signs of my confusion – I also recalled that, to a Londoner, anything with grass in the front, albeit 6 feet square, might qualify as suburban. To a North American, however, even an immigrant like myself, the term meant something else entirely, certainly something more spacious. I had learned, once and for all, that 'suburb' is a slippery term, one that is bounded by history and by culture. My interest in the comparative historical development of suburbs does not date from that moment, but my understanding of the topic – and to some extent of myself – did take a leap forward.

With these personal backgrounds and motivation, we organized two special sessions on suburban development at the annual conference of the (then) Institute of British Geographers in 1995, with the support of the Urban Geography Study Group. To the participants at that conference, some of whom are represented in these pages, we are grateful for discussion and ideas. We invited some presenters from the original conference, and a range of others to help fashion a collection of essays which would examine the twentieth-century suburban experience of Britain and of three ex-British, white settler, colonies: Australia, the United States and Canada. We are grateful to those who responded, and to those who have assisted and offered comments at various stages in the preparation of this manuscript. Richard Harris would like to thank the Australian National University, and especially Pat Troy, for providing an opportunity to undertake research in Australia in 1997, thereby adding an Australian perspective on past experiences in Britain, the United States and Canada. Peter Larkham acknowledges continued support from the School of Planning and Faculty of the Built Environment at the University of Central England, and from colleagues in the Urban Morphology Research Group. Both editors wish to acknowledge the patience and support of Ann Rudkin of Alexandrine Press throughout the development of this volume.

REFERENCES

Hayden, D. (1995) *The Power of Place: Urban Landscapes and Public History.* Cambridge, Mass: MIT Press.
Silverstone, R. (1997) Preface and acknowledgments, in Silverstone, R. (ed.) *Visions of Suburbia.* London: Routledge

CHAPTER I

Suburban Foundation, Form and Function

Richard Harris and Peter J. Larkham

INTRODUCTION

Polymorphous, like the cities of which they are a part, suburbs have offered almost everyone something to praise or, more usually, condemn. Suburbia – a term which, like many suburbs, has not aged well – has attracted attention from a very wide range of people. It has been treated as fair game by urban geographers and historians, by sociologists and political scientists, by makers of documentaries as well as writers of fiction. The result has been a minor academic and popular industry, to the extent that one writer began a review with 'Not another book on suburbs' (Gaskell, 1995)!

Suburbs are important enough for people routinely write books to clear up the myths and misconceptions that previous writers have purveyed (e.g. Wrong, 1967). Over two decades ago Masotti (1973, p. 21) pointed out that 'much of the research and analysis of the sixties, especially the work of Herbert Gans (1959, 1972) and Bennett Berger (1960, 1961) can be interpreted as counter-myth; it served to untangle the web of mythology spun by the social critics of the postwar period'. The work of revision and clarification has continued to this day. For example, one of the present authors has recently offered a reinterpretation of the geography of North American cities and suburbs in the first half of this century (Harris and Lewis, 2000).

Two of the most pervasive, and influential, myths about suburbs are that they are a recent phenomenon and that they take the same form everywhere. Few people appreciate that suburbs have been around for a very long time. In Britain, the inter-war suburbs are often viewed as both definitive and formative. In the United States, there is a popular perception that suburban development is essentially a post-war phenomenon, with the 1950s being the touchstone decade. Historians know that the history of suburbs is much longer, though their insights are rarely brought to bear upon contemporary debates. By bringing together the views of historians and social scientists, one of the purposes of the present volume is to underline the historical depth of suburban development.

If suburbs are widely seen as being of recent origin, they are also seen as generic in character. One of the most common criticisms of suburbs is that they all look the same, from city to city, and nation to nation. Almost all writers have assumed that the process and pattern of suburban development is essentially the same everywhere. At most, they have acknowledged the existence of minor variations, for example in the density of settlement between Britain on the one hand and Australia and North America on the other. The recent fashion for 'historic' architectural styles, sometimes drawing upon local or regional building idioms, has introduced superficial variety, but in the hands of most builders and developers even this new localism can appear somehow generic. But we believe that there are more important ways in which suburbs, and the meaning of suburbanism, have varied from place to place. By commissioning and collecting overviews of suburban development in Britain, Australia, Canada, and the United States, together with treatments of particular issues, we intend the present volume to highlight, and to raise questions about, national differences in the character and meaning of suburban development.

A HISTORIOGRAPHY OF THE SUBURB

There is a perception that the *history* of suburbia is well understood. The situation in Britain is typical in this regard. Certainly, works such as Thompson's classic edited volume *The Rise of Suburbia* (Thompson, 1982a) and Dyos's early and detailed study of the growth of Camberwell (Dyos, 1961) are citation classics in this field. This historical tradition is more recently supported by Beresford's work on Leeds (Beresford, 1988). Such works focus on the suburban development processes, from traditional perspectives and using the traditional data sources of the urban and economic historian. The view of this British literature is summarized by Thompson's introductory remarks that

> Suburbia rose between 1815 and 1939, an unlovely, sprawling artefact of which few are particularly fond. To be sure, there were suburbs long before the nineteenth century in the sense of places beyond city limits, the outskirts of towns hanging on to the central area physically and economically, for the most part composed of the ramshackle and squalid abodes of the poorest and most wretched of the town's hangers-on and its most noxious trades. (Thompson, 1982b, p.2)

Although there is much truth in this view, the manner and language with which it is portrayed perpetuate another suburban myth.

In Britain, key studies of what is often regarded as 'typical' suburbia, principally the London fringe 'Metroland' of the 1930s, have been influential in shaping our understanding of the suburban land development and design processes leading to the characteristic location, growth, densities, street- and block-plans (Jackson, 1973); as indeed was Dyos's pioneering work on Camberwell (1961), where he 'was chiefly concerned to rescue the suburb from historical oblivion and to show that its reputation for insignificant and uninteresting anonymity was unwarranted' (Thompson, 1982*b*, p. 3). Edwards (1981) has made a valiant attempt to set the design of suburbia in a necessary wider (but still suburban) temporal context, drawing together such earlier suburban forms as Victorian villa suburbs and their development into, for example, Bedford Park (London: Jonathan Carr, from 1875) through the classic inter-war speculative semi-detached suburbia to the changing space standards, uses, and architectural and plan forms of the 1960s and 1970s modernism.

But there are gaps in the wider academic understanding of the origins and development of suburbia. Too often is consideration limited temporally, and suburbia dismissed as a (relatively) recent phenomenon. Too often are the mechanisms and processes over-simplified; as, for example,

> the first suburbs were created as a result of a growing antipathy amongst the entrepreneurial middle class to the threats posed to their respectability by the social heterogeneity and lack of order in urban culture. (Chaney, 1997, p. 142)

Too often are the aesthetics of suburbia, and the middle-class suburban lifestyle, derided by a cultural élite – often professional, well-educated and of upper-class origins – such as Osbert Lancaster's well-known caricature of 'Wimbledon Transitional' and 'By-pass Variegated'. Too rarely is the general satisfaction of suburban dwellers with their lifestyle adequately explored, as Ravetz and Turkington (1995) began to do in their wider survey of the British home: suburbia is, after all, home to the many, and a lifestyle to which many aspire. And the characteristics of UK interwar suburbia so well explored by A.A. Jackson (1973), Oliver *et al.* (1994) and others are not typical of other periods, nor of other countries with similar socio-cultural contexts, let alone of quite different national contexts. In short, and as Whitehand and Carr (this volume) note, the suburban experience is dominated by academic and professional myths, based in part on prejudice and in part on lack of knowledge.

SUBURBAN ORIGINS

It is clear that suburbs are not new (cf Thompson, 1982*a*). The term itself derives from *sub urbe*, beneath/below and therefore outside the *urbs*. The *urbs* is not necessarily the 'town' (a later interpretation) but the pre-urban nucleus, often fortified, sometimes a castle. So, in the Western European tradition, many post-Roman towns have suburbs of some form. These mediaeval suburbs sometimes show strong traces of planning in their layouts, as in the regular plots of Corve Street and Foregate Street, in the English towns of Ludlow and Worcester respectively.

These early suburbs were not wholly residential, at least not in the way that we now take for granted. There was functional segregation, with the suburban poor being unable to afford urban taxes and without benefit of urban facilities and the protection of fortifications. Ironically, though, successive waves of urban expansion do swallow up and incorporate previous suburban areas and landforms (a point returned to in a later context). Early suburbs were also (proto-) industrial, with noxious trades such as tanneries regularly banished to the outskirts by city ordinances. Other occupations requiring water access developed between fortification lines and rivers, for example in the Severn valley (Baker, 1997). Thus, in the mediaeval period, there were many thriving and diverse suburbs, as Lilley (1995) has shown in his wider study of Coventry.

The functional segregation of suburbs persisted into the early-modern and industrial period. With developments in city economies and the means of production, in addition to the well-known rural-urban migration, developing suburbs were more attractive than urban cores for residence – and, as Higgins (1995) shows in Newtown, Montgomeryshire, for business and industrial uses too. Higgins explores the ways in which the new built forms of industrial suburbs in the early-industrial period reflected changes in modes of production, and particularly the function of the family unit in the labour supply of early capitalist industrial enterprises.

A new type of suburb began at this point, with the flight of the wealthy from increasingly congested and unpleasant urban cores to the relatively distant semi-rural peace (Fishman, 1987). To show but one example from the English Midlands, in 1776 Arthur Young, having travelled through Wolverhampton from Birmingham, marvelled at the contrast in Tettenhall, which he considered to be 'as retired as the Ohio' (Young, 1932 edition). In 1812, the 'delightful view of Wolverhampton and the adjoining country' was used as a selling-point for a house on the sandstone ridge along which many such villas were springing up (advertisement in the *Wolverhampton Chronicle*, 23rd December 1812). By 1846, Tettenhall was described as

> ... daily more intruded upon by clumsy proprietors of scraps of ground, by imported shopkeepers, and by those architectural affectations, termed 'country houses', in which the hardware gentility of Wolverhampton carries on its evening and Sabbath masquerades, at a convenient distance of a mile and three quarters from the locks, nails, and frying-pans of the productive emporium. (Palmer and Crowquill, *c*. 1846, pp. 33–34)

The growing scale and importance of urban manufacturing, and the associated development of the Romantic movement, made suburban areas more appealing to increasing numbers of people. Bringing nature into the city, they offered ready access to the countryside. From this development arose the notion, commonly expressed and very generally felt in the present century, of suburbs as a sort of marriage of city and country. Ideally, however, they were seen a partial marriage which excluded the basic elements of the new urban economy. The planner Thomas Sharp's critique of Town-Country is relevant here, although it was principally developed as a response to the Garden City Movement (Sharp, 1936, pp. 78ff). Some aristocratic estates were being developed for middle-class residential use, as in Edgbaston, Birmingham (Cannadine, 1980), albeit with considerable control over both form and use. The estates generally laid out streets and plots, and – in Edgbaston – restrictive covenants prohibited any business use, including 'public strawberry-patches'! There was a social dominance of the developing middle classes in these suburbs, caused not least by the need for sufficient disposable income to afford daily travel costs to work in the city. The development of transport innovations was, clearly, fundamental to the growth of this type of suburbia.

Increasingly the suburb, ideally and then to many observers by definition, was purely residential. Indeed, it was a place to which those employed in the city might retreat when day's work was done. Little recognition was afforded to those – almost entirely women – whose often unpaid work supported the suburban lifestyle. As suburbs acquired these specific, and more positive, meanings they attracted more prosperous families. It is widely supposed that, in Anglo-America, the first and definitive suburbs were those built for and occupied by the social élite (Fishman, 1987). According to many writers, the popular desire and opportunity to settle at the fringe came later. It is not clear that this was entirely true in any country. In Australia and North America, for example, it is evident that numerous working-class suburbs existed in the nineteenth and early twentieth centuries (Barrett, 1971; Harris and Lewis, 2000). In European countries (with the exception of England), cities retained their appeal to the élite, while suburbs were often relegated to the socially inferior (Hohenberg and Lees, 1995, pp. 306–307). Paris is a noteworthy case in point. If the reality was complex, however, the idealized conception was usually more simple: especially in the United States, by the beginning of this century, a suburb was a socially-desirable residential area, one which had developed at a relatively low density at the urban fringe.

The social trajectory of the suburb may be traced through changing usage, and in literary accounts. In Britain, Australia and North America the suburb has not always carried the associations of idyllic, quasi-rural and highly private lifestyle that are presently current in much of the English-speaking urban tradition. Along with 'villa', the term 'suburb' has changed markedly: but, while 'villa' has descended the social hierarchy from large upper-class mansions in extensive grounds to suburban industrial terraced housing (cf Slater, 1978), the connotations of 'suburb' have described a parabolic trajectory, from low to high, and then falling. In Britain, the first part of this movement occurred from the eighteenth century onwards.

> In the seventeenth century the suburbs were sometimes equated with the prostitutes'
> quarters of cities . . . by 1817 . . . 'suburban' was used to describe the inferior
> manners and narrowness of views then attributed to residents of the suburbs.
> Thereafter, with the onset of the industrial revolution and the later development of
> new methods of transportation, the meaning of 'suburban' appears to have evolved
> towards its current use and connotation of middle-class lifestyles. (Gray and
> Duncan, 1978, p. 297)

The *Oxford English Dictionary*'s survey of the term[1] begins in the 1380s, with Chaucer's *Canterbury Tales* writing of 'in the suburbes of a toun . . . lurkynge in hernes and lanes blynde', already suggesting a less than salubrious, but probably semi-rural, district. By 1593 Nashe wrote 'London, what are thy Suburbes but licensed Stewes?'; while Shakespeare's Henry VIII of 1613 mentioned the rabble of the suburbs, and Fletcher in 1625 derided 'the suburban strumpet'. Many such references in English literature refer specifically to the disreputable condition and uses of the London suburbs. References are thus explicitly disparaging, and if anything grew worse with Dent, in 1601, using the imagery of 'the suburbs of Hell'.

By the nineteenth century, however, the social status of the suburbs had improved considerably. This may be seen in the landscaper/designer J.C. Loudon's description of London in 1824 where 'the suburban villa . . . [is] of limited extent, but contains a small kitchen garden and stables . . . Such villas are occupied more by professional men and artists'. And, even in England, there are many precedents for the desirability of residing within easy reach of, but not inside, the larger cities: in 1855 Macaulay, in his *History of England*, wrote that 'among the suburban residences of our kings, that which stood at Greenwich had long held a distinguished place'.

In this context, the massive growth of London's suburbs in the late nineteenth century appeared to initiate a democratization of the suburbs, and a downward slide in their social status. By 1875, the fear of suburban growth was evident, with Helps writing 'How this ugly lot of suburbs would join with that ugly lot, and that there would soon be one continuous street'. Shortly afterwards, the *Law Times* stated that 'the speculative builder . . . has become the pest of suburban London'. Suburbs, then, have been around for a very long time; long enough, notably in the case of Britain, for their social status to have passed through several evolutionary phases. What, then, has endured? Indeed, what is a suburb? In addressing these questions it is helpful to adopt not only a historical but also a comparative frame of reference.

SOME SUBURBAN MYTHS

The task of addressing questions about the nature of suburbs is complicated by the development of complex and deep-rooted lay, professional and academic mythologies. Within each of the countries that are surveyed here, myths about suburbs have readily taken on a life of their own. The social image of the suburbs in the United States, and to a lesser extent Canada, is a case in point (Harris and Lewis, 1998). Throughout the twentieth century, North American suburbs have always been socially diverse. Those who studied them in the first quarter of the century were well aware of this diversity (Douglass, 1925; Taylor, 1915). Despite this fact, the popular and academic stereotype came to be that of the middle-class residential enclave. This stereotype was implied in the work of the Chicago sociologists in the 1920s and 1930s, and was perpetuated by the numerous critics of suburbia in the 1950s and 1960s. It was then applied retrospectively by suburban historians in the 1970s and 1980s. Selective historical studies of early, affluent suburbs then confirmed what everyone 'knew': that pre-war suburbs were for the affluent, and that it was only after the war that better-paid workers – a social group which, to Americans, still falls within the broad limits of the 'middle class' – were able to buy into the suburban dream. This has been a powerful myth. It has imparted a strongly progressive image to the Federal Housing Administration (FHA), whose mortgage insurance programmes are thought to have been critical to the development of post-war suburbs. The fact that pre-war suburbs were socially diverse was then conveniently forgotten.

In the same way, suburban myths have also gained widespread acceptance in Britain. Here, the mythology is twofold, covering the production and consumption of suburbia. The pervasive production myths have emphasized the uniformity of suburban character, equating this with dullness, blandness and an impoverishment of the quality of life. Not only were these myths common during the formation of the archetypal suburb, the inter-war speculative semi-detached, but more recent planning and design histories (e.g. Edwards, 1981) have repeated them. Although Whitehand and Carr (this volume) seek to dispel some of these myths, there is still scope for examination of the economics of contemporary building and of taste, and of how builders managed to incorporate significant but small-scale variety within these constraints. Myths of consumption are also prevalent, as can be seen in the marketing of suburbia and all the accoutrements of the new suburban lifestyle, aimed principally at the women, with the unspoken assumption that these would actually be purchased by the male wage-earner, the 'head of the household'. Even those great suburban traditions, the door-to-door salesman and the tupperware party, are rooted in this (increasingly flawed) model of consumption.

Many myths about suburbs also develop out of particular cultural ideals and imagery. The 'picturesque' tradition of the English countryside, for example, is deeply rooted in art and aesthetic appreciation; in the élite cultural icons of Gainsborough and Constable and the production of the unique English landscape of stately home and country park. In responding, consciously or subconsciously, to these influences, suburban myths have been perpetuated – if not originally formed – by a range of professional and lay reactions to earlier suburbs. With the benefit of hindsight, these reactions appear intemperate, ill-informed, and rooted in a false image of an ideal agrarian landscape. In the UK, for example, the industrial historian L.T.C. Rolt, then a young engineer, wrote dismissively of the 'typical' suburbs growing up around Banbury in the 1930s:

> the outskirts of Banbury were a sorry sight, for the sturdy stone heart of the old market town by the Cherwell is besieged on all sides by semi-detached monstrosities whose growth has recently received fresh impetus from new industrial expansion . . . (Rolt, 1944, p. 56)

Rolt was aware of the contradictions of his reactions: he preferred unspoilt, undeveloped countryside, recognized and welcomed the rural-urban migration as it removed a rural development pressure, but then bemoaned the expansion of towns to cope with population redistribution. Professionals, too, eloquently expressed disdain. Thomas Sharp, later to become President of the Town Planning Institute, wrote with horror in his chapter in *English Panorama* on 'Universal Suburbia' that

> a wilderness of semi-detached houses in sham-rural streets are indeed something more than a chaos of romantic individualism in themselves: they are the physical expression of the prime social evil of the age. Everywhere individualism is supreme: and the Street and the Town, those two units in which the quality of man's mass association has always been so clearly symbolised, unmistakably illustrate it – by their very absence. (Sharp, 1936, p. 87)

But myths and misconceptions continue into the present, and modern media imagery allows commentators a more pervasive influence: in the UK a television series presented by the architectural critic Jonathan Glancey scorned the 'odious and selfish' suburbia (Glancey, 1994).

> What is different about current attacks on suburbia is that they combine both self-righteousness and superciliousness in a deliciously irresistible moral frenzy. Suburbia is a Bad Thing . . . so pouring scorn on the appalling habits of the shell-suited, Mondeo-driving classes is given a socially acceptable figleaf of seriousness by paranoia at the prospect of the entire country disappearing beneath an endless carpet of cul-de-sacs of Tudorbethan executive homes, distinguished from one another only by the shape of their satellite dishes. (Sudjic, 1994, p. 2)

These examples of myth-creation or promulgation illustrate several features to which we will return in this Introduction, and which shape the body of this text: the factors causing suburbanization, the aesthetic qualities (or, as some argued, lack of them), individualism, and social issues.

DEFINITIONS: A COMPARATIVE VIEW

'Suburb', like the places that this term denotes, often seems formless. The difficulty is that, to most people, suburbs are characterized along more than one dimension. In varying degrees in different countries, five dimensions are commonly emphasized:

1. Peripheral location in relation to a dominant urban centre.
2. A partly (or wholly) residential character.
3. Low densities, often associated with decentralized patterns of settlement and high levels of owner-occupation.
4. A distinctive culture, or way of life.
5. Separate community identities, often embodied in local governments.

There are obvious connections among these various elements. At the urban periphery, land is usually cheaper, encouraging lower density development and, specifically, the construction of single-family homes for owner-occupation. In the twentieth century, the development of areas at low residential densities has typically depended upon the widespread use of automobiles for commuting, shopping and, increasingly, for other types of trips. Automobiles permit, although they do not inevitably produce, a dispersed pattern of settlement within the suburbs, with few centres of employment and with dispersed nodes of retail activity. Disproportionately, those who choose (and are able) to move to the suburbs are likely to be in households with children, who wish to lead a family-centred life, and to become involved in community organizations, notably through local schools. Through self-selection, then, suburbanites are likely to create what some have referred to as a suburban way of life (Gans, 1972; Thorns, 1972, pp. 111–125, 147–155).

Those who have tried to sort through these various criteria have all begun by commenting that the task is difficult (Dyos, 1961, pp. 20–22; Palen, 1995, pp. 8–13; Rybczynski, 1995, pp. 176–179; Thorns, 1972, pp. 31–34). Aware that the term can be used in various ways, some have insisted on a specific definition. This approach can certainly be revealing. For example, Robert Fishman (1987) has written a penetrating account of Anglo-American suburbs, defining the latter essentially as residential districts at the urban fringe, and in particular areas that were occupied by the more affluent half of the population. Working with this definition, he is able to trace the way in which an originally British phenomenon was imported by, and adapted within, the United States. Other writers, recognizing that a wide range of places have been labelled 'suburban' at one time or another, adopt more eclectic views and definitions. Kenneth Jackson (1985), in what is still the definitive history of US suburbs, adopts a pragmatic approach which – at least in principle – allows him to include just about every type of area that ever developed at or near the changing urban fringe. Inevitably, his account is not as analytically neat as Fishman's, but it is correspondingly more complete. It allows him to write more inclusively about the experience of Americans and, indeed, to make claims about the increasingly suburban nature of American life.

Different definitions of the suburbs serve different purposes and, to some extent, each has its merits. For comparative purposes, it has often appeared to be desirable to use a limited range of criteria, preferably those that can quite readily be translated into measurable variables. Thus, for example, emphasizing density and peripheral location, Clawson and Hall (1973) arrived at some useful (if not very surprising) conclusions about the differences between British and US suburbs: notably, that the latter are less dense and more dispersed, in large part owing to the more widespread use (and from an earlier date) of automobiles, and also to weaker planning controls (cf Cullingworth, 1993). Using similar criteria, Goldberg and Mercer (1986, p. 174) conclude that American suburbs are also more dispersed and auto-dependent than those in Canada. Frost (1991) takes a less conventional approach, arguing that differences among Australian, New Zealand, US and Canadian cities are often more significant than average national differences. He groups together Melbourne, Auckland, Los Angeles and Vancouver, for example, as decentralized 'new frontier' cities, as opposed to older, more dense centres such as Sydney, Philadelphia and Toronto. Although his conclusions are different he, too, assumes that suburbs everywhere are essentially the same, different only in degree. This, we believe, begs the question.

It is not difficult to find evidence which indicates that, underlying the similarities between suburbs in North America, Britain, and Australia, there are also significant differences. The contrasts are most apparent among those who have written about the suburban ideal. British writers almost invariably emphasize that a singular search for closer contact with nature, for privacy and control has been at the core of the suburban ideal (Burnett, 1986, pp. 104–105, 193–199; Dyos and Reeder, 1973, pp. 39–71; Thompson, 1982b, p. 13). In this connection, Lewis Mumford (1966, p. 491), one of the more perceptive observers of the suburbs, cites the example of Mr. Wemmick's father, in Dickens' *Great Expectations*, who lived in a house in one of London's suburbs 'with his castellated house, his moat and his drawbridge'. Here was an Englishman whose home was, almost literally, a castle. In moving to the suburbs, from at least the nineteenth century onwards, British families are thought to have been in retreat – not just from the city, but from wider economic and political engagement.

For much of the nineteenth and twentieth centuries, of course, there was a very gendered dimension to this ideal. In English working-class suburbs the contrasting experiences of men and women were not necessarily all that great. Certainly, many women worked in offices and factories and so experienced the home as a retreat, as well as a workplace in its own right. In middle-class suburbs, the contrasts were clearer. Men shuttled between the private world of the home and the more public worlds of work and politics, while usually women ruled (or, as some feminists have argued, were confined to) the domestic sphere. In such environments, the experiences of men and women were different. Daily, men experienced a wider frame of reference and then retreated to their suburban homes. For women, the contrasts between city and suburb were not underlined with such regularity, and so perhaps meant less. For both, however, the suburban home embodied a search for privacy.

The same themes, of private domesticity, of wishing to live closer to nature, and of retreat from the city, are prominent in the work of those who have written about the suburban ideal in settler societies as well (Ward, 1992). They are routinely emphasized by Canadian (Harris, 1996; McCann, 1996, pp. 266–271; McCann, this volume) and Australian (Davison, 1978, pp. 137–140; 1994), as well as by American writers (Fishman, 1987; Gowans, 1986, pp. 29–30; Jackson, 1985, pp. 45–72; Marsh, 1990, pp. xi–xiv; Sennett, 1970; Stilgoe, 1988, p. 11; Wright, 1981, pp. 104–113). In addition to these considerations, however, in

Australia and North America two other aspects of the suburbs are often thought to be definitive: owner-occupation, and political identity.

Until the third quarter of this century, levels of owner-occupation were much higher in Australia and North America than in Britain (Bourassa, Greig, and Troy, 1995; Harris and Hamnett, 1987; Kemeny, 1981). The contrast among working-class suburbs was especially marked. In Britain, in the inter-war years, the construction of council housing on suburban estates meant that a great many suburban workers were tenants (Turkington, this volume). In working-class suburbs in white settler societies, the majority of families owned their own homes. As far as we can judge, lower rates of working-class owner-occupation in Britain did not reflect any significant difference in aspirations. British-born workers who emigrated proved themselves willing to make enormous sacrifices in order to acquire (or build) homes for themselves (Harris, 1996). The important differences were those of circumstance and opportunity for, by restraining levels of owner-occupation well into the post-war era, these imparted a more limited meaning to suburban residence in Britain. As Jackson (1985, pp. 7, 11) has argued, the opportunity to own a home is almost a defining feature of American suburbs. This is also true in Australia and, to a lesser extent, Canada. In each case, part of the mythology of the suburbs is that it embodies the respective national 'dream' of owner-occupation. The same has not been true in Britain, although this is perhaps a matter which is changing – as the results of the 'right-to-buy' for council tenants, and the earlier Leasehold Reform Act, showed.

A further, and even more vital, meaning to 'the suburbs' in the United States is the notion of community. There, many writers have emphasized the extent to which the suburban ideal has incorporated a desire for community, and for the exercise of democratic control through local government. In his study of Boston's 'first suburbs', the historian Henry Binford (1985, pp. 1–2) writes of the importance of the 'community-building process' which produced 'communities which were defiantly independent in government'. The suburban search for community and grass-roots democracy is a persistent theme.[2] For example, in an influential study of postwar suburbia, the political scientist Robert Wood (1958, p. 18) found a widespread 'faith in communities of limited size'. More recently, when anthropologist Constance Perin wanted to find out what it meant to 'belong' in America, she went to the (middle income) suburbs to find out (Perin, 1988, pp. 4–5, 66–67). Similarly, when the journalist Joel Garreau tried to come to terms with the America's sprawling post-suburban suburbs – what he refers to as 'Edge Cities' – he found it necessary to devote a whole chapter to the new forms of private 'shadow' government that have been created to regulate these areas, and another to the more informal means of creating 'community', using Los Angeles (no less) as his vehicle (Garreau, 1991, chapters 6 and 8). Significantly, in the index entry for 'suburbs' in Garreau's book, 'community and identity' is by far the most significant subheading.

The most effective forms of community are those that possess their own governmental powers. In the United States, nineteenth-century suburbs did not always start out with their own governments but, in many cases, they soon set about creating them. As a result, 'underlying the twentieth-century conception of a suburb is political autonomy' (Keating, 1988, p. 2). The form of this autonomy has varied both historically and geographically over the past century. Services have been provided by special districts, by local and county governments and, increasingly, by private property owner associations (McKenzie, 1994; Teaford, 1997). Despite, or perhaps because of, this often confusing pattern of governance, most American writers assume that political identity is fundamental to the definition of the suburbs (e.g. Ashton, 1984, p. 54). Working from this assumption, they have usually been willing to employ standard census data which, for decades, have drawn a distinction between central cities and the balance of the metropolitan area (e.g. Goldfield and Brownell, 1979, pp. 34–54; K. Jackson, 1985, pp. 8 ff; Schnore, 1962). A few American scholars have acknowledged that some residential districts within central cities do not look very different from those in adjacent suburbs (Sies, 1997). Conversely, some writers have identified a few suburbs which, in terms of their densities, are more similar to central cities than to the stereotypical suburb (Borchert, 1996). 'City suburbs' such as Lakewood, Ohio, and Evanston, Illinois, are seen to be noteworthy because they are exceptions to the rule. In England or Australia, where 'suburb' can easily refer to an older and quite densely-developed part of the city, Evanston would not arouse comment. Although suburbanization is an international phenomenon, then, it means different things in Britain, Canada, Australia, and the United States.

In emphasizing the importance of community for the definition of suburban life, American writers have established a logical tension. If families move to the suburbs in order to retreat from the pressures of the wider society, then suburban life must be characterized as essentially private. To the extent that they seek opportunities to exercise their democratic rights through local and school politics, however, the suburbs are also seen as bastions of civic virtue and grass-roots democracy. The impulses for privacy and for civic engagement are not incompatible, but they must be balanced and reconciled. For Americans, suburbs are places where this difficult task is to be accomplished. Moreover, because this balancing act is so central to a democratic society, and because the democratic ideal is so fundamental to the American identity, the quality of suburban life has taken on a national significance which it lacks elsewhere. Of course in Britain, Australia and Canada, people care a good deal about the character and appearance of the suburbs. Sprawl has long been viewed by some as ugly, and is now often seen as costly and in many eyes environmentally unsound. In Australia and Canada, as well as in the United States, the prospects for suburban owner-occupation are bound up with a national self-image. But it is only in American suburbs that, symbolically, both prosperity and democracy are at stake.

In general, it is the political meaning of 'the suburbs' which is most distinctive from one country to another. If Americans routinely define suburbs in political terms, this is rare in Britain. In Australia, suburbs often do have a political identity, but the significance of this fact is very different (Goodman, 1993). Suburban governments in Australia do not have the powers of their American counterparts, and so political fragmentation does not have the same fiscal and social implications. Moreover, Australian central cities are typically very small, so that older districts which Americans would think of as city neighbourhoods are referred to as 'inner' or 'older' suburbs in Australia (cf. Barrett, 1971; Kendig, 1979). In Australia, then, almost all urban residents (and hence the great majority of the entire population) think of themselves as living in a suburb of some kind. Canadians often follow American practice, distinguishing between city neighbourhoods and politically distinct suburbs (Bourne and Ley, 1993, p. 13; McCann, this volume). As in Britain, however, Canadian local governments have no constitutional powers. They can be made, and unmade, at the will of the provinces. Thus, for example, in Toronto, Ontario centralized some of the functions and powers of suburban governments with the formation of a metro tier of government in 1954. Effective from January 1, 1998, the metro suburbs (as well as the City of Toronto) were abolished with the formation of a single local government. Cultural as well as political considerations have discouraged Canadians from attaching the same significance as their American cousins to suburban government.

In the United States, and especially since the Second World War, any serious discussion of suburbs soon raises a further issue which is of national significance: race. Large-scale migration after the First World War brought large numbers of southern blacks to cities in the northern and western states, in many cases for the first time (Hirsch, 1983; Lehmann, 1991). Although the fact is not generally recognized, a significant number of these migrants found their way into the suburbs and fringe areas of American cities (Wiese, 1993). Most, however, settled and remained in central cities. Increasingly, the socially-significant contrast between city and suburb became their racial composition, a difference which was reinforced by political fragmentation, and only incidentally by their density of settlement. In a society which has always prided itself on the freedom and equality of all people, the persistence of racism is a matter of national shame. Embodied in city-suburb segregation, this issue, too, has helped to make the definition and character of suburbs a national issue. As a result, in the United States, the term 'suburb' has had to carry an unusually large freight of political and cultural meaning.

The above observations rely upon the writings of a literate minority of scholars and journalists. It can be misleading to attach too much significance to the work of such writers. Nations develop intellectual cultures which, to some extent, are independent of the larger society. It is at least arguable that differences of emphasis between, especially, British and American writers might result from distinctive intellectual traditions. By comparison with the US, a large number of the British academics who have written about cities and suburbs have been trained as geographers. For that reason they are, perhaps, more likely to emphasize location, and morphological features, as basic to the definition of suburbs. Sociologists and political scientists have been more prominent in the US, and this might help to account for the greater emphasis there upon the creation of community life, in part through involvement in local politics. It is possible, in other words, that in daily life, local politics and community life are just as important for the residents of Australian or British suburbs as for Americans. This possibility has never been carefully examined. The definitions contained in national dictionaries provide an obvious starting point for such an enquiry.

NATIONAL ETYMOLOGIES: CURRENT USAGES

It is impossible to be certain whether scholarly differences in the way suburbs are discussed are accurate reflections of divergent national experiences. To the extent that popular recent and current usages and meanings are captured by dictionaries, however, it would seem that they are. British and American dictionaries consistently define suburbs in different ways. The *New Shorter Oxford Dictionary* (1993), which might be regarded as the leading British dictionary, defines a suburb as 'a district, especially a residential area, lying (orig.) immediately outside or (now) within the boundaries of a town or city'. This definition acknowledges that an area might be referred to as a 'suburb' even though it lies within the boundaries of a city. By way of contrast, American dictionaries have consistently emphasized the importance of city limits, and also of separate incorporation. *Webster's New Universal*, a leading American dictionary, writes of a suburb as a 'district, usually a residential district, on the outskirts of a city: often a separately-incorporated city or town'. This specific combination of criteria had long been characteristic. In 1944, the *Chicago Dictionary of American English* provided two definitions: the first simply spoke of peripheral location ('outlying'), but the second specified 'a politically independent community, usually residential, located near, and economically dependent on, a larger city'. The term 'community', which implies a degree of social cohesion, is significantly absent from British dictionary definitions of suburb, although it appears in several American ones. Thus, for example, the 1969 edition of the *American Heritage Dictionary* defines a suburb as 'a usually residential area or community outlying a city'. Dictionaries, like urban scholars, speak of a significant national difference.

Entries in Australian, Canadian and international dictionaries, however, also imply the existence of national, cultural differences. The *Macquarie Dictionary* (1981) identifies a suburb as 'a district, usually residential and to some degree remote from the business or administrative centre of a city or large town'. It suggests that such a district is likely to 'enjoy . . . its own facilities, [such] as schools, shopping centres, railway centres, railway stations'. The emphasis on rail transportation is distinctive, reflecting its unusual importance in the early development of several Australian cities, notably Melbourne, but the silence regarding political identity is also characteristic of Canadian dictionaries. The *Gage Canadian Dictionary* (1983) entertains a number of options for a suburb, which might be 'a district, town, or village just outside or near a city or town'. The Canadian suburb, like the American, lies outside city limits but, as in Britain, there is no presumption that it be incorporated. Cutting across such national nuances, international English dictionaries identify only the most basic common denominators. *Websters' Third New International* (1976) writes only of 'an outlying part of a city or town'; *Funk and Wagnall's New Comprehensive International Dictionary* (1971) refers to 'a place adjacent to a city' or, in the plural, simply a city's 'environs'; the *BBC English Dictionary* (1993), compiled as a guide to usage on the World Service, defines a suburb as 'an area of a city, which is away from the centre and where people live'. In each case, it is clear that 'city' refers not, as it would in an American dictionary, to a political unit, but rather to a metropolitan area.

If, as seems clear, 'suburb' does not mean quite the same thing in each country, the difficulties of comparison are greatly compounded. Drawing up accurate comparative data on residential densities or degrees of decentralization, themselves difficult tasks, are insufficient. We also need to know something about the nature and extent of suburban 'community', or the numbers, powers, and cultural significance of suburban government. If, in some respects, we need to extend the bases of comparison, in other respects we must be careful not to assume that other criteria are important everywhere. Americans have consistently found it meaningful to aggregate and analyse a wide range of information for central cities as opposed to suburbs, but this has not consistently been true elsewhere. A truly comparative study of suburbs would need to take account of such differences. In one sense they cannot be 'resolved': the notion of cultural difference implies that certain things are simply non-comparable.

SUBURBS AND CULTURE

When writers have used 'culture' and 'suburb' in the same sentence, they have usually done so with one of two purposes in mind. Those who use 'culture' in the 'high' sense have usually deplored its virtual absence in bland, middlebrow suburbs. The influence of this – often snobbish – critique can be detected even in the defenders of the suburbs such as Joel Garreau, who goes to considerable pains to emphasize how many traditional cultural institutions – from symphony orchestras and theatre to high fashion clothing stores – may be found in Edge City malls (Garreau, 1991, pp. 59–63). Those who use culture in a broader, anthropological sense have discussed the culture of the suburbs (or 'suburbia', a term that is now dated though the idea is not). For much of the present century, and certainly since the Second World War, observers have discussed the character and mentality of the suburban 'way of life' (Gans, 1972). Typically, they have seen this as a private culture, focused upon domesticity and family pursuits, reinforced by home ownership, and increasingly associated with mass consumption. Within a global context, a number of writers have acknowledged the importance of culture to the process of urban development (e.g. Agnew, Mercer and Sopher, 1984). Very few, however, have recognized or explored its varying importance among developed, English-speaking nations. Moreover, to the extent that national differences exist, they are supposed to be of degree, not of kind. Comparing British with American suburbs, for example, it is a commonplace that the former are denser because more tightly regulated; that the latter, because more affluent, are profligate in their use of space, commodities, and energy. No-one disputes, however, that they are essentially, and increasingly, the same. Although there is obviously a good deal of truth to this, from other points of view such a consensus is surprising.

In the political realm, we are continuously reminded of the importance of ethnicity and culture. While ethnicity does not always coincide with national boundaries, we are also accustomed to speaking – sometimes erroneously, often guardedly, but always with the sense of something important being at stake – about differences in national cultures. The British like to think of themselves as being different from Americans, and *vice versa*, while English Canadians have long worked hard to define themselves in relation to both. (French Canadians are a different story.) It would be surprising if the peoples of these nations created cities and suburbs that were essentially the same. Yet, despite a few dissenting voices, this is still what is commonly supposed (cf Agnew, Mercer and Sopher, 1984).

By collecting and juxtaposing accounts of suburban development in four countries – Britain, the United States, Canada, and Australia – we wish to probe the assumption that the modern suburban experience has been essentially uniform. These countries are interesting because they promise to provide variations on a common cultural theme. The common culture is, in varying degrees, British in origin, and the themes are those of romantic anti-urbanism (Bunce, 1994), and of individualism. As a response to the emergence of urban industrial capitalism in the late eighteenth century, the romantic movement was not, of course, unique to Britain; but it was there that it found first and clearest expression in the suburban ideal. From its beginnings in the late eighteenth century, this ideal viewed the suburbs as a marriage of country and city, nature and artifice (Fishman, 1987; Thompson, 1982b, pp. 13–16; Williams, 1975). It was in Britain also that liberal individualism developed, to be transplanted in varying degrees to settler colonies around the world: including the United States and English Canada (Hartz, 1964). Indeed, it has been claimed that Australia was the first true suburban nation (Davison 1995; Dingle, this volume). This individualism was important not only as it affected politics – so that, for example, today writers refer to Anglo-American forms of the welfare state – but also because it shaped cultural attitudes towards property and, in particular, home ownership (Doucet and Weaver, 1991, chapter 4). The ideal of owning one's own home has had a peculiar hold on the national imagination in each of these countries. It is implied in the old adage that an Englishman's home is his castle, and is alluded to as the American/ Australian/Canadian 'dream' (Archer, 1987; Harris and Hamnett, 1987).[3] Cultures, of course, are never transported whole, and in the British colonies romantic individualism was altered by differing circumstances and subsequent patterns of settlement.

Suburban Form

As with culture, comparative studies of suburban form have been few: yet this is rich territory for exploration. It is the morphological characteristics of street layout, plot patterns and building forms and styles which have received much of the criticism of the élite, and shaped the suburban myth, as have the suburban characteristics of community and culture.

There are persistent myths of the uniformity, blandness and monotony of suburban form. In Britain these have been promulgated by the sharp observation of those such as Osbert Lancaster, who drew inspiration from the burgeoning semi-detached suburbia of the inter-war period. In the United States the myth of uniformity arose in the 1950s. It found expression in many ways, perhaps most notably in Malvina Reynolds' song about the 'little boxes' made out of 'ticky tacky' which all looked 'just the same'. In Australia, too, the post-war period was seen as decisive in creating what Robin Boyd called 'the Australian ugliness' (Boyd, 1960; cf Rowse, 1978). Too few writers have challenged the myth of suburban uniformity. In Britain, Whitehand and Carr (1995; this volume) have documented the surprising variety of suburban architecture and form, both within and between towns. For the United States and Canada, there is a growing recognition that, in social terms, suburbs are socially diverse, and indeed that they have been around for a long time (Harris and Lewis, 2000; Harris, this volume). At the same time, surveys and oral histories have found that in Australia, Britain, and North America, many people – including the post-war generation of women who experienced a good deal of isolation – were generally satisfied by the suburban experience (e.g. Allport, 1983; Davison and Davison, 1995; Strong-Boag, 1991; Strong-Boag et al., this volume; Winter et al., 1993).

Compared with the amount of literature on the social character and experience of suburbia, little has been written about its physical form. House types have certainly received some considerable attention (e.g. Foley, 1980; Wright, 1981) but this is usually from an architectural history perspective. Only rarely have writers related buildings to the districts in which they sit, or the uses to which they were put (cf Adams, 1995; Kelly, 1993). Similarly, there is work on 'model suburbs' (Hayden, 1984; Stern, 1981). Yet, as Moudon has observed,

> . . . if these carefully designed, often innovative suburban forms have served as exemplary precursors to later development, they, in effect, bear little resemblance to the mass of developer-controlled subdivisions whose standard designs remain selective interpretations of their famous antecedents. (Moudon, 1992, p. 171)

Indeed, it is Moudon herself who has carried out the most thorough review of suburban forms – and this is limited to US middle-class housing. She has identified a typology of basic types of plot, reviewed the positioning of houses on plots, developments in street patterns, and changing house form and style. In the US context, then,

> in the last seventy years, suburban building has undergone significant changes. The ubiquitous single-family, detached, suburban house for those in the middle-income brackets has given way to semi-detached houses, terrace houses of three or four dwellings, and apartment blocks. More than 40 per cent of the new housing built in North America is now in the form of multiple units. Furthermore, curved streets and culs-de-sac have replaced the traditional gridiron street pattern. (Moudon, 1992, p. 172)

Similar changes, less carefully-documented, are visible elsewhere (cf Edwards, 1981). The critical review of suburban form was sharply focused, particularly in the UK, through influential publications by the critic Ian Nairn during the 1950s. Unacademic, but wide-ranging and rooted in the emerging UK 'townscape' tradition shortly to be focused by Gordon Cullen, Nairn's polemic attacked form and appearance; blandness, monotony, the unplanned spaces and streetscapes (Nairn, 1955). But his main targets were 'spec builders, advertisers, gormless local officials and the general visual squalor of the twentieth-century scene. Architects were still immune' (Esher, 1981, p. 73). In short, Nairn attacked the suburban version of what the *Architectural Review* and Leslie Ginsburg summed up in 1973 as SLOAP – Space Left Over After Planning.

This general neglect of suburban form is changing as, over the last decade or two, suburban forms themselves have undergone substantial change. In Australia, for example, suburban form was roundly criticized by the architect Robin Boyd (1960), who saw the problem as ill-formed public taste and apathy. In particular, he disliked the then-current public taste for the familiar, historic references in style. His own suburban buildings of the 1960s are simple in plan and detail; although his

> attitude to the suburb had been clearly ambivalent. He was prepared earlier to accept a degree of potential quality where certain builder-developers tried L-shaped plans, lower roof pitches and lighter-hued walls. Subsequently he was vehemently opposed to speculative development and what he saw as its debased visual impact. Like the majority of architects he objected to growth which bypassed the professional skills. (Spens, 1992, p. 78)

This says much about professional attitudes, and about the development process. However, his design concepts have been further developed during the 1980s by the architects Peter Corrigan and Ian McDougall who, particularly in Melbourne, have been seeking to provide a new suburban aesthetic to counter the traditional suburban vernacular documented and deplored by Boyd in 1960 (Spens, 1992).

In the UK, one reaction to the criticisms of Nairn and others was to develop 'design guidance', particularly emphasizing local vernacular form, materials and style: the *Essex Design Guide* being probably the most influential example (Essex County Council, 1973; revised January 1998). But these guides did not halt the spread of bland, characterless estates: indeed the spread of guidance, and central government's standards on highways, pavements etc contained in *Design Bulletin 32* (Department of the Environment, 1992) may have further promoted blandness (although this has yet to be researched: and see Southworth and Ben-Joseph, 1997, for US parallels). Again, recent developments have sought to move away from these bland but familiar and traditional suburban forms. In particular, speculative developers working more closely with local planning authorities have introduced more landscaping because of the purchasers' demand for 'instant maturity', more concern for designing against crime – but with open estates for surveillance and self-policing rather than high walls and fences – and less prominence given to roads and parking. 'Soulless estates died with the 1980s. Today's schemes look to create community and security, and to tuck the cars out back' (Smit, 1996, p. 34).

While this detailed redesign of relatively familiar suburban form is going on in the UK, elsewhere there are major changes in what is seen as a post-suburban period. Here, the 'Edge City' of Garreau (1991) has been taken even further. 'Post-suburban America is fragmented and multi-nodal, with mixed densities and unexpected juxtapositions of forms and functions' within which particular forms, such as the private master-planned communities for the wealthy 'are also part of the "post-modern turn" that has been inscribed in the built environment' (Knox, 1992, pp. 207–208). Moudon (1990) has produced a useful summary of the master-planned communities which, *inter alia*, shows the strong impact of neo-traditional design in both layout and style. Seaside is probably the best-known neo-traditional settlement (illustrated by Mohney and Easterling, 1991 and subjected to deconstructivist analysis by Al-Hindi and Staddon, 1997) – it is debatable whether this is a town, resort, suburb or edge city. The neo-traditionalist critique of suburbia (explored in Katz, 1992) is well shown in recent volumes on the design of suburbia which, although rooted in US experience, clearly have resonances with developments elsewhere. These texts discuss consumer dis-satisfaction and how to address it; concentrate on the design of mass-produced houses, and focus on the smaller scales of plots and streets (Wentling, 1995; Girling and Helphand, 1994). Such works strongly suggest that this is the future direction of suburban form. 'Neo-traditional evangelists present this planning model as a remedy for all that is apparently wrong with late-20th century American urbanism, including the crowding, the noxious traffic, the terrifying crime . . . ' (Al-Hindi and Staddon, 1997, p. 349).

Yet they are not without their critics. The neo-traditional 'New Urbanism' has been criticized in particular for its apparent focus on external architectural appearance and its neglect of social concerns and wider regional planning-related issues. And, in the long run, can the traditional lure of even neo-traditional suburbia triumph over calls for more 'sustainable' urban forms (cf Jenks *et al.*,

1996)? There are problems with trying to increase the density of existing suburbs through 'densification' or 'consolidation' (Troy, 1996). And, after all, 'suburbia is where most people live and will continue to live and most of them seem to like it there. Those who do not like it do not have to live there' (Delafons, 1995).

THE STRUCTURE OF THIS VOLUME

The multifaceted character of the suburbs, and the power of suburban mythology, make the subject both difficult and interesting. The difficulties are obvious: there is no agreement even about how suburbs should be defined, still less explained or interpreted. The surprising complexity of the topic, however, encouraged the sort of multi-disciplinary dialogue which too rarely occurs in the modern era of academic specialization. One of the advantages of the study of suburbia, and one of the features of this volume, is its interdisciplinary nature; the ability to make connections and develop new insights; and, through the perspective of mutually-supporting disciplines, to attack the myths of suburbia. History, sociology, geography, and art history are all represented here as major disciplines, with sub-disciplines as diverse as aesthetics, gender studies and urban morphology. In drawing together these strands, we have suggested both a thematic and chrono-logical structure in order to highlight the disciplinary links – although we are aware that no single book can offer comprehensive coverage, and that we have also highlighted gaps in knowledge and coverage.

There is confirmation in recent works that such a broad coalition of arts, humanities and social sciences does have a meaningful contribution to the bur-geoning contemporary academic discourse. Silverstone's recent and particularly wide-ranging edited collection is an example of such a coalition. There, a broad cross-section of disciplinary contributions explores, some in rather eclectic post-modern form, some of the contributions and contradictions of suburbia: its familiarity but facelessness, recognizability but characterlessness, ubiquity but invisibility, security but fragility, and more (Silverstone, 1997). That collection has a focus on cultural issues, uses and representations: the present volume has a broader aim.

We argue, and present a range of evidence to show, that the fusion of historical and contemporary, physical form and sociology, development process and perception and use are stimulating and mutually reinforcing. As with all edited collections, we present only a sample to demonstrate current activity in this long-standing area of investigation. It is encouraging that many facets remain under-investigated, and many interdisciplinary discourses remain unarticulated. The suburb is a fertile field for continuing development.

All of the individual contributions to this volume address our key theme, which is the gap between historical and contemporary treatments of suburbs in the English-speaking cultural tradition: the UK itself, and the former white settler colonies of Australia, the United States and Canada. The contributions are varied in spatial, temporal and disciplinary approach; they approach this gap in different ways. The bringing-together of these approaches, individually concerned with only a part of the overall picture, is the contribution of the entire collection. In exploring the similarities and differences in suburban developments, the gap is narrowed (if not yet completely closed).

The first of two sections deals with early-twentieth century suburbs. The themes explored here range from national overviews, useful for comparative purposes, to detailed treatments of different suburban development processes – principally exploring the difference between private speculative suburbia and municipal developments. It proves difficult to generalize in these national treatments. Nevertheless, there are some common themes and experiences emerging. The treatment is broadly but not rigidly chronological; as several thematic chapters do follow the use and social and physical development of their suburban types from pre-Second World War origins through the post-war period. In thus exploring some of the suburban myths it is necessary not just to examine initial development, but to take a long-term developmental view.

Newby and Turner begin this exploration through discussion of the relationship between the growth in suburbs and of the rise of mass consumerism. Specifically, they address issues of taste and the consumption of design in the production of suburbia. Interior spaces are key to this argument – the numbers, types, furnishing and decor shaped the suburban experience. They examine the transition between the often-caricatured Victorian suburban taste and that of the new century through the products of one significant agency, the Silver Studio. They show many more linkages between these periods than many past commentators would admit, and stress the importance of 'tastemakers', particularly in the newly-developing books and magazines targeted at the status-conscious newly-suburbanizing populace, especially women.

The importance of individual local municipalities in designing and constructing mass affordable housing of a suburban form, following the 'Homes Fit for Heroes' debate, is examined by Turkington, with a particular focus on the example of Norris Green in Liverpool. This 1920s estate was essentially an experimental municipal project, a forerunner of Birmingham's mass estates, where the city built over 50,000 houses before 1939. Turkington focuses on the experiences of the estate and its 37,500 residents, from the first cohort through a post-war consolidation phase to the emergence of physical, social and managerial problems in the 1980s. In taking this long view, Turkington tests the post-First World War desire to create a new and classless society, in which the physical and social setting – the suburban estate – provided a vehicle for social mixing and a new environment within which new social conditions and especially new communities would be generated. The brave new world tarnished over the course of 50 or 60 years.

Whitehand and Carr report on large-scale research which has reviewed the creation and modification of English inter-war private suburbs. They explicitly counter some of the myths prevalent about suburban form, development and experience from the inter-war origins of this development type to the present. Rooted in this detailed research on origin and form, they then explore the nature and scale of change, which has come under increasing pressure for adaptation to changed social, economic and physical conditions. They show that the highest-quality houses and areas are the most susceptible to demolition and alteration. Using detailed local authority data, they develop the concept of the 'life history' of individual roads, relating changes to 'neighbour effects', incomes and incomers. Thus the historical study of origins and early form is explicitly related to current uses and planning issues.

Harris moves to North America to re-construct the making of American suburbs. He reviews the social and morphological diversity of suburbia, and how this can be linked to the development process. Three types of suburb are examined: the stereotypical tree-lined, large single-family house 'middle-class' suburb, the industrial and working-class suburb, to which contemporary commentators appeared more sensitive than many later historians, and the 'unincorporated' areas, less-organized districts at the urban fringe. This raises the issue of suburban definition, and the cultural difference between North America and the UK. Even today, field surveys and insurance atlases can tell us a great deal about suburban evolution in a given area in North America (these atlases do not give suburban coverage in Australia or the UK). Harris' broad generalizations about linking diversity to development are eminently testable, and could form a platform for wider comparative study, again reinforcing the links between history, form, and the present urban landscape.

Looking particularly at Canada, McCann examines the transformation of the residential landscape through the first half of the century; in particular how it became more homogeneous, more middle-class, and more free from non-residential activities through the development and application of development guidelines and by-laws. But this is not just a story of planning history, it also traces how the values and beliefs of both producers and consumers, both the public and private spheres, combined to create suburban lifestyle and character. These are suburbs of desire, of aspiration, as McCann illustrates through fiction, culture and history. But, although the turn-of-the-century suburban landscape was diverse, socially as well as physically (as Harris agrees), the modern suburban landscape is not. McCann's chapter charts this transformation through the formation of policies which, although well-intentioned (in seeking efficiency, providing order, and protecting property) have resulted in zoning and exclusion.

Lewis reviews the development of a particular suburban type, the industrial suburb, in North America over the period 1850–1950. In Europe, he argues, the character and extent of industrial decentralization has been quite well documented. In Canada and the United States, despite some case study evidence, the importance, patterns and processes associated with suburban manufacturing are under-researched. In addressing this omission, Lewis first reviews the work on the rate and extent of industrial suburbanization, then develops a discussion of the three major dynamics driving this change: industrial change, the property market, and institutions. He then develops a fourfold typology of industrial suburbs. First was the informally-created edge-of-town manufacturing district, often an extension of an earlier industrial district that followed a transportation route. Second was the originally separate satellite town, although many were soon absorbed by metropolitan expansion. Third was the company town on a greenfield site. Last was the organized industrial district, planned with ready access to all relevant facilities. Lewis suggests that the industrial suburb was a key component of North American urbanization. As with other suburban types, a variety of forms and processes can be distinguished which broaden our conception of metropolitan development and allow refinement of existing historical and developmental models of urban growth.

In each of the countries surveyed in this collection, the Second World War was a significant watershed. This was especially true in Australia and in North America, where the pace of suburban development had flagged not only during the War but also for most of the preceding decade. Here, especially, the form and process of post-war development seemed novel. Section two focuses on post-war suburbs, and in particular upon some key themes. These include the experience of women, who have been portrayed (sometimes unthinkingly and unsym-pathetically) as the prime users of suburbs; the current pattern of 'edge city' development, recognized first in the United States but, arguably, now spreading more widely; and issues of conservation and management, as these suburbs age and become the familiar and valued homes to a large fraction of the urban population in the countries examined.

A particular, and international, perspective on suburban users is developed by Strong-Boag, Dyck, England and Johnson. They parallel McCann's suburban landscapes of desire, in their view of the 'imagined suburb' which lies at the heart of discourses about post-war modernity. Their critical feminist analysis de-constructs some of the traditional and widely-accepted assumptions of the relationships between women, family, and suburbia. A range of similarities is highlighted through the differing suburbs of Australia, Britain, Canada and the United States. In particular they emphasize the public/private segregation within suburban form, the private domain being supported (or subsidized) by the unpaid domestic work of the 'housewife'. House design, too, supported this segregation and gender division, with men being identified with specific spaces for leisure and a continuation of office-type work. However, in recent years, the increasing participation of women in paid employment, the associated redefinition of 'motherhood' and the role of the 'housewife', and the mixing of socio-economic and ethnic groups in some areas, increasingly questions the dated analyses which distinguished readily between urban and suburban; employed and unemployed; respectable and not-respectable. But, despite the volume of recent feminist analysis, the authors agree that 'relatively little is known about the diversity of

contemporary suburban life, and the concomitant reality of women's lives'
(Baldasarre, 1992).

Dingle reviews the spread of suburbia in post-war Australia; beginning with a
wry commentary on Australian imagery from *Crocodile Dundee* to Edna Everage
which emphasizes that Australian suburban form does differ from the other
national traditions examined here. The 'quarter-acre block' tradition has shaped
the Australian image of suburban form, and the form itself. As elsewhere, the
suburb was mixed; firms migrated to large, cheap sites, forming industrial estates
scattered amongst the residential suburbia. As economic circumstances changed,
homeownership changed from dream to reality for a growing number. They often
went without roads and basic facilities, both because developers were not
compelled to provide them and also because this made the housing cheaper! The
suburbs found increasing intellectual champions in the 1960s and 1970s, just
as the suburban dream began to fade. The oil crisis was a major factor, but other
economic trends have also been significant. Today, the Australian suburb is
criticized, and subject to government policies for 'urban consolidation' which are
fundamentally changing the character and appearance of suburbia in, for example,
Melbourne and Sydney.

In the United States in particular, views of recent suburbs have been
challenged by the journalist Joel Garreau's influential (non-academic) critique of
'Edge Cities' (Garreau, 1991). Jonas reviews the edge-city concept in a detailed
case study of development trends in Moreno Valley, Southern California. This
area had undergone enormous expansion in the 1980s but, by 1996, poor fiscal
management led to a tax base insufficient to pay for basic services. Such
difficulties have been under-explored by Garreau and the many social scientists
who have jumped onto this intellectual bandwagon. The edge city must be built
and managed: what is the reality of the development process, and the quality of
life, in these places? When does the boosterism and place-promotion conflict
with economic reality? In a significant critique of this boosterism Jonas argues
that, in Moreno Valley at least, there were major weaknesses in planning and
management which led to suburban crisis: rising crime levels, job insecurity,
mortgage foreclosures, falling property prices, and other ills traditionally
associated with the city core. And the very process of edge-City development
has led to the loss of valued landscapes and open space. Edge city, he suggests, is
not a sustainable success story; it can be, in Mike Davis' words a 'junkyard of
dreams', in danger of decline into a 'land of abandoned settlements and defeated
colonists'.

The final pair of chapters examine the rise of historical consciousness of
suburbs, and in particular of efforts to preserve suburban environments in
the United States and Britain. Ames explores a topic which has only recently
become fashionable, or indeed possible, in the United States: the preservation of
suburbs as historic landscapes. This raises significant questions concerning both
the practice of historic preservation and the nature and extent of scholarship

required to arrive at accurate assessment of the significance of suburban districts. Protecting post-war suburbs, held in planning and popular myth to be the archetype of dull and poor planning, creates dilemmas for the preservationist. What is to be valued, and how? This chapter is a presentation of Ames' own work for the National Register of Historic Places of the US Department of the Interior, and in particular his development of a Technical Bulletin to inform preservation decision-making. The scholarship necessary to evaluate suburbia necessitates a deeper knowledge of the origin and process of both plan layout and architectural form: in many cases new research or new synthesis allows significant re-evaluation of our knowledge and preconceptions – even if an individual suburb is not, thereafter, protected.

In the final chapter, Larkham takes this concept a stage further, looking at conservation and management in UK suburbs. The philosophical dilemmas and debate are similar; but, in this country where conservation has resulted in more designations and protection than virtually any other, suburban conservation activity is surprisingly well-established. A key difference with the United States is that area designation is a local, not national, process. Older suburbs have been protected from the earliest years of the current system (introduced in 1947 for buildings and 1967 for areas). It is the inter-war suburb which caused intense debate when the first designations were made in the late 1980s; but many more such designations are now being made. The issue is how designation affords protection. Here there are differences between suburban types – Larkham contrasts the wealth and influence of the residents of Hampstead Garden Suburb, very much a resident-driven conservation process, with the top-down attempt in part of 1930s Birmingham. Conflicts between residents' aspirations and the planning system, between residents and local government, and between local and central government characterize this branch of UK conservation. Work on the nature and scale of suburban change generally (cf Whitehand and Carr) suggests that a broader concept of 'management', implying more than 'conservation', would be required.

The chapters by Ames and Larkham explicitly demonstrate the importance of an awareness of continuity: evident in the suburban landscape, in the aspirations of its residents, and in the actions of its planners and managers. In issues of conservation and management, once more, detailed knowledge of origins and processes are vital prerequisites. In this, they reinforce what has become a key theme of this collection: one raised in other contexts, both explicitly and implicitly, by virtually all other contributors.

In conclusion, then, this collection of individually distinctive but closely interlinked chapters is intended to broaden our knowledge of historical and contemporary suburban processes and forms. It has also explicitly developed links between the historical and contemporary analyses, thus beginning to close the gap which the editors identified earlier. After all, as the chapters on conservation and management suggest, one of the key elements in suburbs is their continuity – of form, use, even of actual inhabitants – over extended periods. Values and attitudes do, however, change – witness the emergence of a feminist critique of the suburbs, and a growing suburban nostalgia. Such changes in values and expectations govern the whole approach to the suburb: is its governance or physical form modified in the light of these changes – and is this modification an incremental change or a directed managerial approach (e.g. Turkington; Whitehand and Carr)?

There are similarities in form, process and product in the particular nations which we have selected to represent here. It is too simplistic to suggest that these are a result of shared traditions; the former colonies have sought far too hard for their individual, even nationalistic, self-expression for that to be true. Exploration of these similarities demands still more comparative analysis. It is also instructive to review differences. As Strong-Boag *et al.* suggest, the place of the suburb is closely allied to the national self-image. There are close relationships between Australia and the United States, with their core national visions of independence. The position is more ambiguous in Canada and Britain; although the former centre of the Empire has long held that 'an Englishman's home is his castle' (*sic*) it is now very questionable whether there is any 'national identity' and whether the suburban lifestyle forms any part of it. A new line of research is needed to examine in far greater detail the national similarities and differences, the position of the suburb in national culture, the linkages between history and the present – and, indeed, the implications for the future suburb.

NOTES

1. References in this section may be found in the full *Oxford English Dictionary* entry on 'suburb'.

2. Alexander von Hoffman (1994) has argued that residents of city neighbourhoods have also sought to create community, but this is a minor theme in the American literature.

3. Using a different methodology, Muthesius (1982) has effectively made a similar point about the terraced housing which preceded the semi-detached suburbs.

REFERENCES

Adams, A. (1995) The Eichler home. Intention and experience in postwar suburbia, in Cromley, E.C. and Hodgins, C.L. (eds.) *Gender, Class, and Shelter. Perspectives in Vernacular Architecture.* Knoxville, TN.: University of Tennessee Press, pp. 164–178.

Agnew, J., Mercer, J. and Sopher, D. (1984) Introduction, in Agnew, J., Mercer, J. and Sopher, D. (eds.) *The City in Cultural Context.* London: Allen and Unwin, pp. 1–30.

Al-Hindi, K.F. and Staddon, C. (1997) The hidden histories and geographies of neotraditional planning: the case of Seaside, Florida. *Environment and Planning D: Society and Space,* Vol. 15, pp. 349–372.

Allport, C. (1983) Women and suburban housing: postwar planning in Sydney, in Williams, P. (ed.) *Social Process and the City, 1943–1961.* Sydney: Allen and Unwin, pp. 64–87.

Archer, J. (1987) *The Great Australian Dream.* Sydney: Angus and Robertson.

Architectural Review (1973) Special issue on 'sociable housing', *Architectural Review*, Vol. CLIV, No. 920.

Ashton, P.J. (1984) Urbanization and the dynamics of suburban development under capitalism, in Tabb, W.K. and Sawers, L. (eds.) *Marxism and the Metropolis.* New York: Oxford University Press, pp. 54–81.

Baker, N.J. (1997) History and Archaeology at St Clement's Gate, Worcester. Unpublished paper presented to the conference 'History, Heritage and Urban Design', Worcester.

Baldasarre, M. (1992) Suburban communities. *Annual Review of Sociology*, Vol. 18, pp. 475–494.

Barrett, B. (1971) *The Inner Suburbs. The Evolution of an Industrial Area.* Melbourne: Melbourne University Press.

Beresford, M.W. (1988) *East End, West End: the Face of Leeds during Urbanisation, 1684–1842.* Publications of the Thoresby Society Vols LX and LXI, Nos 131 and 132. Leeds: Thoresby Society.

Berger, B. (1960) *Working-Class Suburb: a Study of Auto Workers in Suburbia.* Berkeley: University of California Press.

Berger, B. (1961) The myth of suburbia. *Journal of Social Issues*, Vol. 17 (November), pp. 38–49.

Binford, H.C. (1985) *The First Suburbs: Residential Communities in the Boston Periphery, 1815–1860.* Chicago: University of Chicago Press.

Borchert, J. (1996) Residential city suburbs. The emergence of a new suburban type. *Journal of Urban History*, Vol. 22, No. 3, pp. 283–307.

Bourassa, S., Greig, A.W. and Troy, P. (1995) The limits of housing policy: home ownership in Australia. *Housing Studies*, Vol. 10, No. 1, pp. 83–104.

Bourne, L.S. and Ley, D. (1993) Introduction. The social context and diversity of urban Canada, in *The Changing Social Geography of Canadian Cities.* Montreal and Kingston: McGill-Queen's University Press, pp. 3–30.

Boyd, R. (1960) *The Australian Ugliness.* Melbourne: Cheshire.

Bunce, M. (1994) *The Countryside Ideal. Anglo-American Images of Landscape.* London: Routledge.

Burnett, J. (1986) *A Social History of Housing, 1815–1985.* London: Methuen.

Cannadine, D. (1980) *Lords and Landlords: the Aristocracy and the Towns, 1774–1947.* Leicester: Leicester University Press.

Chaney, D. (1997) Authenticity and suburbia, in Westwood, S. and Williams, J. (eds.) *Imagining Cities: Scripts, Signs, Memory.* London: Routledge, pp. 140–151.

Clawson, M. and Hall, P. (1973) *Planning and Urban Growth. An Anglo-American Comparison.* Baltimore: Johns Hopkins University Press.

Cullingworth, J.B. (1993) *The Political Culture of Planning: American Land Use Planning in Comparative Perspective.* London and New York: Routledge.

Davison, G. (1978) *The Rise and Fall of Marvellous Melbourne.* Melbourne: Melbourne University Press.

Davison, G. (1994) The past and future of the Australian suburb, in Johnson, L.C. (ed.) *Suburban Dreaming: an Interdisciplinary Approach to Australian Cities.* Geelong, Victoria: Deakin University Press, pp. 99–113.

Davison, G. (1995). Australia. The first suburban nation? *Journal of Urban History*, Vol. 22, No. 1, pp. 40–74.

Davison, G. and Davison, B. (1995) Suburban pioneers, in Davison, G., Dingle, T. and O'Hanlon, S. (eds.) *The Cream Brick Frontier. Histories of Australian Suburbia.* Monash Publications in History, Department of History, Monash University, Clayton, Victoria.

Delafons, J. (1995) review of Quantrill, M. and Webb, B. (1993) *Urban Forms and Suburban Dreams*. Texas University Press Collehe Station. In *Cities*, Vol. 12, No. 1, pp. 79–80.

Department of the Environment (1992) Design Bulletin 32 *Residential Roads and Footpaths: Layout Considerations*. London: HMSO (first edition 1977).

Doucet, M. and Weaver, J. (1991) *Housing the North American City*. Montreal and Kingston: McGill-Queen's University Press.

Douglass, H. (1925) *The Suburban Trend*. New York: Century.

Dyos, H.J. (1961) *Victorian Suburb. A Study of the Growth of Camberwell*. Leicester: Leicester University Press.

Dyos, H.J. and Reeder, D. (1973) Slums and suburbs, in Dyos, H.J. and Wolff, M. (eds.) *The Victorian City. Images and Reality*. Vol. II. London; Routledge and Kegan Paul, pp. 359–386.

Edwards, A.M. (1981) *The Design of Suburbia: a Critical Study in Environmental History*. London: Pembridge Press.

Esher, L. (1981) *A Broken Wave: the Rebuilding of England, 1940–1980*. London: Allen Lane.

Essex County Council (1973) *Design Guide for Residential Areas*. Chelmsford: Essex County Council (the 'Essex Design Guide'; revised edition January 1998).

Fishman, R. (1987) *Bourgeois Utopias. The Rise and Fall of Suburbia* New York: Basic Books.

Foley, M.M. (1980) *The American House*. New York: Harper and Row.

Frost, L. (1991) *The New Urban Frontier. Urbanization and City-Building in Australasia and the American West*. Sydney: University of New South Wales Press.

Gans, H.J. (1959) *The Levittowners*. New York: Pantheon.

Gans, H.J. (1972) Urbanism and suburbanism as ways of life. A re-evaluation of definitions, in Gans, H.J. (ed.) *People and Plans*. Harmondsworth: Penguin, pp. 41–64.

Garreau, J. (1991) *Edge City: Life on the New Frontier*. New York: Doubleday.

Gaskell, S.M. (1995) review of Oliver, P., Davis, I. and Bentley, I. (1994) *Dunroamin: the Suburban Semi and its Enemies*. London: Pimlico, in *Town Planning Review*, Vol. 66, No. 3, p. 336.

Ginsburg, L. (1973) Summing up, *Architectural Review*, Vol. CLIV, No. 920, pp. 263–265.

Girling, C. and Helphand, K. (1994) *Yard-Street-Park: the Design of Suburban Open Space*. New York: Wiley.

Glancey, J. (1994) *Heaven, Hell and Suburbia*, three TV programmes, Channel 4, April.

Goldberg, M. and Mercer, J. (1986) *The Myth of the North American City: Continentalism Challenged*. Vancouver: University of British Columbia Press.

Goldfield, D.R. and Brownell, B.A. (1979) *Urban America: from Downtown to No Town*. Boston: Houghton Mifflin.

Goodman, D. (1993) Comparative urban and suburban history: an interview with Kenneth Jackson. *Australasian Journal of American Studies*, Vol. 12, pp. 65–72.

Gowans, A. (1986) *The Comfortable House: North American Suburban Architecture 1890–1930*. Cambridge, Mass.: MIT Press.

Gray, F. and Duncan, S. (1978) Etymology, mystification and urban geography. *Area*, Vol. 10, No. 4, pp. 297–301.

Harris, R. (1996) *Unplanned Suburbs: Toronto's American Tragedy 1900–1950*. Baltimore: Johns Hopkins University Press.

Harris, R. and Hamnett, C. (1987) The myth of the Promised Land. The social diffusion of home ownership in Britain and North America. *Annals, Association of American Geographers*, Vol. 77, No. 2, pp. 173–190.

Harris, R. and Lewis, R. (1998) Constructing a fault(y) zone. Misrepresentions of American cities and suburbs, 1900–1950. *Annals of the Association of American Geographers*, Vol.88, No. 4, pp. 622–639.

Harris, R. and Lewis, R. (2000) The geography of North American cities and suburbs. A reinterpretation. *Journal of Urban History* (forthcoming)

Hartz, L. (1964) *The Founding of New Societies*. New York: Harcourt, Brace and World.

Hayden, D. (1984) *Redesigning the American Dream*. New York: Norton.

Higgins, J.P.P. (1995) The Emergence of Capitalist Modes of Production: Urban Morphogenesis and Social Theory. Unpublished paper presented to the Institute of British Geographers Annual Conference, Newcastle upon Tyne.

Hirsch, A. (1983) *Making the Second Ghetto: Race and Housing in Chicago, 1940–1960*. Cambridge, Cambridge University Press.

Hohenberg, P.M. and Lees, L.H. (1995) *The Making of Urban Europe 1000–1994*. Cambridge, MA: Harvard University Press.

Jackson, A.A. (1973) *Semi-Detached London: Suburban Development, Life and Transport, 1900–39*. London: Allen and Unwin.

Jackson, K. (1985) *Crabgrass Frontier. The Suburbanization of the United States*. New York: Oxford University Press.

Jenks, M., Burton, E. and Williams, K. (eds.) (1996) *The Compact City: a Sustainable Urban Form?* London: Spon.

Katz, P. (ed.) (1992) *The New Urbanism: Towards an Architecture of Community*. New York: McGraw-Hill.

Keating, A.D. (1988) *Building Chicago. Suburban Developers and the Creation of a Divided Metropolis* Columbus: Ohio State University Press.

Kelly, B. (1993) *Expanding the Dream. Building and Rebuilding Levittown*. Albany, N.Y.: State University of New York Press.

Kendig, H. (1979) *New Life for Old Suburbs*. Sydney: George Allen and Unwin.

Kemeny, J. (1981) *The Myth of Homeownership*. London: Routledge and Kegan Paul.

Knox, P.L. (1992) The packaged landscapes of post-suburban America, in Whitehand, J.W.R. and Larkham, P.J. (eds.) *Urban Landscapes: International Perspectives*. London: Routledge, pp. 207–226.

Lehmann, N. (1991) *The Promised Land: the Great Black Migration and How it Changed America*. New York: Knopf.

Lilley, K.D. (1995) Medieval Coventry: A Study in Town-Plan Analysis. Unpublished PhD thesis, School of Geography, University of Birmingham.

Marsh, M. (1990) *Suburban Lives*. New Brunswick: Rutgers University Press.

Masotti, L.H. (1973) Prologue: suburbia reconsidered – myth and counter-myth, in Masotti, L.H. and Hadden, J.K. (eds.) *The Urbanization of the Suburbs*. Urban Affairs Annual Reviews, Vol. 7. Beverly Hills: Sage, pp.15–22.

McCann, L. (1996) Planning and building the corporate suburb of Mount Royal, 1910–1925. *Planning Perspectives*, Vol. 11, No. 3, pp. 259–302.

McKenzie, E. (1994) *Privatopia. Homeowner Associations and the Rise of Residential Private Government*. New Haven: Yale University Press.

Mohney, D. and Easterling, K. (eds.) (1991) *Seaside: Making a Town in America*. New York and London: Princeton Architectural Press and Phaidon.

Moudon, A.V. (1990) *Master-Planned Communities: Shaping Exurbs in the 1990s*. Seattle: University of Washington Urban Design Program.

Moudon, A.V. (1992) The evolution of twentieth-century residential forms: an American case study, in Whitehand, J.W.R. and Larkham, P.J. (eds.) *Urban Landscapes: International Perspectives*. London: Routledge, pp. 170–206.

Mumford, L. (1966) *The City in History*. Harmondsworth: Penguin.

Muthesius, S. (1982) *The English Terraced House* New Haven: Yale University Press.

Nairn, I. (1955) *Outrage*. Special issue of *Architectural Review*, Vol. 117, pp. 363–454.

Oliver, P., Davis, I. and Bentley, I. (1994) *Dunroamin: the Suburban Semi and its Enemies*. London: Pimlico (originally published 1981 by Barrie and Jenkins).

Palen, J.J. (1995) *The Suburbs*. New York: McGraw-Hill.

Palmer, F.R. and Crowquill, A. (*c.* 1846) *Wanderings of a Pen and Pencil*. (No publisher given).

Perin, C. (1988) *Belonging in America. Reading Between the Lines*. Madison, Wisconsin: University of Wisconsin Press.

Ravetz, A. and Turkington, R. (1995) *The Place of Home: English Domestic Environments, 1914–2000*. London: Spon.

Rolt, L.T.C. (1944) *Narrow Boat*. London: Methuen.

Rowse, T. (1978) Heaven and a Hills Hoist. Australian critics on suburbia. *Meanjin*, Vol. 37, No. 1, pp. 3–13.

Rybczynski, W. (1995) *City Life: Urban Expectations in a New World*. New York: HarperCollins.

Schnore, L.F. (1962) City-suburban income differentials in metropolitan areas. *American Sociological Review*, Vol. 27, pp. 252–255.

Sennett, R. (1970) *Families Against the City. Middle Class Homes of Industrial Chicago, 1870–1890*. Cambridge, MA: Harvard University Press.

Sharp, T. (1936) *English Panorama*. London: Dent.

Sies, M. (1997) Paradise retained. An analysis of persistence in planned, exclusive suburbs 1880–1980. *Planning Perspectives*, Vol. 12, No. 2, pp. 165–192.

Silverstone, R. (ed.) (1997) *Visions of Suburbia*. London: Routledge.

Slater, T.R. (1978) Family, society and the ornamental villa on the fringes of English country towns. *Journal of Historical Geography*, Vol. 4, No. 2, pp. 129–144.

Smit, J. (1996) The car out back. *Building* (Building Homes supplement) August, pp. 34–37.

Southworth, M. and Ben-Joseph, E. (1997) *Streets and the Shaping of Towns and Cities*. New York: McGraw-Hill.

Spens, M. (1992) The riddle of Australian suburbia. *Architectural Review*, No. 11545, pp. 75–79.

Stern, R.A.M. (1981) *The Anglo-American suburb*. Architectural Design Profile. London: Academy Editions.

Stilgoe, J. (1988) *Borderland: Origins of the American Suburb, 1820–1939*. New Haven: Yale University Press.

Strong-Boag, V. (1991) Home dreams. Women and the suburban experiment in Canada, 1945–60. *Canadian Historical Review*, Vol. 72, pp. 471–504.

Sudjic, D. (1994) Nightmare on Acacia Avenue, *The Guardian*, 14 April, p. 2.

Taylor, G. (1915) *Satellite Cities. A Study of Industrial Suburbs*. New York: Appleton.

Teaford, J.C. (1997) *Post-Suburbia. Government and Politics in the Edge Cities*. Baltimore: Johns Hopkins University Press.

Thompson, F.M.L. (ed.) (1982*a*) *The Rise of Suburbia*. Leicester: Leicester University Press.

Thompson, F.M.L. (1982*b*) Introduction, in Thompson, F.M.L. (ed.) *The Rise of Suburbia*. Leicester: Leicester University Press, pp. 2–25.

Thorns, D.C. (1972) *Suburbia*. London: McGibbon and Kee.

Troy, P. (1996) *The Perils of Urban Consolidation*. Sydney: Federation Press.

von Hoffman, A. (1994) *Local Attachments: the Making of an American Urban Neighborhood*. Baltimore: Johns Hopkins University Press.

Ward, S. (ed.) (1992) *The Garden City: Past, Present and Future*. London: Spon.

Wentling, J. (1995) *Designing a Place called Home: Reordering the Suburbs*. New York: Chapman and Hall.

Whitehand, J.W.R. and Carr, C.M.H. (1995) Changing English suburbs. Unpublished paper presented to the Institute of British Geographers Annual Conference, Newcastle upon Tyne.

Wiese, A. (1993) Places of our own. Suburban Black towns before 1960. *Journal of Urban History*, Vol. 19, No. 3, pp. 30–54.

Williams, R. (1975) *The Country and the City*. London: Paladin.

Winter, J., Coombes, T. and Farthing, S. (1993) Satisfaction with space around the home on large private sector estates. *Town Planning Review*, Vol. 64, No. 1, pp. 65–79.

Wood, R. (1958) *Suburbia; its People and Their Politics*. Boston: Houghton Mifflin.

Wright, G. (1981) *Building the Dream: a Social History of Housing in America*. New York: Pantheon.

Wrong, D.H. (1967) Suburbs and the myth of suburbia, in Wrong, D.H. and Gracey, H.L. (eds.) *Readings in Introductory Sociology*. New York: Macmillan.

Young, A. (1932 edition) *Tours in England and Wales by Arthur Young*. Reprints of Scarce Tracts in Economics and Political Science no. 14. London: London School of Economics.

CHAPTER 2

British Suburban Taste, 1880–1939

Peter Newby and Mark Turner

The growth of suburbs is intimately connected with the growth in consumption and the rise of mass consumerism. Two broad processes link these together. First, the sheer increase in the number of houses and households stimulated a demand for products to place in them. Each household would require tables, chairs, beds, crockery, utensils and so on. This process was particularly important in the late nineteenth and early twentieth centuries and again in the interwar period. At these times there was a sustained programme of house building – substantially private but including a small though significant public sector involvement. Between 1901 and 1911, for example, London grew from 6.5 million to 7.2 million and again from 1921 to 1931 from 7.4 million to 8.2 million, growth rates of about 10 per cent in each decade. However, the rates of suburban growth were much higher because of the redistribution of the city's population. For the first decade of the century, Jackson (1991) identifies 25 districts with growth rates of over 25 per cent (and some, such as Southgate in north London and Coulsdon in south London with rates of over 100 per cent). The post-First World War period again saw sustained and even massive growth. Up to 1931 Hendon and Mitcham more than doubled in size, Wembley increased by 260 per cent and Dagenham by almost 900 per cent. In the following eight years (to 1939) the outer suburbs of London were the major sites of expansion and Bexley, Chislehurst, Orpington, Harrow, Hayes, Carshalton and Esher all grew by more than 100 per cent.

In addition to the growth in the number of suburban households, there was a second process at work that linked suburbanization with mass consumption and that was the growing affluence of the inhabitants. Affluence was reflected in the acquisition of more furniture, more equipment, more belongings, in the purchase of higher value and better quality goods and, as we shall show, in the consumption of design. It is the exercise of choice in the consumption of design that is central to our analysis of suburbia. Not only did it permit people to represent themselves in the social milieu more effectively, the very fact that design was a consumption product was a stimulus to further consumption as created designs moved first in and then out of fashion.

These two processes, of growth in the number of households and increasing affluence, were at work also in the United States. Between 1850 and 1950 the twelve largest American cities increased their combined area from 144 square miles to 1267 square miles (Jackson, 1985, p. 140) and the use of design both to segment society and to reflect social position and aspirations was equally strong.

While the focus of this chapter is on the relationship between taste and the consumption of design, the analysis should be considered in the context of the role of the suburb in the macro process of social and economic development. The role of cities as generators of conspicuous consumption is accepted by historians. Burke (1993, p. 157) quotes a claim as early as the sixteenth century for this. However, there is little work on the role of suburbs and an analysis of their part in the consumption process (although Bentley (1994) suggests the scale of the impact with his analysis of the 'planes of choice' facing the new suburbanite). Yet their development was a profound stimulus to consumption (and thus to production) and they were a clearly defined market for the goods the economic system was capable of producing. In other words, they were an engine for economic prosperity and an environment in which to enjoy the fruits of that prosperity. They were also instrumental in the process of social formation. The operation of the housing market (and, as we shall see, the consumption of design) neatly segmented people into groups, and visual appearance, both inside and outside the house, as well as location, clearly represented their social standing. In addition, suburbs functioned as a framework and an environment in which people could learn about the process of consumption, both how to consume and the standards at which to consume. Within the period covered by this chapter there were two distinct foci for this learning. The first, associated with the growth of the Victorian and Edwardian suburbs, was the process of learning to be middle-class consumers. The second, the inter-war period, reflected changed social relations in which suburbanites learned to be modern consumers.

The process of learning to consume is central to our exploration of suburban taste. Our purpose in this chapter is to demonstrate the significance of design for suburban consumers. This significance is closely associated with how consumers wished to represent their social standing. The evidence on which we base our argument is drawn substantially from Middlesex University's Silver Studio Collection. This is a collection of wallpaper and furnishing designs produced for major manufacturers throughout our period. We begin, though, with a review of the consumption of design from a theoretical perspective.

THE CONSUMPTION OF DESIGN

The consumption of design is a particular case of a general conceptualization of consumption. At one level, we consume in order to make use of the functionality of the product or service. However, if this were the sole purpose of consumption there is little merit, within any price range, in producing more than one version of a product; assuming that all versions are equally effective. To understand consumption we must go beyond the job that the product purports to do or that the service seems to give. Manufacturers and service providers seek to establish differences between their offer and others on the market in the hope that the consumer can be persuaded to value some or all of the difference as being additional to the basic function of the product. For material products, the differences can be technological (for example, electronic as opposed to mechanical controls). Alternatively they can be design differences that affect the appearance and attractiveness of the product. Bucock (1993, pp. 154–155) observes that consumerism 'depends on a set of symbols becoming comprehensive to potential customers'. 'These symbols', he notes, 'cannot be simply imposed upon customers by capitalist companies advertising their products, they have to tone in with the potential customers' own ways of life'.

Our selection of products tells us something about the values that individually and as groups we place on the differences. If these differences relate to the functional operation of the product then they can be handled quite effectively in a rational economic decision-making model. However, if they are not functionally based (a glass topped table as opposed to a wooden table, a white chair as opposed to a natural wood finish), then we need a different model in order to understand not just our reasons for choosing but also the purpose of our consuming. Economists have recognized the significance of this in their theorization of demand but, all too frequently, as Douglas and Isherwood (1980) point out, they treat explanation as a 'black box' in which internal processes of causation and influence are not exposed. They do, however, point to some explanations which incorporate the socio-historical concept of 'social emulation' (Douglas and Isherwood, 1980, p. 46). The same concept has been used to explain the consumer revolution in eighteenth century England (see McKendrick *et al.* (1982), discussed in Fine and Leopold, 1993).

Consumption as Symbol

Our ability to purchase goods and services rests on our ability to pay for them. Those who can afford expensive goods mark out their status by their possession of such goods. Goods, then, have both a functional purpose and a symbolic purpose; that is, they represent something which the purchaser wishes to be represented. The existence of a symbolic purpose is not, however, limited to expensive goods. If one can only afford cheap products, then the possession of these and no others is an effective representation of status. In this situation, the representation is determined by the absence of the ability to choose. Where a purchaser can exercise choice, the representation implied by the purchase is not determined solely by economic circumstance but by the values and drives underlying the choices that were made. At this point the argument becomes particularly interesting, since representation ceases to be the consequence of a purchase and becomes its purpose. As Featherstone (1990, p. 5) points out, goods are used 'to create social bonds or distinctions', and he echoes Baudrillard when he states that 'consumption entails the active manipulation of signs' (p. 7). In arguing this, Featherstone both accepts and moves beyond the notion of status cultures. Peterson's review of research into status cultures (Peterson, 1979) demonstrates how products can be used to express social cohesion and, in some cases, an outlook on life. Where theorists such as Bourdieu (1984), Bucock (1993), Featherstone (1990) and others would differ is in seeing this process as part of a broader social determination, rather than as an end in itself. The argument is that, if goods are used as markers, then the aspiration for a particular social position is achieved by the acquisition of an appropriate set of marker goods and the possession of the necessary economic and cultural resources through which to acquire them. At this higher level of theory, the function of consumption is not just to represent social relations but to reproduce and reinforce them.

Design as a Consumption Good

So far, consumption has been explored through the neutral concept of a 'good'. At this point we wish to introduce the notion of design. Notionally, design attractiveness is the product of integrating the functional and the aesthetic. The latter is not, however, absolute. Our selection of design may well be influenced by what others may think of it – and, by implication, what they will think of us for choosing it. Because of this, the consumption of design is inherently symbolic. In some situations it reflects socio-economic status – for example, the ability, consistently, to buy in the art and antiques market of established taste or to support innovative new designers and, through their work, to reflect the *avant-garde*. In other circumstances, wealth can lead to ostentatiousness that offends 'good taste'. At the other end of the spectrum, limited resources need not be a bar to acceptable, creative design solutions. The builders of suburbia, as Davis (1994) and Bentley (1994) point out, made use of the symbolic and representational role of design by creating an ambiguity (or, as Bentley (1994) terms it, 'multivalence') which could appeal to a range of social backgrounds and outlooks. At one level it was an effective marketing tool, at another an opportunity for consumers to express themselves.

Constraints on Taste

The process of choosing design can be represented as a series of influences and forces. In this, the key to the selection of design is the creation and exercise of taste. This is a complex concept. On the one hand it is externally constrained and, on the other, it is internally driven. To exercise taste is not to exercise free will. If nothing else there is an economic control since, like all goods, design has its price in the marketplace. Perhaps as important is the milieu (the status group) which provides examples of the exercise of taste. This constitutes the design character and provides the design standards that inform individual choice. Through time, and with the exercise of taste, there arises a set of experiences that are the consequence of being able to test one's own taste in the broader social environment. The feedback from this (in the context of financial constraints and established benchmarks of design standards) is a major influence upon the development of taste.

There is, however, within this explanation a 'black box' which still has to be explored. Where does the understanding of new design solutions and the ability to ensure that the exercise of one's own taste is effective in design and social terms come from? Underlying this whole process is an aesthetic sensitivity that sets limits on both creativity and the ability to understand design theory, design intentions and design outcomes. The extent to which these limits are tested depends on one's awareness of design principles (both current and from the past) and of the products that flowed from the application of these principles. In the case of suburban taste, learning about design has been particularly important. However, while it is one thing to know about appropriate taste, it is another to be able to exercise it. As with all skills, some people will be effective and others less so. This has been called 'competence' (see Cubitt, 1988, p. 130), the ability to create a design concept and then select the products which will implement the concept. It implies an ability to link theory and practice and to ensure that the design solution is more than a simple aggregation of products.

Consumption Paradigms

So far, the influences that have been discussed represent limits on choice behaviour. They make no statement about the purpose of that behaviour. At a macro theoretical level there are those who would argue that opportunities and experience combine to limit the range of goals one might have. We would accept it as an argument but, in terms of our representation of design choices, it is more useful to see taste as being used to achieve a purpose than to regard it as being constrained to ensure a high degree of class reproduction. Thus the consumption paradigm that is adopted is central to the way taste is exercised. By 'consumption paradigm' we mean the goal orientation of purchasing behaviour – what we use taste to try to achieve. The consumption paradigm can be as broad as the selection of a lifestyle or the desire not to stand out. It can be aspirational or it can be static; it can be alternative or it can be conventional; it can be individual or it can be collective.

The consumption paradigm we follow predisposes our expenditure and selection of goods. Design helps us to position ourselves within that paradigm and, through the paradigm, in society at large. The consumption of design aims at more than social emulation. It is an attempt to say something about our position, importance, aspirations and outlook in ways that can be understood by those whose judgements we value. The choices we make in design represent the way in which we reconcile two competing drives – the drive to conform and the drive to be different. We conform either as an act of solidarity or through a sense of insecurity. If we conform in design terms, we choose within the framework and limits of a prevailing or acknowledged style. A prevailing style is socially conditioned and is an expression of what is socially acceptable. Design is also a medium through which we can express our individuality and free ourselves from the conventions of conforming. Individuality is, sometimes, allied with a drive for leadership; in other situations it is a statement that one is guided by personal values rather than by social pressures. This situation can lead to the adoption of an alternative lifestyle or a move into the design conventions of another (higher) status group. Thus what passes for conformity in one group may constitute individuality if expressed in a different social context.

The Intersection of Influence

This discussion of the influences upon taste is, in many ways, artificial since it is based upon a level of differentiation and separation that in reality does not exist. Income and status are associated and the nature of one's experience depends on life chances – which, in turn, are affected by the cultural attributes of status and the range of opportunities opened up by wealth. All of these influences acting together could affect one's awareness of design influences, and may even affect the development of aesthetic sensitivity. The consumption paradigm that is adopted is unlikely to be independent of socio-economic influences. Zablocki and Kanter (1976) distinguish between economically-based lifestyles and others where the link with income generation is absent. However, whatever the values driving these alternative lifestyles, there is an argument, which Zablocki and Kanter acknowledge, that choice in the character of a lifestyle is enabled by the level of personal capital that has been accumulated. Together these influences form taste and create a predilection and preference within style alternatives. Taste is both a set of standards and a set of aspirations, both mediated through competence. The outcome is a creative and productive process – the selection of design solutions.

Dimensions of Design Choice

The selection of design implies reaching a decision along four dimensions of design choice. Two are strongly influenced by wealth and disposable income and two by aesthetic awareness and sensitivity. The four dimensions are:

- a preference for an individually created product as against a mass produced product;
- the wish to purchase an expensive product as against the ability to buy a cheaper one;

- a desire for a uniform design solution as opposed to an eclectic one; and
- acceptance of prevailing design solutions as against a preference for alternative designs.

The positions we adopt (or are forced to adopt) in respect of these choices define the way in which we enter the market for design. In some cases, our choice is constrained. We might prefer to buy handcrafted Georgian furniture, but if we cannot afford it we may enter the market for Victorian reproductions. Equally important for our argument is that choice is constrained if we are unaware of design alternatives or if we are inhibited from selecting specific solutions. As we shall see, the role of the 'tastemaker' was important for suburban consumers.

Consumption Judgements

The interaction of style (a set of social, artistic and aesthetic conventions) and taste (a disposition to choose and the competence of the choosing) leads to self-expression and self-representation through design. How 'good' one's taste may be depends on a combination of competence and awareness in the selection and combination of design elements. 'Good' in this way is a social judgement that can be made by others of similar or different status. Different groups might make different judgements of the same design conception, and the different judgements are used to establish or reinforce social divisions. What someone from the same status group may find acceptable may be found to be desirable by someone from a lower status group, and may be rejected by someone from a higher status group. What is attractive to someone of an equivalent status might be 'quite nice but not to my taste' to someone in a higher group – a phrase that is recognizably a social 'put-down'. Taste can be used to test and even break the limits of stylistic convention. Taste can value contrast (which produces tensions within a style) and difference (which tests a new style against a prevailing style). It operates along two dimensions, one of coherence and integrity (which ranges from purism to eclecticism) and the other, essentially temporal in nature, which ranges from the conservative adoption of established style to the *avant-garde* anticipation of the next idiom.

The result of the interaction of these dimensions of choice and taste preferences and competencies is a personal design solution whose purpose is social representation. In broad terms, the outcomes can be placed into one of three categories: those that are conformist; those that are individual but accepted and acclaimed; and those that are individual and rejected. The first two can be placed within Bourdieu's (1984) classification of *habitus* – the product of an internalized set of group norms whose effect is to create social distinction. Conformist solutions are the keys to social categorization. Individualist solutions which are accepted are routes to establishing leadership positions through stylistic innovation. Individualist solutions which are not accepted are seen as not having sufficient cultural capital in the expression of taste to establish a worthwhile social position. Douglas and Isherwood (1980, p. 59) quote an example of a New York hostess of the 1890s who, seeking to emulate (or surpass) a rival who had given each dinner guest a jewel as a memento, failed (and was subject to the guests' derision) when she placed a $100 bill in each napkin. The problem for many, as they moved into the suburbs in the nineteenth and twentieth centuries, was to avoid falling into this trap. It is this simple fact that explains the role and importance of tastemakers during this period.

EDUCATING THE CONSUMER

A prevailing style does not just arise; it is created by a complex of tastemakers who, in seeking to influence consumers, serve also to influence each other. Taste-makers work through the media and the design literature to influence both the consumer and producer. They achieve their influence through demonstration, approbation and criticism. The outcomes of this are that, on the one hand, they create style; and on the other, they achieve improved competence in the con-sumption of design. Tastemakers – who have included independent authors, housemaker journals and the promotional literature of manufacturers and retailers – have been particularly influential during the period we are considering.

The creation of style is not the consequence of a random set of aesthetic decisions. As early as the eighteenth century, there were those in the luxury goods trade who recognized that innovation in design (the process by which fashion changes) was a strategy for generating high profits (see Styles, 1993). As Rosenblum (1978) has demonstrated in relation to styles of photography, there is a clear relationship between the style product and the social conditions and relations that gave rise to that product. Through the period covered by this chapter, there was both constancy and change in these conditions. The personal motivations of the tastemakers – to use the process of informing and guiding to establish a position within society, within the design profession and within the media – were constant. In the early part of this period, the principal tastemakers were individuals and promotional literature. By the 1920s, however, journals were the principal influence.

What changed during this period was the pace of stylistic change itself. If we were to force distinctions upon our period, then the nineteenth century reflected stability and uniformity and the twentieth century innovation and variety. Baudrillard (1996) suggests something similar when he says that 'the arrange-ment of furniture (in a traditional environment) offers a faithful image of the familial and social structures of the period' (p. 15) but that with the modern home dweller we are seeing 'man the interior designer ... an active engineer of atmosphere' (p. 26). The shift from one to the other can be understood in terms of the conditions in which the tastemakers operated. Design advice in the nineteenth century was set within the social context of a household with servants (even clerks would have a 'maid of all work') and a domestic and social role for housewives. Much of the advice given to households was aimed at the mistress and was concerned with the management of servants and tradespeople. The clear social context of the advice was the establishment of middle-class values and middle-class behaviour. The role of the tastemaker was to teach people how to act as middle-class consumers. Edwards (1991) points out, from his assessment of furnishing estimates in the late-nineteenth and early-twentieth centuries, that there was a filtering-down of taste which reveals 'how, firstly, established room images remain the same for most parts of society and, secondly, how selected styles are established by taste leaders and are quickly adapted by a wider market' (p. 233). By the end of our period, the tastemakers were dealing with a new type of naïve consumer and a new and dynamic product environment. Many of those who moved to the suburbs after the First World War did so from the inner city. Others came from the depressed industrial or agricultural areas. They had frequently moved from rented accommodation, and their experience of consuming was limited. For these people the range of new products, the move from renting to buying, and the new environment combined to create at best uncertainty and often confusion. The journals which were produced during this time segmented the market and introduced the new products and designs which they thought would appeal to their readers. They reflected the social changes which were taking place.

Tastemakers generally worked in the same way – the demonstration of units of design, the articulation of rules for taste and the presentation of design solutions. As we move to the end of our period these three stages were often rolled into one as photographed display became widespread. Tastemakers informed consumers of new products and new designs. The pace of innovation in this area increased significantly in the inter-war period. With the increased use of pictures there was a tendency for nineteenth-century instruction ('the front door should, of course, never be grained, and it ought in these days to be quite unnecessary for me even to hint at such a thing' (Panton, 1896, p. 39)) to give way to demonstration in the form of actual room settings displayed in full colour.

The success of tastemakers is explained by the naïvety and insecurity of the market they served. Tastemakers persuaded, first, because they were of higher social status than those whom they were advising. Mrs Panton, the doyenne of the late-nineteenth century advisers, was the wife of a successful businessman. They reinforced their position relative to their audience by a combination of apparent authority, condescension and dogmatism. Mrs Panton was amongst the most dogmatic. The purpose of design was, for her, to create an appropriate environment for receiving visitors or for entertaining. She translated the behaviour of the established middle classes for those newly come to the suburbs. She observed that 'if the fresh resident has no introductions, his fate is sealed; the best people don't call' (Panton, 1896, p. 12). Similar publications were to be found in the United States. Catherine Beecher's and Harriet Beecher Stowe's *The American Woman's*

Home (1869) performed a similar role, if not in the same strident way, to Mrs Panton's work. Many of the ideas were imported from Britain. In the exercising of taste, Charles L. Eastlake's *Hints on Household Taste* (originally 1868) was particularly influential and went through six editions between 1872 and 1881. Clarence Cook's *The House Beautiful* (1895 in the United States), was published first in England in 1877.

As suburban dwellers became more established in their roles and more sophisticated in their understanding of the social niceties of consumption, so the character of the tastemakers' advice began to change. The dogmatic rights and wrongs of design and style were gradually replaced by a design vocabulary and an insight into design principles. The authors of the *Book of the Home* (Davidson, 1906) reflected this. 'The hall', they said, 'should not be hung with paper representing great blocks of marble; this would not only offend against the rule concerning one material imitating another . . . but would further be incongruous in an English urban or suburban dwelling' (vol. 1, p. 77). They chose also to reflect the different social functions of rooms in design terms with their advice that 'it is a good plan to introduce as much variety as possible into the different rooms, as this secures a complete change in going from one to the other' (vol. 2, p. 233). By the end of our period, the way in which the tastemakers operated is recognizably modern – informative, demonstrative, picture – rather than text-based. Their approach recognized that, with the number and range of products and designs available, there was, no longer, one design solution.

SUBURBAN TASTE AND DESIGN SOLUTIONS

If the suburbs represented an opportunity for social advancement in the nineteenth century, then living there could be a social nightmare. Far from expressing an improvement in one's social standing, the wrong choices could seriously undermine one's status. The selection of where to live and what to buy was fraught not just with difficulty but also with danger. In this section we review the interaction between fashion, taste and aspiration that led to the clear social basis in the selection and consumption of design from the late-nineteenth century through to the 1930s.

Middle-class Suburbia

In both Britain and the United States, the most important factor in the rapid expansion of suburbia in the 1880s and 1890s was the development of public transport, in particular the railway system. The inner cities were deteriorating socially and the railway enabled those who could afford it (and with a booming economy an increasing number could) to move to cleaner, more pleasant surroundings and still be within easy access of their place of employment. From the 1880s onwards, English railway companies issued regional guide books describing in detail the new suburbs served by their trains (Ward. 1998). They contained much useful information, with local property developers and estate agents being featured prominently. They also provided information on the local geology (always a matter of great importance to Victorians for health reasons[1]), schools, shops, religious provision and rates.

If there was no shortage of advice on choosing either the suburb or the house, it was quite a different matter when it came to guidance on home furnishing and decorating. Many new suburban residents had only recently risen to the ranks of the middle classes, and were anxious that their houses and their interiors should reflect this rise in status. Previously, the majority of Victorians had relied on their local upholsterer and cabinet maker for decorating advice. Household manuals such as Walsh's *Manual of Domestic Economy* (1857 and later editions) listed all the furniture one would expect to find in a middle-class house, and the only variation was in the cost and variety of the wood employed. The householder chose from pattern books supplied by the upholsterer, and durability and cost were the main concerns. It was not, in any case, fashionable to take too much interest in home decoration.

However, as the Industrial Revolution and competition from foreign imports increased, the cost of all household goods began to fall rapidly. There was a corresponding increase in styles and ranges of furnishing and decoration from Louis XV to Aesthetic; and, by 1880, home decorating in Britain and America was a national pastime. The need for advice by the confused but would-be fashionable suburbanite was desperate. The rich had been well-catered for in books such as Robert Kerr's *The Gentleman's House* (1864) and the artistic and aesthetic in William J. Loftie's *Art at Home* series (1876–78). The suburban resident, however, was faced with expanding furniture stores and the rise of the department store. Freed from the tyranny of the upholsterer and his pattern books, she (for it was usually a 'she') was able to wander round a showroom and see furniture arranged in room sets so that she could visualize it in her own home. This, in turn, fuelled the demand from ordinary middle-class people for advice on what they should buy and in what style.

The first publication in Britain to have a serious impact on popular suburban taste was *Cassell's Household Guide*. It first appeared in 1869 and subsequently ran into many editions. The earliest edition carried a series of articles on good taste in furniture and wallpaper, well illustrated with line engravings. As the demand for consumer advice on the subject grew, subsequent editions contained an ever-increasing number of articles on the aesthetics of home decoration. In the 1890 edition, Cassell's employed the most prolific and influential of advisers on suburban home decoration of the day, Jane Ellen Panton. Her books, including *From Kitchen to Garret* (1889) and *Suburban Residences and How to Circumvent Them* (1896) were best-sellers, and provide us with some of the best guides to suburban taste in the late-nineteenth century. While having many imitators, she was unique in both recommending specific patterns for wallpapers and fabrics and naming the stores which supplied them. By no means could she be regarded as *avant-garde*, for the style she recommended was the richly coloured, extremely cluttered look which we now regard as typically Victorian – but which was, in fact, a style unique to the 1880s and 1890s (figure 2.1). It was a style which was based on the use of very demonstrative wallpapers and wallpaper borders and filling the main living rooms of the house with as many small tables, books, plants, ornaments, cushions, hangings and paintings as was physically possible. Sitting rooms, in particular, were divided into sections by creating 'cosy corners' from Japanese screens or fretwork arches. Many architects and designers found the results appalling. A leading designer of the times, Lewis F. Day (whose wallpapers were, ironically, often recommended by Mrs Panton), attacked these lady decorators and wrote that

> their advice is always to buy! buy! buy! . . . but for the artless reference to Fashion one would have been puzzled to imagine the point of view of those who recommended by turns a 'lovely Louis XV rose coloured stripe' for one middle class room, a 'cheap Moorish arch' to outline the recess in another, a ready-made cosy corner for the landing and a stuffed bear to serve as a dumb waiter. (Day, 1893, p. 87)

Figure 2.1. Interior of an affluent household. (*Photograph*: from the archives of the Silver Studio)

The importance of the public rooms and of visiting in this period is revealed by Edwards' assessment of furnishing estimates. He demonstrates that 'the treatment of the public rooms conformed to a pattern, albeit varying in finish and quality, whereas that of the private rooms was much more arbitrary, and it was here that savings could be made' (Edwards, 1991, p. 236). It was important to Mrs Panton, and to those who followed her advice, that the product and the design correctly represented one's status. She was categorical that people should 'never allow themselves to be talked into buying the . . . hideous-patterned linoleum which gives a hopelessly 'bourgeois' appearance to any house' (Panton, 1896, p. 49).

There were several key decorative innovations of this period which together characterize the late Victorian house. First was the division of the wall into three sections by the inclusion of a dado and picture rail. This enabled different design treatments to be given to different sections. Second was the informality of the layouts, the product of decorative objects and mementoes. The present bought on holiday and signed with the name of the town was far more than a memento. It established that one could afford a holiday and, furthermore, it indicated that one could afford to go to better places than one's neighbours. The third design characteristic of this period is the move to dark colour schemes and rich materials. Lastly, as the factory system began to turn out mass-produced reproduction furniture, consumers became able to choose historicist styles appropriate to their design solutions.

These innovations were open to those who were sufficiently well off to introduce change. In the less affluent suburbs, purchasing new furniture was not an option and the incorporation of a dado rail was too expensive. As a result, houses in these areas retained the form and furnishings of the middle of the century; and only in the collection and display of objects did they emulate those who were better off.

A reaction to these ornate cluttered interiors was inevitable. Since the 1870s, architects such as Norman Shaw had been building houses that were based on traditional English vernacular architecture. Inspired by small manor houses and farmhouses of the seventeenth and eighteenth centuries, these houses featured leaded-paned windows, clay tiled gables and roofs, mellow brick and traditional timbers such as oak for doors, floors and window frames. Similarly, for the interiors, designers and architects such as William Morris, Christopher Dresser, C.R. Ashbee and C.F.A. Voysey had designed a range of textiles, wallpapers and furniture that often drew their inspiration from traditional and historic English patterns. Although these products of what was to become known as the Arts and Crafts Movement were beyond the means of the average suburban resident, from the turn of the century onwards, there was increasing interest from a new generation of educated suburbanites who were attracted to this style of architecture and who were learning to appreciate the work of the English cabinet-makers of the seventeenth and eighteenth centuries.

While industry had boomed in Britain in the late-nineteenth century, there had also been a severe agricultural depression which had resulted in the sale of many country estates and farmhouses. One consequence of this was that much seventeenth- and eighteenth-century furniture was now appearing for sale, particularly in the London antique shops. While the works of the famous eighteenth-century cabinet-makers such as Hepplewhite and Sheraton were beyond the reach of all but the rich, country-made furniture of the period was available at a very modest price. Coinciding with this was the highly important advance made in the technique of printing photographs by half-tone block. For the first time the suburban resident could browse through the pages of popular magazines such as *The Lady* or *Country Life*, and see what the inside of a genuine Tudor farmhouse or Georgian manor house really looked like. In America, the *Ladies Home Journal* performed a similar role. By 1890 this had become the most successful magazine, not only in America, but also much wider in the world. It played an enormously

Figure 2.2. Reproduction furniture from Oetzmann and Co.'s catalogue.

significant role in popularizing the bungalow and, from 1895, the editor, Edward Bok, was offering readers full building specifications. Its influence is hard to over-estimate.

By 1910 the demand for a house and interior that looked 'old' was dominating suburbia. The department stores and furniture shops were full of room displays of reproduction antique furniture (figure 2.2) and Oxford Street in London contained at least three large stores given over entirely to the sale of genuine or very carefully faked antique furniture.

By this time the fashion was to have a stylistic theme in furniture running through sitting room, dining room and even the main bedroom. The style of furniture and the overall appearance of rooms was becoming lighter and more controlled. The furnishing of the sitting room, in particular, established a design concept that, in many houses, is still alive today, with a sofa and two armchairs and some upright chairs arranged on a carpet square. The designs of other rooms and areas, though, were clearly of the period. Free-standing bedroom suites with washstands reflected the sparsity of internal sanitary arrangements. The use of papers (textured and painted to resemble wood) below the dado was to disappear soon after the war.

Design studios such as the Silver Studio[2] were kept busy designing fabrics that were based on authentic period designs and, increasingly, the more thoughtful suburban resident gave up using wallpaper as it was not appropriate for an historic interior. Even at the lowest end of speculative suburbia, builders realized that in order to sell their houses at least some vernacular trappings were essential, and were increasingly substituting sash windows with leaded casements and using tiles for gables and roofs instead of slates.

The First World War put an end to both house-building and furnishing and, even after the end of the war, shortages of both labour and materials drove the cost of all household goods to unheard-of heights. Interestingly, however, in the immediate post-war period two highly successful magazines devoted primarily to home decoration were launched. These still flourish today: *House and Garden*, which first appeared in 1919, and *Ideal Home*, which appeared in 1921. Both were aimed primarily at upper-middle class suburbia and interspersed articles and photographs of the houses of the rich, famous and artistic with money-saving tips for those who were well-bred but hit hard by the increases in income tax. *Ideal Home*, recognizing that labour shortages and pressure on middle-class incomes meant that the number of households keeping servants was falling, introduced material on practical household skills. The 1921 issues contained regular monthly features on gardening and keeping poultry, and there were occasional features on electricity (which included advice on how to change a fuse), spring-cleaning and mixing paint. The magazine acted as an information source on new products (the January issue reviewed labour saving devices such as a washer, a 'washing up machine', a plate washer, a knife cleaner, a vacuum cleaner and a cinder sifter). And there was a regular feature on the car, which served to instruct readers on its role and how to use and look after it. *Ideal Home* addressed a readership whose lifestyle and environment had changed greatly from before the war, and this was poignantly reflected in the August issue, which carried an article on the bed-sitting room.

It is from this period that social class in suburban taste can be most easily identified. In the 1860s and 1870s, the interiors of most suburban residences were remarkably similar. It was the size of the house and its grounds that provided the most important clue to the owner's income. Inside, there was a remarkable uniformity to the furnishings. From humble City clerk to successful stockbroker, every suburban drawing room had its gilt pier glass, white marble chimney piece and clock under a glass dome. The rich had rosewood, satinwood and walnut for their furniture, while lower down the social scale, mahogany was the preferred choice.

By the 1920s the prosperous, educated suburban resident furnished with genuine antique furniture, Persian rugs and old Staffordshire earthenware. Lower down the social scale, it was moquette-covered sofas, prints of Highland cattle and spindly tables often referred to as 'Sheraton' (figures 2.3 and 2.4).

In the late 1920s there was a second major suburban house building boom. Its effect was most noticeable in London, which had not been as badly hit by the Depression which had such a disastrous effect on the industrialized cities of the North. Like the late-nineteenth century suburban expansion, it was again largely train-led, particularly in London where there was both the extension of much of the Underground system and the electrification of the Southern Region railway.

In the 1920s and 1930s, a considerable number of substantial houses were being built in the choicest suburban areas of such counties as Surrey and Cheshire, but by far the greatest amount of suburban housing was for the lower-middle classes who worked largely for the expanding service industries or for the light industry companies which sprang up, for example, along London's arterial roads. Thanks to building societies lowering the amount of deposit required to 10 per cent or even 5 per cent, many young couples were able to buy a mock-Tudor semi of their own. This was the period in which the scale of suburban living expanded significantly and the typical suburb, as Cheney (1997) correctly observes, is one where 'the dominant tone of the housing is of a very highly predictable pitched-roof, three bedroomed, detached or semi-detached house'. However, he falls into the trap of seeing only uniformity ('such houses generally lack ornamentation or any distinctive style'), whereas the subtleties of exterior and interior design were and still are significant for the residents. A sundance window or a sailing ship in the hall or a garage window with a sports car were there to be noticed by neighbours who would know that you had had to pay extra for them.

The move into the housing market stretched many family finances to the limit and so, in this period, the furnishing and decoration of the house clearly reflected one's economic position. While the upper-middle class might buy hand-blocked fabrics, put carpets on varnished floors and buy antique furniture, those living in

Figure 2.3. Bedroom of well-to-do middle-class household furnished with old prints and furniture and expensive fabrics. (*Photograph*: from the archives of the Silver Studio)

Figure 2.4. Dining room of a lower middle-class household with reproduction table, modern prints, mirror and carpet square. The chairs and corner cupboard may be older. (*Photograph*: from the archives of the Silver Studio)

the new suburban semis often had to live for many years with what the builder provided – stock wallpaper in the sitting room, dining room, hall and bedrooms and painted walls in kitchen and bathroom. The wallpapers of the 1920s were in bright colours but, by the 1930s, the effect of the Modern and Tudor movements could be seen in the transition to creams and browns. The floors were usually covered in carpet squares with painted or varnished surrounds. The better houses had wood blocks rather than planking for floors in the public rooms. New furniture frequently showed Jacobean influences. This was the period of stained dark oak. Oliver (1994) explores the significance and character of furnishing in this period in more detail.

In the early 1980s, Middlesex University organized an exhibition on design, and interviewed a number of suburban residents in North London who had bought their first house in the 1930s in order to discover what had influenced their furnishing choices and from where they had acquired their furniture. The fashion of antiques and Persian rugs so heavily promoted by *House & Garden* in the 1920s and 1930s was not for this new breed of suburbanite. Most were short of money after buying their houses, and so were obliged to make do with Victorian family cast-offs. However, for those that could afford to buy new pieces, there was a range of home furnishing department stores that specialized in supplying furniture for these new suburban residents. The biggest were The Times Furnishing Store and Drages. Like their more expensive counterparts they, too, showed furniture in room-sets, but tended to offer a much more limited range of furniture styles. They tended to be either a watered-down version of Modernism with much use of chrome and walnut veneer, or a heavy, bulbous version of what became widely known as 'Jacobethan' (figure 2.5). A particularly important influence for purchasers of these houses was the furnished show house. The biggest builders such as Laings, Costain and Wimpey would fully furnish a show house on each of their estates and supply the names of the stores from which the items could be purchased (figure 2.6).

From the mid-1920s onwards, the influence of the Modern Movement on architectural design, interior design furniture and fittings became apparent. Industrial production systems made the design accessible to many moving into the suburbs, though they remained a minority taste. The style is well represented by Ward and Ward (1978), but the examples given were not for the average suburban dweller. As a stylistic innovation, they were taken up more by the 'opinion' leaders who lived in architect-designed flats and houses, and so served to establish social differentiation.

The Second World War and its economic legacy led to the disappearance of design consumption in the 1940s. Yet, in many ways, the manufacture of products with the *utility* mark paved the way for the resurgence of design consumption and the new fashions of the 1950s. The 'no frills' approach to product manufacture created a link between utilitarianism and the post-war emergence of functionalism. With the post-war economic upturn, the process of design consumption

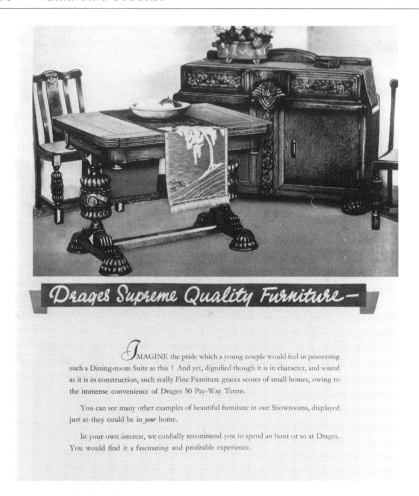

Figure 2.5. 'Jacobethan' dining room suite from Drages' catalogue.

began again; but, whereas Modernism had been a sub-theme in the inter-war period, designs reflecting faith in the future dominated the way in which we decorated and furnished our houses in the 1950s and 1960s (for an assessment of domestic design in this period see MacDonald and Porter, 1990).

SUBURBIA FOR THE WORKING CLASS

Until the early years of the twentieth century, the possibility of a house and garden in suburbia remained a dream for all but the best-paid of blue-collar workers. In the late-nineteenth century in both Britain and the United States, there were philanthropic industrialists who provided better than average homes for their workers (such as Lord Leverhulme's model village, Port Sunlight, on the Wirral

Figure 2.6. Furnished show house bedroom in housebuilder's sales catalogue.

near Liverpool), but these were the exception rather than the rule. Moreover, many workers could not afford the cost of travel to their places of work, and so instead inhabited the inner-city houses vacated by the more prosperous middle classes who had moved to the suburbs in search of more salubrious surroundings. Social reformers at the end of the nineteenth century were both concerned and astonished at the seeming reluctance of the working class to leave their overcrowded city tenements and rooming houses. A writer in *Harper's New Monthly Magazine* stated in 1882 that

> myriads of inmates of the squalid, distressing tenement houses, in which morality is as impossible as happiness, would not give them up for clean, orderly, wholesome habitations in the suburbs, could they be transplanted there and back and free of charge. They are in some unaccountable way terribly in love with their own wretchedness. (*Harper's New Monthly Magazine*, p. 924)

However, there were processes at work in Britain and America which were to change the situation for some working-class families.

In London, from 1889 onwards, the newly-formed London County Council worked tirelessly to keep, and indeed to add to, the provision of cheap workmen's fares on both trains and, subsequently, trams. This had begun in 1864 as a consequence of the demolition of workers' housing to make way for the construction of Liverpool Street Station, and the building of working-class homes in Edmonton. The Great Eastern Railway operated more trains than it was required to with a discounted fare structure and its rates (0.16d per mile (0.06p per mile) compared to LNWR's 0.31d (0.13p per mile) (Jackson, 1991, p. 32)) facilitated working-class commuting. The London County Council adopted a cheap working man's fare on trains for journeys finishing before 8.00 am. Coupled with a policy of building public low-rent housing there was, from the late-nineteenth century onwards, the development of predominantly working-class suburbs (such as Tottenham, Leyton and Edmonton in north and east London). However, within the private housing market, even the small terraced houses in these areas were affordable only by the better-off.

Within these households, a tight household economy meant that there could be little exercise of taste. Colours were plain and drab (in the brown-green range), walls were often painted rather than papered, and furniture was simple, functional and limited in quantity. Expression of the period was possible only with cheap ornaments (from day trips to seaside or fairs), lithographs on walls and family photographs. These circumstances continued through to the twentieth century. Lighter coloured gloss paints might have been used in some rooms (such as the kitchen), and the production of cheap wallpapers may have stimulated some uptake; but, since many in the working classes rented their houses, there was little incentive to improve the landlord's property.

In the United States, the working-class suburb was stimulated not only by cheap transportation but also by cheap accommodation. The development of prefabricated timber bungalows ('balloon' frame houses) and their sale by mail order from companies such as Sears, Roebuck and Montgomery Ward for as little as $800, put home ownership within the means of the skilled workman, who by 1910 could earn as much as $1,000 per annum. In England, Gamages sold similar prefabricated homes, though the uptake was far lower.

In both the United States and Britain, constraints on household expenditure limited personal expression through taste and design. As time went on, the provision of industrially-produced goods provided more scope for this, but the distinguishing feature of the working-class suburb, in design terms, was architectural design. Terraces built at the turn of the century reflected, in a degraded way, an Edwardian style with such vernacular elements as front gables, porches, decorative tiles, glazed front doors and decorative brickwork. Public housing reflected other trends. The provision of public housing by the London County Council began in 1903 at Totterdown in south London. The White Hart estate at Tottenham showed the influence of the garden suburb and, as the twentieth century advanced, improved space standards were reflected in the construction of block terraces of 8–10 units and of semi-detached houses that had the form, but not the ornamentation, of privately-built ones.

In summary, then, working-class suburbs did evolve, but they were identifiable because of absence of design, their plainness and the relative absence of home-making beyond the mere functional, in contrast to middle-class suburbia where decoration and representation were significant.

CONCLUSION

The argument that we have put forward is that design is a 'product' whose consumption can be used to represent our status and our aspirations; the possession of material goods can do so in the same, but more familiar, way. The theoretical framework for this assertion draws on studies from sociologists, cultural analysts and historians. It sees the consumption of design as being influenced by expectations of life and lifestyle as well as socio-economic status and the competence with which one can put design solutions together. The translation of this theoretical perspective into practice highlights the significance of consumer learning and consumer guidance. Guidance was particularly important in the late-nineteenth century and in the inter-war period, because the growth in suburban living was as much a process of societal formation as it was of urban expansion. The significance of suburban growth at these times cannot be underestimated. It was profoundly important in the formation of sets of social values and in the structuring of a modern society, and interior design gave concrete expression to this process. The consumption that suburban growth generated led not only to an expansion in production but also to the development of a modern retailing system and an appreciation of the significance of design as an economic variable. The link between style, socio-economic status, fashion and the consumption of design which has been explored in the sixty years from 1880 is still operative today. Home-making continues to be an economic stimulus, and design is a key element that can induce us to replace something before the end of its functional life. Design has moved on from being the preserve of the public rooms in the late-nineteenth century to include the most private of our own domains in the modern period. Now both kitchen and bathroom are treated to design solutions and the growth in garden centres suggests that the suburban garden and its patio may be the next in line.

It was the architectural critic, writer and former editor of *The Architectural Review*, Sir J.M. Richards,[3] who pioneered the appreciation of suburbia and popular suburban taste in his book *The Castles on the Ground* (1946). It was far in advance of its time in that, instead of pouring scorn on suburban taste, he wrote about why people enjoyed their suburban houses and their contents and the needs that these fulfilled. He succeeded in capturing the charm of suburbia and why so many people wanted to live there.

> The abruptness, the barbarities of the world are far away. There is not much sound, except the musical whirr and clack of a mowing machine being pushed back and forth over a neighbouring lawn and the clink of cups and saucers and a soft foot fall as tea is got ready indoors. (Richards, 1946, p. 13)

Despite the passage of 50 years, these are still the attractions of suburbia; and many who live there continue to adorn their houses as 'Little Palaces'.

NOTES

1. The most expensive suburbs in the nineteenth and early-twentieth century were always on a gravel or chalk subsoil. The cheapest suburbs were on clay which was not well-regarded by middle-class Victorians, who saw it as a source of rheumatism and other illnesses associated with damp and poor drainage.

2. The archives of the Silver Studio are housed at Middlesex University.

3. The library of Sir J.M. Richards is housed at Middlesex University.

REFERENCES

Baudrillard, J. (1996) *The System of Objects* (translated by Benedict, J.). London: Verso (originally published in French, 1968).

Beecher, C.E. and Beecher Stowe, H. (1869) *The American Woman's Home or Principles of Domestic Service*. New York: J.B. Ford & Co.

Bourdieu, P. (1984) *Distinction: A Social Critique of the Judgement of Taste* (translated by Nice, R.). London: Routledge and Kegan Paul.

Bentley, I. (1994) The owner makes his mark: choice and adaptation, in Oliver, P., Davis, I. and Bentley, I. *Dunroamin: The Suburban Semi and its Enemies*. London: Pimlico (first published 1981 by Barrie and Jenkins), pp. 136–154.

Bucock, R. (1993) *Consumption*. London: Routledge.

Burke, P. (1993) *Res et Verba: conspicuous consumption in the early modern world*, in Brewer, J and Porter R. (eds.) *Consumption and the World of Goods*. London: Routledge, pp. 148–161.

Cassell (1869) *Cassell's Household Guide*, Vols 1–3. London and New York: Cassell, Peter and Galpin.

Cheney, D. (1997) Authenticity and suburbia, in Westwood, S. and Williams, J. (eds.) *Imagining Cities: Scripts, Signs, Memory*. London: Routledge, pp. 140–151.

Cook, C. (1895) *The House Beautiful. Essays on Beds and Tables, Stools and Candlesticks*. New York: Charles Scribner & Sons.

Cubitt, S. (1988) Anxiety in public houses: speculations on the semiotics of design consciousness, *Journal of Design History*, Vol. 1, No. 2, pp. 127–139.

Davidson, H.C. (ed.) (1906) *The Book of the Home* Vols. 1–8. London: The Gresham Publishing Company.

Davis, I. (1994) A celebration of ambiguity: the synthesis of contrasting values, in Oliver, P., Davis, I. and Bentley, I. *Dunroamin: The Suburban Semi and its Enemies*. London: Pimlico (first published 1981 by Barrie and Jenkins), pp. 77–103.

Day, L.F. (1893) Decoration by correspondence, *Art Journal* (London), pp. 85–88.

Douglas, M. and Isherwood, B. (1980) *The World of Goods: Towards an Anthropology of Consumption*. Harmondsworth: Penguin

Eastlake, C.L. (1868) *Hints on Household Taste in Furniture, Upholstery and Other Details*. London: Longmans & Co.

Edwards, C. (1991) Furnishing a home at the turn of the century: the use of furnishing estimates from 1875–1910. *Journal of Design History*, Vol. 4, No. 4, pp. 233–239.

Featherstone, M. (1990) Perspectives on consumer culture. *Sociology*, Vol. 24, No. 1, pp. 5–22.

Fine, B and Leopold, E. (1993) *The World of Consumption*. London: Routledge.

Harper's New Monthly Magazine (1882) The problem of living in New York. *Harper's New Monthly Magazine*, Vol. LXV, November.

Jackson, A.A. (1991) *Semi-Detached London: Suburban Development, Life and Transport* (second edition). Didcot: Wild Swan Publications.

Jackson, K.T. (1985) *Crabgrass Frontier: The Suburbanization of the United States*. New York: Oxford University Press.

Kerr, R. (1864) *The Gentleman's House; or How to Plan English Residences from the Parsonage to the Palace*. London (no publisher given).

Loftie, W.J. (1876) *A Plea for Art in the House, with Special Reference to the Economy of Collecting Works of Art, etc* (in the *Art at Home* series, edited by W.J. Loftie). London: Macmillan.

MacDonald, S. and Porter, J. (1990) *Putting on the Style: Setting up Home in the 1950s*. London: The Geffrye Museum.

McKendrick, N., Brewer, J. and Plumb, J.H. (1982) *The Birth of a Consumer Society: The Commercialisation of Eighteenth-Century England*. London: Europa.

Oliver, P. (1994) A lighthouse on the mantelpiece: symbolism in the home, in Oliver, P., Davis, I. and Bentley, I. *Dunroamin: The Suburban Semi and its Enemies*. London: Pimlico (first published 1981 by Barrie and Jenkins), pp. 173–192.

Panton, Mrs J.E. (1896) *Suburban Residences and How to Circumvent Them*. London: Ward and Downey.

Panton, Mrs J.E. (1888) *From Kitchen to Garret*. London: Ward and Downey.

Peterson, R.A. (1979) Revitalising the culture concept. *Annual Review of Sociology*, Vol. 5, pp. 137–166.

Richards, Sir J.M. (1946) *The Castles on the Ground: The Anatomy of Suburbia*. London: Architectural Press.

Rosenblum, B. (1978) Style as a social process, *American Sociological Review*, Vol. 43, pp. 422–438.

Styles, J. (1993) Manufacturing, consumption and design in eighteenth century England, in Brewer, J. and Porter, R. (eds.) *Consumption and the World of Goods*, London: Routledge.

Walsh, J.H. (1857) *A Manual of Domestic Economy, Suited to Families Spending from £100 to £1,000 a Year*. London: Routledge and Co.

Ward, M. and Ward, N. (1978) *Home in the Twenties and Thirties*. London: Ian Allan.

Ward, S.V. (1998) *Selling Places: Marketing and Promotion of Town and Cities 1850–2000*. London: E. & F.N.Spon.

Zablocki, B.D. and Kanter, R.M. (1976) The differentiation of life styles. *Annual Review of Sociology*, Vol. 2, pp. 269–298.

CHAPTER 3

British 'Corporation Suburbia': The Changing Fortunes of Norris Green, Liverpool

Richard Turkington

Between 1919 and 1939, over a million rented homes were built in Britain through state subsidy. Immediately following the First World War, local authorities were handed the responsibility and resources to solve the overlapping housing problems of shortage, quality and affordability. With little or no experience, they plunged into major house building programmes, and became landlord to thousands. The resulting 'council house' and 'housing estate' are taken almost entirely for granted, a reality confirmed by the paucity of scholarly activity in this area. This chapter seeks to remind us of the ambitions and impact of the new and experimental era of council housing, when suburban living was first extended to working-class families. The reality of that experience is examined through a detailed profile of the Norris Green estate in Liverpool. Typical of the larger interwar schemes, Norris Green enables us to explore, at the local level, the long-term impact of the national policies which generated 'Corporation Suburbia'.

THE ROOTS OF CORPORATION SUBURBIA

By 1914, the limited experiments in planned housing had effectively generated two models: the inner-urban and high-density tenement, and the outer-urban and low-density settlement. Both were responses to the nineteenth-century 'slum', whose conditions were held to generate an unhealthiness of both body and mind. Consequently, planned housing had to be both sanitary in structure and reforming of habit. The ideal environment for achieving such ends was beyond the 'city', whose baneful influence could then be overcome. Clearly, this was not a practical solution for the London masses, and the work of Peabody and similar housing trusts are testimony to the attempt to deal with the problems of metropolitan living at source. Elsewhere, though, the settlement solution was preferred, and the 'big three' – Bournville, Port Sunlight and New Earswick – all realized a powerful anti-urbanism through the romantic re-creation of 'village life'.

This outer-urban route to reformed living was confirmed by Howard's 'city in a garden', whose residential principles were translated by the London County Council into the public-sector 'cottage estate'. Immediately prior to the First World War, the suburban developments of Totterdown Fields, Tooting and Old Oak, Hammersmith, demonstrated what could be achieved by public-sector innovation and a subsidy from the rates. Whilst general housebuilding ceased during the 'Great War', the need to house munitions workers provided further opportunities, at Well Hall, Woolwich Arsenal and Gretna Green, to experiment with the layout of planned settlements.

There was by no means a consensus on issues of design and layout, with an effective competition between the Romantic and Formal schools of urban design (Swenarton, 1981). In the former case, represented by Letchworth Garden City and Well Hall, the emphasis was placed on 'picturesque' house designs and free-form layouts, whilst the latter, represented by Gretna Green and Dormanstown, emphasized simple designs and symmetrical layouts.

Both the physical and social ingredients of the residential 'housing estate' were now in place, but the political will to implement them had yet to be achieved. That resolve was generated by the experience of the First World War, whose socially destabilizing influence inspired radical post-war responses. Primary amongst these was the commitment to make available to the returning troops 'Homes fit for Heroes' (Swenarton, 1981). The Tudor Walters Report (Tudor Walters, 1918), commissioned by the wartime coalition government in 1917, dealt in detail with the need for a new policy of state-subsidized housing, and advocated the construction of low-density developments based on the Garden City experience (Oliver *et al.*, 1994).

The design characteristics recommended included houses with private gardens, the use of the cul-de-sac, residential roads with hedges and grass verges, the provision of open space and geometric layouts in reaction to the grid pattern of the bye-law terraced street (Edwards, 1981). The influence of the Formal school of thought can be identified in an emphasis on 'simplicity' in the design and layout of housing and in the 'standardization' of building components. A major area of debate concerned the advisability of building either 'Parlour' or 'non-Parlour' houses. The former were greatly preferred by tenants but, as this 'best room' was little used, non-Parlour houses with a larger living room were recommended in the Report.

The Addison Act of 1919 confirmed the direction of policy and provided the subsidy necessary to realize a state house building programme. Published in the same year, the Local Government Board's *Housing Manual* restated the Tudor Walters recommendations as guidance for local authorities, and the public sector housing programme could now get under way.

BUILDING CORPORATION SUBURBIA

The Addison Act gave local authorities the duty, within 6 months, to survey the housing needs of their areas and make plans to meet them. Within a year, a shortage of over 800,000 homes had been identified in England and Wales alone, and plans for over 160,000 houses had been approved by the Ministry of Health. Bowley (1945) characterized the succession of interwar state housing policies as three 'experiments' in the application of subsidies. Under the 'First Experiment', subsidy levels were open-ended, based on the difference between the product of a penny rate and the income from local 'controlled rents'. 170,000 houses had been built under the 'First Experiment' before the economic collapse of 1921 led to a suspension of subsidies. There then followed a 'see-saw' of Conservative, Labour and coalition administrations, whose experimental policies, whilst shifting the emphasis between private and public sectors, continued to support the building of council housing.

The Conservative government of 1922 focused on slum clearance; and inaugurated under the 1923 Chamberlain legislation a 'Second Experiment' providing 'lump sum' subsidies to the private sector to build either council or owner-occupied dwellings for the 'working classes'. Under this policy, only 76,000 council houses of lower space standards had been added, before the election of a minority Labour administration led to a return to subsidizing 'general needs' council housing. Both the amount and repayment period for subsidies were increased under the 1924 Wheatley Act but, in the interests of controlling rents and increasing access to council housing, the Chamberlain space standards were retained. It was under the Wheatley legislation that the Norris Green estate was to be constructed in Liverpool.

Despite a change to a Conservative government in 1924, the Wheatley Act remained in force until 1933. Subsidies and standards were steadily eroded until 1929, when they were restored by a new Labour administration which embarked on a 'Third Experiment' described as a 'return to a sanitary policy' (Bowley, 1945, p. 135). Under the 1930 Greenwood Act, the emphasis was placed on slum clearance, and the building of tenement flats marked a revival of inner-urban and high-density development. After 1933, the combination of worsening economic conditions and the housing policies of a new Conservative administration restricted the limited resources to dealing with slum clearance and overcrowding, and the large-scale suburban housebuilding programmes came to a halt.

Over 1.1 million council homes were built by state subsidy between 1919 and 1939, almost half under the Wheatley legislation (Burnett, 1986). All but 5 per cent were conventional two-storeyed and, typically, three-bedroomed houses in low-cost suburban locations. Whilst the 'semi-detached' pairing of houses was typical in the first phase of council housing, most were subsequently laid out in groups, thus creating the contradictory style of houses whose individual design was close to the 'semi', but which were laid out in short terraces. Fundamental to the layout of council housing was the 'housing estate', whose organization was shaped by both technical and social considerations.

THE ROLE OF CORPORATION SUBURBIA

The confidence with which the interwar state housebuilding programme was undertaken should not detract from its radicalism as a social and political experiment. Initially, what was being promoted was the reshaping of British society through the form and function of state-subsidized suburban housing. The designation of local authorities as housing providers was a dramatic and far-reaching decision, but the discrediting of the private rented sector was near complete in the political climate immediately following the First World War. In an attempt to overcome the social divisions so agonizingly exposed between 1914 and 1918, the new municipal housing was initially intended to house all social classes. 'It is generally agreed that to cover large areas with houses, all of one size, and likely to be occupied by one class of tenant, is most undesirable' (Tudor Walters, 1918, p. 12, para. 53).

Whilst the 'new communities' of the 'housing estates' were intended to symbolize the new era after the First World War, their achievement appears to have been taken largely for granted. With the sudden and near-overwhelming responsibilities of housebuilder and landlord, it is hardly surprising that local authorities gave little time or attention to the 'provision of amenities and to the development of a sense of community on the new estates' (Daunton, 1984, p. 28). On Becontree, destined to be the largest interwar estate, the London County Council's desire to create 'a new township, complete in itself' did not extend to any recognizable process of community development. In his detailed study of the estate, Terence Young makes the revealing comment that Becontree is a 'dormitory area', a 'housing estate and not a Garden City' (Young, 1934, p. 26). Such definitional niceties were of little consolation to its bewildered 'pioneer' tenants, 'colonists in an area which had no urban facilities' (Young, 1934, p. 45).

By the close of the first decade of council housing, a more sophisticated approach to community development had begun to evolve (Ravetz with Turkington, 1995). In 1929, for example, the National Council of Social Service, in collaboration with the British Association of Residential Settlements and the Educational Settlements Association, formed the New Estates Community Committee. The Committee accepted the legitimacy of the 'housing estate' as a social entity: 'the new estate is not merely a street of houses or a collection of streets of houses: it is a unit of social life' (Barker, 1935, p. 3).

Whilst 'Community Centres' were identified as the key to developing 'social life', the initiative remained largely with local people, especially through the formation of 'tenants' associations' (Thompson and Thompson, 1942). Community development was to remain the poor relation of Corporation suburbia throughout the interwar years.

LIVERPOOL CORPORATION: SUBURBANIZING
THE WORKING CLASSES

The construction of the tenement block St Martin's Cottages, in 1869, marked the beginning of Liverpool Corporation's commitment to innovative public housing. Despite having to rely on subsidies from the local rates, the city had succeeded in building almost 3,000 dwellings by 1914 (City of Liverpool Housing Committee, 1951). With few exceptions, these were high-density and inner-urban tenements, although the Bevington Street scheme, opened in 1911, included three streets of terraced houses which exist to this day.

With such a track record, it is hardly surprising that the Corporation responded with great enthusiasm to the post-war encouragement to build council housing. At 5,808 dwellings, Liverpool succeeded in building more houses under the 1919 legislation than any other municipality (McKenna, 1991). Following the Tudor Walters recommendation of 12 to the acre, the new houses were laid out at low density on estates whose land requirements necessitated a suburban location. Unfortunately, 'there appeared to be no overall structure to the development programme, other than the desire to proceed as rapidly as the Ministry of Health would allow with the development of widely scattered estates as sites became available' (Pooley and Irish, 1984, p. 74).

Fortunately, the Corporation's lack of experience in constructing suburban estates and the initial pursuit of 'a bold, bad wholesale policy' (Reilly, 1938, p. 249) was compensated for by the presence of Liverpool University's School of Architecture and Department of Civic Design (Sharples et al., 1996). The work of William Lever at Port Sunlight, of Charles Reilly as Roscoe Professor of Architecture, of Stanley Adshead and Patrick Abercrombie as first and sub-sequent heads of the Department of Civic Design, ensured that Liverpool was at the forefront of the debate concerning the development of town planning and, not least, planned housing. Through the journal Town Planning Review, the aesthetics of Formal planning were asserted over the Romantic or Picturesque approaches to urban and architectural design. In terms of Corporation housing, such ideas were translated into neo-Georgian council houses in the 'Liverpool manner', and the symmetrical layouts which so characterize the city's interwar suburban housing estates (Pepper and Swenarton, 1980).

Liverpool's interwar housebuilding programme also benefited from the efforts of a dedicated group of officers and councillors. The City Engineer, John Brodie, was joined in 1924 by the architect Lancelot H. Keay, who became Director of the first Housing Department, established in 1926. In collaboration with a dynamic Housing Committee, the Corporation's suburban housing policies were central to its achievements in the interwar years. Keay had a prominent role in the design of both houses and estates, and also greatly preferred designs which were 'Georgian in style' (Caradog Jones, 1934, Vol. 1, p. 263).

With appalling problems of housing shortage and stock conditions, the Corporation might have been excused for some compromise of quantity over quality. In terms of house design, this was largely a choice between 'parlour' and smaller 'non-parlour' houses, but two-thirds of housing built under the 1919 legislation were of the larger type. A similar commitment to quality was evident in the provision of hot water systems, electricity, upstairs bathrooms and indoor toilets. The transformation of the lives of those fortunate enough to gain access to the new dwellings was matched only by the transformation in their living environment, and the new estates became local attractions: 'there were always people walking up and down our road inspecting the houses and, well, they were so cheeky sometimes they would even walk up the path and try and look in through the window' (quoted in McKenna, 1991, p. 178).

Not surprisingly, the demand for the new houses was overwhelming, and the Corporation was able to be highly selective in choosing its new suburban tenants. This was fortunate, as rents were high and wages, in a city dependent on casual port employment, were erratic and low. The initial commitment was to house Liverpool ex-servicemen with families, but the expectation of allocation to predominantly 'working-class' tenants was confounded by the reality. Analysis of the 1919 cohort revealed that almost half of all houses, and mainly the parlour type, were allocated to non-manual workers, including 'a bank manager, master mariners, architects, clerks and artisans. A single lady living by "private means" could even afford the services of a living-in maid' (McKenna, 1991, p. 182).

It was not until the late 1920s that the social balance shifted, when more non-parlour houses were constructed in an attempt to 'build down' to ordinary working-class families. There was still great reluctance to house either the slum dweller or the unemployed, although the slump of the early 1930s brought severe hardship to existing tenants, and soaring rent arrears for the Corporation. Criteria for access were restated in the mid-1930s in order to select tenants with safer, skilled jobs who could afford the rents. This policy coincided with the reverse trend, as those rehoused under the 1930 'slum clearance' Act finally gained access to Corporation housing. Over one-third of tenants on the 1930 estates were un-skilled labourers and 27 per cent were unemployed. For these families, 'enforced suburbanization' only added to their problems. 'The Corporation thought that they were giving the likes of us the world, getting us out of the slums, but they didn't care none of us could afford the bloody houses. They dumped us out here and then forgot about us' (quoted in McKenna, 1991, p. 185).

'Out here' could be up to seven miles from the city centre (figure 3.1), from work on the docks and from the support of extended family and neighbourhood ties; allocation to the new suburban estates could bring about dramatic changes in lifestyle. Despite the wider social ambitions associated with the new estates, and not least the generation of 'new communities', the provision of social amenities lagged far behind. Major problems were associated with the inadequate provision of schools, shops and churches, and the widespread failure to develop transport links aggravated the situation. 'You see there weren't any doctors, clinics or anything at first so it meant that you had to travel for everything, but the problem

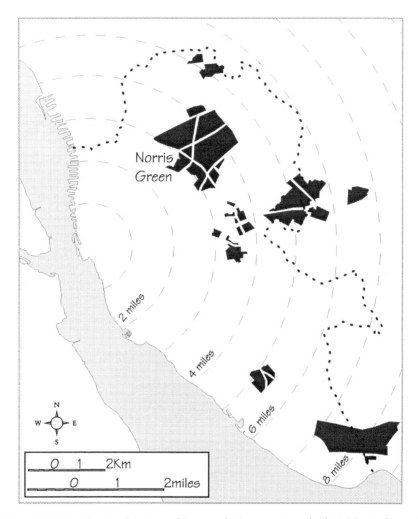

Figure 3.1. Map showing location of Liverpool's 'corporation suburbia'. Norris Green is part of the large grouping at middle centre. (*Source*: Redrawn from Liverpool Council of Social Service (1935))

was there wasn't any trams to take you. It got a lot of people down and they didn't stick it' (quoted in McKenna, 1991, p. 187).

The ideals of those promoting the achievements of the 'new communities' at the national level appear to have had little effect on practice in Liverpool. The type of social provision made, of bowling greens, open spaces and sports fields, appears to have followed a very loosely-defined 'Garden City' tradition, and involved little active promotion of 'community'. Opportunities to socialize were seriously constrained, pubs were banned on the new estates, and even fish and chip shops were excluded until the late 1930s.

In view of the scale of this vast experiment, involving the construction of almost 33,000 houses and 6,000 flats on dozens of sites, it is extraordinary that more mistakes were not made. The interwar period produced an enduring legacy of public housing marked by a distinctiveness of house style and estate layout. The confidence of the assumptions which underpinned its construction were complemented only by the solidity of its construction.

BUILDING NORRIS GREEN

Whilst it is dwarfed by the London County Council's Becontree estate of over 25,000 homes, Norris Green is comparable with the larger interwar estates of up to 10,000 homes including Manchester's Wythenshawe, Bristol's Knowle and Bedminster, and Birmingham's Kingstanding. Originally comprising 680 acres of agricultural land, the Norris Green estate falls into the second Wheatley period of council housing construction, and constituted the largest interwar Corporation housing estate in Liverpool (Liverpool Housing Department, 1937) Located three and a half miles to the north-east of the city centre, work began in 1926 with the construction of over 28 miles of roads and sewers. The estate's layout can be characterized as 'random geometric', and includes an extraordinary series of

Figure 3.2. Aerial photograph showing the 'random geometric' layout of the estate. (*Source*: Caradog Jones (1934))

circles, crescents, horse-shoes and culs-de-sac of housing criss-crossed by roads. Originally, it was bounded by a railway on one side, dual carriageways on two further sides and open country on the final side (figure 3.2).

Built to a low density of 12 to the acre, the housing was of remarkably uniform type. A total of 7,689 dwellings was completed by 1932, all but six of which were three-bedroom family houses in the neo-Georgian style. The only distinction was between 'parlour' housing, which made up 37 per cent of the total, and 'non-parlour' housing, which made up the remainder. The impression of uniformity was reinforced by building in blocks of two, four or six, and by the widespread use of red tiles, unglazed bricks and woodwork painted green and cream (figure 3.3). Unfortunately, the shortage of skilled labour and the desire to progress at speed led to the application of non-standard 'Boot' and 'Boswell' concrete building methods to 3,000 houses concentrated in two neighbourhoods, an innovation which was to prove a poisoned legacy some 50 years later. All of the houses had short front and lengthy back gardens and, internally, electric lighting, gas cookers and a hot water supply represented a high standard of provision. This contrasted with the regressive practice of locating WCs outside the back door, and a continuing reliance on coal fires in the parlour or living room.

Within three years of opening, Norris Green had 25,000 residents, but such massive growth was accompanied by a remarkable lack of social planning and a wholly inadequate provision of local amenities.

Figure 3.3. View of Millbank, Queen's Drive, West Derby, Liverpool. Note retention of mature trees, broad open spaces and streets, and Neo-Georgian house design.
(*Source*: A contemporary hand-tinted postcard)

Some of the estates, especially Norris Green, suffer from the lack of a coherent and centralized plan in their general layout. The streets are in pleasant curves; trees have been planted, adequate open spaces provided. Yet the need is felt, both architecturally and socially, for some kind of focus for the activities of the district. A central square, around which could have been grouped shops, churches, and public buildings, and from which the principal streets might have radiated would perhaps have assisted the development from a heterogeneous collection of people into a social unit which has so noticeably failed to take place. (Caradog Jones, 1934, Vol. 1, p. 264)

Whilst sites were reserved for churches, schools, cinemas, a recreation ground, public library, swimming baths and business premises, their provision lagged hopelessly behind (figure 3.4). It was not until 1929 that the first Broadway shopping centre was opened. Consisting of a crescent of 25 shops and flats, it was located on the west side of the estate, and was subsequently complemented by a further parade of 26 shops on the east side.

Within five years, the population of Norris Green had exceeded that of the county town of Shrewsbury but the failure to develop an infrastructure of amenities appropriate to its size consigned the estate to a primarily residential function. This is a pattern typical for the period, when the process of construction appears to have absorbed all of the Corporation's energy and resources. The consequence for the 'pioneer' tenants was to set the positive experience of a new home against the hardships of life on a new estate.

Figure 3.4. Bowling greens at Muirhead Gardens, West Derby, Liverpool.
(*Source*: A contemporary hand-tinted postcard)

THE 'PIONEERS' OF NORRIS GREEN

In considering the evolution of Norris Green, we are fortunate in having access to the invaluable work of Norman Williams, who researched the early years of the estate (Williams, 1938). He was motivated by a desire to explore the reality of the 'development of new communities by local authorities known as the New Housing Estates Movement' (Williams, 1938, p. 3). His starting-point was the social profile of the first inhabitants or, 'pioneers', of Norris Green, amongst whom he identified an 'economic monotony' determined by having come from similarly inferior housing conditions, by being at the same stage of family growth, and by having similar socio-economic circumstances. Unskilled, semi-skilled and skilled manual workers each contributed around one-quarter of heads of households, 'the remaining fifth is made up of clerks, policemen and shop assistants. There are very few professional classes on the estate' (Williams, 1938, p. 26).

A survey of tenants undertaken in 1937 revealed that, among the 7,900 resident families, 81 per cent of married women were under 40 and 47 per cent were under 30. The number of school-age children quickly overwhelmed the places available, and generated a local crisis of provision. In 1930, there were only 5,200 places for 7,000 children and, consequently, they were not admitted until six or seven years old, and then to classes as large as the middle fifties. Although provision for 10,000 children had been achieved by 1937, there was no nursery provision during these years.

Life must have been particularly difficult for the pioneer residents and, for the first two years, the nearest shops were one-and-a-half miles away. Despite the risk of eviction, an estimated 150 illegal shops were operating from people's homes. 'A woman a few doors away from me sold cigarettes and sweets and another person down the road had a grocery shop in her front room. She sold everything, the room was piled high from floor to ceiling with boxes of stuff' (quoted in McKenna, 1991, p. 187). The poor infrastructure on the estate was compounded by its distance from the city and the initial inadequacy of public transport. The electric tramway was not extended to the estate until 1938, a serious disadvantage for those seeking work. Although unemployment on the estate followed city-wide patterns of 9 per cent in 1930 and 22 per cent by 1937, the rates for those aged 14–18 were twice the city average (Williams, 1938).

In 1929, the additional costs of transport, food and rent were estimated to add at least 10/– (50p) to average expenditure of £3/12/0 (£3.60) per week. An initial problem was the cost of furnishing new and larger homes, and the hazards of Hire Purchase were set out in Williams' study. Savings, could only be made by spending less on food, a trend already identified as a factor in the poor family health of low-income tenants (M'Gonigle and Kirkby, 1936). It is hardly surprising that most of the 30 per cent of tenants who left within the first two years had lower incomes. There was a further 30 per cent turnover in the next six years, and 30 per cent more in the following three; leaving only 40 per cent of the original tenants resident for more than 10 years. Movement also took place within the estate from non-parlour to parlour houses, and to low-cost homes for owner occupation available immediately beyond its boundaries.

Such trends, from the uniformity of class and occupation to the hardship of matching expenditure to income, are recorded in both Young's Becontree study of 1934 and in Jevons and Madge's survey of interwar estates in Bristol (1946). A constant cause of concern was the tenant 'removal rate', which reached a high point of 17 per cent at Becontree in 1928/29. Whilst 'normal' rates were being generated by the realities of tenancy turnover, the underlying concern was to find a measure of the extent of 'settling' on estates.

SETTLING NORRIS GREEN

By the close of the interwar period, the annual turnover of tenants had settled at 6 per cent, and so-called 'replacing tenants' were showing a clear preference to stay. 'There are some very flourishing neighbourhoods in Norris Green, small cul-de-sacs [sic] containing between 40 and 60 houses' (Williams, 1938, p. 101). However, one factor which worked against this 'settling' process was the loss of young people on marriage. Newly-married couples were prevented by tenancy regulations from living with their parents and, as they were not yet eligible for a family home, they had little choice but to leave the estate. As a consequence, over 1,500 young people aged 20 or above moved away between 1930 and 1937. This lack of provision for childless couples, for single and older people, would return to haunt the estate in years to come.

Williams' study emphasized that, whilst new residents had to contend with a range of officials, from the rent-collector to the sanitary inspector, they received little practical advice on living in a suburban estate. Liverpool had, by 1939, only two 'Women Property Managers', and a proposal for two more had been vetoed by the City Treasurer. Denied official help, local people had formed, in 1930, the Norris Green Community Association. Claimed to be one of the first of its kind in the country, a grant from the Carnegie UK Trust had enabled the employment of a full-time organizer, but no support was forthcoming from the Corporation. 'Its only accommodation is a wooden hut containing a small hall to seat nearly 200, an office and cloakrooms' (Williams, 1938, p. 96).

As elsewhere, the rhetoric of forming 'new communities' on the 'new estates' was not reflected in the reality of Norris Green. As Williams makes clear, 'in the early stages of municipal housing the general opinion seems to have been that all that was necessary was to transfer people to new estates where they could live in labour saving homes, and spend their time in their gardens' (Williams, 1938, p. 12). But 'apart from its sociological deficiencies, Norris Green is an estate which can be appreciated for the beauty of its layout. The houses themselves combine utility with artistic simplicity' (Williams, 1938, p. 88). However, when its layout and housing ceased to be such an asset, and when new 'sociological deficiencies' emerged a generation later, the resilience of Norris Green was to be tested to the limit.

THE TRANSFORMATION OF NORRIS GREEN

For a generation following the end of the Second World War, Norris Green maintained its reputation as a settled and desirable Corporation estate. A survey of Liverpool estates undertaken in 1971 (Weinberger, 1973) identified the strength of local ties, and concluded that:

> Norris Green is the most stable and respectable of the study areas. Only a small proportion of the tenants expect to move from the area, and levels of satisfaction are high. Interest in owning is strongest in Norris Green, and levels of income, social class, and savings make it likely that a proportion of young families will leave to buy. (Weinberger, 1973, pp. 81–82)

The report noted ominously that 'More small dwellings suitable for the elderly are needed' (*ibid.*, p.82), but little was done to provide them. Two blocks of 43 two-bedroomed flats were added in 1958, and provided some much-needed diversity to the dwelling stock. A further multi-storey block of 58 three-bedroomed flats was added in 1966, but this new housing describes the limit of development and change over two decades.

The estate's subsequent transformation was now to be shaped by a coincidence of Liverpool's economic decline; the changing role and status of council housing; the consequences of the narrow profile of the estate's population and housing; and by the failure to modernize or reshape the estate.

By the 1960s, the standard of the estate's housing and, in particular, the widespread provision of outside WCs and downstairs bathrooms led to a limited modernization programme. Between 1970 and 1971, prefabricated 'Gilbury Units', incorporating a bathroom, sink and WC were added to the rear of 550 houses. These flat-roofed fibre composite extensions contained one small window and, in solving one problem, they were to create another.

No further modernization took place, and residents had to contend with an estate environment designed for the lifestyles of a pre-war generation. This was particularly the case in relation to the car. No garages or parking spaces had been provided for the houses, and the already narrow and winding streets within the estate were increasingly congested with parked cars, and made dangerous by through traffic. Similarly, no improvements were made to amenities, and the estate's residents had to contend with a level of provision already identified as inadequate in the pre-war years.

The major changes took place after 1979, when a Conservative government was elected that was committed to reducing the role of the State whilst stimulating a market economy. Such economic policies led to a massive reduction in the resources directed at social housing; and, for Liverpool, this policy was translated into a scaling-down of planned maintenance programmes. In 1983, following the election of a 'Militant' Labour council committed to targeted improvement, they were abandoned completely.

The failure to modernize Norris Green, the abandonment of planned maintenance and the consequent increase in the need for repairs coincided with the discovery of serious structural problems affecting the 3,000 houses built to the non-standard Boot and Boswell construction techniques. Structural problems involving the failure of wall ties were also discovered in conventional brick-built housing and, by the early 1980s, the sight of structurally-defective housing with doors and windows protected from vandalism by steel plates began to disfigure the estate (figure 3.5). Furthermore, a new problem was emerging in the deterioration of the Gilbury Units, added to some homes in the early 1970s. Inadequate ventilation from within and water penetration from without had resulted in problems of decay, condensation and mould growth which, in the absence of a heating system, were insuperable. The improvements made in one decade already required replacement in the next.

Such dramatic changes in the physical environment of the estate coincided with an equally momentous social transformation. In 1980, the 'right to buy' scheme was introduced by the Conservative government, enabling local authority tenants to buy their homes at a discount. This discount increased with the length of tenancy which, for the settled residents of Norris Green, proved a great attraction. Within five years, almost one-third of residents had purchased their homes,

Figure 3.5. Dereliction and disfigurement in Norris Green. (*Photograph*: Richard Turkington, 1997)

and frequently embarked on programmes of improvement and modernization. There is no doubt that this activity provided a positive contrast with the City Council's relative neglect of the estate, and helped both to counter the impression of decline and to 'root' settled residents.

At the same time, the social profile of the estate began to change in two important respects. First, the ageing of the settled population resulted, by 1981, in about 20 per cent of the estate's residents being of pensionable age. Secondly, the effective 'rationing' of social housing through the introduction of 'priority needs' allocation led to a significant influx of families dependent on welfare benefits. A social survey undertaken by Merseyside Police highlighted the dramatic change in social conditions in the area including the estate (Jackson, 1987). Drawing on a range of sources, the survey revealed that, amongst a total population of 24,354,

- 19 per cent were over 60 years old;
- 43 per cent were under 24 years old;
- 29 per cent of those of working age were unemployed;
- 75 per cent of tenants were in receipt of means-tested Housing Benefit;
- over 75 per cent of children were receiving free school meals;
- almost 70 per cent of residents did not have access to a car; and
- approximately 10 per cent of houses were classed as 'overcrowded (6+ persons per household).

The Report identified an increasing fear of crime, particularly related to burglary, 'mugging' and car crime, and concluded that Norris Green was a 'community wherein the quality of life is severely eroded and which is, if nothing is done to halt it, set upon a downward spiral of deprivation and communal fragmentation with all that that implies for the health, wealth and well-being of the residents' (Jackson, 1987, p. 1).

By the late 1980s, there were clear signs of a crisis on Norris Green in terms of both physical and social conditions. Over 50 structurally-defective and long-term vacant houses were now randomly located around the estate, and new problems were emerging each week. Furthermore, many residents were finding it difficult to cope with the generous provision of back gardens, and responded by abandoning sections at the end. The effect, especially when repeated, was to create wildernesses within which vermin bred and 'fly-tipping' increased. With a backlog of uncompleted repairs now stretching back for five years, and a continued deterioration in the condition of roads and pavements, the overall impression on Norris Green was one of decline.

REMAKING NORRIS GREEN

The requirement now was to arrest a rapidly deteriorating situation, and an early opportunity arose from the coincidence of two regeneration initiatives based in

Liverpool. In 1983, the City Council launched its 'Urban Regeneration Strategy' (URS), intended to achieve housing and environmental improvement in targeted 'Priority Areas'. One of these was located in the neighbourhoods of Croxteth and Gillmoss, adjoining the eastern boundary of Norris Green. In 1987, Liverpool became one of the participants in the World Health Organization-sponsored 'Healthy Cities Project', a programme intended to identify preventative public health measures (Poon and Turkington, 1991). One of Liverpool's schemes was focused on assessing the health benefits of housing improvement in the Croxteth and Gillmoss 'Priority Area'.

Representatives of the two residents' associations in Norris Green lobbied for the estate to be declared a URS 'Priority Area', and used the increase in social problems and the health consequences of deteriorating housing and environmental conditions in support of their case. In April 1988, the City Council declared its commitment to the improvement of Norris Green under the Urban Regeneration Strategy, and the process of reversing the decline of the estate appeared to be under way. Three of the estate's seven neighbourhoods were designated as 'Priority Areas', and regeneration plans were drawn up for each. Unfortunately, improvements had been made to only two-thirds of the houses in the first Area when the Strategy was abandoned and the necessary resources withdrawn.

It was not until five years later that more comprehensive improvement finally got under way. In 1993, the City Council succeeded in gaining central government funding under the Estate Action Programme for the improvement of the central Sedgemoor neighbourhood. A total of £27m was allocated for the improvement of 1,073 council and 723 owner-occupied properties. This enabled, for example, the provision of central heating and double glazing, and the upgrading of walls and fences. It is noticeable that these Estate Action improvements have had a huge impact on this neighbourhood's fortunes, and have demonstrated the potential of more comprehensive improvement.

The condition of the Gilbury Units was finally tackled in 1990 and, by the end of 1997, all 550 had been replaced by brick-built bathroom/WC extensions. The extent of disrepair elsewhere on the estate has been dealt with by revived planned maintenance programmes, achieving the replacement of roofs in one neighbourhood, of outside toilets in another, and of window frames in a third. However, not one of these programmes has been applied throughout the estate, and it is likely that the new century will be reached with some houses in serious disrepair, still with outside toilets and lead water pipes, and with most homes lacking central heating.

Despite a planned maintenance budget of almost £2m for 1997/98, the cost of bringing all houses up to a habitable state of repair is estimated to exceed £100m. This is quite apart from the resources required to deal with the continuing deterioration of the 3,000 Boot and Boswell pre-cast concrete houses. Renovation of each Boswell house costs in the region of £25,000; but no viable scheme for the renovation of Boot houses has been identified, implying the need for their replacement. £20m has already been spent by the local authority in buying back 'defective' dwellings sold at a discount under the 'Right to Buy' scheme, but which have to be repurchased at full 'market value'. Environmental problems concerned with the need to replace fences, deal with shortened gardens, and improve pavements and roads persist; and recreational provision has declined with the recent demolition of the swimming baths. There is now only one library, two youth clubs and one park, now devoid of its football, tennis, bowling and netball facilities, to serve a population of 25,000; although a multi-purpose sports and community centre is currently under construction.

In the same way that the deteriorated physical condition of the estate has been tackled only belatedly, so too have its changing social conditions. Responsibility for the day-to-day management of over 4,000 rented dwellings rests with the City Council's neighbourhood housing office based on the estate. Its capacity to deal with the changing situation on Norris Green is constrained both by the resources available and by the condition and profile of the stock. An example of the constraints under which the office works concerns the availability of housing either purpose-built or adapted to meet the needs of older estate residents. Known as 'sheltered housing', the first scheme was not opened until 1993, and consists of only 35 units; whilst a further 40 units were added in the following year. Unfortunately, they only provide accommodation for couples, and no specialist accommodation is available for older single people. Both developments are managed by local housing associations, whilst the City Council has no elderly persons' housing on the estate for a retired population several thousand strong.

Older people have little choice but to live in two-storey three-bedroomed family housing, which is too large for their needs, difficult to maintain, and often in deteriorating condition. Consequently, the under-occupation rate on the estate may exceed 20 per cent of all rented houses. Other changes to the dwelling stock have been minimal, and include the addition of 36 housing association houses and bungalows, the conversion of three houses to flats for people with learning difficulties, the transfer of the sole multi-storey block to Liverpool's Housing Action Trust, and the experimental refurbishment of a small number of flats and houses for rent or sale. The limited scale of this activity cannot hope to match the changing needs of the estate's residents.

THE FUTURE FOR NORRIS GREEN

A stroll down the 'leafy lanes' of Norris Green belies the scale of the physical and social problems which threaten to overwhelm the estate (figure 3.6). Their roots lie in the creation, within only a few years, of such a massive local authority residential development, of near uniform housing type, and devoid of adequate amenity planning and provision. A perverse twist to the situation was the construction of several thousand non-standard houses whose physical condition is

Figure 3.6. The positive view of
Norris Green in spring.
(*Photograph*: Richard
Turkington, 1997)

now a massive liability. Had the estate been maintained and modernized over the
years, the coincidence of physical problems might have been prevented, and the
Estate Action improvements in one neighbourhood are testimony to the potential
of their wider application. One major constraint concerns the inflexibility of an
estate environment in which almost every square metre was developed. Creating
space for the addition of any new housing or amenities would almost certainly
require the demolition of existing homes.

The final factor in the estate's future centres on its transformed social
conditions. The ageing of the settled population, and use of local authority
housing for low-income households, have placed the estate under further strain.
The ability of the new poor to manage and maintain ageing and deteriorated
housing is highly questionable, and the allocation of non-family tenants creates
further problems of the under-occupation of homes. The estate now houses
cohorts of residents whose age structure, household composition and economic
circumstances stand in stark contrast: these are 'communities' with little in
common other than a shared 'place' (figure 3.7).

It appears that the limits of Norris Green's physical and social resilience have,
in its present form, been reached. Only radical physical and social restructuring

Figure 3.7. The landscape of individual houses purchased under 'right to buy' legislation and improved piecemeal: fragmentation of character and little sense of shared space in Norris Green. (*Photograph*: Richard Turkington, 1997)

can prevent it from further decline and an uncertain future. From the highly-desirable model estate of the 1930s, Norris Green is in danger of becoming the suburbia of last resort for the 1990s.

REFERENCES

Barker, E. (1935) *New Housing Estates and their Social Problems*. London: New Estates Community Committee of the National Council of Social Service.
Bowley, M. (1945) *Housing and the State, 1919–1944*. London: Allen and Unwin.
Burnett, J. (1986) *A Social History of Housing*. London: Routledge (second edition).
Caradog Jones, D. (1934) *The Social Survey of Merseyside*. London: University Press of Liverpool/Hodder and Stoughton.
City of Liverpool Housing Committee (1951) *Housing Progress 1864–1951*. Liverpool: Liverpool City Council.
Daunton, M. (1984) *Councillors and Tenants: Local Authority Housing in English Cities, 1919–1939*. Leicester: Leicester University Press.
Edwards, A.M. (1981) *The Design of Suburbia: A Critical Study in Environmental History*. London: Pembridge Press.
Jackson, D.S. (1987) *Norris Green: a Social, Demographic and Policing Profile* Unpublished report for Merseyside Police.
Jevons, R. and Madge, J. (1946) *Housing Estates. A Study of Bristol Corporation Policy and Practice Between the Wars*. Bristol: University of Bristol/J.W. Arrowsmith.
Liverpool Council of Social Service (1935) *Liverpool and the Housing Problem*. Liverpool: Council of Social Service.

Liverpool Housing Department (1937) *City of Liverpool Housing*. Liverpool: Liverpool City Council.

McKenna, M. (1991) The suburbanisation of the working class population of Liverpool between the wars. *Social History*, Vol. 16, No. 2, pp. 173–189.

M'Gonigle, G.C.M. and Kirby, J. (1936) *Poverty and Public Health*. London: Gollancz.

Oliver, P., Davis, I. and Bentley, I. (1994) *Dunroamin. The Suburban Semi and its Enemies*. London: Pimlico (originally published 1981 by Barrie and Jenkins).

Pepper, S. and Swenarton, M. (1980) Neo-Georgian maison-type, *Architectural Review*, Vol. 168, pp 87–92.

Pooley, C.G. and Irish, S. (1984) *The Development of Corporation Housing in Liverpool 1869–1945*. Resource Paper. Lancaster: University of Lancaster, Centre for North West Regional Studies.

Poon, Y. and Turkington, R. (1991) *Housing and Environmental Improvements in the Croxteth Health Action Area*. Final Report, Liverpool Healthy Cities Project.

Ravetz, A. with Turkington, R. (1995) *The Place of Home. English Domestic Environments, 1914–2000*. London: Spon.

Reilly, C. (1938) *Scaffolding in the Sky. A Semi-Architectural Autobiography*. London: George Routledge and Sons.

Sharples, J., Powers, A. and Shippobottom, M. (1996) *Charles Reilly and the Liverpool School of Architecture 1904–1933*. Liverpool: Liverpool University Press.

Swenarton, M. (1981) *Homes fit for Heroes: the Politics and Architecture of Early State Housing in Britain*. London: Heinemann.

Thompson, F. and Thompson, G. (1942) *Community Centres: a Survey for the Community Centres Joint Research Committee*. London: Housing Centre Trust.

Tudor Walters (1918) *Report of the Committee . . . to Consider Questions of Building Construction in Connection with Dwellings for the Working Classes*. Cd 9191. London: HMSO.

Weinberger, B. (1973) *Liverpool Estates Survey: A Study of Tenants' Attitudes to their Accommodation and Neighbourhood in Four Selected Council Estate Areas*. Research Memorandum. Birmingham: Centre for Urban and Regional Studies, University of Birmingham.

Williams, N. (1938) *Problems of Population and Education in the New Housing Estates with Special Reference to Norris Green*. Unpublished MA (Education) thesis, Department of Education, University of Liverpool.

Young, T. (1934) *Becontree and Dagenham. The Story of the Growth of a Housing Estate: a Report made for the Pilgrim Trust*. London: Sidders and Son.

ACKNOWLEDGEMENT

The author wishes to recognize the assistance offered by Mr Steve Ryan, Neighbourhood Housing Manager of Norris Green, whose team has the responsibility of seeing the estate into the next century.

CHAPTER 4

England's Garden Suburbs: Development and Change

J.W.R. Whitehand and Christine M.H. Carr

Perhaps the aspect of English cities most taken for granted by English people is their garden suburbs. Garden suburbs, broadly defined, have dominated English cities for three-quarters of a century. They have their roots far enough back for them to be thought of as a normal place in which to live. For some, they are the most striking manifestation of what has been called the closed domesticated nuclear family (Stone, 1979, pp. 7–11) – a type of family unit that was accepted largely without question for several generations. In fact, the cohesive unit of wife, husband and offspring is far from universal, and the garden suburb is even less so, as quickly becomes apparent when we move outside the English-speaking world or outside our own time. Furthermore, a number of assumptions about the way in which English garden suburbs have been created, and the form in which they have continued to the present, has gained widespread credence despite the absence of evidence. This chapter traces the origins of garden suburbs, counters some myths about their form and creation during the period of their great proliferation between the two world wars, and examines some of the physical changes they have undergone since the Second World War.

The Origins of Garden Suburbs

The term 'garden suburb' appears not to have been much used until the end of the nineteenth century, when it became part of the vocabulary of the Garden City movement. Its usage has come to be associated with Ebenezer Howard (1898) and other visionary planners who sought to promulgate an ideal of houses within gardens, as part of a proposed solution to the congestion and squalor that was afflicting Victorian and Edwardian cities. But understanding the physical form and genesis of the garden suburbs that have come to dominate English cities in the twentieth century entails extending the search beyond the history of the Garden City movement.

The social conditions that influenced the rise to dominance of the garden suburb in English-speaking countries were various. Not least there was the separation of home from workplace, of middle class from working class, and the rise of romantic and religious notions favouring the natural and the rural (Fishman, 1987, pp. 239–240). These conditions existed in the late-eighteenth and early-nineteenth centuries, when the Industrial Revolution was in full swing. And it was at that time that the single-family house in its private garden (as distinct from the Georgian 'square' of terraced houses around a communal garden) started to become fashionable for those middle-class families that were rich enough to afford it. Some such single-family 'villas', as they were called at the time in the vicinity of London (London County Council, 1936, p. 77), actually date from even earlier, from the late-seventeenth century (figure 4.1*a*). Many similar houses were constructed in the course of the eighteenth century; most of them were detached rather than semi-detached. Most were bespoke houses – that is, built for a specific client, not as a speculative venture. Their occupiers had looked to the country houses of the aristocracy and the gentry for their exemplars. The earliest detached and semi-detached houses grouped into estates, and conceived as such, were also probably around London (Thompson, 1974, pp. 84–85; 1982, p. 9). There was clear evidence by the early-nineteenth century of a move away from the very urban building forms and layouts that had hitherto dominated London. Trees, private gardens, and houses with names having rural associations, had all become fashionable. Streetscapes were becoming landscapes. It was this change that marked the advent of the suburb, in the sense of garden suburb.

Away from London, similar developments soon occurred in major provincial cities. In the 1810s, the aristocratic Calthorpe family began to develop a garden suburb to the immediate south-west of Birmingham, at Edgbaston (Cannadine, 1980). This low-density estate of detached and semi-detached houses (figure 4.1*b*) was in marked contrast to the terraced houses and row houses, with little if any private garden, that had previously been the homes of virtually all of Birmingham's middle-class population.

However, it was not until the last three decades of the nineteenth century that the suburban villa began to be the norm for new middle-class housing. At Bedford Park, just beyond the western fringes of London, in the 1870s, terraced houses were used on parts of the estate, but it was the individuality of the houses, rather than their unity as a terrace, that was emphasized by the architect. Soon in Bedford Park, detached and semi-detached houses were overwhelmingly predominant (figure 4.1*c*).

At much the same time, 1879, the seeds were being sown in Bournville of what was eventually to become a massive diffusion of the garden suburb down the social hierarchy into the working class. Bournville was, at the time, just beyond the southern fringe of Birmingham. The first houses were built for key workers in the Cadburys' chocolate factory, which had just been moved out from the city centre. They were semi-detached houses in gardens, in marked contrast to the back-to-back houses of inner Birmingham. This experiment in workers' housing by Cadbury Brothers was the beginning of Bournville garden suburb (Bournville Village Trust, n.d.). By the last decade before the First World War the idea of the cottage and the cottage garden had become quite strong in Bournville (figure

Figure 4.1. Early examples of semi-detached houses in garden suburbs. (*a*) The Grove, Highgate, London, built *c*1688 – the two halves of this semi-detached pair are so different in appearance that, viewed from this angle, they appear to be detached houses. (*b*) Frederick Road, Edgbaston, Birmingham, built in the early-nineteenth century.

4.1*d*), as indeed it had elsewhere. It reflected the notion of a private, healthy, quasi-rural existence that lies at the root of English suburbs, although the houses were not likely to be confused with real rural cottages. Bournville's 'cottages' were precursors of much that was to appear in the influential Tudor Walters Report of 1918 (Local Government Boards for England and Wales, and Scotland, 1918) which, while emphasizing local authority housing, gave the official seal of approval to suburbia more generally. Its standards, particularly important for municipal housebuilding, were also, to some extent, those of speculatively-built suburbs.

(c) Fairfax Road, Bedford Park, London, built in the late-nineteenth century. (d) Junction of Laburnum Road and Elm Road, Bournville, Birmingham, built in the late-nineteenth century. (Photographs 1994)

Garden suburbs on a massive scale came into being in England in the years between the two world wars. Nearly all of the 4,200,000 dwellings that Becker (1951, p. 321) calculated were constructed in England and Wales between the end of the First World War and the beginning of the Second World War were single-family houses in private gardens, located on urban fringe sites. It is this phase in the development of the garden suburb that will be considered further in this chapter. Nearly three-quarters of the garden suburbs created at this time were built by private enterprise (Marshall, 1968–69, p. 185), and it is to the physical form of these, largely speculative, developments that attention will be confined. Much of the information upon which the chapter relies has been derived from field surveys and documentary surveys undertaken in six English towns and cities, particularly London and Birmingham (Whitehand, 1997). Local authority building applications and planning applications have been especially important (Whitehand, 1992, pp. 10–13).

MYTHS OF SUBURBIA

The residential growth of towns and cities in inter-war England was practically synonymous with the creation of garden suburbs. These suburbs were hugely land consuming compared with the large majority of earlier residential development. An increase of nearly 50 per cent in the extent of urban land took place in the 20 or so years between the end of the First World War and the beginning of the Second World War (Best, 1964, p. 352). During that time, the urban population had grown by only 10 per cent. The fact that most of this increase in the amount of so-called 'urban' land was accounted for by the transformation of land around towns and cities into suburbs dominated by houses in private gardens accords with the popular conception of the period. In many other respects, however, the popular conception of inter-war suburbs, and indeed the conceptions of many highly educated people, were actually quite wrong. Of the myths that our research has brought to light, two will be examined here. These are that inter-war suburbs were uniform and that architects were rarely involved in their creation.

The first myth is well expressed in the words of the novelist and observer of social conditions, George Orwell (1948, p. 13): 'Always the same. Long, long rows of little semi-detached houses'. Or, in the words of Edwards (1981, p. 134): 'wherever it might be, speculative suburbia was the same'.

In fact, even over very short distances within individual cities, it is often possible to identify a range of inter-war suburban building forms and street plans. Figure 4.2 shows a few of the house types that occurred within a single 25 ha square in Twickenham, London, and figure 4.3 shows the street systems in three squares of the same size that are almost adjacent to one another in south Birmingham.

The notion that the detached and semi-detached house was a universal feature of inter-war suburbs is soon dispelled if systematic observation is undertaken. A field survey of twelve randomly selected 25 ha squares developed in the inter-war period in each of the cities of London and Birmingham suggests that about 19 per cent of the houses in London were terraced (widely referred to as rowhouses in North America), compared with only about 2 per cent in Birmingham. In parts of north London, terraced houses were as numerous as semi-detached houses. These are not always immediately recognized as such because builders have sometimes been at pains to give them the superficial appearance of semi-detached houses which were more fashionable and hence saleable. Detached houses generally sold for more than semi-detached houses, and semi-detached houses sold for more than terraced houses. So, if semi-detached houses could be made to look detached, and terraces to look like a number of pairs of semi-detached, so much the better in terms of saleability. And, of course, all of them – terraced, semi-detached and detached – had sizeable private gardens, averaging a little over 0.04 ha in the sample squares in London. The other major subterfuge was the row or block of several houses disguised as a smaller number of houses. This form of disguise had been employed earlier in Bournville. The commonest variant is what in Glasgow is often referred to as a 'four in a block', which looks at first sight like a semi-detached pair. This type is common in Newcastle upon Tyne, as it is in sizeable parts of Scotland, but it is rare in Birmingham and London. The garden suburb appearance is maintained, but actually these are flats. In the most common variant, two of the entrances are at the front and two are at the sides and there is a private garden for each flat. This is a quite different arrangement from the terrace, or often terraced flat in the case of Newcastle upon Tyne (two-flat rowhouse in American terms), which was characteristic of this level in the housing market before the First World War.

Inter-war suburbs were, therefore, far from being uniform, whether examined locally, regionally or nationally. What commentators were actually recognizing was how extensive inter-war suburbs were compared with development in previous periods. There were great swathes of development around major cities which people could recognize from their characteristics as having been built at much the same time, namely in the 1920s and 1930s. They were in marked contrast to the Victorian and Edwardian terraced houses that dominated development for several decades previously, but when they are examined more closely it is apparent that they vary a great deal in house type, plan, elevations, gardens and architectural style. And these variations include some over very short distances and larger-scale differences between cities and between different parts of the country. The main reason why inter-war suburbs were thought to be uniform was basically that very few people had looked closely at them. They were part of the taken-for-granted backcloth against which people carried out their lives. So much for myth number one.

Myth number two is that architects were rarely involved in the creation of inter-war suburbs. To quote Bradshaw, writing in 1939, 'few suburban houses are built under competent architectural supervision' (Bradshaw, 1939, p. 103). Similarly, the social historian Burnett (1986, p. 259) suggested that 'the vast majority of new houses were designed by the builders themselves, without the benefit of architects'. Again, these views appear to have been wide of the mark. Even many of the cheapest houses – the sort to which the description 'jerry built' was often applied and which were thought to have been run-up by speculative builders who kept well clear of architects – were actually designed by architects, although the percentage of architect-designed houses varied greatly between different areas in the same city (table 4.1).

However, what is meant by 'architect-designed' requires some clarification. For the purpose of table 4.1, houses were deemed to be architect-designed if the

Figure 4.2. Inter-war house types, Twickenham, London. (Photographs 1994)

name of a person with a professional architectural affiliation appeared on the drawings that were submitted to the local authority prior to the commencement of building. If people describing themselves as architects, as distinct from having a professional affiliation, are included, then the proportion is higher still. Of course, the role played by an architect varied. For example, an architect designing a single bespoke house would be operating under different constraints from one preparing designs for a development of 20 semi-detached houses to be erected by a specu- lative builder. Speculative builders were, on the whole, knowledgeable about what were good selling features, and there was often a considerable difference between these and architects' conceptions of good design. For example, designs that were successful in architectural competitions were built as an experiment in

Figure 4.2.

a number of locations by John Laing & Son: they sold less well than the firm's usual type of semi-detached house of the same floor area (*Journal of the Royal Institute of British Architects*, 1936). So what an architect would design given a free hand, and what he actually produced for a speculative builder, were different things. The fact remains, however, that in formal terms architects were involved in the design of a great many houses in inter-war suburbs.

SUBURBAN CHANGE

If the inter-war suburb in England epitomized the closed domesticated nuclear family and an era of unrestrained urban growth, how has it adapted physically

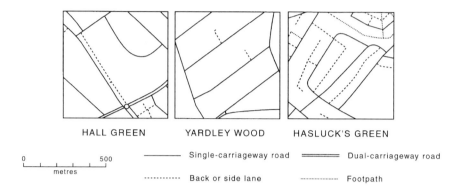

HALL GREEN   YARDLEY WOOD   HASLUCK'S GREEN

0 _____ 500   —————— Single-carriageway road   ═══════ Dual-carriageway road
        metres
                                    ------------ Back or side lane   ··················· Footpath

Figure 4.3. Inter-war street patterns in the Hall Green area of south Birmingham. (*Source*: Ordnance Survey plans at the scale of 1:2,500, revised during the 1950s)

Table 4.1. Houses designed by architects in four areas of Birmingham.

	Number of houses in areas	*Designed by Architects**	
		Number	*Per cent*
Brown's Green	434	217	50
Gilbertstone	576	207	36
Hasluck's Green	314	63	20
Quinton	498	433	87

* Members of the Royal Institute of British Architects or the Birmingham and Five Counties Architectural Association or both.

Sources: Building applications, Kelly's Directories, and Green Books of the Birmingham Architectural Association (later the Birmingham and Five Counties Architectural Association).

in a post-war era characterized by markedly different social and economic conditions? Since the Second World War there has been a strong reaction against the enormous suburban spread of the 1930s (Hall *et al.*, 1973, p. 270). Greenbelt schemes have become major instruments of planning. The consequent shortage of building land around major cities has encouraged higher density development and has focused the attention of house builders upon existing suburban areas, contributing to marked increases in their land values. At the same time, there have been major changes in the number, size and character of households. The average household size in England and Wales has fallen markedly since the end of the inter-war period (from about 3.5 persons to about 2.5 persons), reflecting in particular a pronounced increase in the number of elderly people living alone (Coleman and Salt, 1992, pp. 221, 224).

In the light of such changes it is perhaps surprising that the notion has gained credence that inter-war suburbs have not undergone great physical change.

Like the myths about their creation, however, this partly reflects the paucity of attention that inter-war suburbs have received. They have rarely been deemed particularly newsworthy. They have not, on the whole, been the stuff of great planning controversies. In this respect they are unlike city centres, inner cities and urban fringes. They have changed in piecemeal ways. The changes have, on average, been individually small and often attracted the interest only of people living in their immediate vicinity. Rarely have they been the subjects of highly-publicized planning appeals. Yet the piecemeal changes that characterize suburbs have, when added up, often resulted in substantial change.

The amount and nature of change that has taken place has been greatly influenced by decisions taken when inter-war suburbs were created. When changes in dwelling densities between c1960 and c1990 were examined in areas in the English Midlands that were of different densities when originally developed, significant variations were evident (figure 4.4). Although most of the original houses were still standing at the end of the 1980s and the road systems were still intact, pressures on land had increased over time, and this had been reflected in the construction of additional houses and the subdivision of existing dwellings. This was most evident in the areas that were originally developed at low density. Where plots were large, sometimes existing gardens had been subdivided to make plots for smaller dwellings, leaving the original houses in reduced plots; sometimes the original houses had been demolished and the whole site redeveloped. Paradoxically, the houses that originally had most invested in

LOW DENSITY   MEDIUM DENSITY   MEDIUM / HIGH DENSITY

INCREASE IN DWELLING
DENSITY SINCE 1960

0   100 200 300 400   500 Metres

Figure 4.4. Increases in dwelling densities, c1960–c1990 in sample areas developed at different densities in the inter-war period in the English Midlands. (*Sources*: Planning applications, Ordnance Survey plans and field surveys)

them in terms of design, materials, fittings and size and number of rooms, were most susceptible to demolition because they tended to be also the ones with the largest gardens. Areas of semi-detached houses and small detached houses were less susceptible to demolition and density increases. It made little difference whether the original densities were medium or medium to high: in both cases several plots generally needed to be purchased to make infill or redevelopment economically viable, although open spaces, such as tennis clubs and allotment gardens, were vulnerable to redevelopment. Demolition and 'densification' were being driven by increases in the exchange value of land. The quality and condition of existing houses were frequently irrelevant. The overriding consideration was the market value of land for development compared with existing use value.

The actual physical form in which higher densities have been achieved has been heavily influenced by the form of the original development. Wide plots have encouraged the subdivisions of frontages. Long plots have had culs-de-sac inserted alongside the original house and additional houses have been built in back gardens. The density at which additional dwellings have been added and the amount of demolition have been heavily affected by land values. Redevelopment and infill have taken place at higher densities in south-east England, where pressure on land is high, than in the English Midlands, where pressure on land is significantly lower. Flats in the back gardens of detached houses are not un-common in parts of south-east England, whereas on similar sites in the English Midlands houses are overwhelmingly dominant. The economics of the land market would seem to underlie these differences; the effects of local plan documents appear to have been quite small (Whitehand et al., 1992).

The construction of new dwellings basically within the existing framework of plots and streets is just one aspect of the way in which inter-war suburbs are

Figure 4.5. Changes to inter-war houses. (a) two-storey side extensions to semi-detached houses, creating a continuous two-storey façade spanning several formerly separate pairs,

changing. Less significant individually, but important cumulatively, are changes to existing buildings. The addition of rooms is often the most obvious change of this type, particularly where a separate dwelling is added as a 'granny flat'. Adjacent side extensions can mean that semi-detached houses, in effect, become terraced (figure 4.5a). More minor changes to porches, windows, doors, cladding materials and outbuildings, the changing of front gardens to car parking areas, and a host of other changes also substantially affect the visual character of areas (figure 4.5b).

It is possible to analyse some of these changes over time and space for individual streets using local authority building records. Building applications for changes to the building fabric in a road of semi-detached houses in Reading are shown in figure 4.6.[1] The great period of building change in this road (Balmore Drive) was between the early 1970s and the early 1990s. It affected all parts of the road and was dominated by increases in living space.

However, different roads have significantly different life histories. A similar analysis of a road of semi-detached houses in Newcastle upon Tyne, a less prosperous area, reveals little tendency for the number of building applications to increase towards the present. In this road (Southlands) change has been particularly concentrated in certain parts of the road, sometimes for as long as several decades (figure 4.7). There seems little doubt that the patchy spatial pattern of building changes in this case reflects in part the operation of what in diffusion studies, usually at larger scales, has been referred to as a 'neighbourhood effect' (Hägerstrand, 1965). At the present highly localized scale it might be more aptly described as a 'neighbour effect'. Southlands has had a high proportion of elderly residents in recent decades, which may have combined with the lower incomes of its occupants to make it less susceptible to change in recent

Stoneleigh, Surrey. (Photograph 1994) (b) Multiple changes to one of a pair of semi-detached bungalows, Pakefield, Suffolk. (Photograph 1993)

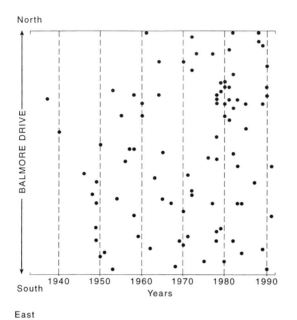

Figure 4.6. Building applications for changes to houses in Balmore Drive, Reading, 1933–92. (*Source*: Borough of Reading Leisure & Environmental Services card index of building applications)

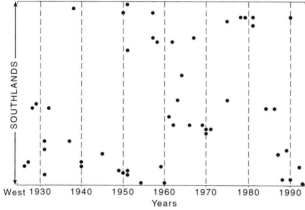

Figure 4.7. Building applications for changes to houses in Southlands, Newcastle upon Tyne, 1925–mid 1993. (*Source*: Local authority building applications (1924–57: Tyne & Wear Archives Service. 1957–93: Building Control, City of Newcastle upon Tyne))

times. A further factor is that this road has had relatively few changes of occupier, which also appears to have had a dampening effect on building change.

In these small-scale changes to individual houses, the motivation for change is different from that in the case of plot subdivision and redevelopment. In the latter the concern is with enhancing the value of the property as real estate, and considerations of exchange value tend to override those of use value (see, for example, Whitehand, 1989, pp. 11–12). In contrast, in the case of small-scale changes, the stimulus for change is primarily the belief on the part of residents that they are enhancing their property for their own use. However, house prices suggest that the enhancement of market value is not commensurate with the cost of the changes. In fact some building changes, if sufficiently idiosyncratic, may have a negative effect on house prices.

CONCLUSION

Well known Edwardian garden suburbs, such as those at Bournville and Hampstead, were stepping stones in the evolution from élite upper-middle-class suburbs over 100 years earlier to what, in England, had by the inter-war period become an almost universal form of urban extension. The scope for creating further suburbs at the fringes of major English cities is now more limited. The story of suburbs has in recent decades become more about changes to existing suburbs than about the creation of new ones. This raises major questions about the adaptation of old suburbs to changed social and economic conditions. Much of this change is taking place in the context of widespread ignorance about both the creation of suburbs in the past, particularly in the inter-war period, and how these suburbs are now being altered. The fact that in general the highest quality houses are actually the most susceptible to demolition should be recognized and addressed, even if the conclusion is reached that the dictates of the land market should be allowed to prevail. Local authorities are on the whole facing a barrage of planning applications for changes that are frequently minor, but cumulatively significant, with little sense of purpose. An awareness of how suburbs have developed and changed in the past can form a valuable basis for forming a planning strategy to which the primarily tactical decisions of development control can relate.

NOTE

1. Data on building applications in this chapter are generally for approved applications. The disapproval of a building application is comparatively rare. A small minority of applications for which the decision was unrecorded have been assumed to have been approved unless there was other, generally circumstantial, evidence to the contrary.

REFERENCES

Becker, A.P. (1951) Housing in England and Wales during the business depression of the 1930s. *Economic History Review*, Series 2, Vol. 3, pp. 321–341.

Best, R.H. (1964) The future urban acreage. *Town and Country Planning*, Vol. 32, pp. 350–355.

Bournville Village Trust (n.d.) *The Bournville Village Trust 1900–1955*. Birmingham: Bournville Village Trust.

Bradshaw, H.C. (1939) The suburban house, in Abercrombie, P. (ed.) *The Book of the Modern House: A Panoramic Survey of Contemporary Domestic Design*. London: Hodder and Stoughton.

Burnett, J. (1986) *A Social History of Housing 1815–1985*. Second edition. London: Methuen.

Cannadine, D. (1980) *Lords and Landlords: The Aristocracy and the Towns, 1774–1967.* Leicester: Leicester University Press.

Coleman, D. and Salt, J. (1992) *The British Population: Patterns, Trends, and Processes.* Oxford: Oxford University Press.

Edwards, A.M. (1981) *The Design of Suburbia: A Critical Study in Environmental History.* London: Pembridge Press.

Fishman, R.L. (1987) American suburbs/English suburbs: a transatlantic comparison. *Journal of Urban History*, Vol. 13, pp. 237–251.

Hägerstrand, T. (1965) On the Monte Carlo simulation of diffusion. *Archives Européennes de Sociologie*, Vol. 10, pp. 43–67.

Hall, P., Gracey, H., Drewett, R. and Thomas, R. (1973) *The Containment of Urban England*, Vol. 1. London: George Allen & Unwin.

Howard, E. (1898) *Tomorrow: A Peaceful Path to Real Reform.* London: Sonnenschein.

Journal of the Royal Institute of British Architects (1936) The architect and housing by the speculative builder. Article 5: Sunnyfields Estate, Mill Hill. *Journal of the Royal Institute of British Architects*, Vol. 43, pp. 299–302.

London County Council (1936) *The Village of Highgate (The Parish of St Pancras, Part I). Survey of London, 17.* London: London County Council.

Local Government Boards for England and Wales, and Scotland (1918) *Report of the Committee Appointed by the President of the Local Government Board and the Secretary for Scotland to Consider Questions of Building Construction in Connection with the Provision of Dwellings for the Working Classes in England and Wales, and Scotland and Report upon Methods of Securing Economy and Despatch in the Provision of Such Dwellings.* London: HMSO.

Marshall, J.L. (1968–9) The pattern of housebuilding in the inter-war period in England and Wales. *Scottish Journal of Political Economy*, Vol. 15, pp. 184–205.

Orwell, G. (1948) *Coming Up for Air.* New edition. London: Secker & Warburg.

Stone, L. (1979) *The Family, Sex and Marriage in England 1500–1800.* London: Weidenfeld and Nicolson.

Thompson, F.M.L. (1974): *Hampstead: Building a Borough, 1650–1964.* London: Routledge and Kegan Paul.

Thompson, F.M.L. (1982) Introduction: the rise of suburbia, in Thompson, F.M.L. (ed.) *The Rise of Suburbia.* Leicester: Leicester University Press, pp. 2–25.

Whitehand, J.W.R. (1989) *Residential Development under Restraint: A Case Study in London's Rural–Urban Fringe.* University of Birmingham School of Geography Occasional Publication 28.

Whitehand, J.W.R. (1992) *The Making of the Urban Landscape.* Institute of British Geographers Special Publication 26. Oxford: Blackwell.

Whitehand, J.W.R. (1997) The Making and Remaking of England's Inter-War Suburbs. Unpublished Final Report to the Leverhulme Trust on Grant No. F.94 AM.

Whitehand, J.W.R., Larkham, P.J. and Jones, A.N. (1992) The changing suburban landscape in post-war England, in Whitehand, J.W.R. and Larkham, P.J. (eds) *Urban Landscapes: International Perspectives.* London: Routledge, pp. 227–265

ACKNOWLEDGEMENTS

The research on which this chapter is based was funded by the Leverhulme Trust. The illustrations were prepared for publication by Mrs A. Ankcorn, Mr K. Burkhill and Mr N. Mudie.

CHAPTER 5

The Making of American Suburbs, 1900–1950s: A Reconstruction

Richard Harris

Recent scholarship has raised – or perhaps it would be more accurate to say that it has renewed – questions about the nature of suburban development in the United States in the first half of this century. The 'traditional' view which, like the traditional family, was largely an invention of the 1950s, is that pre-Second World War suburbs were the preserve of the middle and upper classes. The impression that was created by E.W. Burgess (1925), and developed by later generations of historical scholars, was that only affluent families could afford to acquire new suburban homes (Jackson, 1985; Goldfield and Brownell, 1979; Warner, 1962; cf Harris and Lewis, 1998). Burgess himself knew otherwise, and contemporaries such as Graham Taylor and Harlan Douglass acknowledged the extent of manufacturing employment and working-class settlement in industrial suburbs (Douglass, 1925; Taylor, 1915).[1] For a time, such issues were largely forgotten. In the past decade or so, however, they have been rediscovered and in varying degrees documented (Gardner, 2000; Harris, 1996; Wiese, 1993). It is increasingly accepted that the areas lying beyond the political limits of most United States cities were diverse. Thus the authors of a recent survey argue that, broadly speaking, there were at least three main types of suburbs around North American cities in the first half of this century (Harris and Lewis, 2000). Apart from the affluent residential suburbs of suburban mythology, and the industrial suburbs which many contemporaries discussed, there was also extensive settlement in unincorporated districts at the urban fringe. In historical as well as contemporary research, then, the theme of suburban diversity is in the ascendant.

In theory we might expect that the social and morphological diversity of early twentieth-century suburbs was linked to variations in the manner in which suburbs were developed. In practice, however, the links between pattern and process remain unclear. Those contemporaries who recognized the diversity of early twentieth-century suburbs emphasized their social and economic characteristics. They usually defined diversity in terms of social composition (class, ethnicity, and race) and by the ratio of residents to jobs (Douglass, 1925; Ogburn, 1937; Harris, 1943; Schnore, 1957). On the former criterion they distinguished the élite from the middle- or working-class suburb; using the latter they separated the residential suburb from the industrial. They paid little attention to the forces, and economic agents, that shaped these suburbs. At any rate, they did not think to define suburban types in terms of underlying process. More recently, historical scholars have begun to examine the forces at work in the land market, and especially those who were involved in land subdivision (Doucet and Weaver, 1991; Hise, 1993, 1997; Weiss, 1987). Some have begun to show how subdividers created different types of subdivisions, and hence different types of suburbs, by modulating the constraints that they imposed on builders and buyers, notably through deed restrictions (Burgess, 1994; Keating, 1988). A pair of case studies in Hamilton, Ontario, for example, has shown how a working-class district grew up in the city's east end through a process of unregulated owner-building, while deed restrictions imposed by a land syndicate shaped the development by commercial builders of a middle-class area in the city's west end (Harris and Sendbuehler, 1994; Weaver, 1978). Clearly, different types of suburbs were made in different ways. The implication is that they may be distinguished not only by their form and social character but also by their manner of development. Drawing upon both contemporary writings and also the recent work of urban historians, in this chapter I reconstruct the process and pattern of suburban development in the United States in the first half of this century. My argument is that process and pattern were closely related, and together defined three main suburban types.

The difficulty in constructing this argument is that evidence regarding the connections between form and process is both biased and incomplete. A few case studies have attempted to examine the full range of land development practices in early-twentieth century cities and suburbs, showing how different types of subdivisions were developed in different ways (e.g. Keating, 1988; Sehr, 1981). Most of those who have written general surveys, however, have focused upon the activities of those who created residential, middle-class subdivisions. In the most influential account of suburban land development before the Second World War, *The Rise of the Community Builders*, Marc Weiss (1987) has traced the emergence of large development companies that were involved in all stages of land conversion, from initial subdivision, through construction, to the sale of individual homes. He looks for the origins of the various practices including comprehensive land-use controls and integrated planning – which are now common. Evan McKenzie (1994) has adopted the same approach in tracing the growth of deed restrictions and homeowner associations. The problem is that, as late as the 1950s, such development practices were the exception and not the rule. By including the sorts of subdivision practices which shaped industrial suburbs and unincorporated districts, I seek to provide a more balanced survey of the early-twentieth century scene.

If previous accounts of land subdivision have shown a presentist bias, they have also offered an incomplete picture of the process by which land is converted to urban use. They have focused upon land subdivision at the expense of residential construction. The early classic in the field, Sam Bass Warner's *Streetcar Suburbs* (1962), paid a good deal of attention to the process of housebuilding, but this example has not generally been followed. Here, too, it may be possible to detect a modernist bias. The process of land subdivision was apparently 'modernized' before that of housebuilding. Those looking for the origins of the suburban land development industry have focused upon early initiatives in land subdivision, some inspired by 'Garden City' ideology, and have glossed over the organization of the building industry, which was apparently less progressive.[2] This has left a major gap in our understanding of suburban growth. It is clear that, even in planned suburbs, until the advent of the vertically-integrated developer, homes were typically assembled by a myriad of small builders (Doucet and Weaver, 1991). Fragmentation among builders was even more common in un-planned districts. Recognizing that many builders were amateurs, or operated on a very small scale, and that most were not also involved in land subdivision, in this chapter I try to present not only a more balanced but also a more complete picture of the development of American suburbs.

THREE TYPES OF SUBURBS

There is a stereotype of the United States suburb in the first half of this century, a cliché worn thin with repeated use. The landscape of this suburb is often described as gracious, consisting of broad, tree-lined streets that accommodate substantial single-family homes, and the occasional church, school, and park. Industry has no part in this picture, and even the sorts of commercial activity on which local residents would have depended – grocery and hardware stores, dry cleaners, and so forth – are relegated to the margins of the scene. Socially, this suburb is sometimes described as 'middle class' but, in America this is an elastic term, often stretched to include the better-paid blue-collar worker as well as the teacher, lawyer and business manager. Indeed, it can include all but the poor and the rich. According to stereotype, however, only the mass suburbs of the post-war boom made suburban living accessible to the whole of this middle class. Before then, supposedly, suburbs were more exclusive, accommodating a range of professionals but not, for the most part, the manual worker. In part this was a matter of market forces: it has generally been supposed that only the affluent could afford to buy and commute from new homes at the suburban fringe. Exclusivity, however, was also accomplished through the deliberate efforts of land subdividers and suburban governments who, by instituting and enforcing a variety of land use controls, effectively excluded those with moderate or even middling incomes (Weiss 1987; McKenzie, 1994). In American mythology, a suburb is a prosperous, residential, incorporated place (Fishman, 1987; Jackson, 1985).

There were, of course, many suburbs which fitted this image. Quite a number of them have been described, and indeed such descriptions make up a substantial portion of the historical literature on American suburbs in the first half of this century. We know about the character and development of suburbs like Scarsdale, New York; Cleveland's Shaker Heights; Kansas City's Country Club District, or the whole string of attractive suburbs that extended along the shore of Lake Michigan north of Chicago (Ebner, 1988; O'Connor, 1983; cf Hoffman, 1992). These were not identical, of course. Over time, this type of residential suburb became affordable to wider segments of the middle class. Homes became less imposing, in part because fewer families relied upon servants. Women who had to clean and maintain their own home soon came to place more emphasis upon domestic efficiency (Marsh, 1990). At the same time, and especially during the 1920s, automobiles made it possible for these more modest homes to be situated on somewhat larger lots. Indeed, it was probably during this decade that, as their incomes rose, blue-collar workers in significant numbers began to occupy purely residential suburbs. Around Chicago, for example, during the bungalow boom in the 1920s, many homes were bought by the 'solid working class' (Prosser, 1981, p. 86). Census and other data make it clear that, by 1940, many workers were living in residential suburbs. Using data that were gathered and classified by Grace Kneedler (1945), Harris and Lewis (2000) show that one-quarter of all residential suburbs by 1940 had 'low' rents, while another two-fifths had rents that were about the metropolitan average. Before mid-century, then, the residential suburb had become accessible to a widening range of people.

There were also a great many suburbs which did not fit the residential and middle-class stereotype. Most obviously, there were a growing number of incorporated places which contained a significant numbers of jobs. Contemporaries, who were more alert than many later historians to the diversity of American suburbs before the Second World War, often identified two main types of suburb: the one, affluent and residential, the other industrial and working class (Douglass, 1925; Harris, 1943; Taylor, 1915; cf Walker, 1981). The latter attracted increasing attention after the turn of the century, especially as reformers came to see that it held out prospects for improving the living conditions (and hence the social outlook) of American workers. As early as 1915, using rich but anecdotal evidence, Graham Taylor undertook a nationwide survey of such industrial suburbs, or what he called 'satellite cities'. By the 1920s, most observers, notably Harlan Douglass (1925), had come to recognize industrial suburbs as a common type. Later still, when he undertook the first thorough statistical survey of American suburbs using data from the 1940 census, Chauncy Harris (1943) classified almost as many as industrial (and, by implication, working class) in character as he did suburbs that were, more stereotypically, residential.

The industrial suburbs themselves were diverse. Contemporaries often distinguished between industrial suburbs and satellites (Taylor, 1915; Douglass, 1925; Schnore, 1957). The former were extensions beyond city limits of the main urban centre: city and suburb remained part of a single, or at least an integrated, labour market.[3] In contrast, satellites like Gary, Indiana, were separate communities (Greer, 1976; Mohl and Betten, 1972). Although their industries were often dependent upon linkages to a nearby metropolitan centre – in Gary's case, Chicago – their labour markets were largely self-contained. For some purposes, this is an important distinction. For example, the greater dependency of workers upon local employers in the satellite town could influence industrial relations, community life, and local politics. In terms of housing conditions, however, satellites and industrial suburbs shared a good deal. Except in the case of very large suburbs, and where industries were concentrated in only one district, they did not offer the sorts of pristine environments of the suburban stereotype. At the worst, with homes and industry cheek by jowl, the living – and certainly the air – could be gritty indeed. On the other hand, both sorts of place offered workers cheap land, a lower density of living than in the central city, access to surrounding countryside or bush, and reasonable opportunities for home ownership (cf Harris, 1990).

Home ownership and lower-density living were recognizable, and indeed central, aspects of the suburban dream in the United States. In a survey of Indianapolis in the late nineteenth century, Sehr (1981) contrasted middle-class and élite areas of Irvington and Woodruff Place with the industrial, working-class suburb of Brightwood. In the latter there were no building restrictions 'limiting the buyer's freedom to build whatever and wherever he wished on the property he purchased' (Sehr, 1981, p. 320). The results were much more modest, but recognizably expressed the same sorts of aspirations. Indeed, in more cases than one might expect, the results were quite impressive. Oakwood, which began as a subdivision outside Knoxville, Tennessee, is a case in point (Kane and Bell, 1985). Developed after 1901 alongside the Coster Repair Works of the Southern Railroad, Oakwood was, from the first, an industrial workers' suburb of single-family homes. Homeownership was not universal, but was common enough to be considered the norm. The homes themselves varied in size. Most were quite modest but, Southern style, boasted porches, and were placed on generous 50-foot lots. In a few years, maturing trees made the streetscape almost gracious.

Before it was annexed by the City of Knoxville in 1917, Oakwood was not an incorporated place. It was a subdivision of 531 lots in an unorganized district at the urban fringe. According to the way in which Americans have usually defined the term, it was not really a suburb. Up to a point, an emphasis upon political identity makes sense. In a nation where local governments have constitutional powers, the act of incorporation is significant. In the late-nineteenth and early-twentieth centuries, it greatly facilitated the provision of services, together with the regulation of land use and construction.[4] It also facilitated the creation of distinct communities, setting the seal upon a nascent identity. Even so, it is misleading to exclude unincorporated areas from the ranks of suburbs. They expressed similar aspirations; denied the suburban label, unincorporated fringe areas can then be too easily ignored. To understand what was happening at the fringe of American cities, it is important to recognize the existence and character of places like Oakwood before 1917: unincorporated, variously serviced, and weakly regulated or planned.

It is difficult to obtain a precise sense of the extent of development in unincorporated areas, the third type of suburban place. For 1950, Duncan and Reiss (1956, p. 58) estimated that more than one-third of the urban population that lived outside central cities resided in unincorporated territory. On that reckoning, almost as many people lived in such districts as in residential or industrial suburbs. This fact has been very widely ignored by urban and historical scholars. In part, this neglect has been prompted by the fact that the United States census has reported a much wider range of information for suburbs than for unorganized but urbanized portions of the fringe. It has also followed from the way that scholars have concentrated on the larger metropolitan centres. An exhaustive study by Hawley (1956, p. 58) showed that, by mid-century in the largest metropolitan areas, like Chicago, barely 20 per cent of the urban populations lived in unincorporated areas. In contrast, in the smallest centres, the proportion averaged more than 60 per cent. Around cities like Flint, Michigan, or Peoria, Illinois, most development after the Second World War was occurring in the unincorporated fringe. The absence of systematic evidence for unincorporated areas makes it difficult to identify their social character before mid-century. In a more recent informal survey, John Stilgoe (1988) has implied that many of their residents were quite affluent. Referring only in passing to the existence of some shabby settlements, he paints a picture of borderland gentility. Most contemporaries, however, portray the fringe areas as a refuge for those who were marginal to the urban economy, or who could not afford to live elsewhere. The most typical house seems to have been the shack, not the rambling mansion. This impression is borne out by case studies of the fringe areas around quite a number of cities, including Chicago and Flint, Michigan (Christgau, 1942; Firey, 1946; cf Harris, 1994). These reveal extensive, if scattered, development of very modest homes. For 1950, the social character of these fringe areas was documented directly using census data on incomes. For Chicago, Duncan and Reiss (1956, p. 147) found that the socio-economic status of the labour force was lower at the urban fringe than in the central city, and markedly lower than in the incorporated suburbs. Hoover and Vernon (1962, p. 168) report much the same around New York in 1950, while Lazerwitz (1960, pp. 249, 252) later demonstrated that the pattern was typical nationwide. Recent research by Gardner (2000) has shown what many have long suspected, that throughout the late nineteenth and early twentieth centuries, fringe areas were lower in status than both incorporated suburbs and cities. Unincorporated areas were the third common type of district beyond city limits, and the poorest of them all.

Although residential, industrial, and unincorporated suburbs did differ in terms of their social composition, these differences were not always dramatic. Certainly, by mid century, many residential suburbs were occupied by workers; rather fewer industrial suburbs were occupied by the professional middle class.

The logic of this threefold distinction becomes stronger, however, when we consider more explicitly the manner in which they were developed.

THE MAKING OF SUBURBS

Although systematic evidence is lacking, it would appear that the three types of suburbs were made in very different ways. They differed most obviously in terms of the ways, and extent, to which the process of land development was controlled. Just as important, and even less well-documented, were the varying ways in which individual houses were built.

Land Subdivision and Control

It may be more difficult to generalize about the process of land conversion in the first half of this century than for any other period, before or since. As late as 1900, the average subdivision was small, while most land developers and municipalities exerted little in the way of controls over land use and construction. Today, developers may not reign supreme, but they generally dominate the suburban scene. In both periods, it is possible to speak of a norm but, in the intervening decades, diversity was the order of the day (cf Doucet and Weaver, 1991).

In recent years, scholars have shown that, in the United States, many of the most important initiatives for land use regulation came from those who hoped to make a profit from the subdivision and marketing of land, not from local municipalities (Burgess, 1994; Keating, 1988; McKenzie, 1994; Weiss, 1987). Affluent families wishing to buy a home are naturally concerned about the security of their investment. Since the value of any site depends, to a considerable extent, upon how adjacent parcels are put to use, home buyers care greatly about their neighbours. In this context, land in regulated subdivisions typically commands a premium. Recognizing this, by the turn of this century a growing number of land developers were laying out fairly substantial subdivisions. Through the use of deed restrictions they determined patterns of land use, minimum standards of construction and, until this was declared unconstitutional in 1948, the ethnic or racial composition of the area. These innovations were adopted first at the upper end of the market, and then filtered down. At first, when suburban governments began to adopt planning controls – a trend that gathered momentum in the 1920s – they were merely setting the seal on a pattern of development that developers had already established. Later, when public regulation had become common, suburbs played a more active role in shaping their own destiny. In subtly different ways, then, private and public regulation of the development process together helped to create the stereotypical American suburb.

By way of contrast, it might seem that, in industrial suburbs, there would have been few, if any controls over land development. Local employers were typically eager for workers to find cheap housing close to their work. The cheaper the housing, the less employers would have to pay to provide for a decent subsistence, and companies were in a good position to make their views felt with municipal politicians. Factories enhanced the tax base of industrial suburbs, and provided the jobs on which local businesses and the housing market depended. Politicians must have found it hard to resist when employers pressed them to allow any and all types of development. It would seem, however, that even in industrial suburbs some controls were instituted and enforced. A recent study of Wilmington, Delaware, for example, suggests that, by the 1920s, many of the better working-class districts were subject to deed restrictions, although obviously these were not by any means as exclusive as those used to define middle and upper income areas (Chase, 1995).

Although the connections have not yet been made clear, it is likely that, in many cases, employers supported such controls. Particularly after the First World War, many had come to believe that homeownership was a way of securing a stable and pliant workforce. If workers were to be encouraged to acquire homes, it was surely important that they also enjoy at least the minimal security that deed restrictions might afford. Companies did not welcome unregulated development, and neither did suburban governments, who were naturally concerned about the size and stability of their residential tax base. An untypical, but symptomatic, example was the planned suburb of Torrance, Ca. After the Second World War, Torrance was laid out by a group of industrialists who used zoning and building regulations to segregate homes from industry, to create a salubrious environment for workers and their families (Sidawi, 1997).

The situation in unincorporated districts was quite different. Without municipal government, landowners and developers could do pretty much as they wished. There were little or no municipal services, no zoning or other land use controls, and typically no building regulations to speak of. Land was cheap, and taxes low. This attracted people who could not afford anything better, and deterred people who could. Strapped for cash, farmers severed individual lots along rural side roads; looking for quick profits, speculators bought and sub-divided tracts of varying size. Development was scattered, in more or less random fashion, in small clumps and irregular ribbons. As development within these unincorporated areas grew denser, the pressure for municipal services, including schools and garbage collection, encouraged residents to incorporate, or perhaps to annex themselves to an adjacent municipality. Unplanned development was often a step in the making of a more conventional suburb. From the 1920s to the 1950s, however, the expanding field of exurban settlement outpaced the process of incorporation (Hawley, 1956). The automobile was probably the crucial factor in this trend. During the 1930s, there was a substantial resurgence in what was known as 'part-time farming' (Koos and Brunner, 1945; Rozman, 1930; Tate, 1934; Whetten and Field, 1938). With their hours reduced, industrial workers bought small acreages, and supplemented meagre wages by growing vegetables and fruit, and by raising livestock. With the return of prosperity during the 1940s, metropolitan areas attracted migrants from rural areas, but many of these migrants, as well as city workers, settled at the urban fringe, looking for elbow-room (Firey, 1946). As a result, the amount of development in unincorporated areas grew steadily in importance (Hawley, 1956, p. 58).[5] Looking only at incorporated suburbs, it is possible to speak of the slow rise of community builders in the first half of this century. Looking at the metropolitan area as a whole, however, the persistence of unplanned and uncoordinated development is just as striking.

Housebuilding

If controls over suburban land development were only slowly extended, attempts to 'modernize' the housebuilding industry met with even more limited success. Broadly speaking, there were (and indeed there still are) three ways in which single-family homes could be built. One common method was for a family to pay a general contractor as, in effect, a custom builder. In the case of more substantial dwellings, the family might employ an architect to draw up plans and supervise construction. In more modest projects, the homeowner provided his own plans – often obtained from plan books or magazines – and did the supervision himself. Either way, the process was fraught with difficulty, especially cost overruns. The problem was common enough that it lent itself to the sort of humorous treatment that it received in Ring Lardner's *Own Your Own Home* (1919) and in Eric Hodgins' *Mr. Blandings Builds His Dream House* (1946) which, within two years, was made into a popular movie starring Cary Grant. Alternatively, instead of working for a particular client, the builder could go ahead and erect one or more houses on speculation, and only then advertise to sell. Speculative building – or what the Federal Housing Administration preferred to call 'operative build-ing' – was somewhat riskier but, in planned developments, offered the prospect of realizing efficiencies of scale. Bypassing both types of commercial builder, the third method was for the family to build its own home, using family labour. Unless one or more family members had experience in the construction industry, this method was likely to be inefficient: skills had to be learned by trial and error, on the job. On the other hand, by reducing the amount that families needed to spend, it brought suburban housing, and specifically owner-occupation, within the reach of many more households.

Contemporaries, and most historical scholars, have assumed that the speculative builder was the most efficient and that, largely for this reason, he was also gaining steadily in importance by comparison with the other two. Both assumptions can be questioned (cf Ball, 1988; Schlesinger and Erlich, 1986). It is true that, since the 1950s, speculative builders have gained market share. The trend has not been consistent, however, and until the 1950s even the general direction of change was unclear. Unfortunately, no national data on the social organization of the building industry were published until 1949, and no case studies have been undertaken of specific cities before that date. One reason for the paucity of case studies is that locally-available data rarely make it possible to distinguish clearly between the three types of builder. A difficulty here is that the distinctions which are so clear in principle become blurred in practice. Some commercial builders would begin to build on spec, but seek customers once a foundation was dug. From the 1920s onwards, many of the larger operative builders began to erect model homes which they then used to make sales: subsequently, they built individual homes for specific customers, and sometimes to particular specifications. Some commercial builders catered for the thrifty homeowner by erecting shell homes, which the occupant then finished with his (and her) own labour (e.g. 'Erection of House "Shells" a New Innovation Here': *Home Builders Monthly*, 1950). The distinction between owner-building and custom building was often especially unclear. Although precise evidence is lacking, it was apparently common for owner-builders to subcontract especially onerous or skilled tasks, basement excavation, for example, or wiring. This is eloquently exemplified by the experience of one owner-builder, Emily French, whose diary records the difficulties she faced in scavenging materials and supervising the construction of a modest home in Denver in the 1890s (Lecombe, 1987). At the same time, many of those who employed general contractors might have arranged to do the simpler jobs themselves. In such situations, where one draws the line between custom- and owner-building becomes almost arbitrary, and impossible to reconstruct from routinely-generated records.

Given this uncertainty, the most that we can say is that operative builders seem to have expanded their operations most effectively during boom periods such as the 1920s, when demand was strong and the risks of building on spec were minimized. In the lean years of the Depression, general contractors again took over a larger share of the smaller market. Local evidence pertaining to part-time farmers suggests that there might also have been a resurgence of owner-building during the Depression (e.g. Andrews, 1942, p. 175; Faust, 1942; Firey, 1946, pp. 24–25; Koos and Brunner, 1945, p. 41). What is more clear, though not generally appreciated, is that owner-building underwent a major resurgence after the Second World War, reaching a peak in the late 1940s and early 1950s. Fortuitously, this resurgence is captured by the first thorough national survey of builders, undertaken by the Bureau of Labor Statistics in 1949 (US Department of Labor, 1954).[6] It found that, in that year, owner-builders accounted for 69 per cent of all builders, 27 per cent of all non-farm dwellings units, across the United States, and approaching one-third of new, non-farm single-family homes. Commercial building operations were divided between the two main types of builder, though not quite equally. General contractors slightly outnumbered operative builders. On average, however, the latter built more homes, and so they accounted for about twice as many dwellings. In terms of the social organization of the homebuilding industry, then, no single method prevailed.[7]

The three methods of housebuilding addressed the needs of different home-buyers. Broadly speaking, affluent families were in the best position to hire their own builder or architect. Indeed, at the top end of the housing market, and in the most exclusive suburbs, this manner of construction had long been the norm. When land subdividers first began to lay out whole subdivisions, and to control development through building regulations, their presumption was that buyers would leave it up to individual builders and architects to follow the appropriate guidelines. It is an open question as to how far down the social hierarchy custom building reached. Much of Lardner's humour arose from the assumption that families on very middling sorts of incomes might aspire to hire their own builder. It is unlikely, however, that this was ever a common strategy of those whose incomes placed them below the top third.

At the other end of the housing market, owner-builders dominated the construction scene throughout the first half of this century. Many contemporaries, and most historians, assumed that the filtering process was the way in which low-income families were usually housed: in time, homes built for the affluent deteriorated, declined in value, and eventually fell within the reach of the poor. Recent research has shown that in fact many low-income families, including recent immigrants, acquired homes by building their own. In Toronto in the first quarter of this century, for example, somewhere between one-third and two-fifths of all new homes were owner-built (Harris, 1996). Here, as in other North American cities, the great majority of owner-builders were quite poor. Speaking in the context of Detroit, Zunz (1982) has suggested that, below a certain price, commercial builders were simply not able or willing to operate; applying this idea to Toronto, I have found that the majority of homes at the bottom end of the market were erected by their owners with little or no help from contractors or tradesmen (Harris, 1996). The concentration of owner-builders at the bottom end of the market is not surprising. To be sure, there are periods when minor fashions for owner-building have influenced the middle class. The period around the time of the First World War would appear to have been one of these, while the Depression encouraged attitudes of self-sufficiency even among those who kept their jobs. Building one's own home, however, is a lot of work. It requires skills that many people lack, and time that few are willing to spend, unless they have to do so. For the most part, those who have built their own homes have done so because there was simply no other way of acquiring a home, or even of providing themselves with adequate shelter. The most dramatic expressions of this fact were the shacktowns and Hoovervilles that sprang up during the Depression. As the national builder survey of 1949 showed, however, this remained true into the immediate post-war era (US Department of Labor, 1954). This survey found that, disproportionately, owner-builders tended to erect very modest homes: 28 per cent of the single-family homes that were built by their owners in 1949 were worth less than $6,000 (table 5.1). The equivalent proportion for operative builders was a mere 6 per cent. Consistently, owner-builders addressed a need that commercial businesses could not profitably meet.

Table 5.1. House prices and scale of operations of speculative ('operative') builders, United States, 1949.

Size of Operations	Price Distribution of Single-Family Homes						
	Under $6000	$6000–7499	$7500–9999	$10000–14999	$15000 or more	Unknown	Total
1 house	28	–	–	27	–	–	100
2–4 houses	20	14	19	24	13	10	100
5–9 houses	11	13	24	30	12	10	100
10–24 houses	–	9	30	33	13	11	100
25–49 houses	–	15	34	35	–	–	100
50–99 houses	–	17	48	28	–	–	100
100–249 houses	–	21	51	19	–	–	100
250 or more houses	–	23	39	21	–	10	100
All operative builders	6	16	36	27	7	7	100

– indicates that each builder contributes less than 0.5% of total.
Source: US Department of Labor (1954)

Between the custom builder and the amateur, speculative builders occupied the broad middle range of the housing market. Unfortunately, the 1949 survey did not report the price distribution of homes erected by the sorts of general contractors who erected homes on a custom basis. However, detailed evidence pertaining to the scale of undertakings for operative builders is suggestive. Here it is important to recall the ambiguity of the three main builder types. Among very small commercial builders – those building only one house in 1949 – the distinction between a general contractor and an operative builder was often negligible. They probably addressed much the same segments of market demand: on the one hand they might have been employed by affluent families to erect substantial homes; on the other they might have catered to owner-builders who did not wish to do everything themselves. In contrast, the large operative builders – certainly those responsible for more than 100 homes in 1949 – were surely acting in a speculative capacity. In this context, it is significant that, while the large operative builders concentrated their efforts in the middle segments of the market, small builders distributed themselves at each end of the price spectrum (table 5.1). Just over half of the homes that were built by those who were responsible for 100–250 houses a year fell into the middle price category, $7,500–9,999. In contrast, those who built only one house in 1949 concentrated their efforts either at the very bottom segment of the market, where they were competing for the business of potential owner-builders, or towards the upper end of the market, where more affluent families were looking for one-of-a-kind homes. It would be dangerous to try to read too much into these statistics, which are, after all, subject to sampling error. Nevertheless, they do indicate that different types of builders were active in different segments of the market.

DEVELOPERS, BUILDERS AND SUBURBS

If the three main types of builder were most active in different segments of the housing market, they were naturally concentrated in particular types of suburbs. Many, if not all, studies of affluent residential suburbs indicate that, in such areas, custom building was the norm. Certainly, this was true for the more prominent examples, such as Chicago's Riverside, or Cleveland's Shaker Heights. Part of the appeal of such places was that homes were not only distinguished, but also distinct, one from another. In time, land developers themselves began to cater for this taste by building for their customers on demand. Until at least mid-century, however, they usually contented themselves with setting minimum standards to which owners, together with their builders and architects, then conformed.

At the other end of the housing market, owner-building was concentrated in unincorporated suburbs where, indeed, it was often the norm. There were push as well as pull factors at work. Negatively, speculative builders tended to avoid unregulated areas where homes might prove difficult to sell. Positively, low-income families were attracted to areas where they would not be prevented from building very modest homes, possibly in stages as their finances allowed. As amateurs, they appreciated the fact that they could learn on the job without encountering regulatory disapproval. Together, these sorts of considerations often produced very different housing markets among fringe areas, or between city and suburbs. The best documented case is that of Toronto where, in the first two decades of this century, commercial builders avoided the unregulated suburbs to which owner-builders were drawn in their thousands (Harris, 1996). The same geographical dynamic was at work everywhere, however, and well into the 1940s and 1950s. It differentiated development in the suburbs and unincorporated districts of Chicago in 1940; it highlighted city-suburban contrasts in Flint, Michigan and Peoria, Illinois. In some cases, incorporation changed the dynamics of the housing market. If it happened early enough, the new suburb could strive to re-create itself by enacting tight regulations. Toronto's suburb of Forest Hill was an extreme case in point. More typically, the pattern of development that had been established prior to incorporation continued to define the character of the suburb. The Los Angeles suburb of South Gate, and Chicago's Stone Park, are two of many such examples (Harris, 1994; Nicolaides, 1993).

Speculative builders were not so strongly associated with a particular type of suburb. They built homes in affluent suburbs, especially in those areas which subdividers had targeted to a more middling clientele. A few may have been willing to risk building in unincorporated areas, though it is unlikely that they would have done so unless the land subdivider agreed to provide basic services and to define minimum building standards. It is not clear how commonly they did so. It is certain, however, that speculative builders were much more active in industrial suburbs and in the growing ranks of more modest residential suburbs. In the industrial suburbs, weak deed restrictions and spotty zoning provided some security of investment but, from the builders' point of view, the chief attraction was strong, localized demand. Until automobile ownership became common, workers had a strong incentive to live close to work, especially in suburban districts where public transit was often poor. From the point of view of a builder, and until at least the 1920s, industrial suburbs offered a relatively safe investment. Further removed from employment, residential suburbs could be made appealing to builders if developers imposed tighter private and public regulations, and if they (or suburban governments) provided basic services. Perhaps in different ways, then, both industrial and the middle rank of residential suburbs offered the builder acceptable business risks and the prospect of reasonable profits.

DISCUSSION

I have suggested that there were three main types of suburbs at the fringe of American cities in the first half of this century, and that these were developed, characteristically, in three different ways. If this simplification of a very complex situation is to be useful, we must acknowledge that suburban patterns, and the relation of form to process, underwent significant change. The residential suburb, in particular, went through a steady evolution. Initially, affluent residential suburbs were built by custom contractors in ways which were often tightly controlled by land subdividers. In time, and certainly by the turn of the century, as commercially-built homes became affordable to broader segments of the population, speculative builders became more active. At the same time, deed restrictions in many subdivisions were moderated so that an increasingly wide range of suburbs became possible. Eventually, by the 1950s, speculative builders came to dominate the scene in most residential suburbs, and in many cases the companies in question were involved in both house construction and land development. In contrast, throughout the period in question unincorporated areas grew haphazardly, often through a process of owner-building that was scattered across a landscape where land speculators carved out individual lots and small subdivisions. The extent of this type of development varied greatly, declining in importance during the 1920s but undergoing a resurgence during the 1930s and then again, more spectacularly, in the immediate post-war years.

The third type, the industrial suburb, was always favoured by speculators in both land development and construction. In the early-twentieth century, these suburbs varied a good deal, especially according to whether they were planned or not. Typically, however, land subdividers imposed modest controls upon development, and builders erected large numbers of basic dwellings in a limited variety of styles. The identity of industrial suburbs was eroded by the rising use of automobiles, which allowed workers to travel to suburban jobs from more distant residential suburbs. By the 1940s, the residential portions of the new generation of industrial suburbs were becoming indistinguishable from the new mass residential suburbs (Hise, 1993, 1997). In both cases, large-scale speculative land development was becoming the norm.

Although plausible, the sketch that I have presented should be regarded as a complex hypothesis. Available case studies are consistent with the account that I have presented, but they are few in number. Many broad questions remain unanswered. Were there many affluent suburbs in the first half of this century which managed to evolve in the absence of developer-imposed restrictions; and, if so, how? In more middling residential suburbs, when did the balance shift decisively from contractors to speculative builders? How commonly did commercial builders operate in unincorporated or unregulated areas? In particular, under what circumstances were speculative builders willing to risk investing in such areas? To what extent did the investment decisions of builders in industrial suburbs, where jobs were close by but where incomes were low, differ from those in the more modest residential suburbs, where incomes had to be higher in order to accommodate a longer journey to work? Definite answers to these questions could either confirm or challenge the interpretative framework that I have suggested.

It is time-consuming, and often impossible, to discover exactly how particular subdivisions were actually developed. The records of small land speculators and developers, and of the small amateur and commercial builders who together dominated the construction scene until at least the 1950s, are few and far between. In this context, one of the more promising sources is the built environment itself. More than 30 years ago, Warner (1962) argued that small commercial builders created a distinctive landscape, a 'weave of small patterns' which entailed a myriad of minor variations on a very limited number of general themes. Recently, I have argued that owner-builders created their own landscape, a scattered patterning of modest, frame dwellings with varied setbacks and unique (sometimes eccentric) styles (Harris, 1997). In a general way, it is clear that uniqueness also characterized the more imposing achievements of contractors and architects in affluent suburbs. In this context, the absence of markedly smaller dwellings, and of 'incompatible' land uses, would indicate the use of various types of building restrictions (though they will not reveal whether these were implemented by private land developers or by suburban municipalities). In contrast, uniformity was a striking (and often criticized) feature of speculatively-built subdivisions, whether of cramped workers' dwellings in industrial suburbs or of roomier homes in residential suburbs. To this day, the landscape of early twentieth-century suburbs provides good clues to the way in which they were developed, and for whom.

Undertaken in a systematic fashion, even quite cursory field surveys might tell us a good deal about the evolution of suburbs in a given urban area. Where redevelopment, or substantial renovations, have obscured original details, insurance atlases can provide unusually good clues. In North America – but not in Australia or Britain – these atlases provided irregular but fairly comprehensive coverage right out to the urban fringe. Showing street layout, the overall patterning of development at different points in time, the footprint of each structure on each lot, and providing information about building materials as well as number of storeys, these atlases offer a fair (and very convenient) substitute for field research. Alone or in combination, these methods make it possible, in principle, to begin to test the broad generalizations that I have offered here.

NOTES

1. Burgess refers to the social diversity of fringe settlement, but the logic of his zonal model encouraged others to ignore this fact (Harris and Lewis, 1998).

2. Innovations in housebuilding, as opposed to land subdivision, have been occurring over a much longer period of time and have sometimes appeared minor. For discussion see Ball (1988) and Schlesinger and Erlich (1986).

3. In very large metropolitan areas, and before the widespread use of automobiles, employers in industrial suburbs could draw upon the labour force of the city and their own suburb, but not necessarily upon those living in other industrial suburbs.

4. After the Second World War, the development of special service districts and, in particular, the 'Lakewood Plan', helped to uncouple service provision from municipal incorporation (Miller, 1981).

5. Hawley (1956) presents only disaggregated data for metropolitan areas of different sizes (five categories) and at different zonal distances away from the CBD (eight categories). In the largest metro areas, those with a population of one million and over, and at the 25 mile zone, about 35 per cent of the population lived in unincorporated areas in 1930, rising to almost 50 per cent in 1950. Over the same period, comparable increases in the population share of unincorporated areas occurred in most distance zones and in smaller metro areas.

6. Smaller surveys had been taken previously, but these did not identify owner-builders.

7. In addition to the types of builders already discussed, a number of companies were manufacturing kit houses for local or mail delivery while others were endeavouring, with government assistance, to build completely prefabricated homes of wood, steel, and even concrete. Collectively these accounted for only a small proportion of new dwelling units in the immediate post-war years.

REFERENCES

Andrews, R.B. (1942) Elements in the urban fringe pattern. *Journal of Land and Public Utility Economics*, Vol. 18, pp. 169–183.
Ball, M. (1988) *Construction Rebuilt? Economic Change and the British Construction Industry*. London: Routledge and Kegan Paul.
Berger, B. (1960) *Blue Collar Suburb. A Study of Auto Workers in Suburbia*. Berkeley and Los Angeles: University of California Press.
Burgess, E.W. (1925) The growth of the city, in Park, R.E., Burgess, E.W. and McKenzie, R. (eds) *The City*. Chicago: University of Chicago Press.
Burgess, P. (1994) *Planning for the Private Interest. Land Use Controls and Residential Patterns in Columbus, Ohio, 1900–1970*. Columbus: Ohio State University Press.
Burns, E.K. (1980) The enduring affluent suburb. *Landscape*, Vol. 24, pp. 33–41.
Chase, S.M. (1995) The Process of Suburbanization and the Use of Restrictive Deed Covenants as Private Zoning, Wilmington, Delaware, 1900–1941. Unpublished Ph.D. thesis, University of Delaware.
Christgau, E.F. (1942) Unincorporated Communities in Cook County. Unpublished M.A. thesis, University of Chicago.
Clawson, M. (1971) *Suburban Land Conversion in the United States*. Baltimore: Johns Hopkins University Press.
Davie, M.R. (1937) The pattern of urban growth, in Murdock, G. (ed.) *Studies in the Science of Society*. New Haven: Yale University Press, pp. 33–161.
Doucet, M. and Weaver, J. (1991) *Housing the North American City*. Montreal and Kingston: McGill-Queen's University Press.
Douglass, H. (1925) *The Suburban Trend*. New York: Century.
Duncan, O. and Reiss, A.J. (1956) *Social Characteristics of Urban and Rural Communities 1950*. New York: Wiley.
Ebner, M. (1988) *Creating Chicago's North Shore*. Chicago: University of Chicago Press.
Faust, L.M. (1942) The Eugene, Oregon rural-urban fringe, in *The Rural-Urban Fringe*. *Proceedings of the Commonwealth Conference*. Eugene: University of Oregon, pp. 12–19.
Firey, W. (1946) *Social Aspects to Land-use Planning in the Country-City Fringe. The Case of Flint, Michigan*. Special Bulletin No. 339. East Lansing: Michigan State Agricultural Experiment Station.
Fishman, R. (1987) *Bourgeois Utopias. The Rise and Fall of Suburbia*. New York: Basic Books.

Gardner, T. (2000) The social characteristics of American cities and suburbs. 1850–1950, *Journal of Urban History* (forthcoming).

Goldfield, D.R. and Brownell, B.A. (1979) *Urban America: From Downtown to No Town.* Boston: Houghton Mifflin.

Greer, E. (1976) Monopoly and competitive capital in the making of Gary, Indiana. *Science and Society*, Vol. 40, pp. 465–478.

Harris, C. (1943) Suburbs. *American Journal of Sociology*, Vol. 49, pp. 1–13.

Harris, R. (1990) Working-class home ownership in the American metropolis. *Journal of Urban History*, Vol. 17, pp. 49–54.

Harris, R. (1994) Chicago's other suburbs. *Geographical Review*, Vol. 84, No. 4, pp. 394–410.

Harris, R. (1996) *Unplanned Suburbs. Toronto's American Tragedy, 1901–1951.* Baltimore: Johns Hopkins University Press.

Harris, R. (1997) Reading Sanborns for the spoor of the owner-builder, 1890s–1950s, in Adams, A. and McMurry, S. (eds) *Perspectives in Vernacular Architecture.* Vol. VII. Knoxville, Tennessee: University of Tennessee Press, pp. 251–267.

Harris, R. and Lewis, R. (1998) Constructing a fault(y) zone. Misrepresentations of American cities and suburbs. *Annals of the Association of American Geographers*, Vol. 88, No. 4, pp. 622–639.

Harris, R. and Lewis, R. (2000) The geography of North American cities and suburbs, 1900–1950: a reinterpretation. *Journal of Urban History* (forthcoming).

Harris, R. and Sendbuehler, M.P. (1994) The making of a working-class suburb in Hamilton's East End. *Journal of Urban History*, Vol. 20, No. 4, pp. 486–511.

Hawley, A. (1956) *The Changing Shape of Metropolitan America: Deconcentration Since 1920.* Glencoe: Free Press.

Hise, G. (1993) Home building and industrial decentralization in Los Angeles: the roots of the postwar urban region. *Journal of Urban History*, Vol. 19, pp. 95–125.

Hise, G. (1997) *Magnetic Los Angeles. Planning the Twentieth-Century Metropolis.* Baltimore: Johns Hopkins University Press.

Hodgins, E. (1946) *Mr Blandings Builds His Dream House.* New York: Simon and Schuster.

Hoffman, S.J. (1992) 'A plan of quality': the development of Mt. Lebanon, a 1920s automobile suburb. *Journal of Urban History*, Vol. 18, pp. 141–181.

Home Builders Monthly (1950) Erection of house 'shells' a new innovation here. *Home Builders Monthly*, Vol. 7, No. 8, pp. 2–21.

Hoover, E. and Vernon, R. (1962) *Anatomy of a Metropolis: the Changing Distribution of People and Jobs Within the New York Metropolitan Region.* New York: Anchor.

Howe, R. (1994) Inner suburbs. From slums to gentrification, in Johnson, L.C. (ed.) *Suburban Dreaming. An Interdisciplinary Approach to Australian Cities.* Geelong, Victoria: Deakin University Press, pp. 114–128.

Jackson, K.T. (1985) *Crabgrass Frontier: the Suburbanization of the United States.* New York: Oxford University Press.

Kane, K.D. and Bell, T.L. (1985) Suburbs for a labor elite. *Geographical Review*, Vol. 75, pp. 319–334.

Keating, A.D. (1988) *Building Chicago. Suburban Developers and the Creation of a Divided Metropolis.* Columbus, Ohio: Ohio State University Press.

Kelly, B. (1993) *Expanding the Dream. Building and Rebuilding Levittown.* Albany, NY: State University of New York Press.

Kneedler, G. (1945) Economic classification of cities, in *The Municipal Year Book*, Chicago: International City Managers' Association.

Koos, E. L. and de Brunner, E. (1945) *Suburbanization in Webster, New York.* Rochester: Department of Sociology, University of Rochester.

Lardner, R. (1919) *Own Your Own Home*. Indianapolis: Bobbs-Merrill.

Lazerwitz, B. (1960) Metropolitan community residential belts, 1950 and 1956. *American Sociological Review*, Vol. 25, pp. 245–252.

Lecombe, J. (ed.) (1987) *Emily French. The Diary of a Hard-Working Woman*. Lincoln, Nebraska: University of Nebraska Press.

Marsh, M. (1990) *Suburban Lives*. New Brunswick: Rutgers University Press.

McKenzie, E. (1994) *Privatopia. Homeowner Associations and the Rise of Residential Private Government*. New Haven: Yale University Press.

Miller, G.J. (1981) *Cities by Contract. The Politics of Municipal Incorporation*. Cambridge: MIT Press.

Mohl, R. and Betten, N. (1972) The failure of industrial city planning: Gary, Indiana, 1906–1910. *Journal of the American Institute of Planners*, Vol. 38, pp. 202–215.

Monchow, H. (1928) *The Use of Deed Restrictions in Subdivision Development*. Chicago: Institute for Research in land Economics and Public Utilities.

Nicolaides, B.M. (1993) In Search of the Good Life: Community and Politics in Working-Class Los Angeles, 1920–1955. Unpublished Ph.D. thesis, Columbia University.

O'Connor, C.A. (1983) *A Sort of Utopia. Scarsdale, 1891–1981*. Albany: SUNY Press.

Ogburn, W.F. (1937) *Social Characteristics of Cities*. Chicago: International City Managers' Association.

Prosser, D.J. (1981) Chicago and the bungalow boom of the 1920s, *Chicago History*, Vol. 10, pp. 86–95.

Queen, S.A. and Thomas, L.F. (1939) *The City. A Study of Urbanism in the United States*. New York: McGraw Hill.

Quinn, J. A. (1940) The Burgess zonal hypothesis and its critics. *American Sociological Review*, Vol. 5, pp. 210–218.

Rozman, D. (1930) Part-time farming in Massachusetts. *Massachusetts (Amherst) Agricultural Experimental Station Bulletin*, No. 266, pp. 103–146.

Schauffler, M. (1941) *The Suburbs of Cleveland*. Unpublished Ph.D. thesis, University of Chicago.

Schlesinger, T. and Erlich, M. (1986) Housing. The industry capitalism didn't forget, in Bratt, R., Hartman, C., and Meyerson, A. (eds.) *Critical Perspectives on Housing*. Philadelphia: Temple University Press, pp. 139–164.

Schnore, L.F. (1957) Satellites and suburbs. *Social Forces*, Vol. 36, pp. 121–129.

Sehr, T. (1981) Three Gilded Age suburbs of Indianapolis: Irvington, Brightwood and Woodruff Place. *Indiana Magazine of History*, Vol. 77, pp. 305–333.

Sidawi, S. (1997) Planning environmental racism. The construction of the industrial suburban ideal in Los Angeles County in the early twentieth century. *Historical Geography*, Vol. 25, pp. 83–99.

Stilgoe, J. (1988) *Borderland. Origins of the American Suburb 1820–1939*. New Haven: Yale University Press.

Tate, L. (1934) *The Rural Homes of City Workers and the Urban-Rural Migration*. Bulletin 595. Ithaca, New York: Cornell University Agricultural Experiment Station.

Taylor, G. (1915) *Satellite Cities: a Study of Industrial Suburbs*. New York: Appleton.

Taylor, H.L. (1979) The Building of a Black Industrial Suburb. The Lincoln Heights, Ohio Story. Unpublished Ph.D. thesis, SUNY at Buffalo.

Taylor, H.L. (1993) City building, public policy, the rise of the industrial city and Black ghetto-slum formation in Cincinnati, 1850–1940, in Taylor, H.L. (ed.) *Race and the City. Work, Community, and Protest in Cincinnati, 1820–1970*. Urbana: University of Illinois Press.

Teaford, J. (1979) *City and Suburb. The Political Fragmentation of Metropolitan America, 1850–1970*. Baltimore: Johns Hopkins University Press.

US Department of Labor (1954) *Structure of the Residential Building Industry in 1949.* Bulletin No. 1170. Washington, D.C.: US Department of Labor.

Viehe, F.W. (1981) Black gold suburbs: the influence of the extractive industry on the suburbanization of Los Angeles, 1890–1930. *Journal of Urban History*, Vol. 8, pp. 3–26.

Viehe, F.W. (1991) The social-spatial distribution in the black gold suburbs of Los Angeles, 1900–1930. *Southern California Quarterly*, Vol. 73, pp. 33–35.

Walker, R.A. (1981) A theory of suburbanization: capitalism and the construction of urban space in the United States, in Dear, M. and Scott, A.J. (eds) *Urbanization and Urban Planning in Capitalist Society*. New York: Methuen, pp. 383–429.

Warner, S.B. (1962) *Streetcar Suburbs. The Process of Growth in Boston 1870–1900.* Cambridge, Mass.: Harvard University Press.

Weaver, J. (1978) From land assembly to social maturity. The suburban life of Westdale (Hamilton), Ontario, 1911–1951. *Histoire Sociale/Social History*, Vol. 11, pp. 411–440.

Wehrwein, G.S. (1942) The rural-urban fringe. *Economic Geography*, Vol. 18, pp. 217–228.

Weiss, M. (1987) *The Rise of the Community Builders. The American Real Estate Industry and Urban Land Planning*. New York: Columbia University Press.

Whetten, N.L. and Field, R.F. (1938) *Studies of Suburbanization in Connecticut. 2. Norwich. An Industrial Part-Time Farming Area.* Bulletin No. 226. Storrs: Connecticut State Agricultural Experiment Station.

Wiese, A. (1993) Places of our own. Suburban Black towns before 1960. *Journal of Urban History*, Vol. 19, No. 3, pp. 30–54.

Zunz, O. (1982) *The Changing Face of Inequality: Urbanization, Industrial Development, and Immigrants in Detroit, 1880–1920*. Chicago: University of Chicago Press.

ACKNOWLEDGEMENT

I would like to thank the Social Sciences and Humanities Research Council of Canada (SSHRC) for financial support for part of the research reported here.

CHAPTER 6

Suburbs of Desire: The Suburban Landscape of Canadian Cities, c. 1900–1950

Larry McCann

By the mid-twentieth century, as the full impact of the new industrialism and its modernist tendencies were being felt throughout Canada's economy and society, cities across the country stood more segregated. The urban landscape of the nineteenth-century commercial city was almost completely transformed. Most fundamentally, with the growing power of planners and other government officials who sought an efficient, rational, and orderly city – expressed most forcefully through zoning bye-laws that controlled the location of economic activities and the form of the built environment – distinct places now existed for the exclusive use of separate land-use activities. From a pattern of dense and heterogeneous living spaces in the commercial city, where different classes of people and activities frequently intermingled, the newly-developing, mid-twentieth century neighbourhood had become more homogeneous, decidedly more middle class, and generally free of non-residential activities.

Increasingly, as the twentieth century progressed, the advancing edge of suburbia was the vanguard of this transformed, modern, and segregated urban pattern. With industry, commerce, and especially people moving to the urban periphery in growing frequency and numbers, often creating wasteful sprawl, the calls from citizens and various professional agencies alike for better planning and development regulations grew apace. Change was needed because land developers and house builders of late nineteenth-century suburbanization typically encountered little municipal regulation. Responding eventually to haphazard suburban growth, governments at all levels reacted by expanding, particularly during the inter-war period, a body of regulations that consolidated existing fragmentation and planned for future, orderly development. Federal housing and mortgage legislation, and municipal endorsement of tighter subdivision controls and the zoned-city concept, became common place methods for guiding the expansion and changing shape of the suburban landscape. By the mid-twentieth century, a complex set of development guidelines and bye-laws governed the building of suburbs. But how did interaction between the public and private spheres unfold to shape the modern suburban landscape? Was it simply a matter of government agencies at all levels heeding the call to become even more involved in the city-building process?

SUBURBS OF DESIRE

The very fluidity of the suburban landscape over time denies for the suburb an all-encompassing definition. The evolving character of this landscape embodies the changing interests not only of an all-pervasive government, but of several other groups as well. In fact, suburban residents, land developers, housebuilders, and financial institutions, amongst others, were not just important players on the suburban stage, they were also active participants in the culture of consumer capitalism, of which suburbanization was a major component. According to Leach (1993), this culture of producing commodities and of acquiring material things comprised several important values and beliefs which were common to both the private and public spheres, and which helped to shape the character of suburbs. Through social and geographical mobility, a suburban lifestyle was believed accessible to all consumers who shared in the modern assumption that the acquisition of urban property (rather than land *per se*) was now the measure of personal achievement. Happiness resided in owning a home and enjoying the pleasures of suburban living.

Something of the joy in achieving this lifestyle, and of the consumer culture involved, is captured in Gabrielle Roy's *Street of Riches*, set in St. Boniface, a largely French-Canadian suburb of Winnipeg, just before the First World War. Early in the novel, the narrator Christine reflects that

> in those days on Rue Deschambault we lived as though we were in the country . . . Where our street ended, and which itself was none too built up, a yellow trolley car passed by every fifteen minutes . . . Maman was pleased with the street, with the quiet, with the good, pure air there, for the children, but she objected to the servile copying of our neighbour's house, which was luckily not too close to ours. (Roy, 1957, pp. 1 and 9)

Inside the house, and this was true of Christine's family home, commodities of the new industrialism – for example, sanitary devices, electric appliances, a 'modern' kitchen, or a garage for a new car – offered confirmation of a family's social status within the community (Strong-Boag, 1988). For many individuals who aspired to the suburbs, replacing the old and inefficient with something more technologically advanced became a highly-valued desire. For the public corporation, winning efficiency through new techniques of fiscal management or by applying scientific town planning principles became, ultimately, an equally-prized goal (Schiesl, 1977). The developing consumer culture thus stemmed from private and public desires for the acquisition of the new and modern, whether of changing house styles, household possessions, management techniques, the design of a neighbourhood, or the zoned-city philosophies of planners (Miller, 1987).

This evolving and in time widely-shared culture thus spawned 'suburbs of desire' with distinctive characteristics – all varieties of residential areas at the edge of the expanding city where land could be bought and sold at a profit; where at first individuals of any financial means, family status, or ethnic background could desire and establish equity in a home; where segregated social standing nevertheless stood revealed; and where the presence of local government ensured debate on either the implementation of changing ideals or the preservation of established cultural values. Associated with this culture's advance was the expansion since the late nineteenth century of a new class of brokers (comprising, for example, land surveyors, engineers, landscape architects, planners, contractors, lawyers, and real estate agents) who specialized in different phases of suburban development (Schultz, 1989; Weiss, 1987). Common features of today's suburban tracts – single-family houses, open spaces, curving roads, a hierarchy of streets, parks, recreational facilities, even regulatory mechanisms – owe much to the brokerage power of the new professions over the invisible hand of consumer capitalism. Through this process, for example, corporate developers were among the first to introduce garden suburbs (c. the First World War) and neighbourhood unit schemes (after the Second World War) to Canada. These now serve as standard guidelines for all city planners considering the design of new residential areas.

Taking a cultural perspective, this chapter examines how the different interests, values, and beliefs of important players on the suburban stage – including suburban residents, land developers, housebuilders, planners, financial institutions, and government agencies – have sometimes coalesced, and sometimes clashed, to change the one-time pluralistic character of Canadian suburbs, making them instead more regulated, more planned, and ultimately, but not completely, more segregated and middle class. This was not always the case. Early in the course of twentieth-century suburbanization, suburbs were home to a diversity of Canadians. But as time passed, the forces shaping suburbia shifted in weight, making suburbs less accessible to certain groups, changing a suburb's definition. One of the 'tragedies' of the suburbs, to paraphrase Richard Harris's (1996) recent argument, was the gradual loss of suburban living opportunities for Canada's lower-income, working-class people. For them, the culture of consumer capitalism shifted its focus away from suburban desires, remaining, instead, stranded in inner-city neighbourhoods in search of other material pursuits (Cohen, 1990). The principal benefactors of the newly-emerging culture as it applied to suburban development were the middle and upper classes (Carver, 1962, 1975; Clark, 1966; Fishman, 1987; Seeley et al., 1956). Only they were able to afford the rising entry fee to a suburban world – a fee that increased, not coincidentally, with the widespread acceptance of government as a growing regulatory authority over the suburban environment.

SUBURBAN EXPANSION BEFORE THE FIRST WORLD WAR

The late-nineteenth century suburbs surrounding major Canadian cities were quite different from their mid-twentieth-century counterparts. To begin with, Canada's pre-industrial suburbs were settled only gradually by the bourgeoisie (Rybczynski, 1995, pp. 173–197). The earliest suburbs attracted mainly marginalized groups of immigrants and workers: eighteenth-century Halifax's 'foreign Protestants' and Blacks who located in the North Suburbs (Bell, 1990); the Irish-Catholic lumberers of Saint John's peripheral shanty towns (Wynn, 1981); or the tanners of east end Montréal (Dechêne, 1974). These people were sometimes legislated to the outskirts by colonial officials. When the outward movement of the middle and upper classes did begin in a notable way early in the nineteenth century, it took place very slowly. It was often associated with the seasonal migration of wealthy local residents seeking 'salutary summer breezes', who built countryside estates away from the heat, filth, and stench of the commercial city. In this way, favoured sites of the bourgeoisie were the Northwest Arm of Halifax (Regan, 1908), Rothesay outside Saint John (Hamilton, 1884), the slopes of Montréal's Mount Royal (Hanna, 1980), the shores of Lake St. Louis at Senneville near Montréal (Pratte, 1987), and the Lake Ontario terraces of Toronto's and Hamilton's peripheral zones (Arthur, 1964; Weaver, 1978). Their élite status persists even today. Year-round residence there was restricted by difficult weather conditions that hindered winter-time travel to city jobs. These conditions were not really overcome until the automobile era.

But, as steam railways entered the mid-nineteenth-century scene, the immediate hinterlands of major cities did become more accessible, increasing the range of opportunities for suburban residence. Unlike Britain or the United States, where population and manufacturing growth were much stronger (Kellet, 1964; Stilgoe, 1983), railways never really precipitated a great rush of people or factories to the fringes of Canadian cities. And when this de-centralization did occur in its limited way, particularly around large cities like Montréal and Toronto, the emerging suburban pattern became a patchwork quilt of various land uses (Harris, 1996; Lewis, 1991; Slack *et al.*, 1994). Taking, as an example, the western approach to Montréal (figure 6.1) – a corridor stretching along the terraces of the St. Lawrence River for about 30 miles (50 km) and served daily by as many as sixty trains *c*. 1900 – any one of its sections might comprise a diversity of intermingling land uses: large and small farms, market gardens, isolated factories, villages for industrial workers, race tracks, gravel pits, summer cottages, subdivisions of partially built-up, year-round residential villas on large lots, and unique to Québec, possibly even seminaries, monasteries, or convents (Matthews, 1985). Suburbs, ever-changing, no longer harboured just the outcast.

Except for transportation corridors like these and a few other types of fringe area, Canada's major cities remained quite spatially compact before the arrival of electric streetcars in the 1890s. Previously, the slowness of urban population

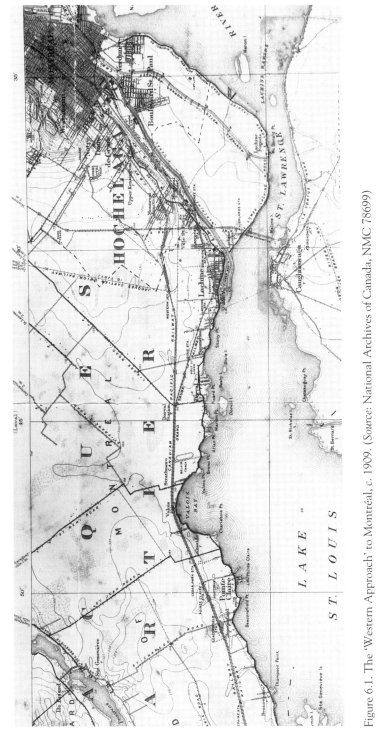

Figure 6.1. The 'Western Approach' to Montréal, c. 1909. (*Source:* National Archives of Canada, NMC 78699)

growth, the reluctance of provincial legislatures to create new municipalities within the political orbit of large cities, the constraints of an arduous climate, the difficulty of securing mortgages, the costliness of providing basic services like water and sewers – these and other factors were drawbacks to suburbanization. As a result, suburbia was often, quite literally, the rural-facing edge of the densely built-up central city, not an expansive area characterized by mixed rural and urban activities. Similarly, detached, single-family houses – the commonly-perceived ideal of suburban desires – were not always an accurate marker of the developing suburbs, particularly in large eastern Canadian cities where row houses marched tightly together into the open countryside. This housing pattern even occurred where municipal boundaries cut through the geographical city, as in the Montréal area where the city's town-house pattern extended continuously into the adjoining eastern and southern districts of the town of Westmount (Gubbay and Hooff, 1979; Rémillard and Merrett, 1987).

The reality of compactness should be born in mind when looking at early twentieth-century maps of Canada's urban areas. As the industrial economy gained momentum in the late nineteenth century, attracting thousands of city-bound immigrants and encouraging substantial rural-urban migration across the country, there was a tremendous rush to provide building lots for the antici-pated population explosion (Saywell, 1975). Suburban land booms flared-up in all major Canadian cities, whether eastern or western, new or old, reaching a frenzy *c.* 1908–1913 (Doucet, 1982*a*; Foran, 1979; Rees, 1974; Selwood, 1988). Land speculation attracted all varieties of capitalist endeavour: foreign and domestic syndicates, railway corporations, banks and trust companies, large and small real estate firms, and hopeful individuals (McCann, 1996). As Beatrice Webb observed while visiting Montréal in 1911, '. . . every man seems to speculate in "lots" and to be the proprietor "on time" of more or less land, which he hopes one day to sell at a profit' (Feaver, 1982). Land registration was controlled by pro-vincial statute, but there was little to stop a would-be speculator from obtaining an option on, or actually purchasing, say, a block of farm land near a city; having it surveyed into lots, usually on a grid base; doing so in a way that complied with local government by-laws; registering the subdivision with municipal or county and provincial officials; and then marketing these building lots for suburban housing (Adams, 1917; Ganton, 1982). In this way, hundreds of thousands – millions – of suburban lots flooded the Canadian market. Most would remain unoccupied, creating a legacy of fragmented development that would take decades to resolve. At the time of registration, there might be no roads passing through the subdivision site; no basic services in place; and no easy way for a potential buyer to reach work in the distant city. But, when legally registered, the subdivision plot could be included as part of the official city plan. Even subdivisions platted well beyond city limits – from three to as many as ten miles away, depending on the size of a city – were displayed (Adams, 1917; Selwood, 1984). Turn-of-the-century maps, many of them designed to advertise a particular subdivision, thus give the impression of an urban area much larger in size than it actually was, with suburban tracts reaching in grid-like fashion far into the countryside (figure 6.2).

Speculation in land was one of the principal ways in which suburban municipalities in Canada came into existence. Whether near Montréal, Toronto, Ottawa, Winnipeg, Saskatoon, Vancouver, or Victoria – to cite examples where the process has been documented – major land owners would sometimes group together and petition the provincial government for incorporation (Artibise, 1975; Elliott, 1991; Kerr and Hanson, 1982; Lemon, 1985; van Nus, 1984; Wynn, 1992). Sometimes they were successful, sometimes they were not. For these brokers of the suburban dream, major participants in the political dimensions of the new culture (Fairfield, 1993), incorporation was a means to an end, a method of protecting an investment. It was accomplished by introducing municipal by-laws that controlled, for example, the type of housing, lot and house sizes, building setbacks, construction materials, and minimum house values. If incorporation was not feasible, some developers sought alternative means of protection. In the exceptional cases of Shaughnessy Heights in Vancouver (a Canadian Pacific Railway project) and the Uplands in Victoria, both upper-class suburbs, special provincial Acts were passed to guarantee the quality of development (Forward, 1973; Ley, 1993). A more common, but not always successful, alternative for controlling the character of better-quality suburbs was to place restrictive covenants on the deed of property sale (Foran, 1975). The nature of these restrictions clearly records the belief of certain property owners that stringent measures were essential for strengthening the suburban face of the new consumer culture. Privately-implemented, these measures would later coalesce in the 1920s with the public sphere's growing interest in zoning and town planning legislation.

Expansive suburbanization, breaking the commercial city's compactness, was facilitated most strongly before the First World War by the development of electric street railway systems. The rush for the suburbs began in earnest once the streetcar companies were formed, franchises awarded, relationships established with municipalities and land developers, and lines actually put down. All manner of pent-up suburban desires, held by many different classes of potential consumers, could now be met by the improved accessibility provided by streetcars. Unlike other essential utilities, including electric, sewer, and water systems, which also played a facilitating role in suburbanization, streetcars gave suburban residents the unprecedented means to travel widely in the city. But the newly-emerging residential patterns varied from city to city, largely because of contrasts in public policy towards streetcar systems and other utilities, the pre-existing subdivision network, and degree to which a consumer culture was ingrained in society.

Some examples from across Canada suggest the variety of possibilities. The slow-growing and financially-strapped Maritimes region illustrates the need for restraint. Practising 'true economy', Halifax's City Engineer vetoed a 1902

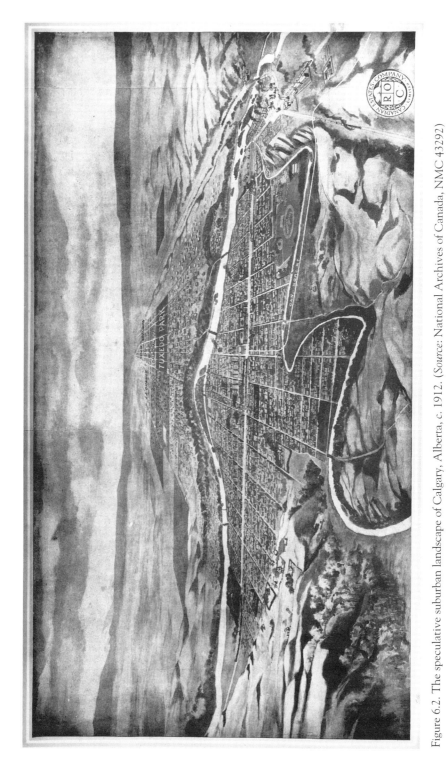

Figure 6.2. The speculative suburban landscape of Calgary, Alberta, c. 1912. (*Source*: National Archives of Canada, NMC 43292)

proposal for several streetcar-oriented suburbs located beyond the built-up city in favour of first repairing dilapidated streets, supplying piped water, and enlarging sewers – in orderly and efficient fashion – in older and previously-settled areas (City of Halifax, 1903). In Québec, it appears that some of the Montréal area's speculative and rapidly-growing suburban municipalities became pawns of the private, powerful, and city-based Montréal Street Railway Company (MSRCo). At first, because municipalities were able to negotiate with several competing suburban rail companies, favourable terms were possible. But, after the MSRCo gained a monopoly in 1911, some of these municipalities soon suffered from poor service, making them less attractive for land development and residence. Here, like elsewhere in suburbanizing Canada, streetcar service operated in a circuitous way: without adequate service, residential growth could be arrested; without housing development (and unless a single-tax was in place), a municipality's potential tax base was diminished; without tax revenue, urban services could not be provided; without services, people might not invest in housing in that suburban district; and without tax-paying residents, a municipality could collapse in bankruptcy. A number of suburban municipalities, over-extended financially before the First World War's end, suffered just this fate, and were annexed by Montréal (Linteau, 1985; Armstrong and Nelles, 1986).

By contrast, in Toronto, first private and later public tramway owners recognized that profits flowed from serving densely-settled neighbourhoods, not from running lines, in speculative fashion, to sparsely-settled suburban tracts (Doucet, 1982b). This policy helped to constrain, at least within Toronto's city limits, a widespread pattern of leap-frogging and inefficient housebuilding; and hence the need to provide other expensive urban services well in advance of their use. Densely-built-up neighbourhoods of small lots could be served efficiently; fragmentation was costly. Still, many rural municipalities freely permitted the platting of subdivisions. And breakaway municipal incorporation was impossible to stop, particularly in the more accessible industrial suburbs to the west of the city. Nor did a lack of streetcars and other amenities restrict, for example, a large number of English immigrants from first buying small, cheap, and unserviced lots just inside Toronto's boundaries and also in rural municipalities lying just north of Toronto's city limits, and from later self-building their family homes (Harris, 1991a; 1996). As this suggests, the immigrant's belief in homeownership was a potent desire recognized fully by astute promoters of suburban lots. By selling cheap, peripheral land to these newcomers, as well as marketing other grades of property to various social classes elsewhere in Toronto and in neighbouring suburbs, the Dovercourt Land, Building and Savings Company – Toronto's largest real estate firm in the pre-war era – was an active broker in the formation of a broadly-based and increasingly ingrained, consumer-oriented culture (Paterson, 1988).

Other variations of the suburban streetcar theme occurred in western Canada. At the height of the early twentieth-century land and housing boom, Edmonton's

City Council did all it could in typical, booster-like fashion to have streetcar lines and related services synchronized with paths of potential real estate development, including some that led to shack-town areas (Weaver, 1984). It was a mistake in policy that would cost Edmonton and other Prairie cities that followed similar strategies many millions of dollars in subsequent decades to consolidate the folly of these early, misdirected urban services (Smith, 1972). Another of many variants occurred further west, in the Victoria area, where all streetcar routes had to be approved by usually cautious municipal councils, such as Oak Bay's, newly-formed in 1906. This did not stop the London-based British Columbia Electric Railway Company from first securing, before approaching the council and laying its tracks, an incentive of 25 acres of choice residential lots from the Winnipeg promoters of the prestigious, 465-acre Uplands district, designed by John C. Olmsted and laid out *c.* 1912 (McCann, 1997). Like all pragmatic real estate promoters, the developers of the Uplands recognized that the value of their land would be considerably enhanced once a streetcar line was built nearby.

Pre-First World War suburban development is thus imprinted indelibly on Canadian cities. The star-shaped form of the streetcar city, built on a frame of gridded streets, lasted well into the 1940s. Apart from a few prestigious and privately-planned neighbourhoods of curving street design, early twentieth-century suburbs typically comprised a landscape of north–south, east–west running streets and rectangular lots imposed upon a region's original survey system – mêtes and bounds in the Maritimes, the long lots of Québec's seigneurial regime, the various shapes of Ontario's townships, and the quarter-section system of western Canada. To the pre-war, cross-Canada traveller and observer of the suburban scene, the street-pattern forms of the country's regional suburbs were thus both familiar and dissimilar, gridded but of varying shapes. Similarly, the astute observer would also have noted the repetitive imprint of a wide variety of social divisions on the suburban landscape. To meet the consumer's desire for building lots – measured chiefly by the ability of different social classes to pay for property by the front footage or area of a lot – large land developers like Dovercourt and the Hudson's Bay Company, and even smaller firms, brokered subdivisions of contrasting lot size, apparently laying the spatial framework for a recognizable, class-divided society. From recent research on the social geography of turn-of-the-century Canadian cities, it is clear that all-variety of social groups resided in all-variety of suburbs which were then emerging on the urban periphery.[1] With the glut of subdivisions on the market, it is not surprising that many, particularly in western Canada, were sparsely settled, unrevealing of their eventual character. In the more densely-occupied suburban tracts of Canada's older cities, on any one street there was sometimes considerable intermingling of classes; in other tracts there was a decidedly segregated tone, comprising mainly but sometimes exclusively, blue-collar workers, middle-class professionals, or upper-income residents.

Residential differentiation also occurred along other lines. Depending upon the regional destination of recent immigrants, the suburban fringe of Canadian cities was host to any number of ethnic or racial groups, not just the native-born. The desire to own a suburban home – the culture of consumption at its most notable – applied to all newcomers to Canada. These included the late nineteenth-century migration of southern Blacks to Halifax's Africville; eastern Europeans residing on the outskirts of Montréal's Lachine Canal factory zone; the English who settled in Earlscourt in north-western Toronto; the Jews and Slavs of Winnipeg's North End; and enclaves of Asians at the edge of Vancouver and Victoria. It is too early in this research to argue decisively which factor – class or ethnicity – was the more important dimension segregating Canada's suburban society in the early twentieth century, but another factor – family structure – does stand revealed. Suburbs were overwhelmingly home to nuclear families of mothers and fathers, sisters and brothers, or a variant of this basic type. While nuclear families with boarders were quite common in the suburbs, multiple, extended, and solitary families, whether with or without boarders, were not. The mother of a family might take responsibility for the boarders, if only because finding a job in the suburbs was quite difficult for a woman. In Toronto, male wage earners had a easier task of finding suburban work than women, but many nevertheless commuted downtown to places of employment (Harris and Bloomfield, 1997).

The distinctiveness of the late nineteenth- and early twentieth-century suburban landscape was made all the more prominent by the impress of residential architecture. Above all else, the choice of a house – its style, interior design, and location – made a strong statement about individual beliefs, family values, and societal attitudes towards material possessions in the ever-strengthening consumer revolution (Damon-Moore, 1994; Gowans, 1986; Rybczynski, 1986). Turn-of-the-century changes in architectural styles comprised the transition from the Victorian house, with its associated meanings of family privacy and social organization, to houses designed for a more open-minded society confronted by increasing levels of 'conspicuous consumption' (Crossman, 1987; Kalman, 1994). Consumer choices were becoming quite substantial, if not overwhelming. Besides self-building, a potential suburban homeowner of even moderate means was able to peruse house plans in any number of popular magazines or pattern books and then consult with a carpenter-builder; purchase pre-fabricated house materials through a building supply firm or even a department store catalogue; or move through the city in search of houses being built on speculation (Doucet and Weaver, 1991). For the middle- or upper-class suburbanite, an architect-designed home was a possibility. Compounding these options, consumers were offered much more than ever before: a greater range of structural types and sizes (for example, rather than row houses, a variety of detached cottages, bungalows, and multi-storeyed houses); a wider offering of culturally-associated designs (for example, English Cottages, California Bungalows, Dutch Colonials, and Tudor Revivals); and louder shouts proclaiming technological change in the arrangement of domestic space, creating, for example, the 'modern suburban house' and the 'model cottage' (Cromley, 1996). But, as building technologies and the construction industry both modernized, another circuitous route of spiralling costs made its suburban appearance: by building a 'modern' house, a wider division of specialized and more expensive labour was needed to install some of the new but costlier electrical, plumbing, and heating technologies; with labour specialization came protective unionization, which further increased labour costs; and by introducing new technologies and materials throughout the housebuilding industry, municipal inspection became even more essential, forcing-up the regulatory fees of building a dwelling (McKay, 1985). In time, these escalating labour, material, and inspection costs became another factor holding back marginal income groups from joining in the suburban experience.

REFORMING THE SUBURBAN LANDSCAPE

The First World War is a benchmark in the Canadian suburban experience. The war slowed immigration and population growth, lessening the demand for housing and halting the rush to the suburbs. It diverted building materials and production facilities to meet more critical needs. The war also drew away a skilled housebuilding labour force – and even brokers of the suburban dream – to join wartime industries, or to fight overseas. With capital diverted to the war effort, interest rates on mortgages and other loans rose, forcing families to reconsider their immediate housing needs (usually to place suburban desires on hold). The effect of the war was to push up, quite significantly, the cost of building a house (Paterson, 1988; Urquhart, 1993) – a factor that would later prompt, from 1918 to 1923, the federal government's first attempt at subsidizing the construction of new housing in the suburbs (Bacher, 1993; Jones, 1978). But, of equal importance, domestic and foreign wartime policies increasingly squashed the flow of capital into the land development industry (Buckley, 1955). On the home front, much less – and much costlier – domestic capital was now lent for speculative land ventures because banks, trust companies, and other financial institutions found funds increasingly harder to muster. Many of these firms and their land development customers even went bankrupt. As a result, fewer land schemes proceeded in what was, at any rate, an already-glutted market. In a similar way, substantial foreign-funded projects, both on-going and proposed, such as the building of Mount Royal (with English capital) and the Uplands (taken over partially by French interests in 1911), were either slowed or halted when the English and French governments put a stop to the wartime export of capital (McCann, 1996, 1997).

The hiatus in rampant suburbanization gave all levels of government the opportunity to take stock of, and confront, a number of problems arising from the pre-war boom in suburban real estate. The important issues facing reform-minded municipalities were largely twofold: first, to consolidate existing areas of wasteful sprawl by providing essential local improvements in an orderly progression; and secondly, to encourage new but efficiently-managed suburbs. Efficiency became the goal of local government. By introducing efficiency, government was acting in the public interest. Few government officials challenged the basic cultural assumption that had precipitated the real estate frenzy in the first place. The belief in property development *per se* was not at issue. In a consumer-based society that adhered to principles of *laissez faire*, the right of an individual to buy and sell land and houses to enhance wealth formation and social mobility, free of unwarranted encumbrance, was unquestionable. Governments were guardians of this culture of property development; they were responsible stewards of the homeownership ethic and of the maintenance of property values. Many reformers believed that, by continually revising a province's land registry and municipal Acts to meet modern, contemporary conditions, order could be restored to older districts and rational progress made when opening new suburbs. To this end, by working within an improved framework of provincial enabling legislation, many local governments in Canada tackled problems of inefficiency and wasteful land development during the 1920s and 1930s by either revising old by-laws or instituting new ones. These measures included strengthening the rules for platting and registering land; enacting local improvement by-laws to control the costs of servicing outlying subdivisions; regulating developers to pay a greater share of any future local improvements traditionally provided by municipalities (road construction, sewer installation, etc); and enforcing a more restrictive system of housebuilding permits. This latter measure was usually justified on the grounds of safety or of protecting property values in the public interest but, where implemented, it was really aimed at controlling the self-built housing associated with 'shack-town' development. The added tasks of following new procedures, complying with the need for permits, and sharing local improvement costs struck a blow at the aspirations of many lower-income groups wanting to reside in the suburbs. In Canada, although not in the United States, the rate of home ownership fell during the 1920s (Harris and Hammett, 1987; Harris, 1996).

Land regulation reform was not implemented equally across suburban Canada. While some communities were zealous in their reforming efforts, others were not. Whether lacking the will or the means, or choosing 'unofficially' to acknowledge the severe housing shortage facing Canadians during the Depression and war years, a number of suburban and rural municipalities surrounding larger places like Vancouver, Winnipeg, Toronto, and Montréal did little to rid the 'suburban jumble' from their midst (Anon, 1925). Most often these were rural-based governments that recognized the critical interweaving of homeownership and self-sufficiency, particularly when the dominant consumer-oriented society waxed and waned in difficult times. The results, on the one hand, were an un-checked mixing of rural and urban land uses; poor service provision; the failure to minimize health and safety (for example, fire) risks; and, in the long run, the likelihood of facing higher costs when rural redevelopment was finally enforced. On the other hand, there is little doubt that the housing aspirations and suburban desires of a number of less well-off people continued to be met; and that inner-city slum and tenement housing problems were kept from deepening (Harris, 1991*b*).

Another reform-directed tack was taken in the early 1920s by a group of professional engineers, land surveyors, health officials, and others, many of whom had either helped to establish or soon joined the Town Planning Institute of Canada. Advocates of utilitarian ideas, they believed that suburban problems could be dealt with efficiently and rationally through the application of scientific town planning principles (Gunton, 1979). These included carefully surveying present conditions, drafting a plan of major land uses, and recommending mechanisms to regulate future growth. This movement was supported primarily by officials working for the federal government's Commission of Conservation (1909–1921), including Thomas Adams, the Commission's tireless Town Planning Advisor from 1914 to 1920 (Armstrong, 1959; Artibise and Stelter, 1980). Building on his English Garden City experience, Adams in particular argued the merits of both conservation and holistic planning, that is, of planning town and country in unision, as an organic whole (Adams, 1922; Simpson, 1985). Suburban problems were not just city problems, they were also rural problems. Town and country planning soon became a rallying point for many reformed-minded people representing professional organizations, business groups, and government bodies, integrating the private and public spheres in a national debate, but bringing few immediate results (Bottomley, 1977).

Before the war, a few cities such as Toronto, Berlin (Kitchener-Waterloo), Calgary, and Regina had commissioned grandiose but impractical City Beautiful plans (Bloomfield, 1982; Foran, 1982; van Nus, 1984). Montréal, Ottawa, and Winnipeg, by contrast, had conducted more singular but useful transportation and park studies (Taylor, 1989; Wolfe and Jacobs, 1991). In many more places, a number of existing by-laws directed at particular nuisances bore the appearance of zoning (Moore, 1979; van Nus, 1979; Weaver, 1978). But the use of powerful legal instruments such as zoning and official town plans for bringing efficiency and order to the development of suburban land had not been implemented. Here, the provinces stood accountable, for they alone were responsible for creating the enabling legislation. Using Britain's Housing and Town Planning Act of 1909 as a point of departure, four provinces – New Brunswick, Nova Scotia, Ontario, and Alberta – established town planning Acts in either 1912 or 1913. A few others followed during the war (for example, Manitoba in 1916). But the British framework of a town planning scheme was hardly sufficient for dealing with Canada's specific suburban conditions. Commenting on Alberta's Town Planning Act of 1913, Peter Smith has argued that 'if the Alberta government really intended that it should be a tool against speculation, they had picked the wrong model' (Smith, 1979, p. 210).

After much debate, more meaningful planning guidelines for suburban development finally prevailed. This time the enabling legislation followed the American model, in which zoning and official city plans from the wartime era had proven all-important (Scott, 1969). More comprehensive town planning Acts were passed first in British Columbia (1925) and later in Alberta (1929). Increasingly, through the 1920s, in these and other provinces where advisory town planning commissions had been established, private planning 'experts' – for example, land surveyors, engineers, landscape architects, and even a few who actually referred to themselves as town planning consultants – were called upon to advise municipal governments on a number of issues. But few town planning exercises that investigated an entire urban region in comprehensive fashion emerged from these actions. An exception was *A Plan for the City of Vancouver* (and several of its adjoining suburban municipalities), produced by an American firm headed by Harland Bartholomew, and published in 1929 (Vancouver Town Planning Commission, 1929). Although pandering at times to business interests that wished to stabilize real estate prices, and not surveying all features in equal depth, it was still the first full-scale study of a major Canadian city to use scientific town planning principles (Bloomfield, 1985). And it did address suburban issues. Unfortunately, this action was not soon repeated in other large cities in other provinces, largely because it was not until after the Second World War that permissive planning legislation was fully repealed in all provinces by town planning Acts with more legal bite. As a result, most municipalities in Canada were not required to put an official town planning by-law in place until the 1940s or 1950s (Dale, 1971).

Zoning, on the other hand, was adopted much more quickly and by many more municipalities (van Nus, 1979). In fact, once the major legal loopholes in zoning by-laws were resolved by the late 1920s, zoning became an essential tool for establishing the type, quality, and extent of new suburban land use development. Zoning, of course, is typically regulated through land use, height, site area, set back, and side yard restrictions; various combinations of these promote the desired effect. Two British Columbia examples – the largely residential districts of Point Grey in Vancouver and Oak Bay in Victoria – illustrate the ways in which zoning could be implemented, as well as its impact on suburban development (figure 6.3).

The Municipality of Point Grey was established in 1908 after the provincial government had commissioned, rather uniquely at the time, a community plan for the well situated, but as yet undeveloped, south-western area of Vancouver. Undertaken by the Montréal landscape architect Frederick Todd, who apprenticed with the Olmsteds, Point Grey was destined to accommodate not only better-quality residences but also the University of British Columbia and its endowment lands (Harris, 1976/77). This process resulted in a picturesque, village-focused plan that linked curving street patterns to undulating topography (Todd, 1908). It is clear that subsequent land developers and housebuilders took note of market trends and paid marked attention to the consumer's desire for single-family homes set on large lots which displayed an English aesthetic of Tudor style houses surrounded by rose gardens. Protecting this desire, restrictive covenants

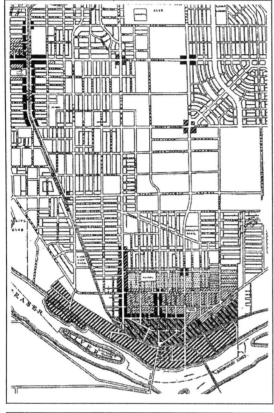

Figure 6.3. Zoning maps for part of Vancouver, 1929 (left) and Oak Bay, 1936 (opposite). (*Sources*: Vancouver Town Planning Commission (1929) and 'a zone map of Oak Bay, 1936' in Oak Bay Municipal Archives)

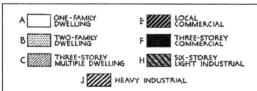

were frequently put in place (Duncan and Duncan, 1984; Holdsworth, 1977, 1986). These private devices later coalesced with the public sphere's will to preserve property values when Point Grey became the first local government in Canada to adopt, in 1922, 'a zoning ordinance as part of a definite town planning policy' (Buck, 1929, p. 297). Here, the large lot, low-density, single-family, and middle-class character of the original suburb was maintained specifically by regulating a substantial proportion of open space on each property, a form of site area restriction. By comparison, the City of Vancouver's zoning policy, made law in 1929 but constrained by small (usually 33-foot) lots, regulated residential areas by the functional use of dwellings, establishing single-family, two-family, six-storey multiple dwelling, etc zones. This was the most typical pattern followed

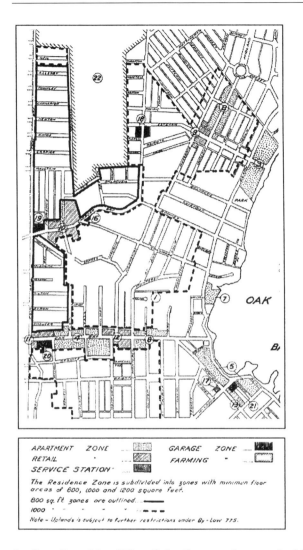

by Canadian cities. When Point Grey amalgamated with the City of Vancouver in 1930, the system of zoning by functional use prevailed, but Point Grey's previously-zoned, single-family character was respected by virtually prohibiting multiple-family housing (Seymour, 1927).

In Oak Bay, which prided itself on being Victoria's premier residential municipality, four different zones were set aside for single-family residential development in the 1936 revision of an earlier 1927 zoning by-law.[2] Taking into account the character of some shack-like, working-class housing built before and shortly after incorporation in 1906, but wanting to restrict the spread of it in favour of enhancing the increasingly publicized, middle-class character of the suburb, Oak Bay officials took the rather extraordinary step of zoning residential districts according to minimum house-size thresholds of 800, 1000, 1200, or 1500 square feet (figure 6.3). This policy continued the earlier council ordinance which barred any residential building of less than 500 square feet from being constructed in the municipality. The lasting effect of these decisions in Oak Bay was to continuously up-grade the quality of housing and middle-class character of the suburb. However, it is worth remembering that not all communities were as zealous in enforcing existing regulations, nor in introducing new guidelines in the first place. For these reasons alone, older, partially built-up suburban areas continued to offer a diversity of housing opportunities through the inter-war period for a diverse group of Canadians – rich and poor, newcomers and native-Canadians, and whole families (Harris and Sendbuehler, 1994).

When applied, the evolving framework of planning and zoning obviously helped to shape the future quality of Canada's suburban growth. Whether building new houses or carving smaller subdivisions out of larger properties, the quality of on-going development was forced to meet stricter standards. But, for the moment, the framework did little to alter the existing, gridded shape of the suburban land-scape. Without an all-encompassing city plan, something which only Canadian resource towns offered in this period (Saarinen, 1986), the shape of suburbia across Canada remained rooted firmly in the past, that is, in the private sector's continued approval of the 'egalitarian' grid. Except for comments on its drab, monotonous appearance, and sometimes on its poor sunlight orientation, particu-larly when combined with Montréal's long lot system (Nobbs, 1926), most reformers had little serious comment to make about the grid's almost universal use. Like local governments, they fully recognized its efficiency in providing services. For subdividers, the grid was likewise acceptable, keeping surveying and other development costs to a minimum, and easing the sale of lots.

Deviation from the grid was therefore the exception, but this situation would be broken dramatically after the Second World War. Through the 1920s and 1930s, there was little Canadian debate to match the American interest in neigh-bourhood units, superblocks, and gridiron redevelopment (Perry, 1929, 1933, 1939). There were those who did see benefits in the designs offered by the variety of picturesque or garden suburb plots, but not always for their utilitarian value. The seeds of the picturesque had been sown, for instance, in post-Confederation Rosedale, then located on the outskirts of Toronto. There was a further round of selective planting of these usually bourgeois suburbs just prior to the First World War, most notably in Halifax, Montréal, Toronto, Ottawa, Winnipeg, Vancouver, and Victoria. Although applauded widely for their attractive layout and park-like beauty, they were hardly a practical solution to suburban problems of waste and inefficiency. Many years would pass before their lots were completely taken-up for residence, suggesting that their intrinsic appeal was limited to the well-to-do; and that, financially speaking, their utility lay well beyond the realistic desires of most consumers. In some cases, their designs would stimulate municipal officials to think about subdivisions other than the gridiron (McCann, 1975).

By contrast, because of its tried association with the urban reform movement in Britain, garden suburb design seemed to offer greater potential. Garden suburbs were highly touted just before and immediately after the First World War by the Commission of Conservation. Thomas Adams extolled their proven utility and even their idealistic virtues. For Adams, they combined pragmatically town and country in a unified design, provided parks and other open spaces, separated land uses, placed houses in attractive street and court-like settings, and offered a variety of internal walkways and streets. But their ability to stop land speculation through community ownership of land and to provide affordable, co-partnership housing was questionable in the cultural context of Canada's *laissez faire* political economy. As shown by the federal government's use of the garden suburb model to rebuild the Hydrostone neighbourhood after the Halifax Explosion of 1917, as well as by its financial support in building Lindenlea in Ottawa, the cost of public, garden suburb intervention proved substantial, if not burdensome (Ross, 1919; Delaney, 1991). The carefully-planned properties of Hydrostone stood well beyond the financial means of the working-class people who had lived in the area before the Explosion, forcing them to live elsewhere (Clarke, 1994; Morton, 1995; Shutlak, 1994; Weaver, 1976). A few planners of middle-class suburbs in the inter-war period, like Horace Seymour, were still swayed by the aesthetic and functional qualities of garden suburbs (Bloomfield, 1985). When suburbanization finally regained momentum after the doldrums of the Depression and war, however, the needs of the 'machine age' and an automobile-oriented society would render many elements of garden suburb design quite obsolete (Elliott, 1991).

Housing, Planning, and the Post-War Suburban Landscape

According to Humphrey Carver (1978, p. 41), one of Canada's most respected authorities on housing reform and the building of suburbs, 'the most *sacred* belief in Canadian public policy has been the idea that *everyone* ought to own a suburban home' [my italics]. Homeownership, even if not won in the suburbs, was also the 'sacred' desire of most Canadians; it was central to the evolving consumer culture. This is shown by the vivid realism portrayed in two classic, historical Canadian novels written in the immediate post-war period. For Sandor Hunyadi, the son of Hungarian immigrants and the protagonist in John Marlyn's *Under the Ribs of Death*, the desire was straightforward: it was to escape from Winnipeg's North End slums and live in the city's wealthy Crescentwood suburb – a rather difficult goal for any immigrant to achieve during the 1920s. Nevertheless, he thought that some day he would

> . . . leave it behind him forever . . . never remembering again this dirty, foreign neighbourhood . . . If the Kostanuiks could . . . move away to a better neighbourhood, why couldn't his own family do the same? . . . They could move away from Henry Avenue. They would have a whole house to themselves. (Marlyn, 1957, pp. 17, 29, 101)

In *The Tin Flute*, set in the slums of Montréal's St. Henri district just as the Depression was closing and the Second World War beginning, the simple wish of Rose Anna Lacasse and her family was to find cheap but decent rental accommodation. But this search was constantly thwarted by the realities of grinding poverty sustained by an unsteady job market, poor health conditions, limited education, ethnic tensions, and family breakdown. For Rose Anna, the suburbs of her desires were places she would never reside in; they were places she would see only when walking through the city (Roy, 1945).

Humphrey Carver, during his long career in Canada from the late 1930s to the mid-1970s as a social activist, academic, and finally senior policy-maker with the federal government's Central Mortgage and Housing Corporation (CMHC), had come to understand well the suburban quest and basic housing needs of people like Sandor Hunyadi and Rose Anna Lacasse (Carver, 1975). But how did the federal government's belief in suburban homeownership evolve to couple with the desires of individuals and families? Carver boldly asserts that the policy on universal suburban homeownership was actively pursued by the mid-1960s, but to what extent was it in place c. 1950, when our study closes? Given Carver's critical assessment of federal housing initiatives on several occasions before 1950, there is every reason to doubt its universality by this time (Carver, 1935, 1937, 1948).

In fact, examination of contemporary housing trends supports this doubt, painting a rather different picture. Meeting pent-up needs and desires, tens of thousands of detached, single-family houses were built in post-war suburbia. They were typically built for a car-owning or bus-riding population that now commuted much greater distances to work (Wolforth, 1965). Most new houses were owner-occupied, not rental units. Between 1941 and 1951, the rate of homeownership in urban Canada jumped from 41 to 56 per cent; the rate in difficult-to-define suburban Canada was, in all likelihood, somewhat higher. In rural areas it rose from 76 to 82 per cent. The housing economist Marion Steele attributes the [sub]urban increase mainly to rapid population growth, substantial gains in real-family incomes, and changes in age of household formation – not to federal initiatives (Steele, 1993). Families moving to the suburbs were mainly of the 'middling classes,' not the Lacasses but sometimes the self-builders, who secured conventional, short-term mortgages from a variety of private lenders (Woodward, 1955). The federal government, acting through CMHC (formed in 1946), had yet to introduce policies implementing mortgage insurance and long-term amoritization of loans to a wide spectrum of Canadians. This would come later, in the mid-1950s, when conventional mortgage sources declined and investment in the house construction industry was used as a new tool for stimulating the national economy.

The federal government's limited moves before 1950 towards designing a policy of universal homeownership in the suburbs nevertheless shaped the social tone of suburbia in a particular and lasting way. It favoured the rich over the poor;

the upper-middle over the lower-middle class; the steadily-employed over the unemployed working class. Something of this situation can be shown by examining, at mid-century, the dynamic edge of suburban development in the mostly English-speaking 'western approaches' residential areas of metropolitan Montréal (figure 6.4). By comparing the population change of census tract areas between 1941 and 1951 with the median family earnings and share of mortgaged dwellings of the same areas in 1951, it is very clear that the most active areas of suburban development are associated with suburban districts of high earnings and more mortgaged dwellings. In older and declining inner-city areas of lower income and

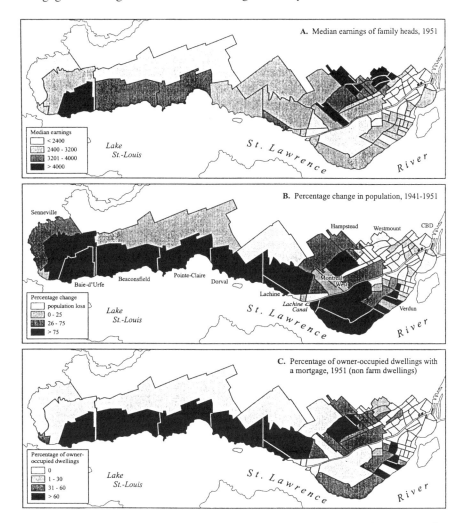

Figure 6.4. The relationship between mortgages, population change, and income in the 'Western Approaches' suburban district of Montréal, 1941–1951. (*Source*: compiled from census tract data in the 1951 *Census of Canada*)

predominantly French-Canadian settlement, owner-occupancy is quite limited and therefore mortgages almost negligible (Choko and Harris, 1990).

One of the reasons for this emerging suburban pattern of middle-class character rests with the federal government's policy of encouraging better-off people to build houses in support of the housing sector as a way of stimulating economic recovery. This policy had been instigated well before 1951; actually, well before the Depression and war years. An initial venture occurred between 1918 and 1923 when Ottawa provided specific guidelines and some $25,000,000 to the provinces for their administration of joint action by municipalities and private contractors, specifically to stimulate the moribund housing industry and to house returning veterans. Given the high standards mandated for construction and their associated costs, most dwellings were bound to be built in better-quality suburban districts (Jones, 1978; McCann, 1996). The debate surrounding this programme nevertheless served as a catalyst for provincial and municipal authorities to consider, and maintain, their long-term, reticent role in housing provision (Purdy, 1997). Another, but even more limited, federal initiative was made through the Dominion Housing Act of 1935 when the federal government, working in close conjunction with the insurance industry, chose to 'top-up' the conventional institutional mortgage of 60 per cent on the value of a house with an additional 20 per cent loan, establish a 5 per cent mortgage rate, and allow the pay-back period to extend to 20 years, providing the residence met stringent building standards (Hulchanski, 1986; Bacher, 1988). But, as John Belec has shown, the conservative nature of the 1935 Act typically supported 'the relocation of households already in well-off suburban districts, to more expensive residences in more remote suburbs' (Belec, 1997, p. 62).

This unique public and private sector relationship in support of high building standards and better-off suburban borrowers was further cemented in successive but slightly more comprehensive National Housing (NHA) Acts (1938 and 1944) and their amendments (1948 and 1949). Even the 1954 NHA, the basis for policy formation in the 1990s, initially supported the principle of a favoured clientele by channelling most federal assistance to the top 20 per cent of Canadian earners (Bacher, 1993). The only major deviation from government support of private housing as an agent of economic take-off resulted from the critical need to provide accommodation for workers involved in the war effort. To offset a drastic housing shortage, caused largely by neglected construction during the Depression and rising wartime housing costs, some 40,000 rental dwellings were built across Canada by the specially-created Crown corporation, Wartime Housing Limited, in operation from 1941 to 1947 (Evenden, 1997; Wade, 1986). Some of their dwellings were built close to downtown industrial sites, some were scattered through older suburbs, and some formed clusters – even satellite communities – at the city's edge (Baker, 1951). Writing at the close of the 1940s, Humphrey Carver offered his approval of this socially-assisted housing project (Carver, 1948), but his long-standing search for ways to promote universal homeownership in the suburbs stood incomplete.

Houses are amongst the most revealing items of cultural expression. Their external face usually projects material tastes and wealth; their interior spaces express attitudes of family structure and privacy – in short, their presence on the suburban landscape is a marker of a society's character, for they are intrinsically bound-up in the culture of consumption as a way of life. To this end, from the late nineteenth to the mid-twentieth century, the ideal suburban house was often promoted in paradoxical ways – for example, as the hallmark of traditional values but also as the showcase of modernity; or as the symbol of private enterprise but also as the product of public, that is, NHA-stewardship.

Through the 1920s, 1930s, 1940s, and into the 1950s, the houses of suburbia waxed and waned in size and style, responding to changing economic conditions or shifting currents of fashion (Gowans, 1986; Kalman, 1994). A variety of consumer-oriented sources – house magazines, department stores, government sponsored architectural competitions, insurance companies, lumber dealers, etc – extolled the virtues of the house and chartered its changing meanings and significance for the consumer culture (Haight, 1996). Gone, for example, was the informality of the Arts and Crafts California Bungalow in favour of the more formal Renaissance English, or the so-called American Colonial. Tudor Revivals lingered through the 1930s, but economical cottages and compact ranchers replaced rambling, multi-storeyed dwellings. Art Deco and Art Moderne of international/modernistic classification were only slight flirtations, never serious suitors for suburban acceptance. By the eve of the Second World War, again to quote Humphrey Carver, the Canadian suburb had become '. . . the most glorious and pathetic hodgepodge [of houses] that the mind of man has ever created' (Carver, 1937, p. 3). This mixture of housing styles existed because most Canadian suburbs had grown and changed through a lengthy process of in-filling over many years, the product of individual decisions, and all with hardly any consideration of the eventual outcome (Pearson, 1956). By extending the period of development, many neighbourhoods also took on a very mixed social character, with different family structures mingling with different socio-economic groups (McCann, 1975). But, only a decade or so later, Carver was lamenting that he '. . . saw NHA mortgage loans being dealt out, one by one, to produce endless rows of small homes. The effect was monotonous because there was no design relationship between the houses' (Carver, 1978, p. 43). What was lacking, according to Carver, was something that lay beyond the image of a single house, something that gave a sense of community to suburbia.

Here, too, the 'Peaceful Path to Real Reform' produced very mixed results. Increasingly, government and the private sector were working hand-in-hand to broker the shape of suburbia. They were guided by a plethora of incentives and regulations such as working within the context of local improvement costs, a zoning by-law, or possibly an official city plan. While the eventual infilling of older suburbs slowly progressed, large parcels of suburban land, both inside and outside of a city's boundaries, were continually coming on the market in the late 1940s. For some developers, this presented the opportunity for doing things differently from before. In the province of Québec, *L'Union economique d'habitations* and its successor, *Les Cités-jardins du Québec Inc.* worked throughout the 1940s to develop a *cité-jardin* on the northern outskirts of Montréal (Choko, 1988). For virtually all others, a more conventional path was followed. The Hudson's Bay Company, for example, one of the largest owners of raw land in western Canadian cities, went about placing lots on the market in a very careful, conservative fashion. The planning principles of William Hobbs in Victoria, and particularly in Oak Bay, illustrate the case. An engineer by training and at one-time the Comptroller of Town Planning in Manitoba, Hobbs joined the

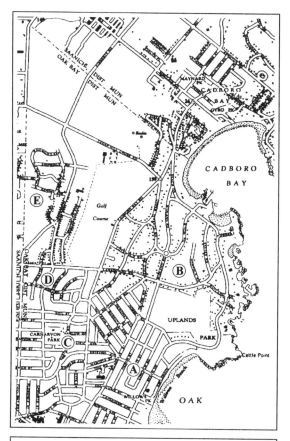

A Grid, pre-1914
B "The Uplands", a residential park
   by, J.C. Olmsted, 1908
C Modified grid subdivision, c.1949
D Modified grid subdivision, c.1945-51
E Modified neighbourhood unit, c.1952-62

Figure 6.5. Types of subdivisions in Victoria (left) and Edmonton (opposite) platted c. 1900–1962. (*Source:* After base maps in the Canadian Cartographic and Architectural Archives Division, National Archives of Canada, and data obtained from the Oak Bay Municipal Archives and Smith (1995))

Hudson's Bay Company in the late 1930s to head its land planning operations in Victoria, where the company still owned thousands of lots (1923). Generally, following Company instructions from London and Winnipeg, Hobbs took a cautious approach. When he could persuade a municipality to share improvement costs more favourably, he took advantage of the assistance; when he could not, he sometimes put-off a development scheme indefinitely. In low-income areas in Victoria during the 1940s, he used the standard grid. Next to the picturesque, high-quality Uplands area in Oak Bay, he followed John Olmsted's example of designing curving streets to match local topography (figure 6.5). At all times,

A   Grid, pre-1914
B   Modified grid neighbourhood, c.1950
C   Independent neighbourhood unit, c.1960

development was carefully budgeted and phased to meet the specific conditions of the local real estate market. But, once lots were sold, the Hudson's Bay Company's task was done. At this point, contractors, building 'on spec' and working to meet either NHA specifications or the mortgage guidelines of major institutional lenders, and with the needs of an average potential homeowner in mind, went about the task of building the type of houses that soon began to earn the chagrin of suburbia's critics, like Humphrey Carver.

There were others before *c*. 1950 that were more exceptional, setting standards and shaping the suburban landscape of the future. In particular, these designs followed the neighbourhood unit principles of Clarence Perry, who worked in the New York region during the 1920s and 1930s (Perry, 1929, 1933, 1939). They diffused only slowly to Canada when planners with American experience or recent university training in planning began working there. Perry's arguments focused on overcoming the shortcomings of gridiron platting, particularly questions of safety arising from increased automobile traffic, the problems of providing essential amenities and services, and the need to create a sense of community. For Perry and his followers, the key to suburban design lay in the neighbourhood unit principle. These were residential districts that included such characteristics as clearly identifiable boundaries; a hierarchy of 'safe,' curvilinear streets; a recognizable centre (usually a school and its grounds); a mixture of residential types; local shopping facilities; and open spaces (figure 6.5). When joined together, they offered the potential of becoming the building 'superblocks' of an efficient, rational, and orderly suburbia. Whether planned for vacant land or on legally replotted property, neighbourhood units made their first appearance at the close of the 1940s in larger centres like Halifax, Winnipeg, Saskatoon, and especially Edmonton (figure 6.5), which had long ago fallen heir to large blocks of tax delinquent land (Smith, 1995).

It was soon realized that these neighbourhood units, sometimes comprising hundreds of acres, required the financial assistance of senior governments, whether provincial or federal. It had become too much of a challenge for developers to meet the tremendous costs associated with assembling large blocks of land and then to provide them with services of a citywide nature: highways, trunk sewers, water mains, and natural gas pipelines. For this reason, senior governments, recognized first by the federal government's amendments in 1949 to the NHA, and later by separate provincial legislation, offered increased assistance to developers engaged in neighbourhood unit building. This kind of assistance paved the way for further innovations in the neighbourhood unit principle that was introduced in the mid-1950s, for example, in the building and brokering of E.P. Taylor's massive corporate suburb of Don Mills, intended as a self-contained community of production and consumption which included a large shopping centre and offices and industrial space (Sewell, 1977, 1993).

The Suburban Landscape in Perspective

As the post-industrial metropolis took shape in the 1980s and 1990s, with a more fragmented pattern of mixed-use schemes at its centre and with an increasing variety of neo-traditional housing projects intended to break its monotonous outer edge, it is as well to recall that, less than one hundred years ago, the obverse was the case. The suburban landscape of Canadian cities stood fragmented, the central business district segregated into quite distinctive zones. The economic forces shaping the city centre and suburbia are still the same. The use of land is still largely determined by the highest bidder. This is part and parcel of the urban land market. The way in which land is used is still governed by political decisions – zoning, official community plans – acting in the public good.

But there is also a cultural dimension that provides both context and agency for understanding the ways in which various forces shape and reshape the urban landscape in an almost constant process of change. As a society, we believe in values that produce efficiency and order; we accept the right of individuals to seek profit in their land-dealing enterprise; and we support the desires of people to express, for example, their fundamental values towards lifestyle choices. Moreover, we are a consuming society that continually seeks status in possessions; we take pleasure in the new and modern; and we are also a society constantly on the move. This is our culture – dynamic and changing. Suburbs are the vivid expression of our culture of consumerism.

The building of the suburban landscape from the late nineteenth to the mid-twentieth century took shape around the almost universal desire of families to own a house in areas free from the problems of the inner city; and from the realization by many individuals that selling land or building houses provided an opportunity for economic success, even social status. The design of suburbs, the architecture of the suburban house, the social and ethnic mix of people who take up residence in suburban districts – all have been shaped by our cultural values. But, in seeking efficiency, in providing order, and in protecting property, we have created a culture that actually denies certain people access to their desires for a better living environment in a suburban setting. The turn-of-the-century suburban landscape was home to all classes of people; the same cannot be said with any certainty about today's suburban districts. At mid-century, this transformation was in process, guided by well-intentioned policies, to be sure, but on its way to becoming the reality of the contemporary Canadian suburban landscape (Bourne, 1996).

Notes

1. The empirical examples discussed in the following few paragraphs are based on results emerging from the Canadian Families Project. Located at the University of Victoria, the research group, drawn from across Canada, has compiled a large database of some 265,000 individuals from the manuscript schedules of the 1901 Census of Canada. By plotting the

precise location of these individuals on maps, it is possible to comment on the social characteristics of people residing in suburban Canada at the turn of the century.

2. The information in this paragraph is based on a close reading of municipal records (bye-laws, engineering studies, etc) contained in the Archives, Municipality of Oak Bay, in Victoria, British Columbia. For further details of sources, see McCann (1997).

REFERENCES

Anon (1925) Manitoba deals with suburban jumble building. *Journal of the Town Planning Institute of Canada*, Vol. 4, No. 2, pp. 12–13.

Adams, A. (1993) Eden Smith and the Canadian domestic revival. *Urban History Review/ Revue d'histoire urbaine*, Vol. 21, No. 2, pp. 104–115.

Adams, T. (1917) *Rural Development and Planning*. Ottawa: Commission of Conservation.

Adams, T. (1922) Modern city planning: its meaning and methods. *National Municipal Review*, Vol. 11, No. 6, pp. 157–176.

Armstrong, A.H. (1959) Thomas Adams and the Commission of Conservation. *Plan Canada*, Vol. 1, No. 1, pp. 14–23.

Armstrong, C. and Nelles, H.V. (1986) Suburban street railway strategies in Montreal, Toronto and Vancouver, 1896–1930, in Stelter, G.A. and Artibise, A.F.J. (eds.) *Power and Place: Canadian Urban Development in North American Context*. Vancouver: University of British Columbia Press, pp. 187–218.

Arthur, E. (1964) *Toronto: No Mean City*. Toronto: University of Toronto Press.

Artibise, A.F.J. (1975) *Winnipeg: A Social History of Urban Growth*. Montreal: McGill-Queen's University Press.

Artibise, A.F.J. and Stelter, G.A. (1980) Conservation planning and urban planning: the Canadian Commission of Conservation in historical perspective, in Kain, R.J.P. (ed.) *Planning for Conservation: An International Perspective*. London: Mansell.

Bacher, J. (1986) Canadian housing policy in perspective. *Urban History Review/Revue d'histoire urbaine*, Vol. 15, No. 1, pp. 3–18.

Bacher, J. (1988) W.C. Clark and the politics of Canadian housing policy, 1935–1952. *Urban History Review/Revue d'Histoire Urbaine*, Vol. 17, No. 1, pp. 5–15.

Bacher, J. (1993) *Keeping to the Marketplace: The Evolution of Canadian Housing Policy*. Montreal: McGill-Queen's University Press.

Baker, K. (1951) Ajax: planning a new town in Ontario. *Community Planning Review*, Vol. 1, February, p. 1–6.

Belec, J. (1997) The Dominion Housing Act. *Urban History Review/Revue d'histoire urbaine*, Vol. 25, No. 2, pp. 53–62.

Belec, J., Holmes, J., and Rutherford, T. (1987) The rise of Fordism and the transformation of consumption norms: Mass consumption and housing in Canada, 1930–1945, in Harris, R. and Pratt, G. (eds.) *Housing Tenure and Social Class*. Gävle, Sweden: National Swedish Institute for Building Research, pp. 187–237.

Bell, W.P. (1990) *The 'Foreign Protestants' and the Settlement of Nova Scotia*. Fredericton: Acadiensis Press.

Binns, R.M. (1973) *Montreal's Electric Streetcars: An Illustrated History of the Tramway Era, 1892–959*. Montreal: Railfare Press.

Bloomfield, E. (1982) Reshaping the urban landscape?: Town planning efforts in Kitchener-Waterloo, 1912–1926, in Stelter, G.A. and Artibise, A.F.J. (eds.) *Shaping the Urban Landscape*. Ottawa: Carleton University Press, pp. 256–303.

Bloomfield, E. (1985) Ubiquitous town planning missionary: The careers of Horace Seymour, 1882–1946. *Environments*, Vol. 17, No. 2, pp. 29–42.

Bottomley, J. (1977) Ideology, Planning and the Landscape: The Business Community, Urban Reform, and the Establishment of Town Planning in Vancouver, British Columbia. Unpublished Ph.D. thesis, University of British Columbia.

Bourne, L.S. (1996) Reinventing the suburbs: Old myths and new realities. *Contemporary Perspectives on Urbanization*, Vol. 46, Part 3, pp. 163–184.

Buck, F.E. (1929) Planning the municipality of Point Grey, in Vancouver Town Planning Commission. *A Plan for the City of Vancouver, British Columbia, including a General Plan of the Region*. Vancouver: The Commission.

Buckley, K. (1955) *Capital Formation in Canada, 1890–1930*. Toronto: McClelland and Stewart.

Carver, H. (1935) A housing programme, in Research Committee. *Social Planning for Canada*. Toronto: League for Social Reconstruction.

Carver, H. (1937) Analysis of planning and housing. *Journal of the Royal Architectural Institute of Canada*, Vol. 14, No. 5, pp. 7–11.

Carver, H. (1948) *Houses for Canadians*. Toronto: University of Toronto Press.

Carver, H. (1962) *Cities in the Suburbs*. Toronto: University of Toronto Press.

Carver, H. (1975) *Compassionate Landscape*. Toronto: University of Toronto Press.

Carver, H. (1978) Building the suburbs: A planner's reflections. *City Magazine*, Vol. 3, No. 7, pp. 40–45.

Choko, M.H. (1988) *Une cité-jardin à Montréal*. Montreal: Méridien.

Choko, M.H. and Harris, R. (1990) The local culture of property: A comparative history of housing tenure in Montreal and Toronto. *Annals of the Association of American Geographers*, Vol. 80, No. 1, pp. 74–95.

City of Halifax (1903) *Annual Report of the City of Halifax 1902–03*. Halifax: City Council.

Clark, S.D. (1966) *The Suburban Society*. Toronto: University of Toronto Press.

Clarke, E. (1994) The Hydrostone phoenix: Garden city planning and the reconstruction of Halifax, 1917–1921, in Ruffman, A. and Howell, C.D. (eds.) *Ground Zero: A Reassessment of the 1917 Explosion in Halifax Harbour*. Halifax: Nimbus, pp. 389–408.

Cohen, E. (1990) *Making a New Deal: Industrial Workers in Chicago, 1919–1939*. New York: Cambridge University Press.

Cromley, E. (1996) Transforming the food axis: Houses, tools, modes of analysis. *Material History Review*, No. 44, pp. 8–22.

Crossman, K. (1987) *Architecture in Transition: From Art to Practice, 1885–1906*. Montreal: McGill-Queen's University Press.

Dale, E. (1971) Decision making at Edmonton, Alberta, 1913–1943: Town planning without a plan. *Plan Canada*, Vol. 11, No. 2, pp. 134–147.

Dalzell, A.E. (1926) Should shack towns be encouraged? *Journal of the Town Planning Institute of Canada*, Vol. 5, No. 2, pp. 23–29.

Damon-Moore, H. (1994) *Magazines for the Millions: Gender and Commerce in* The Ladies' Home Journal *and* The Saturday Evening Post, *1880–1910*. Albany: State University of New York Press.

Davis, D. (1978) Mass transit and private ownership: an alternative perspective on the case of Toronto. *Urban History Review/Revue d'histoire urbaine*, Vol. 3, pp. 60–98.

Davis, D. (1992) Technological momentum, motor buses and the persistence of Canadian street railways to 1940. *Material History Review*, No. 36, pp. 6–17.

Dechêne, L. (1974) *Habitants et marchands de Montréal au XVII siècle*. Paris: Plon.

Delaney, J. (1991) The garden suburb of Lindenlea, Ottawa: A model for the first federal housing policy, 1916–1924. *Urban History Review/Revue d'histoire urbaine*, Vol. 19, pp. 151–165.

Delaney, J. (1996) The garden suburb of Lindenlea, Ottawa: A model project for the first federal housing policy, 1918–1924. *Urban History Review/Revue d'histoire urbaine*, Vol. 19, pp. 151–165.

Doucet, M. (1982*a*) Urban land development in nineteenth-century North America: Themes in the literature. *Journal of Urban History*, Vol. 8, No. 3, pp. 299–342.

Doucet, M. (1982*b*) Politics, space and trolleys: Mass transit and early twentieth-century Toronto, in Stelter, G.A. and Artibise, A.F.G. (eds.) *Shaping the Urban Landscape*. Ottawa: Carleton University Press, pp. 356–381.

Doucet, M. and Weaver, J. (1991) *Housing the North American City*. Montreal: McGill-Queen's University Press.

Duncan, J. and Duncan, N.G. (1984) A cultural analysis of urban residential landscapes in North America: The case of the anglophile élite, in Agnew, J., Mercer, J. and Sopher, D. (eds.) *The City in Cultural Context*. London: Allen and Unwin, pp. 255–276.

Elliott, B.S. (1991) *The City Beyond: A History of Nepean, Birthplace of Canada's Capital, 1792–1991*. Nepean: City of Nepean.

Evenden, L.J. and Walker, G.E. (1993) From periphery to centre: The changing geography of the suburbs, in Ley, D. and Bourne, L.S. (eds.) *The Changing Social Geography of Canadian Cities*. Montreal: McGill-Queen's University Press, pp. 234–251.

Evenden, L.J. (1997) Wartime housing as cultural landscape: National creation and personal creativity. *Urban History Review/Revue d'histoire urbaine*, Vol. 25, No. 2, pp. 41–52.

Fairfield, J. (1993) *The Mysteries of the Great City: The Politics of Urban Design, 1877–1937*. Columbus: Ohio University Press.

Feaver, G. (1982) The Webbs in Canada: Fabian pilgrims on the Canadian frontier. *The Canadian Historical Review*, Vol. 57, No. 3, pp. 261–274.

Fishman, R. (1987) *Bourgeois Utopias*. New York: Basic Books.

Foran, M. (1975) Land speculation and urban development in Calgary, 1884–1912, in Rasporich, A.W. and Klassen, H.C. (eds.) *Frontier Calgary: Town, City and Region*. Calgary, University of Calgary Press, pp. 203–220.

Foran, M. (1979) Land development patterns in Calgary, 1884–1945, in Artibise, A.F.J. and Stelter, G.A. (eds.) *The Usable Urban Past*. Toronto: Macmillan, pp. 293–315.

Foran, M. (1982) The Mawson report in historical perspective. *Alberta History*, Vol. 28, No. 3, pp. 31–39.

Forward, C.N. (1973) The immortality of a fashionable neighbourhood: The Uplands, in Forward, C.N. (ed.) *Residential and Neighbourhood Studies in Victoria*, Western Geographical Series No. 5. Victoria: Department of Geography, University of Victoria, pp. 1–39.

Ganton, I. (1982) The subdivision process in Toronto, 1851–1883, in Stelter, G.A. and Artibise, A.F.J. (eds.) *Shaping the Urban Landscape*. Ottawa: Carleton University Press, pp. 200–231.

Gilpin, J. (1986) The land development process in Edmonton, Alberta, 1881–1917, in Stelter, G.A. and Artibise, A.F.J. (eds.) *Power and Place*. Vancouver: University of British Columbia Press, pp. 151–172.

Gowans, A. (1986) *The Comfortable House: North American Suburban Architecture, 1890–1930*. Cambridge, MA: MIT Press.

Gubbay, A. and Hooff, S. (1979) *Montreal's Little Mountain: A Portrait of Westmount*. Montreal: Trillium.

Gunton, T. (1979) The ideas and policies of the Canadian planning profession, in Artibise, A.F.J. and Stelter, G.A. (eds.) *The Usable Urban Past*. Toronto: Macmillan, pp. 177–195.

Haight, S. (1996) Machines in suburban gardens: The 1936 T. Eaton Company architectural competition for home designs, *Material History Review*, No. 44, pp. 23–44.

Hamilton, J.R. (1884) *Saint John and the Province of New Brunswick: A Handbook for Travellers, Tourists and Businessmen*. Saint John: Hamilton.

Hanna, D. (1980) Creation of an early Victorian suburb in Montreal. *Urban History Review/Revue d'histoire urbaine*, Vol. 2, No. 2, pp. 38–64.

Harris, R. (1990) Self-building and the social geography of Toronto, 1901–1913: A challenge for urban theory. *Transactions of the Institute of British Geographers*, NS Vol. 15, No. 4, pp. 387–402.

Harris, R. (1991*a*) A working-class suburb for immigrants, Toronto, 1909–1913. *Geographical Review*, Vol. 81, No. 3, pp. 318–332.

Harris, R. (1991*b*) The impact of building controls on residential development in Toronto, 1900–40. *Planning Perspectives*, Vol. 6, pp. 269–296.

Harris, R. (1996) *Unplanned Suburbs: Toronto's American Tragedy, 1900–1950*. Baltimore: Johns Hopkins University Press.

Harris, R. and Bloomfield, V. (1997) The impact of industrial decentralization on gendered journey to work, 1900–1940. *Economic Geography*, Vol. 73, pp. 94–117.

Harris, R. and Hammett, C. (1987) The myth of the promised land: The social diffusion of home ownership in Britain and North America. *Annals of the Association of American Geographers*, Vol. 77, No. 2, pp. 173–190.

Harris, R. and Sendbuehler, M. (1994) The making of a working-class suburb in Hamilton's east end, 1990–1945. *Journal of Urban History*, Vol. 20, No. 4, pp. 486–511.

Harris, R.C. (1976/77) Locating the University of British Columbia. *BC Studies*, No. 32, pp. 106–125.

Hobbs, W.E. (1923) East Kildonan, Manitoba: Town Planning Scheme. *Journal of the Town Planning Institute of Canada*, Vol. 2, No. 6, pp. 6–8.

Holdsworth, D.W. (1977) House and home in Vancouver: Images of West Coast urbanism, 1886–1929, in Stelter, G.A. and Artibise, A.F.J. (eds.) *The Canadian City: Essays in Urban History*. Toronto: McClelland and Stewart, pp. 186–211.

Holdsworth, D.W. (1982) Regional distinctiveness in an industrial age: Some California influences in British Columbia architecture. *American Review of Canadian Studies*, Vol. 12, pp. 64–81.

Holdsworth, D.W. (1986) Cottages and castles for Vancouver home-seekers. *BC Studies*, Nos. 69–70, pp. 11–32.

Holdsworth, D.W. (1993) Revaluing the house, in Duncan, J. and Ley, D. (eds.) *Place/Culture/Representation*. London: Routledge, pp. 95–109.

Hulchanski, J.D. (1986) The 1935 Dominion Housing Act: Setting the stage for a permanent federal presence in Canada's housing sector. *Urban History Review/Revue d'histoire urbaine*, Vol. 15, No. 1, pp. 19–40.

Kalman, H. (1994) *A History of Canadian Architecture*, Vol. 2. Toronto: Oxford University Press.

Jones, A.E. (1978) *Beginnings of Federal Government Housing Policy, 1918–1924*. Occasional Paper No. 1/78. Ottawa: Carleton University, Centre for Social Welfare Studies.

Kellet, J. (1964) *The Impact of Railways on Victoria Cities*. London: Routledge and Kegan Paul.

Kerr, D. and Hanson, S. (1982) *Saskatoon: The First Half Century*. Edmonton: NeWest Books.

Leach, W. (1993) *Land of Desire: Merchants, Power and the Rise of a New American Culture*. New York: Pantheon.

Lemon, J.T. (1985) *Toronto Since 1918: An Illustrated History*. Toronto: Lorimer.

Lewis, R. (1991) The segregated city: class patterns and the development of industrial districts in Montreal, 1861 and 1901. *Journal of Urban History*, Vol. 17, No. 2, pp. 123–152.

Ley, D. (1993) Past elites and present gentry: Neighbourhoods of privilege in the inner city, in Ley, D. and Bourne, L.S. (eds.) *The Changing Social Geography of Canadian Cities*. Montreal: McGill-Queen's University Press, pp. 214–233.

Linteau, P-A. (1985) *The Promoters' City: Building the Industrial Town of Maisonneuve, 1883–1918*. Montreal: Lorimer.

Linteau, P-A. (1987) Canadian suburbanization in a North American context: Does the border make a difference? *Journal of Urban History*, Vol. 13, No. 3, pp. 252–274.

Maryln, J. (1957) *Under the Ribs of Death*. Toronto: McClelland and Stewart.

Matthews, B.R. (1985) *A History of Pointe Claire*. Pointe Claire, Que.: Brianor.

McCann, L.D. (1975) *Neighbourhoods in Transition*. Occasional Paper No. 2. Edmonton: Department of Geography, University of Alberta.

McCann, L.D. (1996) Planning and building the corporate suburb of Mount Royal, 1910–1925. *Planning Perspectives*, Vol. 11, No. 2, pp. 259–301.

McCann, L.D. (1997) John C. Olmsted, 'The Uplands,' and the Planning of a Suburban Landscape, 1907–1950. Paper presented at the Seventh National Conference on American Planning History, Seattle.

McCririck, D. and Wynn, G. (1990) Building self-respect and hopefulness: The development of blue-collar suburbs in early Vancouver, in Wynn, G. (ed.) *People, Places, Patterns, Processes: Geographical Perspectives on the Canadian Past*. Toronto: Copp, Clark, Pitman, pp. 267–284.

McKay, I. (1985) *The Craft Transformed*. Halifax: Formac.

Miller, D. (1987) *Material Culture and Mass Consumption*. Oxford: Blackwell.

Miron, J. (1988) *Housing in Post-War Canada*. Montreal: McGill-Queen's University Press.

Miron, J. (1993) *House, Home and Community: Progress in Housing Canadians, 1945–1986*. Montreal: McGill-Queen's University Press.

Moore, P. (1979) Zoning and planning: the Toronto experience, 1904–1970, in Artibise, A.F.J. and Stelter, G.A. (eds.) *The Usable Urban Past*. Toronto: Macmillan, pp. 316–342.

Morton, S. (1995) *Ideal Surroundings: Domestic Life in a Working-Class Suburb in the 1920s*. Toronto: Toronto University Press.

Nobbs, P.E. (1926) The subdivision of residential property. *Journal of the Town Planning Institute of Canada*, Vol. 5, No. 2, pp. 10–16.

Paterson, R. (1985) The development of an interwar suburb: Kingsway Park, Etobicoke. *Urban History Review/Revue d'histoire urbaine*, Vol. 13, No. 3, pp. 225–235.

Paterson, R. (1988) Creating Suburbia: Processes of Housing Production and Consumption in Toronto, 1911–1941. Unpublished Ph.D. thesis, York University.

Pearson, N. (1956) Hell is a suburb: what kind of neighbourhoods do we want? *Community Planning Review*, Vol. 7. No. 3, pp. 124–128.

Perry, C. (1929) *The Neighbourhood Unit*. New York: Regional Plan of New York and Its Environs.

Perry, C. (1933) *The Rebuilding of Blighted Areas*. New York: Regional Plan Association.

Perry, C. (1939) *Housing in the Machine Age*. New York: Russell Sage.

Pratte, F.G. (1987) *Country Houses for Montrealers, 1892–1924: The Architecture of E. and W.S. Maxwell*. Montreal: Meridian Press.

Purdy, S. (1997) Industrial efficiency, social order and moral purity: Housing reform thought in English Canada, 1990–1950. *Urban History Review/Revue d'histoire urbaine*, Vol. 25, No. 2, pp. 31–40.

Rees, R. (1974) The 'Magic City on the Banks of the Saskatchewan': The Saskatoon real estate boom. 1900–1913, *Saskatchewan History*, Vol. 27, pp. 51–59.

Regan, J. (1908) *Sketches and Traditions of the Northwest Arm, Halifax, Nova Scotia.* Halifax: McAlpine.

Rémillard, F. and Merrett, B. (1987) *Mansions of the Golden Square Mile, Montreal, 1850–1930.* Montreal: Meridean Press.

Ross, G.A. (1919) The Halifax disaster and the re-housing. *Construction*, Vol. 12, pp. 293–307.

Roy, G. (1945) *The Tin Flute*. Toronto: McClelland and Stewart.

Roy, G. (1957) *Street of Riches*. Toronto: McClelland and Stewart.

Rybczynski, W. (1986) *Home: A Short History of an Idea*. New York: Viking.

Rybczynski, W. (1995) *City Life: Urban Expectations in a New World*. Toronto: Harper Collins.

Saarinen, O.W. (1986) Single-sector communities in northern Ontario: The creation and planning of dependent towns, in Stelter, G.A. and Artibise, A.F.J. (eds.) *Power and Place: Canadian Urban Development in North American Context*. Vancouver: University of British Columbia Press, pp. 219–264.

Saywell, J.T. (1975) *Housing Canadians: Essays on the History of Residential Construction in Canada*. Discussion Paper No. 24. Ottawa: Economic Council of Canada.

Schiesl, M. J. (1977) *The Politics of Efficiency: Municipal Administration and Reform in America, 1880–1920*. Berkeley: University of California Press.

Schultz, S.K. (1989) *Constructing Urban Culture: American Culture and City Planning, 1800–1920*. Philadelphia: Temple University Press.

Scott, M. (1969) *American Planning Since 1890*. Berkeley: University of California Press.

Seeley, J.R., Sim, R.A., and Loosley, E.W. (1956) *Crestwood Heights: A Study of the Culture of Suburban Life*. Toronto: University of Toronto Press.

Selwood, H.J. (1984) Invisible landscape: Premature urban subdivision in the Winnipeg region, in Selwood, H.J. and Welsted, J. (eds.) *Landscape Development and Boundary Influences in the Canadian Prairies*. Regina Geographical Studies, No. 4. Regina: Department of Geography, University of Regina, pp. 41–57.

Selwood, H.J. (1988) Lots, plots and blocks: Some Winnipeg examples of subdivision design. *Bulletin of the Society for the Study of Architecture in Canada*, Vol. 11, pp. 6–8.

Sewell, J. (1977) The suburbs. *City Magazine*, Vol. 2, No. 6, pp. 19–55.

Sewell, J. (1993) *The Shape of the City*. Toronto: University of Toronto Press.

Seymour, H.L. (1927) The progress of town planning in Vancouver and Point Grey. *Journal of the Town Planning Institute of Canada*, Vol. 6, No. 6, pp. 215–216.

Shutlak, G. (1994) A vision of regeneration: Reconstruction after the Halifax Harbour explosion, in Ruffman, A. and Howell, C.D. (eds.) *Ground Zero: A Reassessment of the 1917 Explosion in Halifax Harbour*. Halifax: Nimbus, pp. 421–426.

Simpson, M. (1985) *Thomas Adams and the Modern Planning Movement*. London: Mansell.

Slack, B., Meana, L., Langford, M. and Thornton, P. (1994) Mapping the changes: the spatial development of industrial Montréal, 1861–1929. *Urban History Review/Revue d'histoire urbaine*, Vol. 22, pp. 97–112.

Smith, P.J. (1972) Changing forms and patterns in the cities, in Smith, P.J. (ed.) *The Prairie Provinces*. Toronto: University of Toronto Press, pp. 99–117.

Smith, P.J. (1979) The principle of utility and the origins of planning legislation in Alberta, in Artibise, A.F.J. and Stelter, G.A. (eds.) *The Usable Urban Past*. Toronto: Macmillan, pp. 196–225.

Smith, P.J. (1986) American influences and local needs: Adaptation to the Alberta planning system in 1928–1929, in Stelter, G.A. and Artibise, A.F.J. (eds.) *Power and Place: Canadian Urban Development in North American Context*. Vancouver: University of British Columbia Press, pp. 109–132.

Smith, P.J. (1995) Planning for residential growth since the 1940s, in Hesketh, B. and Swyripa, F. (eds.) *Edmonton: Life of a City*. Edmonton: NeWest, pp. 243–255.

Steele, M. (1993) Incomes, prices, and tenure choice, in Miron, J. (ed.) *House, Home and Community: Progress in Housing Canadians, 1945–1986*. Montreal: McGill-Queen's University Press, pp. 41–63.

Stilgoe, J. (1983) *Metropolitan Corridor: Railroads and the American Scene*. New Haven: Yale University Press.

Strong-Boag, V. (1988) *The New Day Recalled: Lives of Girls and Women in English Canada, 1919–1939*. Markham, Ontario: Penguin.

Taylor, J. (1989) City form and capital culture: Remaking Ottawa. *Planning Perspectives*, Vol. 4, pp. 79–105.

Todd, F.G. (1908) Point Grey, British Columbia: A new departure in laying out a townsite. *The Canadian Municipal Journal*, Vol. 4, pp. 146–147.

Urquhart, M.C. (1993) *Gross National Product, Canada, 1870–1926*. Montreal: McGill-Queen's University Press.

Vancouver Town Planning Commission (1929) *A Plan for the City of Vancouver, British Columbia, including a General Plan of the Region, 1928*. Vancouver: The Commission.

van Nus, W. (1977) The fate of City Beautiful thought in Canada, 1890–1930, in Stelter, G.A. and Artibise, A.F.J. (eds.) *The Canadian City: Essays in Urban History*. Toronto: McClelland and Stewart, pp. 162–185.

van Nus, W. (1979) Towards the city efficient: The theory and practice of zoning, 1991–1939, in Artibise, A.F.J. and Stelter, G.A. (eds.) *The Usable Urban Past*. Toronto: Macmillan, pp. 226–247.

van Nus, W. (1984) The role of suburban government in the city-building process: the case of Notre Dame de Grâces, Quebec, 1876–1910. *Urban History Review/Revue d'histoire urbaine*, Vol. 13, No. 2, pp. 91–103.

Wade, J. (1986) Wartime Housing Limited, 1941–1947: A Canadian housing policy at the crossroads. *Urban History Review/Revue d'histoire urbaine*, Vol. 15, No. 1, pp. 41–60.

Weaver, J.C. (1976) Reconstruction of the Richmond district in Halifax: A Canadian episode in public housing and town planning, 1918–1921. *Plan Canada*, Vol. 16, pp. 36–47.

Weaver, J.C. (1978) From land assembly to social maturity: The suburban life of Westdale (Hamilton), Ontario, 1911–1951. *Histoire Sociale/Social History*, Vol. 11, pp. 411–440.

Weaver, J.C. (1979) The property industry and land use controls: The Vancouver experience, 1910–1945. *Plan Canada*, Vol. 19, No. 3, pp. 211–225.

Weaver, J.C. (1984) Tomorrow's metropolis revisited: A critical assessment of urban reform in Canada, 1880–1920, in Stelter, G.A. and Artibise, A.F.J. (eds.) *The Canadian City: Essays in Urban History*. Toronto: McClelland and Stewart, pp. 456–477.

Weiss, M. (1987) *The Rise of the Community Builders*. New York: Columbia University Press.

Wolfe, J. and Jacobs, P. (1991) City planning and urban beautification, in The Metropolitan Museum of Fine Arts, *The Architecture of Edward and W. S. Maxwell*. Montreal, Metropolitan Museum of Fine Arts, pp. 50–56.

Wolforth, J. (1965) *Residential Location and the Place of Work*. Vancouver: Tantalus.

Woodward, H. (1955) *Canadian Mortgages*. Toronto: Collins.

Wynn, G. (1981) *Timber Colony*. Toronto: University of Toronto Press.
Wynn, G. (1992) The rise of Vancouver, in Wynn, G. and Oke, T. (eds.) *Vancouver and Its Region*. Vancouver: University of British Columbia Press, pp. 69–148.

Acknowledgement

This chapter has been supported by research funds granted to the author and to the Canadian Families Project by the Social Science and Humanities Research Council of Canada, and is gratefully acknowledged.

CHAPTER 7

Running Rings Around the City: North American Industrial Suburbs, 1850–1950

Robert Lewis

The development of suburban industrial districts has been an important element of the changing character of European, American and Canadian metropolitan fringe belts since the middle of the nineteenth century. In Europe, the character and extent of industrial decentralization has been well documented. Lace, hosiery, silk and shoes were manufactured in the industrial satellite villages surrounding the East Midland cities of Nottingham, Derby and Leicester (Palmer and Neaverson, 1992). Significant clusters of chemical, metal-working and textile firms were to be found in the Paris fringe areas of Saint-Denis, Saint-Ouen and Clichy from as early as the 1850s (Fontanon, 1988). The emergence of industrial suburbs such as Moabit and extensive industrial development elsewhere on the city periphery contributed to Berlin's tremendous growth in this period (Waterhouse, 1993). Similarly, a range of suburban industrial districts has been identified as surrounding American and Canadian cities from as early as the middle of the nineteenth century. Agglomerations of manufacturing firms populated the expanding fringe of cities as different as highly compact Milwaukee and Montréal, and spread out Los Angeles and Chicago (Buder, 1967; Lewis, 1991, 1994; Muller and Groves, 1979; Viehe, 1981). Unfortunately, we know little about the patterns and processes associated with suburban manufacturing in the United States and Canada. Despite the existence of a few case studies, the question of the role and importance of manufacturing on the urban fringe after 1850 has been neglected.

The purpose of this chapter is to show the extent of industrial development on the urban fringe and, in particular, the importance of industrial suburbs in the 100 years after 1850. This period is important for two reasons. First, industrial capitalism featuring the rise of manufacturing, technological innovation, massive population growth and new social classes transformed the American and Canadian city after 1850. These changes to urban society had a decisive impact on the character and scale of urban form, one element of which was the development of extensive fringe manufacturing districts. Secondly, the dominant characteristic of the outward thrust of metropolitan areas between 1850 and 1950, according to most writers, was middle-class residential suburbanization. Most models and descriptions of the geography of industry have emphasized the concentration of industry and working-class districts in the city centre. Before the Second World War, 'by far the largest expansion of urban employment occurred in central locations' (Ward, 1971, p. 86). The ascendancy of the truck and the automobile coupled with working-class suburbanization opened the urban fringe to manu-facturing after the Second World War, 'free[ing] many firms from traditional central locations' (Warner, 1972, p. 118). There is little doubt that industrial and working-class suburbanization have been important features of post-war metro-politan expansion. The point to be made here, however, is that manufacturing on the fringe has been part of urban growth from the small mid-nineteenth-century city hugging the waterfront to the sprawling mid-twentieth-century metropolis.

The focus of this chapter is upon the sprawling empire of industrial suburbs ringing the central core. Even though some firms were scattered across the periphery, a great deal of manufacturing was to be found clustered in specific areas of the urban fringe. The chapter begins with a review of the various attempts to assess the rate of North American industrial suburbanization between 1850 and 1950. This is followed by a discussion of the three major sets of dynamics producing industrial suburbs: industrial change, the property market, and insti-tutions. Next, an outline of the major types of industrial suburbs is presented. In the conclusion, I discuss the ways in which manufacturing decentralization has shaped the historical geography of American and Canadian metropolitan development.

Identifying Industrial Suburbanization

Industrial suburbs became firmly entrenched in the fabric of North American urban districts after 1850. The cumulative effects of 100 years of industrial suburbanization had become such a problem for central cities by the Second World War that city after city commissioned reports to establish the extent, character and impact of the diffusion of manufacturing to the suburbs (Chicago Plan Commission, 1942a; Cincinnati, 1946; Reid, 1951; Beauregard, 1993). In Chicago, as elsewhere, one of 'the chief problems' of the early decades of the twentieth century was 'the trend towards decentralization of Chicago's industries to adjacent and nearby suburbs' (Chicago Plan Commission, 1942a, p. 5). With the aim of assessing empirically the declining importance of the central city, scholars have examined the basic lineaments of the changing geography of American metropolitan manufacturing (Creamer, 1935; Kitagawa and Bogue, 1955; McLaughlin, 1938; Woodbury and Cliffe, 1953). Although decentralization was recognized by many as the 'chief problem', it has been extremely difficult to calculate the degree of industrial suburbanization that has taken place since the rise of industrial capitalism. In a detailed review of the American secondary evidence, Woodbury and Cliffe state that the question 'admits of no clear answer' (Woodbury and Cliffe, 1953, p. 286). Still, they, along with most other writers, agree that slow but gradual industrial suburbanization had been occurring since the end of the nineteenth century. For example, between 1899 and 1947 the central cities' share of the nation's production workers declined from 40 per cent to only 32 per cent, while the suburban share rose slightly from 18 per cent to 22 per cent (table 7.1). Similarly, the relative share of total metropolitan manufacturing employment between central city and suburbs changed slowly over the 50-year period, dropping from 68 per cent to 59 per cent. In Canada, although there may have been a greater degree of industrial suburbanization in the decades before the mid-twentieth century, the trend paralleled that of the States (Slater, 1961).

The slow but discernible diffusion of manufacturing employment from central cities to the suburbs was characterized by some important variations. First, there were significant differences in the balance of central and suburban jobs between cities. The central cities of Cleveland and Chicago between 1879 and 1954 retained a large share of employment (table 7.2). In contrast, jobs in Boston and Pittsburgh were widely spread throughout the metropolitan region (McLaughlin, 1938; Muller, forthcoming; Orum, 1995). Likewise, manufacturing employment in Canada was more dispersed through the Toronto metropolitan region than in Montréal (Slater, 1961). Secondly, cities specializing in durable goods industries such as Detroit and Pittsburgh tended to have higher shares of suburbanized firms than those specializing in non-durable goods (Kitagawa and Bogue, 1955; Chicago Plan Commission, 1942a; Reid, 1951). Thirdly, even while industrial suburbanization was increasing overall, there was great variability between cities over time. Between 1929 and 1954, for example, while the overall trend was for the movement of manufacturing firms to suburban municipalities, almost a third of American cities experienced a centralization of employment (Kitagawa and Bogue, 1955; Zelinsky, 1962).

Table 7.1. Manufacturing employment of U.S. metropolitan districts, 1899–1947.

	Production Workers as % of Total U.S. Employment				Production Workers as % of Metropolitan Employment		
	Metropolitan						
Year	City	Suburb	Total	Other	City	Suburb	Total
1899	39.5	18.3	57.8	42.2	68.3	31.7	100.0
1919	36.1	22.2	58.3	41.7	61.9	38.1	100.0
1929	35.1	21.1	56.2	43.8	62.4	37.6	100.0
1939	32.0	23.0	55.0	45.0	58.2	41.8	100.0
1947	32.2	22.2	54.4	45.6	59.2	40.8	100.0

Source: Compiled from Woodbury, 1953, p. 253 and Zelinsky, 1962, p. 254.

Table 7.2. Manufacturing employment in selected U.S. metropolitan districts, 1879–1947.

| Metropolitan District | Production Workers (%) | | | | | | | |
| | Central City | | | | Suburbs | | | |
	1879	1899	1929	1954	1879	1899	1929	1954
Cleveland	90.0	85.8	81.4	62.8	10.0	14.2	18.6	37.2
Chicago	89.4	88.2	73.6	65.3	10.6	11.8	26.4	34.7
St. Louis	84.4	82.3	70.7	64.1	15.6	17.7	29.3	35.9
Philadelphia	82.5	79.3	65.7	56.0	17.5	20.7	34.3	44.0
Detroit	78.7	83.3	75.2	53.5	21.3	16.7	24.8	46.5
Buffalo	78.6	76.2	59.8	43.3	21.4	23.8	40.2	46.7
New York	74.6	68.9	60.0	55.7	25.4	31.1	40.0	44.3
Pittsburgh	66.8	45.2	27.1	22.5	33.2	54.8	72.9	77.5
Providence	55.3	63.5	57.6	57.5	44.7	36.5	42.4	42.5
Boston	29.8	27.8	26.6	25.8	70.2	72.2	73.4	74.2

Source: Compiled from various censuses of the United States.

There appears to be strong evidence that industrial suburbanization was a slow and relatively unimportant, although variable, process before 1950. But was this the case? There are several reasons for questioning the validity of this claim. One is that the census data used to chart the long-term trends of industrial suburbanization are susceptible to the changing boundaries of city and suburbs. Methodological problems inherent in the generally accepted census definition of these spatial units are ignored by writers on suburbanization. Based, as they are, on an artificial division between the central city and the surrounding area, census data provide information at a scale inappropriate for detecting the geography of manufacturing at a disaggregated level. Furthermore, they tell us very little about the processes behind suburbanization. This is not to deny that political boundaries have important effects, but these effects often cut across industrial districts, separating areas that have significant internal coherence (Muller, 1996; Teaford 1979). This point was acknowledged by New York's Regional Plan Association: 'the natural economic unity of the New York Metropolitan Region . . . is split by political boundaries into a number of artificial segments which are separate entities only for governmental purposes' (New York Regional Plan, 1944, p. 10).

Another issue, and one rarely noted, is that suburban districts contained a significant amount of metropolitan manufacturing employment in the period before the studies began to document industrial decentralization. As early as 1899, suburban districts accounted for almost a third of metropolitan employment (table 7.1). While the trend of decentralization may have been relatively slow after 1899, it was continuing a long-term process that reaches back into the middle of the nineteenth century. In the textile towns of Paterson and Passaic, manufacturing 'at a very early date became established near the outer margins of the spreading communities . . . Thus, the present decentralization [1950s] of industry is not new, but . . . is the present manifestation of a trend as old as the settlement itself' (Kenyon, 1960, p. 22). This has been confirmed in several other cities. In Baltimore, New York and Montréal, substantial industrial suburban development was taking place by the 1850s (Lewis, 1991, 1994; Muller and Groves, 1979; Stott, 1990). After the 1880s, and continuing through the first half of the twentieth century, it has been documented for places as different as Montréal, New York, Toronto, Pittsburgh, San Francisco and Los Angeles (Gad, 1994; Lewis, forthcoming; Muller, forthcoming; Pratt, 1911; Taylor, 1916; Walker, forthcoming; Viehe, 1981). The general point can be illustrated by the example of New York. Manhattan's share of manufacturing fell from almost two-thirds in 1869 to less than a third in 1954, while the boroughs of Brooklyn and Queens and the satellite areas of New Jersey grew dramatically (table 7.3). Attracting industries such as food processing, textiles and metalworking, these suburban industrial districts formed an impressive set of manufacturing and working-class areas ringing the central core of metropolitan New York City.

Annexation also affected the identification of industrial suburbanization. From the middle of the nineteenth century through the opening decades of the twentieth, most cities undertook an extensive campaign of annexation, both residential and industrial (Jackson, 1985; Teaford, 1979). One effect of the incorporation of manufacturing suburbs into the jurisdiction of the central city was to reduce the suburban industrial base in favour of the central city. Annexation of the metal working towns of Pullman and South Chicago to Chicago in 1889, and the manufacturing suburbs of Saint-Henri, Sainte-Cunégonde and Maisonneuve to Montréal between 1905 and 1918 sharply reduced, in terms of the census defini-tion, the degree of suburban manufacturing in those metropolitan areas (Jackson, 1985; Linteau, 1985). Different rates of annexation also led to significant differ-ences between the size of central cities, thus affecting the relative share between centre and suburb. It is impossible, for example, to make meaningful comparisons between Chicago with its 200 square miles and Boston with its 45 square miles.

An illustration of the effects that annexation had on the city-suburb balance of industry can be found in Philadelphia. In 1854 the annexation of a large surrounding territory brought the textile suburbs of Kensington, Moyamensing and Southwark under Philadelphia's control. These suburban districts contained 87 per cent of the Philadelphia region's textile employment in 1850 (table 7.4). Their incorporation into the central city in 1854 transformed the city-suburban share of textile manufacture. By 1893, the 'city' contained more than 78 per cent of textile employment, compared to just 12 per cent in 1850. The old suburbs of Kensington and others that were annexed to the city in 1854, however, contained most of these jobs; while new suburbs ringing Philadelphia became increasingly important by the end of the century. In other words, although the city officially contained the bulk of the area's jobs after 1854, the vast majority of it was not in the original mid-nineteenth-century city, but in the annexed textile suburbs. Even

Table 7.3. The geography of manufacturing employment in New York Metropolitan Area, 1869–1954.

District	Wage Earners (%)				Wage Earners (No.)			
	1869	1899	1929	1954	1869	1899	1929	1954
New York City								
Manhattan	62.0	51.2	36.8	32.5	129,577	285,265	328,230	397,286
Brooklyn	8.8	15.7	16.4	16.1	18,545	87,445	146,648	196,205
Queens	1.2	1.9	6.2	8.1	2,534	10,684	55,166	99,197
Bronx	–	–	2.8	3.5	–	–	24,958	42,990
Richmond	0.5	0.9	0.9	0.7	1,033	5,192	8,247	8,235
Total	72.5	69.7	63.1	60.9	151,689	388,586	563,249	743,913
Environs								
New Jersey	23.0	27.7	33.9	35.9	48,003	154,455	302,685	438,807
Westchester	4.4	2.6	2.9	3.1	9,162	14,586	26,136	38,412
Total	27.4	30.3	36.8	39.0	57,165	169,041	328,821	477,219
Grand Total	100.0	100.0	100.0	100.0	208,854	557,627	892,070	1,221,132

Source: Ninth Census of the United States, 1870. Washington: Government Printing Office, 1972. Vol. III, Table IX. pp. 493–584: New York Regional Plan, 1940, p. 40.

Notes:
1. The metropolitan region is defined as the City of New York, and the counties of Westchester (N.Y.), Bergen, Essex, Hudson, Middlesex, Passaic, and Union (N.J.).
2. In 1869 and 1899 the Bronx included in Manhattan.

Table 7.4. The geography of the Philadelphia region's textile industry, 1850–1934.

District	1850 Number	%	1893 Number	%	1916 Number	%	1934 Number	%
Old City	1,537	12.4	1,324	2.1	2,201	2.8	2,376	3.4
Pre-1854 annex suburbs								
Kensington	3,977	32.2	26,024	40.4	33,856	43.4	21,429	31.0
Other Old Suburbs	6,855	55.4	23,110	35.8	26,409	33.8	22,230	32.2
New Suburbs	NA	NA	14,008	21.7	15,591	20.0	22,993	33.3
Philadelphia Region	12,369	100.0	64,466	100.0	78,057	100.0	69,028	100.0

Source: Scranton, 1983, p. 184; Scranton, 1989, pp. 121, 123, 300, 464–465.

as cities such as Philadelphia were intent on acquiring large chunks of the surrounding area, some industrial suburbs resisted annexation. In Milwaukee, for example, the attempt by the city to annex the industrial suburbs of West Allis and Cudahy were met with fierce and successful resistance (Orum, 1995, pp. 78–80). Different rates of annexation were important in shaping the metropolitan geography of manufacturing.

To be able to decipher the actual rate, timing, and character of industrial suburbanization, the broad picture provided by the census needs to be complemented by case studies of particular cities and industries. It is one thing to know that industry in Pittsburgh was widely dispersed throughout many small industrial towns and suburbs; it is another to describe and explain the actual historical-geographic processes behind widespread industrial suburbanization. Despite this, two things are quite clear. First, a definition of suburban which includes only those areas with political autonomy adjacent to a large city is inadequate. Accordingly, the definition used here refers to politically separate areas, annexed suburban districts and the expanding fringe of the central city itself. Secondly, industrial suburbanization was a long-term process reaching back to the early days of industrial capitalism. Although it is difficult to draw out generalizations or trends of industrial decentralization, it is possible to identify some critical processes behind the development of industrial suburbs after 1850.

INDUSTRIAL SUBURBS AND INDUSTRIAL CHANGE

The beginnings of industrial suburbanization were intimately tied to the emergence of industrial capitalism after the mid-nineteenth century. Initially concentrated in the mill towns of New England, the Mid-Atlantic and the St. Lawrence valley, the factory system shifted to larger cities from the 1840s. In these expanding urban centres, industrial capitalism initiated a rationalization of urban space. The development of new production technologies, a more specialized division of labour, increased investment in manufacturing, and the growing scale of the workplace broke down the artisanal character of manufacturing. Changes to, and the growth of, industrial markets were set into motion by the proletarianization of the workforce and changing consumption patterns. New transportation networks widened the scope of product markets and inter-firm linkages through their greater speed and lower costs. These changes affected the logic of locational decisions within cities. In the mercantile city, manufacturing and artisanal production were concentrated in central districts and along the waterfront (Muller and Groves, 1979; Stelter, 1982). Capitalist industrialization after 1850 led to increasing demand for new work sites, many of which were to be created at greenfield sites on the city edge.

Greenfield sites on the city fringe and in surrounding suburban districts presented several advantages. They gave firms the opportunity to install new production technologies and organizational forms on large plots of land. The increasing scale and complexity of industrial production placed strong pressure on firms to seek new manufacturing sites where large-scale machinery, through-flow and assembly line production processes, new building forms (the single-storey factory for example), and large workforces could be more easily and profitably located. The increasingly extensive set of major transportation networks snaking out of the downtown core and encircling the central city allowed more rapid and easier access throughout the metropolitan district (Chinitz, 1960; Hoover and Vernon, 1959; Jackson, 1985; Mayer, 1944). In late nineteenth-century Nashville, for example, manufacturing districts formed along the railroad on the city's periphery. Once the nucleus was in place, new lines and spurs were added as demand increased, resulting in a suburban 'maze of switches and sidings' (Marshall, 1975, p. 71). Suburban industrial districts allowed firms to gain greater political suzerainty over the suburb and to escape the labour conflict of the city (Gordon, 1984). In 'company' towns such as Pullman, West Allis, Vandergrift and Gary, the firm's power could be almost absolute; but even in suburban districts that were not dominated by one company, the influence of manufacturers was ever present (Buder, 1967; Greer, 1976; Mosher, 1995; Orum, 1995).

The movement of manufacturing to industrial suburbs after 1850 generated suburban agglomeration economies. While the benefits of greenfield sites allowed individual firms to gain reductions in their operating costs and greater political control over the labour force, they also frequently translated into a series of collective economies open to any firm willing to move to the fringe. Over time, increasing inter-firm linkages, the emergence of localized labour markets, and better access to transportation networks accelerated the formation of manufacturing clusters on the metropolitan fringe. The growth of a textile, food-processing, leather and metal district in Montréal's east end was generated by the initial establishment of a few large firms on the city's edge before 1880 (Lewis, 1994).

To take advantage of existing economies, new industrial suburbs in Milwaukee after 1900 extended from older fringe districts in a wedge pattern (McClelland and Junkersfeld, 1928). Many industrial districts ringing Los Angeles coalesced around early oil production sites (Viehe, 1981). The move to the suburbs or satellite cities did not mean cutting ties with the central city. Technological changes to communication (the telegraph and the telephone) and transportation (the railway, electric streetcar and the auto) allowed effective connections between city and suburb. These changes lengthened intra-metropolitan flows of information, goods and capital, extended the commuting range of workers, and allowed for better inter-industry networks (Harris, 1993; Kenyon, 1960; Moyer, 1977; Muller, forthcoming; Platt 1991). As the writers of the New York Regional Plan stated,

> each of the political segments of the New York Metropolitan Region performs a function for the other segments. There is a great daily flow of goods, services and people crossing the political boundary lines within the Region but this circulation is necessary in order to maintain the life of the greater economic organism. (New York Regional Plan, 1944, p. 10)

Leading the outward thrust of industrial suburbanization was the large, integrated firm. Most writers have stressed that the city and suburbs were differentiated in terms of small, labour-intensive firms and large, capital-intensive firms (Scott, 1982). It is commonly believed that the opportunities presented by industrial suburbanization were more easily taken up by the large corporations which emerged in the late nineteenth century. In the forefront of industrial reorganization and the development of new markets, these corporations, with their greater financial resources, were more able than smaller firms to establish factories in new suburban locations. There is little doubt that the large firm could take advantage of the opportunities opened by spatial relocation. Propulsive industries such as chemicals, steel and automotive production, with their continuous-process, high-volume methods and large workforces, shaped the capitalist imperative through the reorganization of work and their need for large manufacturing sites. For these firms, the use of greenfield sites in industrial suburban districts after 1850 was one element in their strategy of efficiency, cost reduction and political control. Chicago's Calumet district exemplifies this process. Between 1880 and 1920 a series of industrial suburbs ringing the southern edge of Chicago developed an integrated, suburban production system based on heavy industry. Gary, South Chicago, Chicago Heights and East Chicago specialized in steel production, while Harvey and Blue Island concentrated on fabricated metal products and heavy equipment (Appleton, 1927; Greer, 1976; Meyer and Miller, 1956; Mohl and Betten, 1972).

Although large firms increasingly viewed industrial suburbs as having great potential for installing new and efficient working spaces, firms of all types could be found on the urban fringe after 1850. It is true that small, labour-intensive, consumer non-durable industries remained concentrated in the core to take advantage of a large labour market, close face-to-face contacts, and external economies of scale. As numerous studies have shown, these factors spawned distinct central clusters of vertically disintegrated firms in cities such as Baltimore, New York and Toronto (Hiebert, 1990; Muller and Groves, 1976; Selekman *et al.*, 1974). Yet there is evidence to suggest that suburban intra-urban networks developing after 1850 also allowed the growth of small and medium sized firms on the suburban fringe. Some of these were new starts, while many were refugees from the central city. In nineteenth-century Pittsburgh, firms of all sizes in the glass, steel, and railroad equipment industries coexisted throughout the various industrial suburbs and satellite towns. The result was the development of an extensive set of metropolitan inter-firm linkages (Muller, forthcoming). In the New York men's clothing industry, more than 82 per cent of jobs were found on Manhattan Island, south of 42nd Street, in 1900 (table 7.5). Twenty-two years later, its share had fallen to 58 per cent; while the number in Brooklyn, Queens and the New Jersey portion of the metropolitan district was 26,000, or almost 40 per cent of the industry. During the 1920s, the industrial suburbs next to Chicago's boundaries reaped the rewards of the agglomeration effects of the periphery. Many of Chicago's small firms sought locations 'in the suburbs immediately outside the city limits, notably in Clearing' (Mitchell, 1933, p. 62). In the Calumet district, many small 'dependent fabricating plants' making an assortment of finished products clustered close to the large integrated steel mills (Appleton, 1927, pp. 15, 29). In Detroit, the small- to medium-sized machine tool

Table 7.5. The employment geography of selected industries in the New York Metropolitan Area.

| Industry | Employment (%) | | | | | | | |
| | Manhattan, S | | Rest of NYC | | New Jersey | | Other | |
	1900	1922	1900	1922	1900	1922	1900	1922
Printing	85.5	74.0	9.8	15.2	2.1	7.4	2.6	3.5
Women's Clothing	83.4	70.4	6.1	18.1	4.5	6.2	6.0	5.2
Men's Clothing	82.2	57.7	15.2	30.8	2.6	8.3	–	3.2
Fine Chemicals	52.2	25.9	6.9	35.5	31.5	31.4	9.4	7.2
Light Metal	33.5	17.3	22.4	36.5	25.9	29.1	18.2	17.1
Instruments	30.4	22.5	18.9	18.8	39.1	45.7	11.5	13.0
Knit Goods	25.8	14.1	32.7	63.3	41.2	21.3	0.4	1.3
Heavy Metal	18.2	6.4	28.1	28.8	40.5	46.5	13.3	18.3
Silk Goods	6.0	3.5	8.8	12.4	81.0	78.2	4.2	5.9
Heavy Chemicals	4.6	1.4	34.1	5.1	60.6	93.2	0.7	0.2
All Selected Industries	48.8	37.8	16.7	24.9	25.9	27.9	8.6	9.4

Source: Compiled from various reports in Regional Plan of New York and Its Environs, 1974.

and fabricating metal firms moved out to the suburbs to service the large automobile factories (Reid, 1951).

A highly differentiated and specialized industrial suburban landscape resulted from the convergence of these processes. From the mid-nineteenth century, suburban industrial districts in cities such as Baltimore and Montréal were distinct from each other and from the more centrally-located ones with regard to their industrial structure, labour composition, degree of mechanization and scale (Lewis, 1991, 1994; Muller and Groves, 1979). The specialization of suburban manufacturing was to be found throughout most other North American metropolitan districts, although the larger and more diverse ones tended to have a much more complex geography. Again, the case of New York neatly illustrates this. Between 1900 and 1922, many manufacturing firms left Manhattan, south of 59th street (table 7.5). Although it retained large shares of clothing and printing, many other industries left the core for the industrial areas of Brooklyn, Queens and the Bronx. Industry was also seeking space further out in the New Jersey satellite towns of Paterson, Passaic and Newark. The decentralization of chemical, metalworking and textile firms between 1900 and 1922 extended the metropolitan specialization created during the nineteenth century. This specialization continued over the following decades. In 1950, each of the industrial suburbs ringing New York City occupied a niche within the metropolitan economy: Bergen specialized in transportation equipment, textiles and instruments, Middlesex in chemicals and apparel, and Passaic in textiles and apparel (Kenyon, 1960).

INDUSTRIAL SUBURBS, LAND AND WORKING-CLASS HOUSING

The dynamics of the property market were critical to the growth of industrial suburbs. Investments in, and marketing of, suburban land set the basis for the outward thrust of industry and working-class housing. Occurring within cycles, the industrial suburban landscape was quickly developed in times of expansion as speculation, housing and factory construction, and transportation building forced their way into the open spaces of the fringe (Hoyt, 1933; Monchow, 1939; Warner, 1962). The result was an extensive new fringe belt consisting of a mix of residential, industrial and retailing land uses (Whitehand, 1987). In times of bust, building and subdivision activity usually concentrated on infilling the interstices of the earlier growth period. The uneven development of the property market on the urban fringe laid down rings, sectors and wedges of suburban development at different times. Each new bust created distinct industrial and residential landscapes. The various areas making up the new fringe belts were distinguished from each other and from the central city by different building forms, industries, occupations, ethnic structures, and infrastructures.

Suburban working-class residential land development was part of the outward thrust of the capitalist urban land market. Most studies of residential suburbanization have emphasized its middle-class character (Fishman, 1987; Jackson, 1985; Warner, 1962; Weaver, 1978; Weiss, 1987). In fact, significant working-class suburbanization had been taking place since the mid-nineteenth century (Kane and Bell, 1985; Lewis 1991; Stott, 1990), and continued through the first decades of the twentieth (Harris, 1996). Greenfield sites, especially in unincorporated municipalities with minimal regulations and cheap land, offered large profits for property speculators, and facilitated easy assemblage of working-class housing. Working-class suburbanization over time generated an extensive, and often dependent, labour market, and further consolidated the potency of the suburban production system (Muller, forthcoming). Many blue-collar workers employed in suburban manufacturing lived in working-class residential and industrial suburbs. Fringe working-class residential areas offered an accessible labour force for those firms wishing to settle outside the city core. Likewise, with their labour force, bonuses and infrastructures, the industrial suburbs, small towns and satellite cities ringing the central city acted as magnets for firms seeking new locations. Not only were direct production motives and savings to be made by the move to the suburbs, but the formation of fringe working-class neighbourhoods gave greater impetus to those hesitant about the advantages of the periphery.

Industrial suburban working-class housing was built under a variety of conditions. Until the Second World War, most working-class suburban housing – cottages, row housing, and small, detached housing – was built by small-time builders and contractors. Working-class suburban growth was a product of the search by workers for affordable, decent housing and jobs. In cities such as Montréal, Los Angeles and Pittsburgh, as elsewhere, suburbanizing firms acted as a magnet for working-class settlement (Fogelson, 1967; Hise, 1997; Lewis, 1991; Linteau, 1985; Muller, forthcoming). Working-class housing, however, was not always forthcoming. Sometimes, firms in industrial suburbs had to rely on workers commuting from elsewhere, because of the tight character of the local suburban housing market (Harris and Bloomfield, 1997; Taylor, 1916). In other cases, employers, spurred on by housing shortages and attempts to control both their workforce and the politics of the suburb, built company housing (Buder, 1967; McKiven, 1995; Mohl and Betten, 1972; Silcox, 1994). As one contemporary observer noted of housing provision by U.S. Steel in Birmingham, the firm wanted 'ideal living conditions for its employees, appreciating the fact that better home conditions mean better labor, more contented labor – an actual return in dollars and cents in dividends and interest' (quoted in McKiven, 1995, p. 138). Employers and small builders were not the only house builders, however. In Toronto, in the early decades of the twentieth century, and possibly in many other places, as much as a quarter to a third of new housing was owner-built (Harris, 1996).

Class, occupational and ethnic distinctions characterized the social geography of industrial suburbs. Although industrial suburbs could contain a wide range of classes, most were dominated by a blue-collar population living in low-rent

Table 7.6. Social characteristics of industrial areas on the Chicago urban fringe, 1939.

District	Owner Occupied Dwellings	Monthly Rent < $25	House Value < $3000	Foreign Born	Black
Chicago	26.2	31.4	72.4	28.1	7.5
Pullman	43.3	56.4	94.8	54.6	0.0
South Deering	37.6	45.4	92.0	44.4	0.1
South Chicago	36.4	41.5	74.9	35.9	1.6
West Pullman	48.6	34.0	87.8	47.1	0.3
Clearing	44.2	23.2	67.1	28.0	0.0
West Lawn	72.3	12.2	73.3	25.0	0.0

Source: Compiled from Chicago Plan Commission, 1942*b*, pp. 4–69.

housing. The housing market served to segregate middle-class housing from working-class industrial districts through income, zoning and deed restrictions. But even within the blue-collar industrial suburb, there was segregation by ethnicity and skill. The functioning of the ethnic division of labour within firms, in combination with the cultural advantages of the clustering of people from different ethnic origins was translated onto the suburb's social geography (Golab, 1977; Greenberg, 1981; Hiebert, 1991; Schreuder, 1989; 1990; Zunz, 1982). A large foreign-born, non-black home-owning population living in low-rent dwellings settled the industrial districts on Chicago's fringe (table 7.6). In Birmingham's industrial suburbs, 'race, ethnicity, and occupational status defined the spatial distribution of workers': unskilled blacks lived in the worst housing in the shadow of the mills, while the skilled Anglo-Americans resided in the better neighbourhoods (McKiven, 1995, p. 135).

Tying home and work together was the journey to work. Long journeys to work were not unknown before 1950. Many workers in working-class residential suburbs commuted downtown (Harris and Bloomfield, 1997), while the increasing size of the city, and the growing use of the automobile and public transit, contributed to the lengthening of the journey to work (Ericksen and Yancey, 1979; McShane, 1994). In the process, firms could draw upon a larger labour market. Nonetheless, proximity to work was a defining feature of industrial suburbs. There was a particularly strong home-work relationship in satellite towns and suburbs with a diverse industrial base, but isolated greenfield sites tended to draw workers from all parts of the city. While there is little empirical evidence setting out details of the journey to work before 1950, the importance of a close home-work relationship has been confirmed for several cities. In nineteenth-century Philadelphia, manufacturing employment on the urban fringe was associated with the development of local labour markets (Golab, 1977; Greenberg, 1981). This persisted over the following decades. Philadelphia's 'workplace locations were an important influence on the residential locations of manufacturing workers' as late as 1930 (Ericksen and Yancey, 1979, p. 178). The same relationship was to be found elsewhere. In Birmingham, black and white workers employed by the companies in its industrial suburbs, 'lived near their workplaces because most walked to and from work' (McKiven, 1995, p. 56). While many workers walked to work in the nineteenth century, most relied on public transit in the twentieth. Public transit in Detroit in 1940 was 'the most important means of movement for workers between the industrial districts of the metropolitan area' (Reid, 1951, p. 10). Twenty years earlier, only 12 per cent of Milwaukee's workers drove to work; 61 per cent took public transit and 27 per cent walked (McClelland and Junkersfeld, 1928).

INDUSTRIAL SUBURBS, INFRASTRUCTURES AND INSTITUTIONS

The growth of manufacturing and residential capital on the expanding urban periphery was made possible by the actions of local growth coalitions. Critical to the formation of an extensive ring of industrial suburbs was a series of infrastructure developments that enabled local governments, manufacturers and property developers to convert fringe areas into industrial and residential districts. The success of industrial suburbs depended upon their relationship with other parts of the metropolitan area and with regional and national markets. This was achieved through the development of networks of communication, transportation and sanitation that would fulfil both the requirements of everyday production and residence, and extend the reach of industrial suburbs to other areas. The nature, direction, and timing of these infrastructures did not proceed willy-nilly. Alliances made up of an assortment of railway companies, industrialists, land developers, financiers, merchants and several levels of government established the legal and institutional framework around which extensive metropolitan districts formed (Fogelson, 1967; Linteau, 1985; Orum, 1995; Platt, 1983; Weiss, 1987).

   The political context in which industrial suburbs developed changed over the period. During the nineteenth century, formal economic and social planning was virtually non-existent at the metropolitan level. Local alliances were generally temporary; shifting groups coming together for specific purposes underlay city growth and changes to urban form. The emergence of urban political machines, and their emphasis upon the expansion of public works as a motor of urban growth, accelerated the extension of infrastructure to the urban fringe (Schultz, 1989; Tarr, 1984). The urban reform movement after 1880, together with the growth of corporate forms of industry and the professionalization of society, led to more formal and ordered forms of urban regulation. These new governance structures, as with the political machine system, was based on the view that the city was a vehicle for business activity. The more efficient and faster circulation of goods and people through the 'engineered metropolis' tied the central city and the suburban areas into a highly connected, powerful machine (Schultz, 1989). By the early twentieth century, zoning, planning and government bureaucracies provided shape to the development process. The creation of regional associations and metropolitan plans by the 1920s, and large-scale federal intervention in urban affairs during the 1930s, further facilitated the reordering of metropolitan space (Chicago Plan Commission, 1942*a*; Fairfield, 1993; Logan and Molotch, 1987; Mollenkopf, 1983). While the State became increasingly tied to the fortunes of urban places over the period, most decisions functioned within an ideological environment that pitted the interests of most of the urban population against corporate and political interests.

Industrial suburbs emerged within these broad institutional changes. Tied to decisions made by business interests and governments, they were products of the demands of business (Buder, 1967; Mohl and Betten, 1972; Taylor, 1916). The process of private and State investment in the urban landscape was important in attracting industry and working-class settlement to suburban locations. Local alliances between the State and business developed a comprehensive system of infrastructure that facilitated industrial suburbanization. Behind the formation of suburban infrastructure networks were funds channelled from all levels of the State and the actions of local business interests. By the end of the nineteenth century, municipal government and private utilities diverted vast funds to the provision of water, sewer systems, streetcar tracks and electricity. In the process, they further extended the perimeters and connections of the networked metropolis (Moyer, 1977; Platt, 1991; Tarr, 1984). The ensuing attraction of the suburbs for manufacturing, in turn, contributed to the nature and direction of the metropolitan area's outward thrust. Underwriting industrial suburbanization were projects such as the extension of Montréal's docks into the industrial suburb of Maisonneuve, the building of bridges and tunnels connecting Manhattan with Brooklyn and New Jersey, and the construction of radial and belt railroad lines into the suburban districts of Chicago. At the same time, this infrastructure wove the different areas of the expanding metropolis into a tighter functional unit. The drawing power of the suburbs was further advanced through promiscuous use of municipal tax subsidies and bonuses, land giveaways, other forms of financial inducements to business, and few business and housing regulations (Harris, 1996; Monchow, 1939). In short, industrial suburbs were created through the efforts of local alliances that sought to reproduce a set of productive relations on the periphery. These suburbs were products of utility companies and land developers seeking profit, manufacturers wanting greenfield sites, politicians drumming up financial and electoral success, and workers desiring homes and work.

TYPES OF INDUSTRIAL SUBURBS

Between 1850 and 1950, the processes of manufacturing investment, land development, working-class suburbanization and institutional practices resulted in a diversity of industrial suburbs. Four major types can be identified. The first was the informally-created manufacturing complex on the edge of the existing urban fabric (Kenyon, 1960; Lewis, 1991, 1994; McKiven, 1995; Muller and Groves, 1979; Thomas, 1927). Often it was a wedge-like extension of an earlier industrial district, running along the railroad tracks or waterways, and spilling over the political boundary separating central city from suburban municipality. Sometimes it was an attempt by manufacturers to escape the labour and property disadvantages of the central city. Part of the informal process of suburban land development and industrial decentralization, these districts ranged from the large, diversified suburb such as Chicago's Cicero, consisting of many firms from several industries, to the small suburb with a few companies from a select set of industries such as East St. Louis and Wauwatosa outside Milwaukee (Cramer, 1952; Thomas, 1927; McClelland and Junkersfeld, 1928; Taylor, 1916). These informal industrial suburbs were replicated all over North America, and were the most common form of landscape development arising from industrial change.

In contrast, the satellite town was a relatively self-contained entity some distance from the major city that functioned within the orbit of a large metro-politan district (Orum, 1995; Taylor, 1916). Established originally as separate urban places, satellite towns were drawn into an expanding metropolitan district. Nonetheless, they were dependent upon the central city for financial and other high-level business information and transactions. Satellite towns had a well-developed local labour market, transportation network, retailing services and municipal authority. Examples include Joliet and Waukegan outside Chicago, South Milwaukee and Cudahy ringing Milwaukee, Alton and East Alton across the Mississippi from St. Louis, and Passaic and Paterson on the New Jersey shore facing New York City (Thomas, 1927; Kenyon, 1960; Chinitz, 1960; Orum, 1995; McClelland and Junkersfeld, 1928).

Another type was the company suburb or town such as Tacony (Philadelphia), Gary and Pullman (Chicago), West Allis (Milwaukee) and Vandergrift (Pittsburgh). Established by a large and solitary firm on a greenfield site, the company suburb was often some distance from the built-up area of the city (Buder, 1967; Greer, 1976; McClelland and Junkersfeld, 1928; Mosher, 1995; Silcox, 1994). Although they differed in some significant ways, there were com-mon features to their use of suburban land. They sought large plots of cheap land where they could build large, integrated plants with modern manufacturing methods. They also functioned as a means to gain direct control over the labour force and to keep other employers and unwanted labour out.

The final type was the organized industrial district. Established on the edge of the city by real estate and railway companies, the numbers of organized districts grew from a handful before the First World War to over 122 located in 84 cities by the middle of the century (Mitchell and Jucius, 1933; Wrigley, 1949). The organized industrial districts offered a package of cheap land, low taxes, transportation facilities, building design, and credit. Districts such as Clearing

(Chicago) and Central (Vernon, Los Angeles) were extremely attractive to small-to medium-sized firms seeking a safe, regulated environment. The organized district with its highly developed set of external economies, adjacent labour force, and access to the central city's information networks and financial institutions was, in many ways, a replica of manufacturing districts located in the city core.

CONCLUSION

A major gap in our understanding of urban growth is the timing, nature and scale of industrial suburbanization. Studies portraying industrial suburbanization as a relatively slow process before 1950 suffer from a series of problems. A principal problem relates to the definition of city and suburb. The generally accepted definitions, with their simple political jurisdictional boundaries, force the internal components of metropolitan areas into census-defined boxes that are easy to fill, but are difficult to sustain historically. Moreover, while we know quite a lot about the changing dynamics of specific industries and the forces behind the cyclical pattern of property development, studies of the formation of industrial suburbs before 1950 are few and far between. This is especially true when our knowledge of the processes producing industrial suburbs is contrasted with that of the residential suburb. If we are to know more about urban growth and the role of industrial suburbanization in this growth, there are important questions that need to be satisfactorily answered. How much decentralization took place and when? What sorts of firms were decentralizing and why? How was manufacturing land developed and by whom? How did suburban collective economies develop? At what point did these economies turn into large-scale suburban production complexes? What was the relationship between industrial and working-class suburbanization? What were the implications of this for emerging metropolitan scale?

The material discussed in this chapter goes part of the way towards answering these questions. As in England, France and Germany, industry has been an important component of the formation of Canadian and American suburban areas since the mid-nineteenth century. Three important and interacting set of dynamics underpinned the formation of suburban industrial clusters. After 1850, industrial capitalism set in motion a series of changes to manufacturing, notably the growing scale of firms, increased capital investment, frequent technological innovation, and accelerating capital-labour conflict. These changes, in turn, fuelled demands for new industrial locations. Greenfield areas on the edge of expanding cities and in surrounding suburbs and satellite towns increasingly became attractive sites for both new and relocating firms. The ability to establish a satisfactory environment for industry on the periphery was made possible through the working of the property market and the development of an infrastructure network. Each wave of suburban development increased the stock of land available for manufacturing and for working-class housing, leading to the development of industrial and working-class residential corridors. Furthermore, the property market functioned to segregate spatially class and ethnic differences. Holding all of this together were the actions of private and public groups working in concert. The laying-down of infrastructures, the giveaway of bonuses and tax exemptions, and the building of working-class housing made possible the development of industrial suburbs ringing the central city.

More generally, answers to the questions outlined above will broaden our understanding of the historical geography of metropolitan development in the United States and Canada in two important ways. First, examination of industrial suburbs will provide the basis for a reinterpretation of existing economic geography models of the industrial metropolis. The simple, yet commonly accepted, polarization between small, labour-intensive firms located in the city centre and large, capital-intensive firms located on the urban fringe misrepresents the location of manufacturing firms and the processes producing the geography of industrial suburbs. One remedy for this is to build upon the small number of existing case studies of individual metropolitan areas and industries. As these studies suggest, extensive clusters of manufacturing firms from most sectors and scales appeared on the suburban fringe after 1850. Secondly, grappling with these questions will also provide a different perspective on the supposed dominance of middle-class residential suburbanization. The movement of industry and workers to the urban fringe was a central component of urban expansion. Hitched to the waterfront and railway lines, these districts formed a primary corridor of metropolitan growth after 1850. Industrial suburbs composed of extensive housing areas, retail strips, community institutions and factories were magnets for industrial and residential agglomerations outside the central city. Examination of the role of industrial suburbs will broaden our picture of metropolitan growth and provide the basis for the reassessment of prevailing models and descriptions of urban growth. Without intensive research framed around the questions laid out above, our understanding of the suburban landscape will continue to be clouded by questionable generalizations.

References

Appleton, J. (1927) *The Iron and Steel Industry of the Calumet District: a Study in Economic Geography*. Urbana: University of Illinois Press.
Beauregard, R. (1993) *Voices of Decline: the Postwar Fate of U.S. Cities*. Oxford: Blackwell.
Buder, S. (1967) *Pullman: an Experiment in Industrial Order and Community Planning, 1880–1930*. New York: Oxford University Press.
Chicago Plan Commission (1942a) *Industrial and Commercial Background for Planning Chicago*. Chicago: Chicago Plan Commission.
Chicago Plan Commission (1942b) *Residential Chicago*. Chicago: City of Chicago.
Chinitz, B. (1960) *Freight and the Metropolis. The Impact of America's Transport Revolutions on the New York Region*. Cambridge, MA: Harvard University Press.

Cincinnati (1946) *The Economy of the Cincinnati Metropolitan Region*. Cincinnati: City Planning Commission of Cincinnati.

Cramer, R. (1952) *Manufacturing Structure of the Cicero District, Metropolitan Chicago*. Research Paper No. 27. Chicago: University of Chicago, Geography Department.

Creamer, D. (1935) *Is Industry Decentralizing?* Philadelphia: University of Pennsylvania.

Ericksen, E. and W. Yancey (1979) Work and residence in industrial Philadelphia. *Journal of Urban History*, Vol. 5, pp. 147–182.

Fairfield, J. (1993) *The Mysteries of the Great City: the Politics of Urban Design, 1877–1937*. Columbus: Ohio State University Press.

Fishman, R. (1987) *Bourgeois Utopias: the Rise and Fall of Suburbia*. New York: Basic Books.

Fogelson, R. (1967) *The Fragmented Metropolis: Los Angeles, 1850–1930*. Cambridge, MA: Harvard University Press.

Fontanon, C. (1988) L'industrialisation de la banlieue parisienne, in Fourcaut, A. (ed.) *Un siècle de banlieue parisienne (1859–1964): Guide de recherche*. Paris: Éditions l'Harmattan, pp. 49–80.

Gad, G. (1994) Location patterns of manufacturing: Toronto in the early 1880s. *Urban History Review*, Vol. 22, pp. 113–38.

Golab, C. (1977) *Immigrant Destinations*. Philadelphia: Temple University Press.

Gordon, D. (1984) Capitalist development and the history of American cities, in Tabb, W. and Sawers, L. (eds.) *Marxism and the Metropolis*. New York: Oxford University Press, pp. 21–53.

Greenberg, S. (1981) Industrial location and ethnic residential patterns in an industrializing city: Philadelphia, 1880, in Hershberg, T. (ed.) *Philadelphia: Work, Space, Family and Group Experience in the Nineteenth Century*. New York: Oxford University Press, pp. 204–232.

Greer, E. (1976) Monopoly and competitive capital in the making of Gary, Indiana. *Science and Society*, Vol. 40, pp. 465–478.

Harris, R. (1993) Industry and residence: the decentralization of New York City, 1900–1940. *Journal of Historical Geography*, Vol. 19, pp. 169–190.

Harris, R. (1996) *Unplanned Suburbs: Toronto's American Tragedy, 1900–1950*. Baltimore: Johns Hopkins University Press.

Harris, R. and Bloomfield, A.V. (1997) The impact of industrial decentralization on the gendered journey to work, 1900–1940. *Economic Geography*, Vol. 73, pp. 94–117.

Hiebert, D. (1990) Discontinuity and the emergence of flexible production: garment production in Toronto, 1901–1931. *Economic Geography*, Vol. 66, pp. 229–253.

Hiebert, D. (1991) Class, ethnicity and residential structure. The social geography of Winnipeg, 1901–1922. *Journal of Historical Geography*, Vol. 17, pp. 56–86.

Hise, G. (1997) *Magnetic Los Angeles: Planning the Twentieth-Century Metropolis*. Baltimore: Johns Hopkins University Press.

Hoover, E. and Vernon, R. (1959) *Anatomy of a Metropolis: the Changing Distribution of People and Jobs Within the New York Metropolitan Region*. New York: Anchor.

Hoyt, H. (1933) *One Hundred Years of Land Values in Chicago 1830–1933*. Chicago: University of Chicago Press.

Jackson, K. (1985) *Crabgrass Frontier: the Suburbanization of the United States*. New York: Oxford University Press.

Kane, K. and Bell, T. (1985) Suburbs for a labor elite. *Geographical Review*, Vol. 75, pp. 319–334.

Kenyon, J. (1960) *Industrial Localization and Metropolitan Growth: the Paterson-Passaic District*. Research Paper No. 67. Chicago: University of Chicago, Geography Department.

Kitagawa, E. and Bogue, D. (1955) *Suburbanization of Manufacturing Activity Within Standard Metropolitan Areas*. Studies in Population Distribution No. 9. Oxford, OH: Scripps Foundation, Miami University.

Lewis, R. (1991) The development of an early suburban industrial district: the Montreal ward of Saint-Ann, 1851–1871. *Urban History Review*, Vol. 19, pp. 166–180.

Lewis, R. (1994) Restructuring and the formation of an industrial district in Montreal's east end, 1850–1914. *Journal of Historical Geography*, Vol. 20, pp. 143–157.

Lewis, R. (forthcoming)A city transformed: Manufacturing districts and suburban growth in Montreal, 1850–1929. *Journal of Historical Geography*.

Linteau, P-A. (1985) *The Promoter's City. Building the Industrial Town of Maisonneuve, 1883–1918*. Toronto: Lorimer.

Logan, J. and Molotch, H. (1987) *Urban Fortunes: the Political Economy of Place*. Berkeley: University of California Press.

Marshall, J. (1975) Railroads and urban growth, in Blumstein, J.F. and Walter, B. (eds.) *Growing Metropolis: Aspects of Development in Nashville*. Nashville: Vanderbilt University Press, pp. 65–80.

Mayer, H. (1944) Localization of railway facilities in metropolitan centers as typified by Chicago. *The Journal of Land and Public Utility Economics*, Vol. 20, pp. 299–315.

McClelland and Junkersfeld Inc. (1928) *Report on Transportation in the Milwaukee Metropolitan District*. New York: McClelland and Junkersfeld Inc.

McKiven, H. (1995) *Iron and Steel: Class, Race, and Community in Birmingham, Alabama, 1875–1920*. Chapel Hill: University of North Carolina.

McLaughlin, G. (1938) *Growth of American Manufacturing Areas*. Pittsburgh: University of Pittsburgh, Bureau of Business Research.

McShane, C. (1994) *Down the Asphalt Path: the Automobile and the American City*. New York: Columbia University Press.

Meyer, A. and P. Miller (1956) Manufactural geography of Chicago Heights, Illinois. *Proceedings of the Indiana Academy of Science*, Vol. 66, pp. 209–229.

Mitchell, W. (1933) *Trends in Industrial Location in the Chicago Region Since 1920*. Chicago: University of Chicago Press.

Mitchell, W. and Jucius, M. (1933) Industrial districts of the Chicago region and their influence on plant location. *Journal of Business*, Vol. 6, pp. 139–156.

Mohl, R. and Betten, N. (1972) The failure of industrial city plannning: Gary, Indiana, 1906–1910. *Journal of the American Institute of Planning*, Vol. 38, pp. 203–214.

Mollenkopf, J. (1983) *The Contested City*. Princeton: Princeton University Press.

Monchow, H. (1939) *Seventy Years of Real Estate Subdividing in the Region of Chicago*. Evanston: Northwestern University Press.

Mosher, A. (1995) 'Something better than the best': industrial restructuring, George McMurty and the creation of the model industrial town of Vandergrift, Pennsylvania, 1883–1901. *Annals of the Association of American Geographers*, Vol. 85, pp. 84–107.

Moyer, J. (1977) Urban growth and the development of the telephone: some relationships at the turn of the century, in Pool, I. (ed.) *The Social Impact of the Telephone*. Cambridge, MA: MIT Press, pp. 342–369.

Muller, E. (1996) The Pittsburgh Survey and 'Greater Pittsburgh': a muddled metropolitan geography, in Greenwald, M. and Anderson, M. (eds.) *Pittsburgh Surveyed: Social Science and Social Reform in the Early Twentieth Century*. Pittsburgh: University of Pittsburgh Press, pp. 69–87.

Muller, E. (forthcoming) Industrial suburbs and the growth of metropolitan Pittsburgh, 1870–1920. *Journal of Historical Geography*.

Muller, E. and Groves, P. (1976) The changing location of the clothing industry: a link to the social geography of Baltimore in the nineteenth century. *Maryland Historical Review*, Vol. 71, pp. 403–420.

Muller, E. and Groves, P. (1979) The emergence of industrial districts in mid-nineteenth century Baltimore. *Geographical Review*, Vol. 54, pp. 159–178.

New York Regional Plan (1944) *The Economic Status of the New York Metropolitan Region in 1944*. New York: Regional Plan Association, Inc.

Orum, A. (1995) *City-Building in America*. Boulder: Westview Press.

Palmer, M. and Neaverson, P. (1992) *Industrial Landscapes of the East Midlands*. Chichester: Phillimore.

Platt, H. (1983) *City Building in the New South: The Growth of Public Services in Houston, Texas, 1830–1910*. Philadelphia: Temple University Press.

Platt, H. (1991) *The Electric City: Energy and the Growth of the Chicago Area, 1880–1930*. Chicago: University of Chicago Press.

Pratt, E. (1911) *Industrial Causes of Congestion of Population in New York City*. New York: Columbia University Press.

Regional Plan of New York and Its Environs (1974) *Regional Survey of New York and Its Environs*. Vols 1A and 1B. New York: Arno Press.

Reid, P. (1951) *Industrial Decentralization: Detroit Region 1940–1950*. Detroit: Detroit Metropolitan Area Regional Planning Commission.

Schreuder, Y. (1989) Labor segmentation, ethnic division of labor, and residential segregation in American cities in the early twentieth century. *Professional Geographer*, Vol. 41, pp. 131–143.

Schreuder, Y. (1990) The impact of labor segmentation on the ethnic division of labor and the immigrant residential community: Polish leather workers in Wilmington, Delaware in the early twentieth century. *Journal of Historical Geography*, Vol. 16, pp. 402–424.

Schultz, S. (1989) *Constructing Urban Culture: American Cities and City Planning, 1800–1920*. Philadelphia: Temple University Press.

Scott, A. (1982) Locational patterns and dynamics of industrial activity in the modern metropolis, *Urban Studies*, Vol. 19, pp. 111–142.

Scranton, P. (1983) *Proprietary Capitalism: The Textile Manufacture at Philadelphia, 1800–1885*. New York: Cambridge University Press.

Scranton, P. (1989) *Figured Tapestry: Production, Markets and Power in Philadelphia Textiles, 1885–1941*. Cambridge: Cambridge University Press.

Selekman, B., Walter, H. and Couper, W. (1974) The clothing and textile industries, in Regional Plan of New York and Its Environs *Regional Survey of New York and Its Environs*. Vol. 1B. New York: Arno Press.

Silcox, H. (1994) *A Place to Live and Work. The Henry Disston Saw Works and the Tacony Community of Philadelphia*. University Park: Pennsylvania State University Press.

Slater, D. (1961) Decentralization of urban peoples and manufacturing activity in Canada. *Canadian Journal of Economics and Political Science*, Vol. 27, pp. 72–84.

Stelter, G. (1982) The city-building process in Canada, in Stelter, G. and Artibise, A. (eds) *Shaping the Urban Landscape*. Ottawa: Carleton University Press, pp. 1–29.

Stott, R. (1990) *Workers in the Metropolis: Class, Ethnicity and Youth in Antebellum New York City*. Ithaca: Cornell University Press.

Tarr, J. (1984) The evolution of the urban infrastructure in the nineteenth and twentieth centuries, in Hanson, R. (ed.) *Perspectives on Urban Infrastructure*. Washington: National Academy Press. pp. 5–66.

Taylor, G. (1916) *Satellite Cities: a Study of Industrial Suburbs*. New York: Appleton.

Teaford, J. (1979) *City and Suburb. The Political Fragmentation of Metropolitan America, 1850–1970*. Baltimore: Johns Hopkins University Press.

Thomas, L. (1927) *The Localization of Business Activities in Metropolitan St. Louis*. Washington University Studies. New Series. Social and Philosophical Sciences No. 1. St. Louis: Washington University.

Viehe, F. (1981) Black gold suburbs: the influence of the extractive industry on the suburbanization of Los Angeles, 1890–1930. *Journal of Urban History*, Vol. 8, pp. 3–26.

Walker, R. (forthcoming) Industry builds the city: the suburbanization of manufacturing in the San Francisco Bay area, 1850–1945. *Journal of Historical Geography*.

Ward, D. (1971) *Cities and Immigrants*. New York: Oxford University Press.

Warner, S.B. (1962) *Streetcar Suburbs. The Process of Growth in Boston 1870–1900*. Cambridge, MA: Harvard University Press.

Warner, S.B. (1972) *The Urban Wilderness: A History of the American City*. New York: Harper and Row.

Waterhouse, A. (1993) *Boundaries of the City: the Architecture of Western Urbanism*. Toronto: University of Toronto Press.

Weaver, J. (1978) From land assembly to social maturity. The suburban life of Westdale (Hamilton), Ontario, 1911–1951. *Histoire Sociale/ Social History*, Vol. 11, pp. 411–440.

Weiss, M. (1987) *The Rise of the Community Builders. The American Real Estate Industry and Urban Land Planning*. New York: Columbia University Press.

Whitehand, J.W.R. (1987) *The Changing Face of Cities*. Institute of British Geographers Special Publication No. 21. Oxford: Blackwell.

Woodbury, C. (ed.) (1953) *The Future of Cities and Urban Development*. Chicago: Chicago University Press.

Woodbury, C. and Cliffe, F. (1953) Industrial location and urban redevelopment, in Woodbury, C. (ed.) *The Future of Cities and Urban Redevelopment*. Chicago: University of Chicago Press, pp. 102–288.

Wrigley, R. (1949) Organized industrial districts with special reference to the Chicago area. *Journal of Land and Public Utility Economics*, Vol. 23, pp. 180–198.

Zelinsky, W. (1962) Has American industry been decentralizing? The evidence for the 1939–1954 period. *Economic Geography*, Vol. 38, pp. 251–269.

Zunz, O. (1982) *The Changing Face of Inequality: Urbanization, Industrial Development, and Immigrants in Detroit, 1880–1920*. Chicago: University of Chicago Press.

CHAPTER 8

What Women's Spaces? Women in Australian, British, Canadian and US Suburbs

Veronica Strong-Boag, Isabel Dyck, Kim England
and Louise Johnson

Women, families, and suburbia: for more than one hundred years the three
have been intertwined in Australia, Britain, Canada, and the United States.
Suburbs exist in that critical fluid region between city centres and rural spaces.
While individual suburbs may change remarkably over time and range widely
in their specifics, their quintessential representation identifies them as low-
density, family-centred residential spaces, sometimes revealingly characterized
as 'bedroom' or 'dormitory' communities. Although differentiated in many
ways across the four countries, such imagined suburbs lie at the heart of many
discourses about modernity, forecasting either national promise or nightmare.
Women and their work, or, more broadly, gender relations haunt the majority
of these accounts. However, sustained deconstruction of the 'taken-for-granted'
association between women and 'the family' within residential suburbs had to
await the arrival of feminist scholars in the late-twentieth century.

Feminist analysis recasts suburban areas as socio-spatial spaces experienced
differently by women and men, as well as constituted within complex localized
webs of meanings and relationships. Initially, suburban women appeared as
victims of spatial constraints and cultural norms that naturalized their domestic
roles. More recently, women emerge as active agents with diverse experiences of
'suburban life'. The family home remains a central motif, but socio-economic
change and theoretical insights have complicated and challenged long-standing
assumptions. The concept of the home as refuge from paid labour is contested by
studies demonstrating women's experience of it as a domestic, and sometimes
paid, workplace, and by the widespread reality of domestic violence (Hanson and
Pratt, 1995; Johnson, 1981; Matthews, 1984; Pain, 1991). Feminists working
from a post-structuralist perspective are breaking down, universalizing and
essentializing images of women's lives and embracing the simultaneity of gender,
class, 'race'/ethnicity, age, religion, sexuality, and other differences (Johnson,

1994; Weedon, 1987). Such reappraisals require a rethinking of conventional categories: this chapter became not so much an examination of suburbs from the outside in (as is usually the case), but rather from the inside out. Perhaps suburban women and children, but some men as well, see the suburb as central and the city as peripheral to their everyday lives?

What follows provides only a brief survey of feminist thinking about residential suburbs. We highlight the national similarities, as well as some differences, among Australia, Britain, Canada and the United States. The interplay of gender, family, work, and national identity in inner and outer, largely residential, predominantly single-family suburbs from the 1880s to the 1990s is of special interest. Our review is largely limited to what Robert Fishman (1987) describes as 'bourgeois utopias' – suburbs that are low-density, family-oriented 'bedroom communities'. This reflects the pivotal place of these suburbs in assumptions about the creation and preservation of the 'good life' and national identity. We begin with an overview of suburban studies, observing how gender is taken for granted. We move to review women's lives from the 1880s to the 1990s. This is followed by a woman-centred assessment of changing suburbs and reflections on their meaning for women.

CHARACTERIZING 'SUBURBAN STUDIES': MISSING WOMEN

The emergence of distinct residential space around modern cities attracted early attention. Critics of industrialization, such as the Clapham Sect and the Owenites in nineteenth-century Britain, made critical connections between morality and housing removed from the urban core. Citizens of Britain's loyal and rebellious colonies were also ambivalent about cities (Fishman, 1987; Isaacson, 1988). Yet the charms of wilderness (whether they be the Australian bush, Canadian forests, or the United States' plains), regardless of their celebration in national mythologies, were ultimately insufficient. Located between city and country, residential suburbs could partake, their champions hoped, of the virtues of both and the evils of neither. To varying degrees, ideologies about the modern nations of Australia, Britain, Canada, and the United States took shape on the outskirts of cities, fuelled by growing populations, new technologies, and intensely conservative assumptions about the proper relations of classes, 'races', and genders.

Of the four countries, American suburbia seems to exemplify national aspirations most clearly. By the mid-twentieth century, commentators on the United States were remarking that '[s]uburbia symbolizes the fullest, most unadulterated embodiment of contemporary culture' (Jackson, 1985, p. 4). The construction of Levittown on Long Island in the late 1940s ushered in a multitude of social science studies that were often ambivalent about the private and familial preoccupations of modern suburbanites (see, for example, Gans, 1967; Whyte, 1957). The mounting sense of crisis, of a growing gulf between rich and poor, between whites and blacks, was captured in 1967 with the appointment of an ultimately ineffective national task force on the suburbs (Haar, 1974). At the end of the twentieth century, suburbs in the United States are problematized as insecure refuges, confirming national cleavages and calling into question consumer society. Of the four countries, while the United States seems the most ideologically committed to equality, it is also the most devoted to suburban expansion and its deepened gulf between 'haves' and 'have nots' of various kinds.

By contrast, Australian, British and Canadian suburbs have rarely competed with cities and rural areas in the national imagination (notwithstanding Britain's nomination as the birthplace of suburbia in Fishman, 1987, p. 9). In spite of Australians having been largely urban or suburban since the 1850s, an artistic and ideological obsession with the bush has flourished (Ward, 1965; Schaffer, 1988). The island continent was hailed in the nineteenth century as a 'Working Man's Paradise' where high wages, secure employment, abundant land, and easy financing made suburban housing a possibility for many (Johnson, 1984; Davison, 1994). Since at least the 1940s, suburban home ownership has been posited as a vehicle for class mobility and social inclusion for European and, more recently, Asian and Middle Eastern migrant groups (Burnley, 1974; Forster, 1995). Commentators have linked Australian suburbanization to class equality, a home-owning democracy, and monoculturalism rather than to a particular gender order, despite the privileging of the bread-winner family and the differentiation of suburbs by class and, more recently, by ethnicity.

In Canada and Britain, suburbs also appear significant in affirming class and, to a more limited degree, ethnic and racial divisions. While the middle class in the nineteenth century turned to private builders, workers were the preferred beneficiaries of initiatives by both pioneering housing philanthropists such as George Cadbury and W.J. Lever in England, and a few early state initiatives such as Ottawa's Lindenlea suburb after the First World War. Post-1945 'new towns' in Britain and 'corporate suburbs' in Canada reflect a later type of class politics in the two nations (Clark, 1966; Isaacson, 1988). British and Canadian suburbanites are sometimes represented as retreating from industrializing and blighted inner cities, but the desire for improved domestic space has been acknowledged as the stronger influence (see Harris, 1996). Preoccupied with class, and latterly 'race' relations in the city overall, British observers seem to draw few sustained distinctions between core and periphery. In Canada, massive suburban expansion after the Second World War brought the first sustained attention to suburbs of any kind (Clark, 1966). Later studies on Ontario, Quebec, and western Canada confirmed the diversity which S.D. Clark had observed (Doucet and Weaver, 1991; Linteau, 1985). Canadian suburbs tend to evoke particular concern when they further the general unmanageability of cities, but the implications of class or racial divisions are rarely spelled out (see, for example, Lemon, 1996).

Over the course of the century, suburban landscapes have been emblematic of wider developments shaping the nations as a whole. Changes from a walking to a public transport and thence to a private car city occurred at similar times, in the process providing women with new opportunities and constraints. On the other hand, the extent of suburban 'privilege' over city and country ranged tremendously over time and space, as did policies with respect to mortgages, local government, and transportation. Despite very real differences in the structure and support for suburban living, women everywhere were taken for granted as its main custodians and beneficiaries and separated, appropriately enough it was assumed, from male-dominated economic and political activity in the city.

Women's unpaid domestic work underpinned the suburban home as a 'private' haven. Since the 1880s, urban areas have been increasingly designed around the spatial and functional separation of the 'public' from the 'private' sphere. Reinforced by restrictive covenants and by pricing, many (but by no means all) twentieth-century suburbs were marked by cultural, economic, and racial homogeneity. Planners and social scientists have been preoccupied with the cultural and physical shortcomings of post-1945 suburbs (for example Boyd, 1960; Carver, 1962; Gans, 1967; Seeley *et al.*, 1956), while critics of 'mass society' belittled suburban aesthetics and morality (see Thompson, 1982; Strong-Boag, 1991).

Whatever their perspective, early commentators everywhere, with the conspicuous exception of Betty Friedan (1963), generally took suburbia's gendered landscapes for granted. This had changed by the 1980s. Scholars identified women and gender relations as lying near the centre of the early suburban story (Marsh, 1989, 1990; Stilgoe, 1988). The appearance of a special issue of the American journal *Signs* on women and the city (Vol. 5 No. 3, 1980; republished as Stimpson *et al.*, 1981), the Australian special section on 'Feminism and the built environment' in *Urban Policy and Research* (1984), the British book *Geography and Gender* (WGSG, 1984), and the Canadian *Life Spaces. Gender, Household, Employment* (Andrew and Moore-Milroy, 1988) highlight a growing awareness of women's place in the suburbs. Perhaps MATRIX – a British collective of feminist urban designers – best summed up feminist sentiments: 'in the final decision-making, women's real needs, desires and aspirations are not taken as seriously as male-dominated ideas about the "appropriate" house for the family' (MATRIX, 1984, p. 80). At the close of the twentieth century, feminist scholars in all four countries are creating interpretations of suburban space that centre on women's experiences.

THE CHANGING CONTEXT OF WOMEN'S LIVES: 1880s–1990s

The connections between women's everyday lives and suburbia over the century help to shape, and are shaped by, larger demographic, social and economic shifts. In these years, American, Australian, British and Canadian women became increasingly 'modern'. While timing and specifics differed, shifts in women's experiences were, in many ways, transnational in character. For instance, although motherhood and domesticity remained central themes, women's lives were increasingly marked by formal education, paid employment, greater occupational choice, and the hope of (indeed campaign for) more equitable gender relations. Technological changes, such as 'the Pill', also brought major new opportunities for many (Gordon, 1976; McLaren and McLaren, 1985; Mitchell, 1971).

Not all women have shared equally in these changes. Racialized and ethnicized groups, many working-class women, and those with disabilities, among others, have often been deprived of resources and opportunities (for an outstanding effort to make these critical distinctions, see Amott and Matthaei, 1991). Yet, for all the sometimes stark differences in their lives, in the 1990s many women remain caught between demands from the family and their need and desire to earn a cash income.

Throughout the twentieth century, formal educational opportunities have been unequal. Although North American girls have been more likely than those in Australia and Britain to graduate from secondary and post-secondary institutions, opportunities were nowhere equal to their brothers (Prentice and Theobald, 1991; Tyack and Hansot, 1990). Curricula confirmed the 'naturalness' of women's place in the home; for example, domestic science remained a staple in many schools. Girls were also encouraged in more subtle ways to limit ambitions (Arnot, 1986; Gaskell, 1992). The Australian Germaine Greer spoke for many in remembering that to be an intellectual girl during the 1950s meant 'constant recriminations, lamentations that she is missing out on what makes being a girl such fun' (Greer, 1970, pp. 132–133).

Advice from child study experts such as the New Zealander Sir Frederick Truby King, and the American 'baby doctor' Benjamin Spock, reinforced the international gospel of full-time mothering. The spread of Mother's Day signalled motherhood's growing cultural significance throughout the English-speaking world. Its very real demands, particularly the growing expectation that children required extensive maternal supervision, contributed to the century-long drop in fertility, which was only briefly interrupted after the Second World War. Nor were children the only responsibility of women. In the ideal middle-class world, men were full-time wage-earners, women were full-time homemakers and community volunteers. The 'traditional nuclear family' and domestic women were bulwarks against depressions, wars, and economic and political change. In the years after 1945, housewives were popularly represented as essential to western democracy's Cold War (Allport, 1986; Coontz, 1992; Strong-Boag, 1991). On the other hand, the collapse of the Soviet Union, the trend to globalization, and the continuous demographic shift that saw women in Australia, Britain, Canada and the United States marrying later, more likely to divorce, with fewer or no children, meant new roles, and thus new housing needs and desires, for many.

If Americans, Australians, Canadians, and the British treasured the ideal of domesticated womanhood, they also increasingly regarded paid work outside the home as 'real'. Domestic labour, in contrast, had little economic or social value.

Women's paid labour force participation rates in all four countries have increased since the end of the nineteenth century. In the first decades of this century, women's labour force participation rates were around 25 per cent, largely consisting of single women. Flooding into white-collar jobs, teaching and nursing, women changed the urban landscape and their own prospects. In the 1950s and 1960s, the increased employment of married women with older children pushed the rate up. Since then, employment, both full- and part-time, has been fuelled first by women with school-aged children and, more recently, by mothers of pre-schoolers. Now dual earners make up approximately half of all married couples in all four countries (Bowlby, 1990; Frances *et al.*, 1996; Goldin, 1990; Probert, 1990).

Despite increasing participation in wage labour, women often find that male partners do little more domestic labour than those in male breadwinner families (Bittman, 1995; Hanson and Pratt, 1995; Marshall, 1994; Pinch and Storey, 1992). New household technologies promised respite from domestic labour, but did more to change labour's specifics than its extent (Hayden, 1986; Iremonger, 1989; McDaniel, 1993; Matthews, 1984; Schwartz-Cowan, 1983). In the nineteenth and early twentieth centuries, domestic servants lightened the load for some middle-class mistresses. A few 1990s women employ cleaning services and nannies, with the critical difference that the 'mistress' is also likely to be in paid employment. The recent resurgence in paid domestic labour has not, however, changed the more general picture of women performing housework alone and relatively unaided (Arat-Koç, 1995; England and Stiell, 1997; Gregson and Lowe, 1994). This prompts McDaniel (1993, p. 429) to remark that, for dual-earner couples, 'there emerges a 1990s pattern of work outside the home combined with a modified 1950s division of labour at home'.

Women attempt to balance domestic labour and cash requirements in a variety of ways. This helps to explain the steady appeal of part-time work in all countries. Both permanent part-time and casual jobs, as well as seasonal labour, allow time for the family. Also significant, and often ignored (and un- or under-reported) is women's paid labour at home. Women, particularly, but not only, among the poorer classes, have long been accustomed to operating small businesses from their homes, everything from childcare to dressmaking and clerical services. Contributions have often been essential to the family's standard of living (Matthews, 1984; Roberts, 1986; Strong-Boag, 1994). Paid home-based work may sometimes form a natural extension of any other domestic work, or be ultimately irreconcilable (for example Bradbury, 1993; Christensen, 1993; Genovese 1980; Mackenzie, 1987; Oberhauser, 1995). Even for middle-class women, this accommodation is not entirely new (Ahrentzen, 1997), and at the end of the twentieth century paid home-based work shows no signs of diminishing: quite the contrary (Dawson and Wirth, 1989; Driscoll, 1994; Gardner, 1994). Such jobs transform the conventional definition of the paid workplace, unsettling assumptions about what is 'private' and 'public', and further complicate decisions for planners who rely on supposed dichotomies between residential and non-residential uses.

Women active in the late-nineteenth and early-twentieth century urban reform campaigns often focused on mothers and children (Fitzgerald, 1987; Frances *et al.*, 1996; Gittell and Shtob, 1980; Mark-Lawson *et al.*, 1985; Wolfe and Strachen, 1988). Activists strove to upgrade urban and suburban public health, educational and political systems and institutions in efforts to guarantee safer childrearing. In the 1920s and 1930s and later, women founded and led parent-teacher/home and school groups whose ambitions also centred on children's welfare (Pederson, 1996; Sutherland, 1974). The strategy of tying demands to the defence of home and family brought benefits, especially to white women. After the suffrage campaigns of the late nineteenth and early twentieth centuries, however, partisan politics divided female voters in all four nations.

Consciousness of women's oppression never disappeared. Two internationally influential volumes, Simone de Beauvoir's *The Second Sex* (1949) and Betty Friedan's *The Feminine Mystique* (1963), helped to refocus attention. Feminism's second wave first appeared among young American, Australian, British and Canadian women, often students, in the 1960s but spread quickly to other groups. Recognition of the extent of women's poverty and of violence against women and children mobilized large numbers of new feminist activists. By the 1980s they were battling the neo-conservative threat to the social security system and pervasive misogyny (Black, 1993; Dahlerup, 1986; Rowbotham, 1989; Vickers *et al.*, 1993). As it developed, contemporary feminism gave rise to an unprecedented generation of scholars, including those who study the suburbs, committed to the recovery and improvement of women's lives.

SUBURBAN WOMEN IN TRANSITION – SIMILARITIES AND DIFFERENCES

Feminist analyses have recognized the powerful association between gendered human beings and the built environment, and have highlighted the physical and social separation from opportunities and resources of women, particularly mothers of young children. Marsh (1989, 1990) suggests that, by the end of the nineteenth century, suburbs in Britain and the United States were closely associated with the defence of the ideal middle-class family. The spatial separation of 'private' homes and 'public' cities, as captured in the ideas of the Garden City movement, influenced suburban development in the 1920s and 1930s. The ideal of separation was further reinforced with the spread of Le Corbusier's influence after the Second World War. In constructing post-war suburbs, estate agents, government housing agencies, and financiers helped to entrench ideologies of (suburban) homes as 'private' havens, away from the harsh realities of 'public' life. Post-war reconstruction focused on restoring women to the nuclear family, and the family to new housing in suburbs or New Towns, as in Levittown on Long

Island and Aycliffe and Peterlee in County Durham. In Australia, where the rate of home ownership had fallen as a result of rent controls, depression, and war shortages, the Federal Government championed suburban housing ownership for the new world of the Cold War for both the middle class (through the provision of finance) and the working classes (by way of the State housing authorities) (see Allport, 1986, 1987; Kass, 1987).

Heterosexuality was assumed: suburbs (for that matter, like workplaces) were places where heterosexual social relations were enacted and ultimately enforced – not only through social expectation and opprobrium, but also more formally through regulations detailing who has access to housing finance and public housing (Allport, 1986, 1987; Knopp, 1992). In contrast, the inner city became the locale for the expression of diverse sexualities as much as the location of the poor, the newly-arrived immigrant, and the racially marginalized (Knopp, 1992). More generally, the inner city was often regarded as the special site of female sin, a place to be avoided by the would-be 'respectable' (Peiss, 1986; Stansell, 1986; Strange, 1995). In the 1910s, Toronto's middle-class matrons avoided the Ward, an immigrant ghetto, and Hampstead ladies avoided London's East End.

Early on, except for an élite who benefitted from hired-help and the most up-to-date technologies, women felt the constraints of suburban living (Miller, 1983, 1991; Summers, 1977; WGSG, 1984). Certain aspects – transportation services, housing design and location, and provision of childcare, health care delivery and other services – have significantly restricted women (England, 1991; Harman, 1983; Lang, 1992; Pickup, 1984; WISH, 1991). Isolation, both physical and social, has sometimes aggravated loneliness, depression and low self-esteem (Doyal and Elston, 1986; Egar et al., 1985). Recognition of suburbia's short-comings has matured to include consideration of domestic violence (Johnson, 1981; Pain, 1991).

Early house design reflected and reaffirmed traditional gendered divisions of labour. While the bungalows, and in some instances semi-detached housing, simplified aspects of housekeeping, they left the housewife in charge of the kitchen. Later in the century, modernist-inspired designs and layouts typical of ranchers and split levels, large windows, open-plan settings, fire-places, and galley kitchens added to housework's visibility and simultaneously helped raise standards (Adams, 1995; Clark, 1986; Dovey, 1994; Johnson, 1992, McDowell, 1983; Strong-Boag, 1995). Much of this space was to be supervised by women from kitchen 'headquarters'. By contrast, men were much more identified with leisure (in transformed basements), the outdoors (the garage and the garden shed) or space behind closed doors (dens or studies): their task was to recover from paid work. Women acting as families' chief consumers were targeted by advertisers, and they helped to construct a suburban culture with remarkable world-wide similarities (Leslie, 1993; McDowell, 1983; Miller, 1991; Wright, 1993). In homes and catalogues from Adelaide to Regina, Chicago and Manchester, housewives picked through the housewares, furniture, and clothing options presented by modern industry. Australian women's choice of particular styles of home furnishing in the 1950s and 1960s, like those in Toronto in the 1930s (Wright, 1993), marked a place of family security and collective well-being, as well as a showplace of relative prosperity.

The familial ideology tying 'good' women to homes and childrearing was reinforced by transportation systems. Early suburbs, dependent on trolleys, trams, and trains, remained readily connected to their urban centres; but the first generation of married suburban women rarely worked outside the home. Their daughters, in contrast, increasingly could and did. However, the schedules and routes of public transit tend to have been designed to get employees, usually men and single women, to and from downtown workplaces. Public transit planners rarely recognized the much more complicated requirements of housewives and mothers. Australia and, still more, the United States seem to have been especially poorly served (Newman and Kenworthy, 1989).

The low-density, car-dependent suburbs of the 1950s and early 1960s were not initially accompanied by a comparable expansion in female car ownership and drivers' licences. The proliferation of the private automobile thwarted public transportation systems, expanded suburbs, and furthered physical and social isolation (Jackson, 1985). Men's near monopoly of their family's automobile furthered gender differentiation in the experience of urban space. Uniquely privileged, men could move freely, from home to paid work, from domesticated wives to women subordinated in employment. The car became a powerful symbol of freedom. Americans led the four countries in ownership but then too in waste, extravagance and alienation (Newman and Kenworthy, 1989). As Silicon Valley families sometimes confirmed, California emerged as among the fullest expressions of car culture (Fishman, 1987; Stacey, 1990). Although suburban spatial entrapment is less the case in the 1990s, there remains a gender gap. For example, in New South Wales in 1991, 42 per cent of licensed drivers were women, but they had licences at the rate of 75 per cent of men (Lang, 1992).

Home-ownership in a residential suburb remains a goal for many women and men in the four countries (Davison, 1994; Dyck, 1989; Evenden and Walker, 1993; Harris and Hamnett, 1987; Richards, 1994). The ideology of familism, with its support for the traditional nuclear family and different gender roles, has been persistently and firmly linked to this tenure choice. However, well into the 1980s, the prominent image of suburban women was as omnipresent, but near silent, full-time childrearers and homemakers in two-parent, one-car families, hampered by inadequate public transportation, and a lack of local resources and adult company.

In fact, suburban women and landscapes have become both more similar to those found closer to city centres and internally more diverse. In the past, there were significant intra-urban variations in women's labour force participation rates, but rates have converged. In 1951, the rate for women living in Canada's inner cities was 36 per cent greater than that for the metropolitan areas as a whole (a difference probably even higher in earlier decades). By 1981 the gap had narrowed to just 3 per cent (Ram *et al.*, 1989). In North America, older industrial suburbs historically offered some nearby jobs, but local employment has become more readily available in today's 'suburban downtowns' and 'edge cities' (Garreau, 1991; Relph, 1991). Accessible by public and private transport, they (and associated leisure industries) continue to fuel economic growth, and provide employment for women and youth. In Britain, McDowell (1983, p. 67) noted that 'as the economy expanded, the pool of married women on suburban estates proved an attractive and flexible source of labour for light assembly industries that also began to decentralize and expand in the suburbs'. In Australia, office employment has expanded in the more affluent suburbs (Fincher, 1989, 1991). This move has exacerbated class differences, as the decline in manufacturing has hit particular working-class suburbs while office employment has gone to leafy middle-class areas. In the United States, about 60 per cent of all jobs are now located in the suburbs (England, 1993). In 1971, about one-third of Montréal women's workplaces were suburban; by 1981 this was 48 per cent (Rose and Villeneuve, 1993). Despite a greater variety of services and local jobs, suburban women in dual-earner couples and lone mothers in paid employment continue to be especially hindered by the near-absence of public transportation and of accessible, quality childcare (Fincher, 1991, 1993; Truelove, 1996).

In the late-twentieth century, the male breadwinner nuclear family is also challenged especially by lone-parent, blended, and dual wage-earner households and by lesbian, gay, and multi-generational families. While such alternatives have always existed (see, for example, Bradbury, 1993; Faderman, 1981), today their presence is beginning to be acknowledged. Marginalized by dominant discourses of 'the family', they may well experience suburban space differently and encounter special isolation and difficulty (Chan, 1983; Wekerle and Mackenzie, 1986). However, with the exception of mother-led families (Rose and Le Bourdais, 1986), and some work on suburban gay men (Hodge, 1995), relatively little is known about the diversity of contemporary suburban life, and the concomitant reality of women's lives (Baldasarre, 1992).

Suburban diversity has been enhanced by the arrival of different radicalized and ethnicized groups. While the post-1945 immigration waves characterizing Australia and Canada first enriched inner cities, contemporary new immigrants are often suburbanites (Lemon, 1996; Ley *et al.*, 1992; Smart and Smart, 1996). When they turn their attention to today's suburbs, house and neighbourhood designers regularly offer a range of lot and house sizes and types. The large suburban 'migrant' house of Australia and Vancouver's 'monster' home, intended to accommodate extended or larger families, like apartments, townhouses, and condominiums with their somewhat different clientele, provide alternatives to earlier bungalows, ranchers, and split levels (Smart and Smart, 1996; Thompson, 1994). Even high-rise public housing forms part of the suburban landscape in some Canadian cities (Lemon, 1996), as do occasional instances of women's co-operative housing (Wekerle, 1993).

While women have often been identified as especially unhappy (Gans, 1967), neighbourhood satisfaction surveys in the United States in the 1980s also reveal a range of opinion here, with some women preferring suburbs (Spain, 1988). Richards' (1990, 1994) study of 'Green Views', Australia suggests that women find compensations for personal isolation in realizing home ownership in an area good for childrearing, a finding shared in interviews and questionnaires from Canadian veterans of 1950s suburbs (Strong-Boag, 1991; see also Harris 1996). Not surprisingly, women's needs differ according to whether they are commuters or primarily at home childraising, and also according to previous accommodation and (dis)satisfaction with their spouses.

Although traditional 'bourgeois utopias' are now harder to find, familism remains a dominant discourse, constructing understandings of the everyday. As women's wage labour participation rates have increased, contradictions arise between assumptions underpinning suburban communities and the reality of female residents' lives. Homemakers who desire suburban environments for childrearing may be isolated as women wage-earners go out to jobs. Others may face chaotic lifestyles, accommodating the competitions of family life and wage labour (Berry *et al.*, 1996; Bowlby, 1990; Dowling, 1995; Dyck, 1989, 1990, 1996; England, 1993, 1996; Richards, 1994). Increasingly, female suburbanites emerge as creative urban actors rather than merely victims of spatial structures: they actively attempt to renegotiate ways of living, 'the family', the conditions of childraising, and their need/desire for paid employment. For example, Strong-Boag (1991) shows how post-war female suburbanites in Canada campaigned to keep streets safe for their children. Hanson and Pratt's (1995) study of working families in Worcester, Massachusetts, discusses strategies used in addressing familial and economic needs, and Dyck (1989, 1990, 1996) explores how the ideal of motherhood is redefined as women create 'safe' spaces in suburban Vancouver and build social networks to combine childrearing and wage labour (also see England, 1993, 1996; Stacey, 1990). Ideologies distinguishing urban and suburban, employed and 'unemployed' women, and even the 'unrespectable' and the 'respectable', are increasingly brought into question.

SOME FINAL REFLECTIONS

As feminist scholars have directed attention to women in suburban studies, women appear variously as victims and as active agents. In the hundred years covered in this chapter, women's childrearing activities have been central to the negotiation of spatial understandings and arrangements. Suburban spaces have been continuously reconstructed as women moved throughout these landscapes, and between them and centre cities. At the end of the twentieth century, the ideal of familism is again reworked and interpreted. More mothers are trying to weave paid employment into their negotiation of suburban life. Earlier assumptions about the separation of the 'public' and the 'private' spheres are even less appropriate than in the past. Today's suburbs show growing diversity in family, class, and ethnic/'racial' make up.

Continuity, as well as change, shapes suburbs. More than ever, space is implicated in on-going negotiation of social practices and cultural representations such as the 'good mother', 'family' and 'family life'. Throughout the twentieth century, the Australian, British, Canadian and United States governments expanded their provision of health, educational and leisure services, as well as physical infrastructures. Suburbanites have been the chief beneficiaries. In the 1990s, most governments are withdrawing, downsizing, and privatizing; and the private sector increasingly provides (or fails to provide) critical services to those who can pay. Privately supplied services, finding their fullest contemporary expression in the United States, promise to widen the gulf dividing suburbanites from the rest of society. Equally problematic is the re-emergence of an anti-suburban rhetoric and pro-city dwelling hype, also familiar from the 1950s, which blames 'suburbanization' for spiralling urban costs and resulting deficits. Whether women will be able to co-operate in countering the trends toward social fragmentation remains to be seen. Just as in the past, women activists are attempting both to fill in the gaps and to force states to meet the needs of citizens. The result is additional hours of female labour as women seek ways to balance the multiple demands in their lives.

Women's efforts to secure suburbia's advantages for themselves and their children are not unprecedented. In new suburbs throughout the century, women often coped with everything from the lack of sewers to over-crowded schools, limited services, and shortfalls in family income. 'Good mothering' has required active intervention. That requirement has not changed. What has changed is the unprecedented recognition of the *active* role that women play in negotiating and constructing suburban landscapes. Residential suburbs can no longer be understood as isolated enclaves segregated from the 'real' work of the 'public' sphere.

Almost twenty years of feminist scholarship in Australia, Canada, Britain, and the United States emphasizes experiences common to many suburbs in the English-speaking world. Women overwhelmingly come to the suburbs for the sake of children. Once there, some find the burden of being 'good' wives and mothers worsened by a landscape that has regularly ignored them. Those who deviate from the middle-class, 'white bread' ideal have been especially vulnerable. Others have flourished, able to mobilize community and kin resources in ways they experience as rewarding. What we need to know now is whether these patterns hold with respect to the *new* groups and family forms which increasingly distinguish the suburban landscape. That is the work of the future.

What have been the differences among suburbs located in the four nations? Few have cared to ask. This more comparative research is largely in the future. Part of the answer lies in the past, in the way that each country has chosen to make sense of the suburb. Suburbs have loomed larger in some countries and meant different things. To some extent, their physical form differs, as do their ethno-cultural composition, their relationship to central cities, their governance, and their services. In Australia, and especially in the United States, suburban life stands somewhere near the core of the national vision. The Canadian and British situations are more ambiguous. Canadian and British suburbs do not embody the nation in the same way. What might all this mean for women? Depending on their social and political location and their acceptance of prevailing notions of the 'good life', women may well invest somewhat differently in the landscape. Australians and Americans may expect more; Canadians and the British may expect to find something less or merely something different. Although women in all four countries may be held effectively responsible for family and home, their sense of anticipation and enthusiasm, disappointment and guilt reflects, in part at least, the value their society ascribes to the landscape they inhabit. Suburbia's moral terrain may well weigh more heavily in two nations on different continents that in some ways see themselves in suburbia's mirror.

REFERENCES

Adams, A. (1995) The Eichler home: intention and experience in postwar suburbia, in Cromley, E.C. and Hudgins, C.L. (eds.) *Gender, Class, and Shelter. Perspectives in Vernacular Architecture, V*. Knoxville: University of Tennessee Press, pp. 164–178.

Ahrentzen, S.B. (1997) The meaning and materiality of home workplaces for women, in Jones, J.P., Nast, H. and Roberts, S. (eds.) *Thresholds in Feminist Geography: Difference, Methodology, and Representation*. Lanham, Maryland: Rowman and Littleford.

Allport, C. (1986) Women and suburban housing: post-war planning in Sydney, 1943–61, in McLoughlin, J.B. and Huxley, M. (eds) *Urban Planning in Australia: Critical Readings*. Melbourne: Longman Cheshire, pp. 233–250.

Allport, C. (1987) Castles of security: the New South Wales Housing Commission and home ownership, 1941–1961, in Kelly, M. (ed.) *Sydney: City of Suburbs*. Sydney: New South Wales University Press in association with the Sydney History Group, pp. 95–124.

Amott, T. and Matthaei, J. (1991) *Race, Gender and Work. A Multicultural Economic History of Women in the United States*. Boston: South End Press.

Andrew, C. and Moore-Milroy, B. (1988) *Life Spaces. Gender, Household, Employment*. Vancouver: University of British Colombia Press.

Arat-Koç, S. (1995) The politics of family and immigration in the subordination of domestic workers in Canada, in Nelson, E.D. and Robinson B.W. (eds.) *Gender in the 1990s. Images, Realities, and Issues*. Toronto: Nelson Canada, pp. 413–442.

Armstrong, P. and Armstrong, H. (1994) *The Double Ghetto. Canadian Women and Their Segregated Work*. Toronto: McClelland and Stewart.

Arnot, M. (1986) State education policy and girls' educational experiences, in Beechey, V. and Whitelegg, E. (eds.) *Women in Britain Today*. Milton Keynes: Open University Press, pp. 132–172.

Baldasarre, M. (1992) Suburban communities. *Annual Review of Sociology*, Vol. 18, pp. 475–494.

Berry, M., Kerkin, K., Jackson, J. and Johnson, L. (1996) *The Social Production of Outer Suburbia*. Canberra: Australian Government Publishing Service.

Bittman, M. (1995) *Recent Changes in Unpaid Work*. Occasional Paper ABS Catalogue No. 4154.0. Canberra: Australian Government Publishing Service.

Black, N. (1993) The Canadian women's movement: the second wave, in Burt, S., Corde, L. and Dorney, L. (eds.) *Changing Patterns*. Toronto: McClelland and Stewart, pp. 151–176.

Bowlby, S. (1990) Women, work and the family: control and constraints. *Geography*, Vol. 15, Part 1, pp. 17–26.

Boyd, R. (1960) *The Australian Ugliness*. Melbourne: Cheshire.

Bradbury, B. (1993) *Working Families: Age, Gender and Daily Survival in Industrializing Montreal*. Toronto: McClelland and Stewart.

Burnley, I. (1974) *Urbanization in Australia: The Post-War Experience*. Cambridge: Cambridge University Press.

Carver, H. (1962) *Cities in the Suburbs*. Toronto: University of Toronto Press.

Chan, K.B. (1983) Coping with aging and managing self-identity: the social world of the elderly Chinese woman. *Canadian Ethnic Studies*, Vol. 15, No. 3, pp. 36–56.

Christensen, K. (1993) Eliminating the journey to work: home-based work across the life course of women in the United States, in Katz, C. and Monk, J. (eds.) *Full Circles: Geographies of Women over the Life Course*, London: Routledge, pp. 55–87.

Clark, C.E. Jr. (1986) *The American Family Home, 1800–1960*. Chapel Hill: University of North Carolina Press.

Clark, S.D. (1966) *The Suburban Society*. Toronto: University of Toronto Press.

Coontz, S. (1992) *The Way We Never Were. American Families and the Nostalgia Trap*. New York: Basic Books.

Dahlerup, D. (1986) *The New Women's Movement: Feminism and Political Power in Europe and the USA*. London: Sage.

Davison, G. (1994) The past and the future of the Australian suburb, in Johnson, L.C. (ed.) *Suburban Dreaming: An Interdisciplinary Approach to Australian Cities*. Geelong: Deakin University Press, pp. 99–113.

Dawson, W. and Wirth, L. (1989) *When She Goes to Work She Stays at Home*. Canberra: Department of Employment, Education and Training.

de Beauvoir, S. (1949) *The Second Sex*. New York: Vintage Books.

Doucet, M. and Weaver, J. (1991) *Housing the North American City*. Montreal: McGill-Queen's University Press.

Dovey, K. (1994) Dreams on display: suburban ideology in the model home, in Ferber, S., Healy, C. and McAuliffe, C. (eds.) *Beasts of Suburbia*. Melbourne: Melbourne University Press, pp. 127–147.

Dowling, R.M. (1995) Placing Identities: Family, Class and Gender in Surrey, British Columbia. Unpublished Ph.D. thesis, University of British Columbia.

Doyal, L. and Elston, M.A. (1986) Women, health and medicine, in Beechey, V. and Whitelegg, E. (eds.) *Women in Britain Today*. Milton Keynes: Open University Press, pp. 173–209.

Driscoll, J. (1994) *Financially Yours: Women who Work from Home*. Monograph No. 3. Geelong: Australian Women's Research Centre.

Dyck, I. (1989) Integrating home and wage workplace: women's daily lives in a Canadian suburb. *The Canadian Geographer*, Vol. 33, No. 4, pp. 329–341.

Dyck, I. (1990) Space, time and renegotiating motherhood: an exploration of the domestic workplace. *Environment and Planning D: Society and Space*, Vol. 8, pp. 459–483.

Dyck, I (1996) Mother or worker?: women's support networks, local knowledge and informal child care strategies, in England, K. (ed.) *Who Will Mind the Baby? Geographies of Child Care and Working Mothers*. London: Routledge, pp. 123–140.

Egar, R., Sarkissian, W., Male, D. and Hartmann, L. (1985) Coping with the suburban nightmare: developing community supports in Australia. *Sociological Focus*, Vol. 18, pp. 119–125.

England, K. (1991) Gender relations and the spatial structure of the city. *Geoforum*, Vol. 22, No. 2, pp. 135–147.

England, K. (1993) Changing suburbs, changing women: geographic perspectives on suburbanization and the everyday lives of suburban women. *Frontiers: A Journal of Women's Studies*, Vol. 14, No. 1, pp. 24–43.

England, K. (1996) Mothers, wives, workers: the everyday lives of working mothers, in England, K. (ed.) *Who Will Mind the Baby? Geographies of Child Care and Working Mothers*. London: Routledge, pp. 109–122.

England, K. and Stiell, B. (1997) 'They think you're as stupid as your English is': constructing foreign domestic workers in Toronto. *Environment and Planning A*, Vol. 29, No. 2, pp. 195–215.

Evenden, L.J. and Walker, G.E. (1993) From periphery to centre: the changing geography of the suburbs, in Bourne, L. and Ley, D. (eds.) *A Social Geography of the Canadian City*. Kingston: McGill-Queen's University Press, pp. 234–251.

Faderman, L. (1981) *Surpassing the Love of Men. Romantic Friendship and Love Between Women from the Renaissance to the Present*. London: Junction Books.

Fincher, R. (1989) Class and gender relations in the local labor market and the local state, in Wolch, J. and Dear, M. (eds.) *The Power of Geography: How Territory Shapes Social Life*. London: Unwin Hyman, pp. 93–117.

Fincher, R. (1991) Caring for workers' dependents: gender, class and local state practice in Melbourne. *Political Geography Quarterly*, Vol. 10, No. 4, pp. 356–381.

Fincher, R. (1993) Women, the state and the life course in urban Australian, in Katz, C. and Monk, J. (eds.) *Full Circles: Geographies of Women over the Life Course*, London: Routledge, pp. 243–263.

Fishman, R. (1987) *Bourgeois Utopias: The Rise and Fall Of Suburbia*. New York: Basic Books.

Fitzgerald, S. (1987) *Rising Damp: Sydney 1870–90*. Melbourne: Oxford University Press.

Forster, C. (1995) *Australian Cities: Continuity and Change*. Melbourne: Oxford University Press.

Frances, R., Kealey, L. and Sangster, J. (1996) Women and wage labour in Australia and Canada, 1880–1980. *Labour History/Le Travail*, Vol. 71, pp. 54–89.

Friedan, B. (1963) *The Feminine Mystique*. New York: Norton.

Gans, H. (1967) *The Levittowners: Ways of Life and Politics in a New Suburban Community*. New York: Pantheon.

Gardner, A. (1994) *The Self-Employed*. 'Focus on Canada' series, Statistics Canada. Scarborough, Ontario: Prentice Hall.

Garreau, J. (1991) *Edge City: Life on the New Frontier*. New York: Doubleday.

Gaskell, J. (1992) *Gender Matters from School to Work*. Toronto: OISE Press.

Genovese, R.G. (1980) A women's self-help network as a response to service needs in the suburbs. *Signs*, Vol. 5, pp. S248–256.

Gittell, M. and Shtob, T. (1980) Changing women's roles in political volunteerism and reform of the city. *Signs*, Vol. 5, pp. S67–78.

Goldin, C. (1990) *Understanding the Gender Gap: An Economic History of American Women*. New York: Oxford University Press.

Gordon, L. (1976) *Woman's Body, Woman's Right: A Social History of Birth Control in America*. New York: Grossman.

Greer, G. (1970) *The Female Eunuch*. London: MacGibbon and Keen.

Gregson, N. and Lowe, M. (1994) *Servicing the Middle Classes: Class, Gender and Waged Domestic Labour in Contemporary Britain*. London: Routledge.

Haar, C.M. (ed.) (1974) *Final Report*. Cambridge, MA: Ballinger.

Hanson, S. and Pratt, G. (1995) *Gender, Work, and Space*. London: Routledge.

Harman, E. (1983) Capitalism, patriarchy and the city, in Baldock, C.V. and Cass, B. (eds.) *Women, Social Welfare and the State in Australia*. Sydney: Allen and Unwin, pp. 104–129.

Harris, R. (1996) *Unplanned Suburbs. Toronto's American Tragedy, 1900–1950*. Baltimore: Johns Hopkins University Press.

Harris, R. and Hamnett, C. (1987) The myth of the promised land: the social diffusion of home ownership in Britain and North America. *Annals of the Association of American Geographers*, Vol. 77, No. 2, pp. 173–190.

Hayden, D. (1986) *Redesigning the American Dream: The Future of Housing, Work and Family Life*. New York: Norton.

Hodge, S. (1995) 'No fags out there': gay men, identity and suburbia. *Journal of Interdisciplinary Gender Studies*, Vol. 1, No. 1, pp. 41–48.

Iremonger, D. (1989) *Households Work*. Sydney: Allen and Unwin.

Isaacson, P. (1988) *The Garden City and New Towns: Ideology and the British New Towns Policy, 1800–1970*. Lund: Department of Economic History, University of Lund.

Jackson, K.T. (1985) *Crabgrass Frontier: The Suburbanization of the United States*. New York: Oxford University Press.

Johnson, L. (1984) *Gaslight Sydney*. Sydney: Allen and Unwin.

Johnson, L. (1992) Housing desire: a feminist geography of suburban housing. *Refractory Girl*, Vol. 42, pp. 40–46.

Johnson, L. (1994) Colonizing the suburban frontier: place-making on Melbourne's urban fringe, in Gibson, K. and Watson, S. (eds.) *Metropolis Now: Planning and the Urban in Contemporary Australia*. Sydney: Pluto, pp. 46–59.

Johnson, V. (1981) *The Last Resort: A Women's Refuge*. Melbourne: Penguin.

Kass, T. (1987) Cheaper than rent: aspects of the growth of owner occupation in Sydney, 1911–1966, in Kelly, M. (ed.) *Sydney: City of Suburbs*. Sydney: University of New South Wales Press, pp. 77–94.

Knopp, L. (1992) Sexuality and the spatial dynamics of capitalism. *Environment and Planning D: Society and Space*, Vol. 10, pp. 651–669.

Lang, J. (1992) Women and transport. *Urban Policy and Research*, Vol. 10, No. 4, pp. 14–25.

Lemon, J. (1996) *Liberal Dreams and Nature's Limits: Great Cities of North America Since 1600*. Toronto: Oxford University Press.

Leslie, D. (1993) Femininity, post-Fordism, and the 'new traditionalism'. *Environment and Planning D: Society and Space*, Vol. 11, pp. 689–708.

Ley, D., Hiebert, D. and Pratt, G. (1992) Time to grow up? from urban village to world city, 1966–91, in Wynn, G. and Oke, T. (eds.) *Vancouver and its Region*, Vancouver: University of British Columbia Press, pp. 234–266.

Linteau, P.A. (1985) *The Promoter's City*. Toronto: Lorimer.

Mackenzie, S. (1987) Women's responses to economic restructuring: changing gender, changing space, in Hamilton, R. and Barrett, M. (eds.) *The Politics of Diversity: Feminism, Marxism And Nationalism*. London: Verso, pp. 81–100.

Mark-Lawson, J., Savage, M. and Warde, A. (1985) Gender and local politics: struggles over welfare policies, 1918–1939, in Murgatroyd, L. and the Lancaster Regionalism Group (eds.) *Localities, Class and Gender*. London: Pion, pp. 195–215.

Marsh, M. (1989) From separation to togetherness: the social construction of domestic space in American suburbs, 1840–1915. *Journal of American History*, Vol. 76, pp. 506–527.

Marsh, M. (1990) *Suburban Lives*. New Brunswick: Rutgers University Press.

Marshall, K. (1994) Household chores, in Thompson, K. (ed.) *Canadian Social Trends: A Canadian Studies Reader* (Volume 2). Toronto: Thompson.

MATRIX Collective (1984) *Making Space. Women and the Man-Made Environment*. London: Pluto Press.

Matthews, J.J. (1984) *Good and Mad Women: The Historical Construction of Femininity in Twentieth Century Australia*. Sydney: George Allen and Unwin.

McDaniel, S.M. (1993) The changing Canadian family, in Burt, S., Code, L. and Dorney, L. (eds.) *Changing Patterns: Women in Canada*. Toronto: McClelland and Stewart, pp. 422–451.

McDowell, L. (1983) Towards an understanding of the gender division of urban space. *Environment and Planning D: Society and Space*, Vol. 1, pp. 59–72.

McLaren, A. and McLaren, A.T. (1985) *The Bedroom and the State: The Changing Practices and Politics of Contraception and Abortion in Canada, 1880–1980*. Toronto: McClelland and Stewart.

Miller, R. (1983) The Hoover in the garden: middle-class women and suburbanization, 1850–1920. *Environment and Planning D: Society and Space*, Vol. 1, pp. 73–87.

Miller, R. (1991) Selling Mrs. Consumer: advertising and the creation of suburban socio-spatial relations, 1910–1930. *Antipode*, Vol. 23, No. 3, pp. 263–301.

Mitchell, J. (1971) *Woman's Estate*. New York: Vintage.

Newman, P.W.G. and Kenworthy, J.R. (1989) Gasoline consumption and cities: a comparison of U.S. cities with a global survey. *Journal of the American Planning Association*, Vol. 55, No. 1, pp. 24–37.

Oberhauser, A.M. (1995) Gender and household economic strategies in rural Appalachia. *Gender, Place and Culture*, Vol. 2, No. 1, pp. 51–70.

Pain, R. (1991) Space, sexual violence and social control: integrating geographical and feminist analyses of women's fear of crime. *Progress in Human Geography*, Vol. 15, No. 4, pp. 415–431.

Pederson, D. (1996) Providing a woman's conscience: the YWCA, female evangelicalism, and the girl in the city, 1870–1930, in Mitchinson, W., Bourne, P., Prentice, A., Cuthburt-Brandt, G., Light, B. and Black, N. (eds.) *Canadian Women: A Reader*. Toronto: Harcourt Brace Canada, pp. 194–210.

Peiss, K.L. (1986) *Cheap Amusements: Working Women and Leisure in Turn-of-the-Century New York*. Philadelphia: Temple University Press.

Pickup, L. (1984) Women's gender-role and its influence on their travel behaviour. *Built Environment*, Vol. 10, No. 1, pp. 61–68.

Pinch, S. and Storey, A. (1992) Who does what, where? A household survey of the division of domestic labour in Southampton. *Area*, Vol. 24, No. 1, pp. 5–12.

Prentice, A. and Theobald, M. (eds.) (1991) *Women Who Taught: Perspectives on the History of Women and Teaching*. Toronto: University of Toronto Press.

Probert, B. (1990) *Working Life*. Ringwood, Victoria: McPhee Gribble.

Ram, B., Norris, M.J., and Skof, K. (1989) *The Inner City in Transition*. Ottawa: Supply and Services Canada.

Relph, E. (1991) Suburban downtowns of the Greater Toronto area. *Canadian Geographer*, Vol. 35, No. 4, pp. 421–425.

Richards, L. (1990) *Nobody's Home: Dreams and Realities in a New Suburb*. Melbourne: Oxford University Press.

Richards, L. (1994) Suburbia: domestic dreaming, in Johnson, L.C. (ed.) *Suburban Dreaming: An Interdisciplinary Approach to Australian Cities*. Geelong: Deakin University Press, pp. 114–128.

Roberts, E. (1986) Women's strategies, 1890–1940, in Lewis, J. (ed.) *Labour and Love: Women's Experience of Home and Family, 1850–1940*. Oxford: Blackwell.

Rose, D. and Le Bourdais, C. (1986) The changing conditions of female single parenthood in Montreal's inner city and suburban neighbourhoods. *Urban Resources*, Vol. 3, No. 2, pp. 45–52.

Rose, D. and Villeneuve, P. (1993) Work, labour markets, and households in transition, in Bourne, L.S. and Ley, D.F. (eds.) *The Changing Social Geography of Canadian Cities*, Montreal: McGill-Queen's University Press, pp. 153–174.

Rowbotham, S. (1989) *The Past is Before Us. Feminism in Action since the 1960s*. London: Penguin.

Schaffer, K. (1988) *Women and the Bush: Forces of Desire in the Australian Cultural Tradition*. Cambridge: Cambridge University Press.

Schwartz-Cowan, R. (1983) *More Work for Mother: The Ironies of Household Technology from the Open Hearth to the Microwave*. New York: Basic Books.

Seeley, J.R., Sim, R.A. and Loosley, E.W. (1956) *Crestwood Heights: A Study of the Culture Of Suburban Life*. Toronto: University of Toronto Press.

Smart, A. and Smart, J. (1996) Monster homes: Hong Kong immigration to Canada, urban conflicts, and contested representations of space, in Caulfield, J. and Peake, L. (eds.) *City Lives and City Forms: Critical Research and Canadian Urbanism*. Toronto: University of Toronto Press, pp. 33–46.

Spain, D. (1988) The effect of changing household composition on neighborhood satisfaction. *Urban Affairs Quarterly*, Vol. 23, No. 4, pp. 581–600.

Stacey, J. (1990) *Brave New Families: Stories of Domestic Upheaval in Late Twentieth Century America*. New York: Basic Books.

Stansell, C. (1986) *City of Women: Sex and Class in New York, 1789–1860*. New York: Knopf.

Stilgoe, J.R. (1988) *Borderland: Origins of the American Suburb, 1820–1939*. New Haven: Yale University Press.

Stimpson, C., Dixler, E., Nelson, M. and Yatrakis, K. (eds.) (1981) *Women and the American City*. Chicago: University of Chicago Press.

Strange, C. (1995) *Toronto's Girl Problem: The Perils and Pleasures of the City*. Toronto: University of Toronto Press.

Strong-Boag, V. (1991) Home dreams: women and the suburban experiment in Canada, 1945–60. *Canadian Historical Review*, Vol. 72, No. 4, pp. 471–504.

Strong-Boag, V. (1994) Canada's wage-earning wives and the construction of the middle class, 1945–60. *Journal of Canadian Studies*, Vol. 29, No. 3, pp. 5–25.

Strong-Boag, V. (1995) 'Their side of the story': women's voices from Ontario suburbs, 1945–60, in Parr, J. (ed.) *A Diversity of Women*. Toronto: University of Toronto Press, pp. 46–74.

Strong-Boag, V. (1996) Independent women, problematic men: first and second wave anti-feminism in Canada from Goldwin Smith to Betty Steele. *Histoire sociale/Social History*, Vol. XXIX, No. 57, pp. 1–22.

Summers, A. (1977) *Damned Whores and God's Police: The Colonization of Women in Australia*. Ringwood, Victoria: Penguin.

Sutherland, N. (1974) *Children in English-Canadian Society*. Toronto: University of Toronto Press.

Thompson, F.M.L. (1982) Introduction: the rise of suburbia, in Thompson, F.M.L. (ed.) *The Rise of Suburbia*. Leicester: Leicester University Press.

Thompson, S. (1994) Suburbs of opportunity: the power of home for migrant women, in Gibson, K. and Watson, S. (eds.) *Metropolis Now: Planning and the Urban in Contemporary Australia*. Sydney: Pluto, pp. 33–45.

Truelove, M. (1996) The locational context of child care centers in metropolitan Toronto, in England, K. (ed.) *Who Will Mind the Baby? Geographies of Child Care and Working Mothers*. London: Routledge, pp. 93–108.

Tyack, D. and Hansot, E. (1990) *Learning Together. A History of Coeducation in American Public Schools*. New York: Russell Sage Foundation.

Vickers, J., Rankin, P., and Appelle, C. (1993) *Politics as if Women Mattered*. Toronto: University of Toronto Press.

Ward, R. (1965) *The Australian Legend*. Melbourne: Oxford University Press.

Weedon, C. (1987) *Feminist Practice and Poststructuralist Theory*, Oxford: Blackwell.

Wekerle, G. and Mackenzie, S. (1986) Reshaping the neighborhood of the future as we age in place. *Canadian Woman Studies/Les cahiers de la femme*, Vol. 6, No. 2, pp. 69–72.

Wekerle, G.R. (1993) Responding to diversity: housing developed by and for women. *Canadian Journal of Urban Research*, Vol. 2, No. 2, pp. 95–111.

WGSG (Women and Geography Study Group of the Institute of British Geographers) (1984) *Geography and Gender: An Introduction to Feminist Geography*. London: Hutchinson.

Whyte W. (1957) *The Organization Man*. Garden City, N.Y.: Doubleday.

WISH (Women In Supportive Housing) (1991) *Speaking of Housing . . . A Report on a Consultation with Victorian Women on Housing for the Minister of Planning and Housing*. Victoria: WISH.

Wolfe, J. and Strachan, G. (1988) Practical idealism: women in urban reform: Julia Drummond and the Montreal Parks and Playgrounds Association, in Andrew, C. and Moore-Milroy, B. (eds.) *Life Spaces. Gender, Household, Employment*. Vancouver: University of British Colombia Press, pp. 65–80.

Wright, C. (1993) *The Most Prominent Rendezvous of the Feminine Toronto: Eaton's College Street and the Organization of Shopping in Toronto, 1920–1950*. Unpublished Ph.D. thesis. University of Toronto.

CHAPTER 9

'Gloria Soame': The Spread of Suburbia in Post-War Australia

Tony Dingle

In the late nineteenth century, Australian painters and nationalist writers looked increasingly to the bush and to those who lived there in their search for the essential Australia. Most of these artists were city dwellers in what had already become an urbanized nation, but they were unable or unwilling to create an urban myth which could capture the imagination: indeed, many of them recoiled from the squalour of the city (Davison, 1978). Australians continued to look to the outback in search of their distinctiveness. Historian Russel Ward, in his influential *The Australian Legend* (1958), celebrated the male bush worker as the typical Australian; laconic, practical, easy going, egalitarian and anti-authoritarian. More recently, this myth has been commercialized. It has been used in successful advertising campaigns to attract tourists to Australia, sometimes using Paul Hogan, the Sydney comedian and actor whose *Crocodile Dundee* films projected the same message overseas. No urban or suburban myths have succeeded in capturing the popular imagination in this way, but they have been created in the second half of the twentieth century in belated recognition of the essentially suburban nature of life in Australia. These have been as savage and hostile as the 'typical Australian' has been amiable.

Edna Everage became Australian suburbia's most famous inhabitant, especially once she became a Dame and a superstar and appeared regularly on television in Britain and America to mock her home, her neighbours and the emptiness of a married woman's life in suburbia. The typical suburban man was described by Allan Ashbolt in an often-quoted passage.

> Behold the man – the Australian man of today – on Sunday morning in the suburbs, when the high-decibel drone of the motor-mower is calling the faithful to worship. A block of land, a brick veneer, and the motor-mower beside him in the wilderness – what more does he want to sustain him, except a few beers with the boys, marital sex on Saturday nights, a few furtive adulteries, an occasional gamble on the horses or the lottery, the tribal rituals of football, the flickering shadows in the lounge-room . . . (Ashbolt, 1966, p. 323)

There were other critics of suburbia in the 1960s. They complained of the visual ugliness, the intellectual, cultural and spiritual poverty, and the conformity of the place and of the people who lived there (Gilbert, 1988). Their criticisms were sharpened by the realization that, in the words of Robin Boyd, architect and critic, 'the suburb was the major element of Australian society'. He defined suburbia as 'a half-world between city and country in which most Australians lived', and regretted that 'in a land of rolling plains and wide blue skies, a race of cheerful agoraphobes grew up in little weather-sealed boxes' (Boyd, 1987, pp. 4–5).[1] As he wrote in the early 1950s, more Australians than ever before were choosing to go to the furthest reaches of suburbia to create their 'gloria soame' on a rectangular quarter-acre block of land, enclosed on three sides by high paling fences.[2]

URBAN DEMOGRAPHICS

Australia's population rose from 7,579,358 in 1947, the year of the first post-war census, to 17,292,000 in 1991. Already, by 1947, a highly urbanized society, 69 per cent of the population lived in towns and cities. This proportion grew rapidly during the next few years to 82 per cent in 1961 and a peak of 86 per cent by the mid-1970s; although since then it has fallen back fractionally. Most of these urban dwellers have lived in either Sydney, Melbourne, Brisbane, Adelaide, Perth or Hobart, the capital cities of the six states of the Australian federation; half of them did so by 1947, rising to about 65 per cent by 1961 before again dropping slightly below this subsequently. It is these capital cities upon which this chapter focuses, for it has been here that suburbia in Australia has spread and flourished, but such developments have also been experienced on a lesser scale in the smaller cities. All of the capital cities have at least doubled in size since the end of the Second World War, with the most rapid growth coming before the 1970s; Perth has quadrupled its population in this period. They differ greatly in size. Sydney and Melbourne, with metropolitan populations today of three and a half and three millions respectively are large cities, followed at a considerable distance by Brisbane, Adelaide and Perth, all with one to one and a half million people. Hobart has not grown rapidly during the twentieth century and, at less than 200,000, has long been smaller than Newcastle, Gold Coast, the national capital Canberra, and Wollongong. Nevertheless, since the 1970s, two in every three Australians have lived in one or other of these capital cities, two in every five of them in Sydney and Melbourne.

Natural increase and internal and overseas migration have all made some contribution to urbanization, but their relative importance has changed over time and from one city to another. Broadly, immigration was more important than natural increase in fuelling urban growth up to the 1970s. Sydney and Melbourne have gained most from overseas immigration, much of it from Italy, Greece and other parts of Europe from where few migrants had come previously, and latterly from south-east Asia. This has been counterbalanced somewhat by a net outflow of Australian born, particularly during the last three decades. Adelaide and Perth also experienced big inflows of foreign migrants, but from predominantly British backgrounds. They were also the main beneficiaries of the internal migrations of the Australian born, along with Brisbane (Neutze, 1981; Burnley, 1974; Merrett, 1978).

Movements within cities are somewhat more difficult to identify than those into and out of cities, but the overall picture is clear. From the late 1940s, population growth was highest in the newest suburbs on the urban fringe, as they filled rapidly with people and houses. The main engine of growth was out-migration of young adults from the inner and middle suburbs where they had grown up, to build a home and start a family. They did so in sufficient numbers to halt population growth in their parents' suburbs and also to push birth rates in the outer suburbs well above the metropolitan average. In both Sydney and Melbourne by the early 1970s, the outer ring of suburbs, broadly defined as those which had developed since the war, already held around half of the total population of both cities (Maher, 1982; Neutze, 1981, p. 31). This outward movement appears to be a repetitive and generational pattern. The offspring of the young couples who moved in the 1950s and 1960s are themselves moving further out in the 1980s and 1990s, from what have become middle suburbs to the new suburban frontier. In the process, they are stimulating rapid growth in the new suburbs and also starting a population decline in the early post-war suburbs where they grew up. These movements have given Australian suburbs a distinctive demographic life cycle which has been analysed by Max Neutze. The graph of population growth over time in each local government area is roughly S-shaped, with an initial period of very rapid early growth giving way to a phase of slower growth leading to a population peak around 30–40 years later. This is then followed by a slow but immediate decline rather than a plateau. There have been enormous variations in the rapidity of this growth, with some areas sustaining population growth rates of more than 8 per cent per year for several decades, while others have filled up at less than a quarter of that rate (Neutze, 1981, pp. 69–77; Dingle, 1996).

THE RUSH TO THE SUBURBS: MOTIVES AND MEANS

In the decades after the end of the Second World War, many countries faced the challenge of deciding where their growing urban populations should live. Britain, for example, chose to create new towns and also to build high-density accommodation within existing cities; while, in the United States, low-density suburbs of detached homes were built outside city boundaries. Australia, whose urban population grew at a faster rate than Britain's, chose this latter approach.[3] This has sometimes been explained as the result of a lack of planning and foresight which allowed developers to do as they wished, but this ignores the many pressures and inducements which drew people out to suburbia. The most obvious attraction was the force of tradition. Almost from the beginning of European settlement, people chose to live in suburbs, giving Australia strong claims to being the pioneer suburban nation (Davison, 1994). During the late nineteenth century and again in the building boom of the 1920s, people opted to buy their own detached house in the suburbs if they could afford it. By the 1920s, State governments were actively trying to increase the number of those who could afford suburbia by offering subsidized housing loans to low-income earners.

The Depression of the 1930s halted the growth of suburbia. The building industry was slow to recover and had not reached pre-depression levels of output in most areas when the Second World War brought a complete halt to residential building. There was a serious housing shortage at the end of the War, the result of fifteen years of population growth which had not been matched by increases in the housing stock. People of modest means who might normally have expected to have a home of their own in suburbia, as their parents had done before them, had been forced instead to live with their parents or in rented rooms. High-density living in flats was considered to be decadent, European, something from which people escaped when they migrated to Australia. This message was strengthened by housing reformers, who equated slums with high-density living. There was some justification for this, as people looking for accommodation during the Depression had gone to the old inner suburbs, cramming themselves into what was already often overcrowded and substandard housing (Howe, 1988).

The whole thrust of public health and housing reform had long been to give people space both within the home and between houses, so that air could circulate and light enter, and germs would not find their hosts in too close proximity to each other (this can be contrasted with the critics of suburbia mentioned earlier, some of whom assumed that urban areas grew more interesting and culturally and intellectually stimulating in direct proportion to their population density). The perceived benefits of suburbia were reiterated after the war. Physically, economically, morally and psychologically, this was a superior environment for living. Life expectancy was higher than in the city because people were far away from polluted industrial areas. Widespread home ownership would distribute national wealth more evenly, making another depression less likely, it was claimed (Chapman, 1944). The moral degradation of city life, which fascinated artists such as Albert Tucker, was also absent in the suburbs. Instead there was 'air, sun, comfort and quiet', in the words of a Melbourne planning exhibition of 1943 (Darian Smith, 1990, p. 112). Sydney psychologist Henry Lovell reinforced the preference for low-density living when he argued in a report to the Commonwealth Housing Commission that space was vital for personal well-being; 'a man deprived of space is reduced in stature' (Brown, 1995, p. 128). Ownership of space generated self-respect, contentment and responsible citizenship. This was something which conservative politicians well understood. Robert Menzies, a past and future prime minister in 1942 when he made his 'Forgotten People' speech on radio, believed that the 'real life' of the nation was to be found 'in the homes of the people', and he had in mind the suburban house owned by its occupant. The home was 'the foundation of sanity and sobriety . . . the indispensable condition of continuity; its health determines the health of the nation as a whole' (Menzies, 1943; Brett, 1992). During the boom years of the 1950s and 1960s, his governments consistently supported the interests of suburban home owners and those aspiring to that state, although this concern did not extend to adequate financing of public infrastructure.

Motive was matched by an ability to pay. The widespread employment of women and increasingly full employment of men during the war was combined with rationing and a lack of consumer goods on which to spend this income. The result was a high level of wartime saving. After 1945, young men and women used their savings to buy subdivided suburban building land and to put a deposit on the dream home they would buy or build once they were married. While there were serious shortages of materials and labour for at least a decade after the war, this initial burst of post-war spending kick-started the building industry. With only minor, cyclical, interruptions it then maintained high levels of activity until the boom ended in the early 1970s. Conditions could hardly have been more favourable. Real household incomes per head rose at more than 1 per cent per year during the 1950s, rising to nearly 4 per cent during the 1960s and early 1970s, while levels of unemployment hovered around 1 per cent throughout. Furthermore, the distribution of incomes was probably less unequal than it had been (Boehm, 1993, p. 325; Jones, 1975).

This prosperity owed much to the growth of manufacturing as the Australian economy finally industrialized. By the early 1950s, 40 per cent of the jobs in Melbourne and 37 per cent of those in Sydney were in manufacturing. Even in the least industrialized cities of Brisbane, Perth and Hobart, over a quarter of all jobs were in manufacturing, while much employment in the service sector was linked to the growth of industry. Manufacturing expanded by replacing imports in a policy of local industry protection by means of import controls and tariffs which Australian governments had followed for much of the twentieth century (Anderson, 1987). This encouraged large multinational companies, who could not import competitively over rising tariff barriers, to set up Australian subsidiaries. Car manufacturing companies such as General Motors and Ford would far rather have imported their cars, but they were induced to bring in capital and skills to produce locally, with profound consequences for both employment and the spatial organization of suburbia, as we will see. Governments also stimulated urbanization, and therefore suburbanization, by a programme of large-scale assisted immigration. Most migrants remained in the metropolitan areas and underpinned the expansion of manufacturing by becoming both factory workers and consumers. Between 1947 and 1961, 73 per cent of additions to the labour force as a whole was provided by immigration, a proportion that then fell back to almost 50 per cent during the following decade. Because manufacturing migrated to the suburbs, the immigrants went there also.

SHAPES ON THE GROUND

Firms migrated to the suburbs because it made commercial sense for them to do so. In most cities, the old inner ring of industrial suburbs had become increasingly congested with road traffic. There was little unused land available for expansion and land prices were high. The parameters of industrial location were changing. The use of electrical power in place of steam had already widened location choice, while the increasing use of road transport by truck was reducing the need to be close to a railway line. Many of the newer industries had special site requirements which could no longer be accommodated in the inner areas dominated by multi-storey factory buildings. Assembly-line techniques required large single-storey buildings to house the continuous mechanized flow of production. The increasing use of the fork-lift for moving materials reinforced the advantages of single level-plants. Manufacturers, especially the multinationals making cars, electrical goods, building materials, plastics and other consumer goods, looked increasingly to the suburban fringe and beyond to find the large sites and cheap land which they needed (Dingle, 1984, pp. 226–230; Spearritt, 1978, pp. 121–127). Land-use zoning prevented the promiscuous mixing of housing and factories typical of the older industrial areas, and so distinct industrial estates emerged, scattered throughout the new suburbs. Governments saw this as good urban planning and strategically sensible, for dispersed industry made more difficult targets for bombers in the event of another war.

These developments are exemplified most clearly by the car industry. Its activities in Melbourne indicate clearly its importance in shaping suburban growth. In 1952, General Motors-Holden built its new plant beyond the suburban frontier, to the south-east of the city, near the market town of Dandenong, on land provided on favourable terms by the State government. While the public housing authority built a village of detached cottages to house some of the workforce, many more built their own homes nearby, pulling suburbia out towards the factory. H.J. Heinz and International Harvester set up plants nearby, followed by Volkswagen, Bosch, Dulux paints, Repco spare parts and other car-linked firms to create an extensive industrial complex with automotive manufacture at its core. In 1959, Ford made an identical move to the north of Melbourne, with similar consequences. Possibly a third of the residents on the suburban fringe owed their livelihood directly or indirectly to the car. If they did not help assemble it, they made parts, paint or tyres, or serviced or wrecked it. They also increasingly relied on it to take them to work, for shopping and for recreation, because the old radial public transport networks of train and tram were of limited use to those journeying across suburbs.[4] Motor-vehicle ownership increased rapidly to a ratio of one for every 2.8 people by 1968, better than one for each family, and at a cost which had fallen to the equivalent of 30 weeks' work on the average wage (Whitwell, 1989, p.3).

Australia's post-war suburbs have been shaped to the requirements of the car, just as earlier suburbs were moulded by the train and the tram, the dominant forms of transport when they were created. Every house needed a driveway from the street and a garage or carport; so house blocks had to be widened to make room for the car as well. Streets, too, were widened, and car-parking spaces had to be provided wherever the car stopped; aerial photographs demonstrate vividly the massive acreages turned over almost exclusively to car use. The corners of busier suburban streets acquired petrol filling stations. Drive-in movie theatres, motels and bottle shops followed. Australia's first drive-in shopping centre was at Chermside in Brisbane, built in 1957 in conscious imitation of American models. With its 700 car parking spaces, it claimed to be the first large-scale drive-in shopping centre outside the United States. Chadstone in Melbourne, opened in 1960 after careful research into United States precedents, was the first to approach an American scale of operation with its 2,500 parking spots. Its rapid success sparked off a boom in the construction of regional shopping centres during the 1960s and early 1970s. The proportion of retail spending in the central business district of Melbourne fell from 34 per cent in 1957 to 20 per cent in 1969, and half that again a decade later (Spearritt, 1996). This was but one indication of the declining importance of old city centres and the growing self-sufficiency of the suburbs.

Housing is the heart of the suburb. Families began buying their own homes in unprecedented numbers after the Second World War. This had not been anticipated. Plans to overcome the post-war housing shortage envisaged that around half of all accommodation would be publicly financed for rental to low-income earners. The worst of the shortage had been overcome by the mid-1950s, with the construction of almost 700,000 dwellings. Only one in seven of these was financed by public authorities. Private enterprise built and paid for the rest; over a third of all houses were built by their owners in an unprecedented burst of self-help activity (Dingle, 1999). During the 1950s and 1960s, investment in private housing amounted to around 20 per cent of all fixed capital expenditure each year, compared with around 16 per cent in manufacturing. This was a measure of the importance people placed on property ownership. In the years between 1947 and 1961, levels of owner occupation jumped from around 50 per cent, where they had been for the previous three decades, to 70 per cent, a level which has not been exceeded subsequently (Troy, 1991, p.2).

There has been much debate about the causes of this increase in home ownership. While no consensus has emerged, there is at least wide agreement on the major forces at work (Allport, 1980; Berry, 1988; Bethune, 1978; Kass, 1987; Kemeny, 1986). Although house and materials prices rose sharply, so too did incomes, so that only 10–12 per cent of household expenditure was going on housing. At little more than half of pre-war levels, this represented an historic low; for expenditures on housing rose again in the 1970s and 1980s (Dewhurst, 1990; Podder, 1971; Whitwell, 1989, p. 30). It also appears to have been very low by international standards at the time. Government subsidies also lowered the barriers to home ownership. The War Service Homes scheme, which offered low-interest housing loans to former military personnel, financed almost 18 per cent of all housing advances between 1945 and 1956 (Hill, 1959, p. 128). After 1956, a new Commonwealth and State Housing Agreement encouraged State housing authorities to sell public housing to sitting tenants on favourable terms. Large amounts of public housing fell into private hands in most States and this, too, boosted home ownership. Governments were reducing the supply of private as well as public rental property. After the war, rent controls kept rents at pre-war levels in an inflationary environment. Landlords making little or nothing from their properties sold them to their sitting tenants or anyone who would buy them. As a result, the number of private rental properties in Sydney shrank by 44,000 and in Melbourne by 39,000 between 1947 and 1961. If all these converted to owner occupation, as was likely, this alone would have raised ownership levels by 8 per cent in the two cities (Bethune, 1978, pp. 165–7).

It has often been noted that Australian suburbs were not well planned (Boyd, 1987, p. 129). The pioneers frequently went without made roads, sewers and other basic facilities because developers were not forced to provide them when they subdivided; but this also meant that land was cheaper. In effect, this lowered the financial threshold for those wishing to live in suburbia at the cost of a temporary lack of infrastructure. People could defer the cost of services for several years until their home had been built and furnished and they could accumulate savings to pay for streets and footpaths and sewer connections.

Intending home owners choose what kind of house they will build or buy, but they do so within the parameters set by their perceptions of what constitutes an appropriate house, both internally and externally. Prevailing fashion, as well as the depth of their purse, also limited the possibilities. Materials shortages and government-imposed limitations on house size restricted their choice even further for a decade or so after the war. Once these were relaxed, average house sizes rose gradually while the numbers of people living in each house declined slowly, giving a ratio of people per room which fell from 0.76 in 1947 to 0.57 in 1976 (Neutze, 1981, p. 151). One of the striking features of Australian suburbia is its uniformity. In any locality, block sizes and house sizes and styles tend to be similar. This is, perhaps, surprising when housing is the outcome of many individual decisions of home owners rather than of a public housing agency, but the pressures towards conformity have been powerful (Dingle, 1993). Localities typically filled with houses before fashions had time to change significantly and bring variety to house design. Building regulations encouraged houses to be set back a uniform distance from the street and from neighbouring blocks – each of which was approximately the same size, although not always as large as the quarter acre derided by the critics – and also led to uniformity in window sizes and in the heights of ceilings and roofs. People on similar incomes have tended to cluster together, affording housing of similar size and with the same range of equipment. In this way, suburbanites could disguise wealth inequalities.

Housing styles and layouts changed gradually but steadily. During the period of austerity after the war, the challenge was to squeeze as much as possible into a small house. This provided an opportunity for Modernist architects to offer clean, simple, functional, box-like designs, 'machines for living in' in Le Corbusier's famous phrase, in place of the traditional house. Verandahs could be dispensed with, so too could high pitched roofs, hallways and sitting rooms. Open-plan interiors would give much-needed flexibility. This campaign had some impact in shaping the suburban house, but most people were not enthusiastic about flat roofs or open-plan interiors. Popular compromises appeared embracing some of what was new, such as built-in cupboards, a combined lounge and dining alcove and larger windows, while retaining much that was felt to be old and familiar and essential to a sense of domesticity (Dingle and O'Hanlon, 1996). As materials became more freely available, timber weatherboards, fibrous cement sheeting, and corrugated iron roofing – the cheapest of house cladding materials – rapidly gave way to bricks and roof tiles, the traditional materials for wall and roof. But there were differences. The tiles were often concrete rather than terracotta, while the house was a brick veneer rather than solid brick; that is, it had a timber frame which bore the weight of the roof. In this way a traditional preference for brick as a building material could be achieved more cheaply. The brick veneer became ubiquitous in the suburbs. The double-fronted and triple-fronted brick veneers were the dominant styles during the 1960s, before being joined by ranch style houses in the 1970s.

If we can accept that houses are 'chosen, modified, and decorated so that they are symbolically appropriate for their residents' (Sadalla *et al.*, 1987, p. 570), so too are gardens. Indeed, they are perhaps more immediate and sensitive indicators of the preferences and social identity of their owners, because it is far easier and cheaper to alter a garden than a house. Gardening, for long an important suburban recreation, became quicker and less arduous as a result of motorized rotary grass cutters, chemical fertilizers and weed killers, and improved watering systems. Much of the variety and richness in the streetscape of post-war suburbia comes from front gardens (Seddon, 1990; Seddon and Davis, 1976). Fashions have changed. From the 1960s long-favoured British flowers and shrubs began to make way for natives. Few suburban gardeners planted pure native gardens, but natives and exotics were mingled, along with the traditional lawn. Trees became increasingly popular so that, within ten years of a street being built, the foliage and branches of predominantly native tree species in gardens and on nature strips hid roof and fence lines, softening and greening the neighbourhood. Backyards changed also as higher incomes and refrigerators allowed people to dispense with the hens and vegetable patch for which the space was formerly used, and turn it over to recreational pursuits; lawn and barbecue and swimming pools of all shapes and sizes taking their place. As a part of a general move outside, house architecture rediscovered its links with the garden; glass doors, full-length windows, pergolas, patios and verandahs sought to integrate the two.

FADING DREAMS

The bulk of Australia's population continues to live in the band of post-war
suburbs which ring their cities. Young married couples still go to the suburban
fringe, where a house and land package offers them a first home of their own more
cheaply than anywhere else in the urban area; but they can no longer do so with
the simple enthusiasms or the confidence with which their parents moved three
decades earlier. The suburban dream has been interrupted by a host of troubling
realities since the early 1970s. This is ironic, for some of the most obvious
physical deficiencies of suburbia had finally begun to be addressed at that time.
The election of the Whitlam Labor government in 1972 resulted in more money
going into urban infrastructure enabling, for example, the sewering of many of the
new suburbs which had been relying on inadequate septic tanks (Dingle and
Rasmussen, 1991). The suburbs had also found intellectual defenders at last.
Craig McGregor insisted that 'the self-contained house on its own block of land is
the most satisfactory solution to man's living needs that we have yet been able to
evolve'. It is 'by far the best locale for raising children', provides 'more space,
freedom and room to expand than any other form of housing', keeps people in
touch 'with the bush and things that grow' and, 'above all, it gives you complete
independence'; advantages of which most suburbanites had long been aware
(McGregor, 1968, pp. 49–50). Hugh Stretton subsequently elaborated on these
and other benefits of suburban life in his influential *Ideas for Australian Cities*
(Stretton, 1970). He was doing so just as the foundations upon which suburbia
was built began to be subjected to new strains.

The first OPEC oil crisis in 1973 marked the end of three decades of rapid
economic growth throughout most of the developed world. In the same year, a
large balance of payments surplus in Australia provoked an across-the-board
tariff cut of 25 per cent, which marked the beginning of the end of the policy of
high protection for local industry. The proportion of the urban workforce in
manufacturing had begun to decline from the end of the 1950s. Under the impact
of recession, increased mechanization and tariff cuts, the absolute number of jobs
in manufacturing began to decline during the 1970s. By 1991, manufacturing
provided only 14 per cent of Sydney's jobs, 18 per cent of Melbourne's, and 13
per cent of Brisbane's, less than half the proportion it had employed four decades
earlier. Other sectors of the urban economy took up some of the slack. Wholesale
and retail employment expanded, so too did work in health and education. This
was not enough to prevent a tripling in average levels of unemployment to 6 per
cent by the late 1970s, and 10 per cent by the early 1980s. Unskilled and semi-
skilled factory workers of both sexes were the main victims. Significant
unemployment came to the post-war suburbs for the first time. It was, and is,
worst where there was a heavy reliance on manufacturing, and particularly those
sectors such as textiles, clothing and footwear, as well as car production, which
have shed most labour. Places like Elizabeth on the outskirts of Adelaide, which

began as a planned new town in the 1950s, suffer badly, as does Broadmeadows in Melbourne (Peel, 1995).

Recent research into income variations between neighbourhoods in Australian cities has found evidence of large increases in inequality. Between 1976 and 1991, household incomes in the poorest 5 per cent of areas have fallen by 23 per cent, while in the richest areas they have risen by the same amount; so that the income gap between the two has almost doubled. Higher incomes and jobs are being captured by richer areas and lost by poorer areas; in the poorest 5 per cent of neighbourhoods, the proportion of men in employment has fallen by 42 per cent but the proportion of women in employment has also declined spectacularly. The causes of these changes remain to be disentangled. The loss of manufacturing jobs has had an impact as has the location of public housing. It may also be that double-income families have been moving to more affluent suburbs, while single-income families have moved to cheaper housing in poorer areas (Gregory and Hunter, 1995).

For those remaining in work, income growth since the early 1970s has been far slower than it had been in earlier decades, but the impact of this on suburbia is unclear. Housing appears to have become gradually less affordable relative to income since the end of the 1960s, so that is it has been necessary to work progressively longer at average weekly wages to acquire a deposit and service a mortgage. This suggests that home ownership in suburbia has become inaccessible to a growing number of people. Levels of owner occupation have not fallen, but many factors apart from affordability affect them, including an ageing population and a decline in the rate of family formation in recent years (Troy, 1991, pp. 39–46). These may well be masking a decline in the proportion of newly-formed families able or desirous of owning their own home in suburbia.

Demographic changes are altering the pattern of housing demand. The most significant trend has been the growth of smaller households. In 1954, less than a third of all households contained only one or two people, yet by 1991 slightly more than half did so. Various demographic trends have contributed to this – later first marriages, smaller families, higher divorce rates and more single-parent families, as well as lower mortality and the ageing of the population. As a result, the large detached post-war suburban home has satisfied the housing needs of a progressively smaller proportion of the population. Smaller households are now clustered increasingly into the older inner suburban areas in medium-density and high-density accommodation (AURDR, 1995, pp. 45–47).

Before the 1970s, there were few alternatives to a detached house in post-war suburbia for most people. A flat-building boom during the 1960s in the larger cities offered alternatives to affluent young and not so young singles both in inner areas and some suburbs (O'Hanlon, 1996). During the 1970s, as the charms of suburbia began to fade, some of the affluent middle class discovered the attractions of the older near-city neighbourhoods, often those which had been given a lift by the influx of Greek or Italian migrants, who recreated a lively European cafe and street life. Run-down terraced houses and cottages were bought up and renovated. This process of gentrification offered an attractive alternative to outer suburbia, especially for smaller households (Logan, 1985). It also pushed up land values, causing some of the previous inhabitants to leave for outer suburbia. More recently, large-scale high- and medium-density private developments close to city centres and on former industrial land in older inner suburbs has widened housing options still further. The old opposition to high-density living mentioned earlier has been replaced by a preference for the compact convenience and ambience of the nineteenth-century walking suburbs.

The economic, social and environmental costs of car dependence in suburbia have become more obvious during the last quarter of a century. The OPEC upheavals threatened reduced supplies and higher prices for petrol; fears that have not yet been realized. But there is an increased awareness of the costs as well as benefits of relying upon exhaustible fossil fuels. Cars are an example of what economist Fred Hirsch called 'positional goods' (Hirsch, 1977). Full enjoyment of them depends on their rarity. As more cars drove along suburban roads, traffic congestion increased and travelling times were extended. Ambitious plans to build networks of freeways to relieve the congestion were challenged, and sometimes defeated, by resident action groups. This typically pitted the interests of older inner suburbs, through which the freeway would slice, against the convenience of car commuters from the outer post-war suburbs. Freeways which were built destroyed homes, parks and neighbourhoods. The car also disappointed in other ways as it emitted pollutants and greenhouse gases into the suburban atmosphere.

For the last decade and a half there has been a debate about the direction in which Australian cities should move in the future. There had long been criticism of typical Australian low-density suburban development by planners and urban commentators (but not by suburban dwellers); 'urban sprawl' was their pejorative description. This verdict took on added relevance for State governments in the early 1980s as they reluctantly contemplated the need to finance a new generation of dams, roads, sewage treatment plants and other infrastructure to service expanding suburbia, particularly as the Commonwealth government was less likely to help than previously. Their answer was 'urban consolidation'. This meant increasing population densities within existing urban areas in order to make fuller use of the existing infrastructure, which was considered to be under-utilized. Planning codes were amended and other incentives offered to encourage higher-density housing. One particular amendment was to allow 'dual occupancy', that is, a second dwelling could be built on a suburban building block, to the rear of the original house, provided that there was enough room for car access. In some suburbs in Melbourne and Sydney, dual-occupancy buildings have gone up in sufficient numbers to change fundamentally the landscape of suburbia; trees in spacious backyards are replaced by houses. Neighbours, deprived of any power to halt backyard building, complain bitterly that the quality of their suburban life is being compromised fatally. The savings from urban consolidation may be far smaller, and the costs far higher, than governments anticipated (Troy, 1996), but it is perhaps the greatest challenge yet to the survival of the traditional low-density Australian suburb.

NOTES

1. The word 'suburb' is commonly used in Australia to refer to a residential area. This usually means that the area possesses the characteristics classically associated with suburbia, such as detached houses set in their own gardens. This is, indeed, the dominant form of Australia's housing stock; but in the old 'inner suburbs' it can also include terraces and flats. Most of Australia's major cities suffer from fragmented local government, with many municipalities existing within the metropolitan area; and suburbs are usually known by the name of the municipality in which they are located. There is, consequently, no sense of a suburb being something outside of and apart from the city, as is the case in the United States.

2. An Australian rendition of 'glorious home', defined in Afferbeck Lauder's *Let Stalk Strine* (1974 edition, p. 20) as 'a spurban house of more than fourteen squares, containing fridge, telly, wart wall carps, payshow, and a kiddies' rumps room'.

3. It could be argued that the programme of public housebuilding in the various States was similar in some respects to the policies followed in Britain. Elizabeth in South Australia was a new town, based on British ideas, and the Cumberland Plan of 1949 in New South Wales proposed satellite towns, probably in imitation of Abercrombie and Uwin's proposals for London. Public housing authorities also later built high-rise public housing, with consequences similar to those experienced in Britain. The big difference is that, in Australia, the public sector housed a far smaller proportion of the population.

4. In all of the Australian capital cities, except Melbourne, competition for road space between car and tram resulted in the elimination of the tram.

REFERENCES

Allport, C. (1980) The unrealised promise: plans for Sydney housing in the forties, in Roe, J. (ed.) *Twentieth Century Sydney. Studies in Urban and Social History*. Sydney: Hale and Iremonger, pp.48–68.

Anderson, K. (1987) Tariffs and the manufacturing sector, in Maddock, R. and McLean, I. (eds.) *The Australian Economy in the Long Run*. Cambridge: Cambridge University Press, pp. 165–194.

Ashbolt, A. (1966) Godzone: 3 myth and reality. *Meanjin Quarterly*, No. 107, Vol. 25, No. 4, pp. 373–388.

AURDR (Australian Urban and Regional Development Review) (1995) *Places for Everyone: Social Equity in Australian Cities and Regions*. Canberra: Australian Urban and Regional Development Review.

Bethune, G. (1978) Urban Home Ownership in Australia: Some Aspects of Housing Demand and Policy. Unpublished Ph.D. thesis, Australian National University.

Berry, M. (1988) To buy or rent? The demise of a dual tenure policy in Australia 1945–60, in Howe, R.(ed.) *New Houses for Old: Fifty Years of Public Housing in Victoria 1938–1988*. Melbourne: Ministry of Housing and Construction, pp. 95–122.

Boehm, E.A. (1993) *20th Century Economic Development in Australia*. Melbourne: Longman Cheshire.

Boyd, R.(1987) *Australia's Home: Its Origins, Builders and Occupiers*. Melbourne: Pelican (first published 1952).

Brett, J. (1992) *Robert Menzies' Forgotten People*. Chippendale: Macmillan Australia.

Brown, N. (1995) *Governing Prosperity. Social Change and Social Analysis in Australia in the 1950s*. Cambridge: Cambridge University Press.

Burnley, I.H. (1974) Internal migration and metropolitan growth in Australia, in Burnley, I.H. (ed.) *Urbanization in Australia: The Post-War Experience*. London: Cambridge University Press, pp. 99–118.

Chapman, A.A.S. (1944) *Buying or Building Your Postwar Home*. Sydney: Mingay Publishing Company.

Darian Smith, K. (1990) *On the Home Front: Melbourne in Wartime 1939–1945*. Melbourne: Melbourne University Press.

Davison, G.J. (1978) Sydney and the Bush: an urban context for the Australian legend. *Historical Studies*, Vol. 18, No. 71, pp. 191–209.

Davison, G.J. (1994) The past and future of the Australian suburb, in Johnson, L.C (ed.) *Suburban Dreaming; An Interdisciplinary Approach to Australian Cities*. Geelong: Deakin University Press, pp. 99–113.

Dewhurst, J.H. (1990) An analysis of consumers' expenditure in Queensland: 1948–1985. *Economic Analysis and Policy*, Vol. 20, No. 2, pp. 169–188.

Dingle, T. (1984) *The Victorians: Settling*, Sydney: Fairfax, Syme and Weldon.

Dingle, T. (1993) Who has shaped 'bald brick-veneerdom'? in Garden, D. (ed.) *Created Landscapes: Historians and the Environment*. Melbourne: History Institute, Victoria, pp. 17–27.

Dingle, T. (1996) People and places in post-war Melbourne, in Davison, G.J., Dingle, T. and O'Hanlon, S. (1996) *The Cream Brick Frontier: Histories of Australian Suburbia*. Monash Publications in History No. 19. Monash: Monash University, pp. 27–40.

Dingle, T. (1999) Self-help housing and co-operation in postwar Australia, *Housing Studies*, forthcoming.

Dingle, T. and Rasmussen, C. (1991) *Vital Connections: Melbourne and its Board of Works 1891–1991*. Melbourne: McPhee Gribble/Penguin.

Dingle, T. and O'Hanlon, S. (1996) Ten per cent Modern? Reshaping Melbourne's small homes 1945–1960, in Griffiths, T. (ed.) *People and Place: Australian Heritage Perspectives*. London: Sir Robert Menzies Centre for Australian Studies, pp. 25–52.

Gilbert, A. (1988) The roots of Australian anti-suburbanism, in Goldberg, S.L. and Smith, F.B. (eds.) *Australian Cultural History*. Cambridge: Cambridge University Press, pp. 33–49.

Gregory, R.G. and Hunter, B. (1995) *The Macro Economy and the Growth of Ghettos and Urban Poverty in Australia*. Australian National University, Centre for Economic Policy Research, Discussion Paper no. 325.

Hill, M.R. (1959) *Housing Finance in Australia 1945–1956*. Melbourne: Melbourne University Press.

Hirsch, F. (1977) *Social Limits to Growth*. Cambridge, MA: Harvard University Press.

Jones, F.L. (1975) The changing shape of the Australian income distribution 1914–15 and 1968–9. *Australian Economic History Review*, Vol. 15, No. 1, pp. 21–34.

Howe, R. (ed.) (1988) *New Houses for Old: Fifty Years of Public Housing in Victoria 1938–1988*. Melbourne: Ministry of Housing and Construction.

Kass, T. (1987) Cheaper than rent: aspects of the growth of owner-occupation in Sydney 1911–1966, in Kelly, M. (ed.) *Sydney: City of Suburbs*. Kensington: New South Wales University Press, pp. 77–94.

Kemeny, J. (1986) The ideology of home ownership, in McLoughlin, J.B. and Huxley, M. (eds.) *Urban Planning in Australia: Critical Readings*. Cambridge: Cambridge University Press, pp. 251–258.

Lauder, A. (1974) *Let Stalk Strine*. Sydney: Ure Smith.

Logan, W.S. (1985) *The Gentrification of Inner Melbourne: A Political Geography of Inner City Housing*. Brisbane: University of Queensland Press.

Maher, C.A. (1982) *Australian Cities in Transition*. Melbourne: Shillington House.

McGregor, C. (1968) *People Politics and Pop: Australians in the Sixties*. Sydney: Ure Smith.

Menzies, R.G. (1943) *The Forgotten People and other Studies in Democracy*. Sydney: Angus and Robertson.

Merrett, D.T. (1978) Australian capital cities in the twentieth century, in McCarty, J.W. and Schedvin, C.B. (eds.) *Australian Capital Cities: Historical Essays*. Sydney: University of Sydney Press, pp. 171–198.

Neutze, M. (1981) *Urban Development in Australia*. Sydney: Allen and Unwin.

O'Hanlon, S. (1996) Six packs and villa units: the 1960s Melbourne flats boom, unpublished typescript.

Peel, M. (1995) *Good Times, Hard Times: The Past and the Future in Elizabeth*. Melbourne: Melbourne University Press.

Podder, N. (1971) Patterns of household consumption expenditure in Australia. *Economic Record*, Vol. 47, pp. 379–398.

Roe, J. (1980) *Twentieth Century Sydney. Studies in Urban and Social History*. Sydney: Hale and Iremonger.

Sadalla, E.K., Vershure, B. and Burroughs, J. (1987) Identity symbolism in housing. *Environment and Behavior*, Vol. 19, No. 5, pp. 569–587.

Seddon, G. (1990) The suburban garden in Australia. *Westerly*, No. 4, pp. 5–13.

Seddon, G. and Davis, M. (1976) *Man and Landscape in Australia: Towards an Ecological Vision*. Canberra: Australian Government Publishing Services.

Spearritt, P. (1978) *Sydney Since the Twenties*. Sydney: Hale and Iremonger.

Spearritt, P. (1996) Suburban cathedrals: the rise of the drive-in shopping centre, in Davison, G.J., Dingle, T. and O'Hanlon, S. (1996) *The Cream Brick Frontier: Histories of Australian Suburbia*. Monash Publications in History No. 19. Monash: Monash University, pp. 96–103.

Stretton, H. (1970) *Ideas for Australian Cities*. Adelaide: The author.

Troy, P.N. (1991) *The Benefits of Owner Occupation*. Australian National University, Urban Research Program Working Paper No. 29.

Troy, P.N. (1996) *The Perils of Urban Consolidation*. Leichardt: Federation Press.

Ward, R. (1958, reprinted 1974) *The Australian Legend*. Melbourne: Oxford University Press.

Whitwell, G. (1989) *Making the Market: The Rise of Consumer Society*. Melbourne: McPhee Gribble/Penguin.

Chapter 10

Making Edge City: Post-Suburban Development and Life on the Frontier in Southern California

Andrew E.G. Jonas

> . . . These new urban areas are marked not by the penthouses of the old urban rich or the tenements of the old urban poor. Instead, their landmark structure is the celebrated single-family detached dwelling, the suburban home with grass all around that made America the best-housed civilization the world has ever known.
>
> I have come to call these new urban centers Edge Cities. Cities, because they contain all the functions a city ever has, albeit in a spread-out form that few have come to recognize for what it is. Edge, because they are a vigorous world of pioneers and immigrants, rising far from the old downtowns, where little save villages or farmland lay only thirty years before. (Garreau, 1991, p. 4)

During the 1980s, the City of Moreno Valley (see figure 10.1) in Riverside County, California, experienced a spectacular rate of development, growing in population from 28,000 in 1980 to 115,000 in 1990. As William Fulton – a California-based planning author and critic – suggested, Moreno Valley was at the time the fastest-growing city in the fastest-growing county in the United States (Fulton, 1991). Demographic projections showed that the city's population was likely to reach 250,000 by the year 2020, overtaking Riverside as the largest city in Riverside County. Such projections contributed to the popular image that Moreno Valley had become California's latest boomtown, an emergent edge city in the burgeoning post-suburban landscape of Southern California. In coining the term Y-CHOP (Young Commuting Home-Owning Parent) to describe the typical Moreno Valley resident, an article in *Time Magazine* in 1991 captured the essence of that image. Moreno Valley, it suggested, '. . . is the place for hardworking parents, with wagon-train hearts, seeking picket-fenced yards, swing sets and quiet streets, for people who can endure temperatures in the 100s and can drive three hours a day to work and back' (Lee, 1991, p. 99).

Such an image, however, did not endure for very long. In 1996, the *Los Angeles Times* declared that Southern California's boomtown had gone bust (Gorman, 1996). Moreno Valley faced substantial revenue shortfalls, and

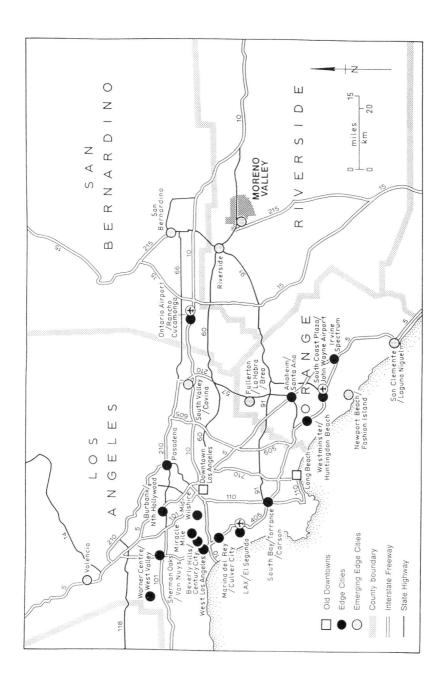

Figure 10.1. Moreno Valley: Edge City emergent. (*Source:* After Garreau, 1991, pp. 262–263))

politicians had appealed to local voters to pass a controversial utility tax increase. Whereas other cities had managed to ride Southern California's property market slump relatively unscathed, Moreno Valley no longer had a sufficient tax base to pay for basic services. The *Times* article suggested that locally-elected officials were responsible for the city's fiscal crisis. Poor planning and lack of proper fiscal management had turned a suburban dream into a post-suburban nightmare.[1]

Moreno Valley's predicament presents a neglected dimension of the edge-city phenomenon. Following the publication of Joel Garreau's influential treatise in 1991, the edge-city concept captured the imaginations of academics and popular writers alike. Social scientists have subsequently gone to great lengths to provide the latest empirical evidence of the phenomenon, including up-to-date lists and profiles of places which supposedly meet the edge-city criteria. But they have given rather less of their time to examining the processes and politics underlying the making of edge cities. An edge city does not simply materialize in the sub-urban landscape as a *fait accompli*; it must first be built. There is, I suggest, a politics to this building process, a politics in which discourse and material reality do not always converge. The aim of this chapter is to examine, by means of a case study, the contradictory and conflictual nature of edge-city building processes.

With regard to urban development politics in the United States, regime theorists suggest that the coherence and effectiveness of local development and fiscal policies are contingent upon a consensus forged within the local governing coalition (Cummings, 1988; Elkin, 1987; Pecorella, 1987; Stone, 1989, 1993; Stone and Sanders, 1987). A characteristic feature of urban development politics in the context of the United States is that it is often dominated by pro-growth governing coalitions: those interest groups that profit from the sale of land parcels to prospective investors (Logan and Molotch, 1987; Molotch, 1976; see also Jonas and Wilson, 1999). These coalitions mobilize to ensure that local land-use and development policies encourage inward investment. Such activity is often a threat to vested land-use interests, particularly in suburban areas where local residents generally enjoy open space, lower taxes and high-quality services such as education and police protection (Cox and Jonas, 1993; Logan and Molotch, 1987). Nevertheless, despite some evidence of mounting opposition to develop-ment and growth in suburban areas (Logan *et al.*, 1997), property developers have found various ways of avoiding suburban growth restrictions either by building in areas not subject to growth restrictions or by circumventing legal obstacles to growth (Jonas, 1991; Warner and Molotch, 1995). For their part, local politicians tend to be favourably disposed towards land development activity – and inward investment more generally (Cox and Mair, 1988) – because local governments are fiscally dependent upon property taxes, developer fees, and sales taxes, all of which tend to increase with new development and investment in the locality. This fiscal local dependence inclines elected municipal officials towards approving development projects, even if this means overlooking the concerns and demands of local residents and electorates.

Mindful, therefore, that the form of suburban development is contingent upon the character of the local political regime, I have chosen to divide the governance of Moreno Valley's development into three periods. The first period, 1980–84, was when a local growth coalition was galvanized by a move to incorporate the valley as a new municipality; but the emergence of growth factions compromised the coherence of the local development and fiscal policies that were pursued. During the second period, 1985–1991, concerted efforts – including the defeat of a local growth control measure – were made by the local growth regime to transform Moreno Valley into a major suburban employment centre. In the third period, 1992–1996, contradictions in Moreno Valley's development and fiscal policies were exposed by the property market crash in Southern California and the threatened closure of a local military installation. Moreno Valley's current fiscal predicament raises questions about the sustainability of edge-city developments in a rapidly-growing region such as Southern California.

ORGANIZING GOVERNANCE, 1980–1984

A typical edge city need not necessarily be a legally-incorporated place having clearly-defined political boundaries. Rather, such places are governed by a 'shadow government' (Garreau, 1991, p. 185) comprising a mixture of private and quasi-public agencies or special districts. Special districts have powers to raise taxes, provide local services, and set regulations with only minimal recourse to the local electorate. An edge city thus can have a strong territorial identity, but its residents may well lack any control or voice in its day-to-day management.

When Moreno Valley first began to attract the attention of developers in the 1970s, it was not a legally-incorporated place. Rather, the valley consisted of three unincorporated communities: the relatively poor community of Edgemont; a more affluent residential area known as Sunnymead; and the eastern end of the valley, known as Moreno, which was comprised of smallholdings, poultry farms and horse ranches. All decisions affecting land-use planning, development and service provision in these communities came within the jurisdiction of the Riverside County Board of Supervisors. The county, however, had failed to provide adequate services; indeed development was encouraged with little regard to the needs of local residents.

One county land-use policy, in particular, had a dramatic impact on development in Moreno Valley during the 1980s. This was the introduction of R-6 (medium-to-high density residential) zoning. R-6 zoning was Riverside's answer to the State of California's requirement that local governments should take measures to contain suburban sprawl and promote housing affordability. State law mandated that cities and counties include an Adopted Housing Element in their general plans, laying out in detail how much new housing would be provided for households at different income levels (Fulton, 1991). Around 1981, Riverside County adopted R-6 zoning as its affordable housing policy. The aim was to 'build on smaller lots and therefore save on the infrastructure costs as well as the acreage costs, and get the houses down in what the [State] call[ed] the "affordable price range"' (Riverside County Supervisor, personal interview, October, 1994). What this meant in practice was that, in order to keep housing costs low, many of the usual planning regulations were suspended (Fulton, 1990). This involved allowing developers to use smaller setbacks, double the square footage on exist-ing lots, and build much narrower access roads, some of which lacked sidewalks and were little more than dirt tracks.

House prices in Riverside County were, at the time, much lower than in Orange County and Los Angeles, where local municipalities had passed growth-control ordinances restricting further residential development. During the 1970s, devel-opers had been accumulating land banks in unincorporated parts of western Riverside County, and the introduction of R-6 zoning encouraged a wave of speculative development in these areas, fuelling a massive building boom in places like Moreno Valley. Much of this development was poorly planned, with minimal provision for basic infrastructure and services. Moreover, the speculative nature of R-6 development meant that house prices in Moreno Valley began to increase rapidly, exceeding the rate of increase in other parts of Southern California.

It transpired that 60 per cent of all the land in Riverside County zoned for R-6 residential units was located in Moreno Valley. The sheer pace of development of R-6 housing units, and the high density nature of development (figure 10.2), became the catalyst for an incorporation campaign in the valley, which attracted supporters and opponents alike, including the following:

1. *Long-time residents, retirees and smallholders.* These groups were concerned that incorporation would increase their tax burden. Resistance to incorporation was strongest amongst farmers and smallholders who wanted to retain the rural/equestrian character of the valley.
2. *Recent residents and young families.* Mainly residents in R-6 housing, these groups comprised a growing political constituency concerned about the poor quality of local infrastructure and services. They wanted a more managed approach to growth.
3. *Residential developers.* R-6 housing developers were comfortable dealing with the county and were, therefore, opposed to any attempt to shift control of land-use planning in the valley to municipal government.
4. *The Moreno Valley Chamber of Commerce.* The Chamber's support for incorporation was galvanized by an attempt by the Riverside Chamber of Commerce to merge with the Moreno Valley Chamber, a move which was interpreted as the first step towards the annexation of the entire valley to the City of Riverside.

Supporters of the incorporation campaign formed the Moreno Valley Incorporation Committee (MVIC) in January 1981. The MVIC comprised a local

Figure 10.2. R-6 'affordable' housing development in Moreno Valley.
(*Photograph*: A. Jonas)

developer, a realtor, the publisher of the valley newspaper, a local banker, a local
manager of a major regional utility, a school district official, and a local property
owner. These seven founding members were what could be described as
locally-dependent businesses; that is to say, they were likely to benefit from
any expansion in the local market for their goods and services (Cox and Mair,
1988). The interest-group profile of the MVIC matched that of the classic growth
machine as described in Logan and Molotch (1987).

The MVIC viewed successful incorporation as a necessary precondition
for controlling future investment opportunities in the valley, and so set about
obtaining signatures for a petition to the Local Agency Formation Commission
(LAFCO).[2] Despite receiving more than $10,741 in campaign contributions,
the MVIC's initial attempt to incorporate the valley was defeated in April
1982, by popular referendum. The vote was 3,001 in favour of incorporation
and 3,314 against, with a turnout of 50 per cent of eligible voters (*Riverside Press
Enterprise*, 14 April, 1982). Under State law, a two-year moratorium was
immediately imposed on any further incorporation initiative in the valley.

The outcome of the 1982 incorporation vote appeared to be influenced by the
political tactics of R-6 housing developers. At a very late stage in the campaign,
developers contributed $49,875 to an anti-incorporation group known as Save
Our Valley (SOV). Another such group, Incorporation No, received $1,166
from poultry farmers based in the eastern part of Moreno Valley. Together,

these campaigns received five times more in funds than that raised by the MVIC, an amount sufficient to tip the balance of the popular vote against incorporation.

Those developers and builders which contributed the most to SOV included Woodhaven Developers of Riverside, Myerscough Builders of Redlands, and Lewis Homes of Upland. All were involved in R-6 development projects in the valley. Despite bitter objections from residents in Sunnymead, these projects were approved by the County Board of Supervisors immediately prior to the incorporation election (*Riverside Press Enterprise*, 7 April, 1984). Indeed, it was the prospect that approval for such projects would not be forthcoming in the future which most likely encouraged R-6 developers to back the anti-incorporation campaign.

After this initial setback, pro-incorporation campaigners renamed their organization United Citizens for Cityhood (UCC), and geared up for a referendum in November 1984. On this occasion they were successful. In favour of incorporation were 11,316 voters, whereas 3,664 voted against. This represented a turnout of 70 per cent of eligible voters – very high by most standards. A crucial factor in swinging the popular vote in favour of incorporation was support from non-local developers. These raised $120,000 in campaign contributions compared to $500 for anti-incorporation groups, in other words a ratio of 240:1!

It appears that, in this instance, members of UCC – Moreno Valley's *de facto* growth coalition – were instrumental in mobilizing external support for their campaign, a not unusual tactic for thwarting the local opposition (see Molotch and Logan, 1984). At issue was the possibility that Riverside would annex all or part of the valley, and place limits on commercial and industrial development. As one Moreno Valley city councillor later put it,

> I firmly believe that one reason [for incorporation was] that the County was involved in the creation of Moreno Valley as a bedroom community for Riverside . . . And what leads me to believe that is the fact that the major jobs which came down from the State to the county . . . went directly to Riverside. Then of course it's in our area so Moreno Valley people are going to work there. We were basically developed as little-to-no businesses . . . (Moreno Valley City Councillor, personal interview, May, 1994)

Although the incorporation campaign was funded by growth interests, the concerns of local residents still had to be addressed. The statement for incorporation had provided for a council-manager system of government, with five council members being elected on a district basis. Council elections were held at the same time as the incorporation vote, but these operated on a 'first past the post' system, such that the five candidates with the most votes would form the new city council. Three of the newly-elected city councillors – each with close business ties to developers and all members of UCC – refused to introduce council districts as mandated in the November 1984 election. The three councillors were, as a result, subjected to a recall vote.[3]

The recall election was held in February of 1986. The 'No on Recall' campaign – supported by the Moreno Valley Chamber of Commerce – received $144,000 in donations, most of it from developers and the local Building Industry Association. This compared to $3,170 raised by the Alliance for Responsible Government, which backed the recall campaign. The recall was successful, and new councillors were elected to replace the three recalled officials.

The entire election had been cast as a case of growth versus no-growth. But, as an editorial in a local newspaper was quick to point out, Moreno Valley had '. . . come under the influence of big developers' (*Riverside Press Enterprise*, 29 November, 1985). The election itself highlighted a conflict around what type of growth would be pursued and how it would be financed. This conflict became internalized in local politics even as Moreno Valley's emergent growth regime set about the task of attracting investment to the city.

In Pursuit of Growth, 1985–1991

Garreau's list of edge cities in the Los Angeles area included three places in the Inland Empire (a region which includes the western portions of Riverside County and San Bernardino County). These were Ontario Airport-Rancho Cucamonga; San Bernardino; and Riverside (Garreau, 1991, p. 431). Moreno Valley did not appear on the list, and yet, by 1991, local boosters were already predicting that it would eventually become Riverside County's largest city.[4] Growth activists wanted to change the city's image as a dormitory suburb of Riverside, and to transform Moreno Valley into a major employment centre serving the Inland Empire. This meant using the city's newly-acquired land-use powers to earmark prospective sites for inward investment. Indeed, in the latter part of the 1980s there was a concerted effort to transform Moreno Valley into a major edge-city employment centre.

The city, however, had been built for outgoing rather than incoming commuters. Located at the intersection of Highway 60 and Interstate 215, Moreno Valley was relatively accessible to major employment centres in Orange County and Los Angeles (figure 10.1). Indeed, a labour market study commissioned by the City of Moreno Valley in 1986 had shown that at least 41 per cent of wage earners living in Moreno Valley commuted to places outside Riverside County. In a follow-up survey, it was found that 36 per cent of residents surveyed – who had recently moved to Moreno Valley – had done so to take advantage of cheaper housing costs, while only 18 per cent moved for job reasons (City of Moreno Valley, 1989). The survey noted, however, that in the meantime the number of residents commuting to places outside Riverside County had declined slightly (8 per cent between 1986 and 1989). Responding to the study's findings, local planners and city boosters began to talk about a 'population-jobs imbalance' which, supposedly, required inward investment to correct.

The establishment of the city's redevelopment agency in 1987 was viewed by

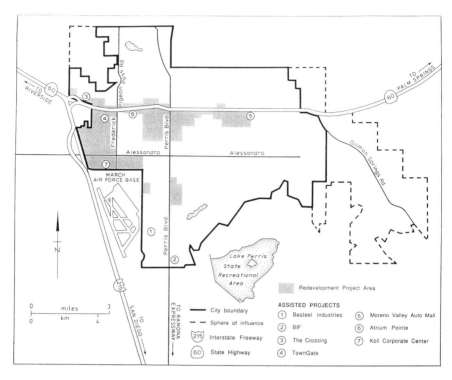

Figure 10.3. Moreno Valley redevelopment area and assisted projects. (*Sources*: Based on fieldwork and City of Moreno Valley, 1991)

local boosters as a significant step towards attracting commercial and industrial development to Moreno Valley.[5] The City Council loaned the redevelopment agency approximately $10 million to kick-start local redevelopment projects. The agency's jurisdiction covered nearly one-fifth of the total area of the city (figure 10.3), including the community of Edgemont, various sites adjacent to Route 60 and I-215, and the site of the former Riverside International Raceway, where plans to build a town-centre development (TownGate) were already under way.

TownGate was designed as a major mixed-use development, featuring a regional shopping mall, the Moreno Valley Mall at TownGate. The mall was developed as a joint venture involving the Homart Development Company, a subsidiary of Sears of Chicago, and the Fritz Duda Company of Dallas. It followed the Urban Land Institute's 'town centre' design concept, with provision made for offices, retail outlets, parking space, and medium- and medium-to-low-income housing development. The entire TownGate development included plans for over 4 million square feet of commercial/retail space, 2,000 housing units, a medical centre, restaurants, recreational facilities, and private security arrangements (figure 10.4).

Figure 10.4. Security watchtowers at the TownGate Mall in Moreno Valley. (*Photograph*: A. Jonas)

In terms of siting commercial and industrial development, the City of Moreno Valley invited small-firm guru David L. Birch[5] to its annual Economic Development Conference in 1991. Birch suggested that Moreno Valley had the potential to be a competitive location for the kinds of small-to-medium sized firms considered essential to economic growth in the post-mass production economy. To encourage investment by such firms, two master-planned industrial estates were featured in the city's economic development plans; CenterPointe Business Park and the Oleander Industrial Complex (figure 10.5). CenterPointe included a 345-acre mixed-use business park with office, retail and industrial space, and the Koll Corporate Center, a 32-acre master-planned, multi-use business centre. The Oleander Industrial Complex was a 1,500-acre master-planned industrial estate adjacent to March Air Force Base. The City offered a $1.5 million subsidy to Borneo International Furniture (BIF) of South Korea to locate its first production facility in the United States in the complex. A further $7.4 million in industrial development bonds was made available to finance the construction of a 123,000 square feet manufacturing facility for Besteel Industries. Indeed, local officials went to great lengths to court new business. A local delegation was sent to South Korea to negotiate the BIF deal and attract other investors to Moreno Valley.

But, in agreeing to subsidize commercial and industrial development, the City Council was placing the city in a financially precarious situation. The problem was that operating revenues were tied to developer fees which meant that, in terms of fiscal policy, the emphasis was on encouraging residential rather than commercial or industrial development. In fact, the city was already committed to several major planned community developments, including Moreno Valley Ranch (12,500 housing units), Sunnymead Ranch (3,029 units) and Hidden Springs

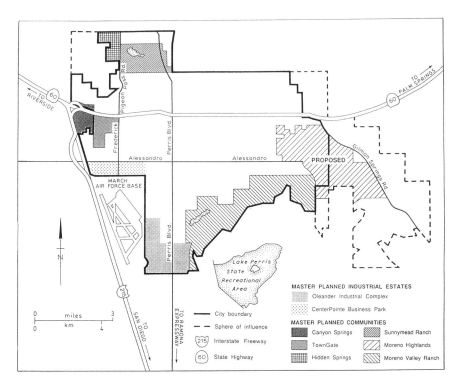

Figure 10.5. Master planned developments in Moreno Valley. (*Sources*: Based on fieldwork and City of Moreno Valley, 1991)

(1,200 units) (figure 10.5). Further large-scale residential developments were in the planning phase. To paraphrase the city's motto of the time, 'the excitement [was] building [more houses]'.

Attempts to introduce more controlled and fiscally-sound development policies were thwarted by Moreno Valley's growth regime. One growth control measure – so-called Measure J – was put before the voters in 1990. Had it passed, Measure J would have provided for managed growth policies and increased citizen participation in the development process. Amongst other issues, the measure called for limits on population growth, improvement of transport and public services, adequate provision for parks, equestrian trails and open space, preservation of sensitive habitats, and annual growth reports including projected costs of services. However, the measure was soundly defeated at the polls, thanks largely to opposition from the Chamber of Commerce and a significant injection of cash into the anti-growth control campaign by developers (*Riverside Press Enterprise*, 20 June, 1990).

What proved to be a decisive moment in the campaign was the linking of Measure J to a wider movement to set aside open space on private property for the protection of a locally-endangered species known as the Stephen's Kangaroo Rat (SKR). The SKR conservation plan received much negative publicity in the local media, with developers and farmers being opposed to it on the grounds that it not only threatened growth, but also involved the uncompensated taking of private property (Feldman, 1995). In the event, a voluntary agreement between Riverside County, Moreno Valley and other local jurisdictions released most of the land in Moreno Valley from development controls pertaining to SKR habitat.

The failure of Measure J was considered to be a mandate for uncontrolled growth. The city could issue bonds and encourage development in the expectation that growth would be more than adequately subsidized by developer fees. As it transpired, the anticipated revenues were not forthcoming.

MANAGING CRISIS, 1992–1996

Moreno Valley's growth proponents had successfully thwarted a major growth control initiative even as plans for a massive new mixed-use project, Moreno Highlands, were unveiled. But the year of 1992 marked a downturn in Moreno Valley's economic fortunes.

The first major blow was the slump in the Southern California housing market. New housing starts in the Greater Los Angeles Area had declined from over 120,000 annually in 1988 to less than 40,000 annually by 1992 (Jonas, 1997). The property market slump put several residential developers operating in Moreno Valley out of business. This was the fate of Woodhaven Developers, opponents of the first incorporation move in 1982. It also befell the Warmington Company and the Landmark Land Company, which lost their interests in the Moreno Valley Ranch master-planned community development. As a result, large areas of the development remained undeveloped as recently as 1996. Many other projects fully permitted in 1991 were still not completed by 1996. Of those completed, only Hidden Springs (1,200 dwelling units) and Sunnymead Ranch (3,029 units) were developed as originally planned.

Commercial and industrial property was also affected by the property market crash. T&S Development, the developer of Canyon Springs Plaza, experienced problems and, in 1996, the Homart Development Company sold its interests in the Moreno Valley Mall at TownGate to General Growth Companies, based in Des Moines, Iowa. Investors, including BIF and Besteel Industries, withdrew from projects in the Oleander Industrial Complex and the CenterPointe Business Park. By far the biggest project to fall victim to the deflated property market was Moreno Highlands, a 3,038-acre master-planned mixed-use development proposed for the eastern end of the valley – although, in this instance, factors other than the economic downturn came into play. A series of public hearings on the proposed development were held before the Moreno Valley City Council in 1992. Given the state of the property market, the investment consortium and the City Council were eager to go ahead without any delays. The project was potentially a significant boost to local revenues from developer fees, an area in which the city had already begun to encounter problems (*Riverside Press Enterprise*, 7 December, 1990). In addition, plans for a 500-acre business centre to be included in the project were considered to be a boost to local employment.

With an investment of some $2 billion and 24,000 new jobs projected, Moreno Highlands was presented to the public as a development gain. However, the development faced some serious objections from a coalition of local home-owners, farmers, hunters and conservationists (McDonnell, 1992). Concerns included the loss of the rural character of the eastern end of the valley, the threat to local farming interests, loss of habitat of endangered species, and seismic risk (the proposed development lay adjacent to a series of geological faults). Local residents voiced particular concerns that the housing element of the project would be completed before the business centre, few permanent local jobs would be created, and the development would contribute to further congestion on local freeways. Despite these concerns, the development plans were approved by the City Council in March of 1992. However, facing a contracting market as well as a court case initiated by the local chapter of a national wildlife conservation organization, which had objected to the proposed development, the development consortium eventually withdrew from the Moreno Highlands project.[6]

Another blow to Moreno Valley's economy was the threatened closure of March Air Force Base (MAFB). Although located outside the city's boundaries (see figure 10.3), social and economic ties between the base and the city were strong. A major local employer, the base was operated by the United States Air Force and the National Guard as home to the 452nd Air Refuelling Wing, 455th Air Lift Wing, and the National Guard Air Refuelling Wing. In 1994, the base was added to the federal Base Realignment and Closure Committee (BRACC)'s list of possible base closures. This listing prompted the formation of the March Air Force Base Support Group, which included representatives from the cities of Moreno Valley, Perris and Riverside, and the county. The MAFB Support Group made a presentation at the San Diego meeting of the BRACC, and organized a tour of the base for committee members and California's Governor Pete Wilson. BRACC eventually decided against closure. Instead, part of MAFB would be converted into an Air National Guard and Reserve Base, leaving 2,066 civilians and 4,889 military personnel stationed at the base, with an estimated local economic impact of $301 million. A Joint Powers Authority was set up to manage the conversion of the remainder of the base into commercial and industrial uses.

Uncertainties over the future of MAFB contributed to the more general economic malaise facing the city. Indeed, in 1996 the city faced a fiscal crisis. According to a public memo released by the Office of the City Manager in April of that year (City of Moreno Valley, 1996), the cause of the crisis was revenue shortfalls rather than increased costs. The main shortfall was in developer processing fees (a one-time charge for each building permit issued). During its growth phase, 1985–89, the city had netted over $36 million in developer fees.

But, after peaking in 1990, development fees declined from $11.5 million in 1990–91 to $1 million between 1994 and 1996. Total General Fund revenues (utility, sales, property and other taxes) were projected to decline by a further $700,000. The memo noted that income would have been greater but for existing sales tax agreements on the TownGate Mall and the loan of funds to the re-development agency. Meanwhile, public safety costs (police, fire, etc) had increased from $9.8 million in 1989–90 to $20.7 million in 1996–97.

The City Manager's memo claimed that the city's problems were exacerbated by unrealistic revenue projections. The city had over-estimated revenues from development fees by $8 million in 1990–91. The fees were supposed to help repay $12 million in capital improvement bonds issued in 1989. The repayment schedule was based on a projected rate of home construction of 900 homes per year. In 1993, however, only 173 units had been built and, in 1994, 236 were constructed. In other words, development fee income was insufficient to meet the city's future obligations.

In 1991, the city had introduced a 6 per cent utility tax to make up for revenue shortfalls. Subsequent changes in State law required that such taxes had to be subject to a public referendum and, as a consequence, a vote on the utility tax was set for November 1996. If it passed, the so-called Measure O would have allowed the continuation of the utility tax. Another measure called for the continuation of the city's business license tax. In the event, both measures failed in the November elections, placing the city in a precarious financial situation.

Since 1996, the recovery of the Southern California housing market has done little to improve Moreno Valley's prospects of becoming a major employment centre. Vacant space abounds in the city's two major industrial estates (figure

Figure 10.6. Oleander Institute complex in 1995. (*Photograph*: A. Jonas)

10.6). These two locations are now in competition with sites at March Air Force Base as well as in neighbouring Riverside. Although Moreno Valley recently signed a 'no competition' pact with the City of Riverside, there is little evidence that this agreement has had a net positive effect in terms of total jobs created in the area. While a major local aircraft parts supplier recently expanded its Riverside facility, this occurred only after it had closed down its Moreno Valley operations. More recently, a manufacturer of truck parts and bodies relocated more than 100 jobs from Riverside to Moreno Valley.

'POST-SUBURBAN IDYLL' OR 'JUNKYARD OF DREAMS'?

Compared with the boom times of the 1980s, the mood in the Moreno Valley of the 1990s is far more self-restrained and introspective, as suggested by the city's new motto (figure 10.7). The city is at a key moment in its brief history; a history which has seen its governing coalition and attendant policies transformed from the pursuit of growth to the management of economic restructuring. One scenario for the future would see the city as a major employment centre, with more people commuting in than out, local firms capitalizing on the pool of local entrepreneurial talent, and demand for commercial and office space rising; see, in other words, Moreno Valley become a 'mature' edge city. Such a scenario would perhaps involve closer co-operation between Moreno Valley and Riverside, particularly with regard to development along the I-215 corridor as well as the conversion of March Air Force Base. It would involve more realistic financial and growth management policies, including less reliance upon developer fees and a more co-ordinated approach to redevelopment. Under these conditions, Moreno Valley may yet fulfil the aspirations of even its most ardent promoters. But at what cost?

A second – and arguably more likely – scenario is that the city will continue its downward economic and social trajectory, or at least attract little in the way of new investment and jobs. Tensions and distrust between pro-growth interests and local residents might increase, jeopardizing any chance of the city developing coherent economic and fiscal policies. Local citizens would face a future of job insecurity and deteriorating quality of life. In this scenario, historic rivalries between Riverside and Moreno Valley might be revived by local boosters, fuelled perhaps by the view that Moreno Valley is little more than a bedroom community for other employment centres in the region.

How should social scientists assess Moreno Valley? What does it tell us about similar edge-city developments? One lesson is that social scientists need to be far more 'up-front' about the politics and contradictions of edge-city building processes. The insights into local governance provided by urban regime theory are certainly helpful in this regard, as is related work on the city as a growth machine (Molotch, 1976), particularly those versions of the growth machine thesis that are attuned to urban ideologies and the wider regulatory context (Jonas

People · Pride
Progress

— Another —
PUBLIC WORKS PROJECT
~ Thank You For Your Patience ~

MAYOR   MAYOR PRO TEM
Cynthia A. Crothers   Denise V. Lanning

COUNCIL MEMBERS
Bonnie Flickinger   Richard A. Stewart
Gregory G. Lefler

Figure 10.7. Moreno Valley:
people, pride and progress.
(*Photograph*: A. Jonas)

and Wilson, 1999). It is important, then, to move beyond banal rules and lists. These, by their very nature, encourage over generalization and a lack of sensitivity to ideology and context. Rather, it is necessary to examine what is involved in the making of edge cities; to see such places as socially produced and politically contested.

A first step on the path to a reconceptualization of the making of edge cities is to question their sustainability; to consider, in other words, their economic viability as well as their capacity to support a quality of life acceptable to local citizens. As the planning critic William Fulton has recently suggested (Fulton, 1996), edge-city developments are not likely to succeed commercially unless they become more liveable places. He goes on to argue that the competitive advantage over traditional downtowns that many such developments enjoyed in the 1980s has all but disappeared in the harsher economic climate of the 1990s. If Fulton's assessment of the current predicament of edge cities is correct, then those places such as Moreno Valley, which aspire to be both commercially successful and liveable edge cities, face even greater challenges.

But Fulton's assessment of the edge-city phenomenon does not amount to an outright rejection of this contemporary form of suburban development. Yet we know that such development is neither necessary nor indeed inevitable; it arises from a particular confluence of political and economic processes. In considering where and how more sustainable suburban landscapes may materialize, it is important to identify the political alternatives. In this regard, Robert Beauregard has recently pointed out that middle-class Americans have held a deep ambivalence towards their central cities, an ambivalence which the edge-city phenomenon serves to reinforce (Beauregard, 1996). The irony is that, in the 1990s, many of the ills previously associated with inner-city America have found their way to the outer edges of the metropolis. Southern California is no exception in this regard. In places like Moreno Valley, crime levels have risen steadily, job insecurity is prevalent, many homeowners are on the brink of foreclosure, and the local fiscal situation remains unstable. When these ills are added to existing concerns, such property values, loss of open space and destruction of valued landscapes, one has the ingredients of politically un-sustainable post-suburban development. If, as some scholars like to claim, Southern California is a paradigm for the contemporary urban condition, then we can expect middle-class Americans to become as ambivalent towards their edge cities as they currently are towards their central cities. Whether this ambivalence translates into a movement to create more liveable and democratic spaces within post-suburbia and/or elsewhere remains an open issue, although currently the prospects do not look very promising.

All, then, is not entirely well in edge city. For further evidence of this condition, the reader is referred to Mike Davis' account of life and politics in Los Angeles (Davis, 1990). In the final chapter of *City of Quartz*, Davis extends his critical gaze beyond the borders of Los Angeles County and into San Bernardino County. There, in the City of Fontana, he finds evidence of a new crisis. This is not a crisis of the inner-city *barrio* or ghetto; it is a crisis of the residential sub-division and the suburban employment centre. It is, in other words, a crisis of the *edge* city. Perhaps, then, a more appropriate metaphor for the edge-city phe-nomenon is not the 'vigorous world of pioneers and immigrants' (Garreau, 1991, p. 4), but rather the 'land of abandoned settlements and defeated colonists'. Like the City of Fontana, Moreno Valley perhaps has become a 'junkyard of dreams' (Davis, 1990) for those Southern Californians who have aspired to transform poultry farms and citrus groves into a latter-day Arcadian dream.

NOTES

1. The term 'post-suburban' is used by Kling, Olin and Poster (1991) to describe development in Southern California that has occurred beyond the borders of Los Angeles County. While they refer mainly to Orange County, Riverside County has attracted a similar sprawling and fragmented pattern of development.

2. In Riverside County, a petition for incorporation must contain at least 25 per cent of registered voters in the affected territory. This petition is filed with the county and reviewed by the Local Agency Formation Commission (LAFCO) which determines whether the boundaries are appropriate and adequate provision is made for services. Two useful studies of the incorporation process in California are Hoch (1984) and Miller (1981). In his study, Hoch argues that the legal structure of municipal incorporation favours property owners: only those who own property can initiate the process of municipal formation. Miller suggests that incorporation has made it possible for property owners and residents to lower their tax bills by externalizing fiscal responsibility for certain

services to the county. In this manner it has been possible, on the one hand, to exploit economies of scale in service provision and, on the other hand, to adopt exclusionary zoning polices that ensure demands on local services remain low. LAFCOs often approve incorporations that follow proper legal procedures without a full assessment of the fiscal capacity of the jurisdiction in question to provide adequate services to its population. The question of local fiscal capacity has become much more of an issue in the wake of the passage of Proposition 13 in 1978 which had the effect of limiting the amount of revenue generated from property assessments. In this context, municipalities and counties in California have increasingly turned to other local revenues sources such as sales taxes and developer impact fees. In addition, redevelopment has become more widely used as a fiscal regeneration tool by suburban municipalities (see note 5 below, and Althubaity and Jonas, 1998).

3. In California, petitions to recall certain named councillors and bearing the signature of 25 per cent of registered voters may be presented if the electorate is not satisfied with the procedure and/or the result of a local election. The concept of 'recalling an elected public official' was first introduced in California in 1911. A Progressive Era concept, recall by petition arose in response to public distrust of local politicians, who were often seen to be influenced by special interests (e.g. political machines, greedy railroad monopolies, etc) (see Milau, 1966). In Moreno Valley, certain councillors were recalled because it was felt that they had not responded to the electorate's request for district elections and were unduly influenced by local business interests.

4. Figure 10.1 is my attempt to update the map of emerging edge cities in Southern California with the inclusion of Moreno Valley. No doubt other places could be added to the list, including Palmdale in Los Angeles County, Victorville in San Bernardino County, and Temecula in Riverside County, all of which have experienced quite dramatic growth rates in recent years.

5. In California, cities and counties can establish their own redevelopment agencies. Redevelopment projects are funded by the tax increment resulting from any increase in property values over and above a base value established at the start of a redevelopment project.

6. Birch is the author of an influential study on the contribution of small firms to the employment generation process (Birch, 1979).

7. Nevertheless, planning permission and development options on Moreno Highlands remain in place. Construction of the project could recommence at any time with the backing of a new development consortium.

REFERENCES

Althubaity, A. and Jonas, A.E.G. (1998) Suburban entrepreneurialism: redevelopment regimes and co-ordinating metropolitan development in Southern California, in Hall, T. and Hubbard, P. (eds.) *The Entrepreneurial City: Geographies of Politics, Regime and Representation*. Oxford: Wiley, pp. 149–172.

Beauregard, R.A. (1996) Edge cities: peripheralizing the center. *Urban Geography*, Vol. 16, pp. 708–721.

Birch, D.L. (1979) *The Job Generation Process*. Cambridge, MA: MIT Program on Neighborhood and Regional Change.

City of Moreno Valley (1989) *Demographic and Labor Analysis*. Moreno Valley, CA: City of Moreno Valley Economic Development Department.

City of Moreno Valley (1991) *Moreno Valley Statistical Profile*. Moreno Valley, CA: City of Moreno Valley Economic Development Department.

City of Moreno Valley (1996) *Memorandum: 1996–97 Budget Message*. Moreno Valley, CA: Office of City Manager, April 12 (copy available in Moreno Valley Public Library).

Cox, K.R. and Jonas, A.E.G. (1993) Urban development, collective consumption and the politics of metropolitan fragmentation. *Political Geography*, Vol. 12, pp. 8–37.

Cox, K.R. and Mair, A.J. (1988) Locality and community in the politics of local economic development. *Annals of the Association of American Geographers*, Vol. 78, pp. 307–325.

Cummings, S. (ed.) (1988) *Business Elites and Urban Development: Case Studies and Critical Perspectives*. Albany, NY: State University of New York Press.

Davis, M. (1990) *City of Quartz: Excavating the Future in Los Angeles*. London and New York: Verso.

Elkin, S.L. (1987) *City and Regime in the American Republic*. Chicago: University of Chicago Press.

Feldman, T. (1995) Local Solutions to Land Use Conflict Under the Endangered Species Act: Habitat Conservation Planning in Riverside County. Unpublished Ph.D. thesis, University of California at Riverside.

Fulton, W. (1990) The long commute. *Planning* (U.S.), July, pp. 6–11.

Fulton, W. (1991) *Guide to California Planning*. Point Arena, CA: Solano Press.

Fulton, W. (1996) Are edge cities losing their edge? *Planning* (U.S.), May, pp. 4–7.

Garreau, J. (1991) *Edge City: Life on the New Frontier*. New York: Doubleday.

Gorman, T. (1996) Moreno Valley: boomtown going bust turns to voters. *Los Angeles Times*, 28 October.

Hoch, C. (1984) City limits: municipal boundary formation and class segregation, in Tabb, W.K. and Sawers, L. (eds.) *Marxism and the Metropolis*. New York: Oxford University Press, pp. 298–322.

Jonas, A.E.G. (1991) Urban growth coalitions and urban development policy: postwar growth and the politics of annexation in metropolitan Columbus. *Urban Geography*, Vol. 12, pp. 197–226.

Jonas, A.E.G. (1997) Regulating suburban politics: 'suburban-defense transition', institutional capacities, and territorial reorganization in Southern California, in Lauria, M. (ed.) *Reconstructing Urban Regime Theory: Regulating Urban Politics in a Global Economy*. Thousand Oaks, CA: Sage, pp. 206–230.

Jonas, A.E.G. and Wilson, D. (eds.) (1999) *The Urban Growth Machine: Critical Perspectives Two Decades Later*. Albany, NY: State University of New York Press.

Kling, R., Olin, S. and Poster, M. (eds.) (1991) *Postsuburban California: The Transformation of Orange County Since World War II*. Berkeley: University of California Press.

Lee, G. (1991) Moreno Valley: Home of the Y-CHOP. *Time Magazine*, 18 November.

Logan, J.R., Bridges Whaley, R. and Crowder, K. (1997) The character and consequences of growth regimes: an assessment of 20 years of research. *Urban Affairs Review*, Vol. 32, pp. 603–630.

Logan, J.R. and Molotch, H.L. (1987) *Urban Fortunes: The Political Economy of Place*. Berkeley: University of California Press.

McDonnell, P.J. (1992) Backlash hits growth-loving Moreno Valley, *Los Angeles Times*, 13 January.

Miller, G. (1981) *Cities by Contract: The Politics of Municipal Incorporation*. Cambridge: MIT Press.

Milau, G.T. (1996) *State and Local Government: Politics and Processes.* New York: Scribners.

Molotch, H.L. (1976) The city as a growth machine: towards a political economy of place. *American Journal of Sociology*, Vol. 82, pp. 309–331.

Molotch, H.L. and Logan, J.R. (1984) Tensions in the growth machine: overcoming resistance to value-free development. *Social Problems*, Vol. 31, pp. 483–499.

Pecorella, R.F. (1987) Fiscal crisis and regime change: a contextual approach, in Stone, C.N. and Sanders, H.T. (eds.) *The Politics of Urban Development.* Lawrence, KS: University of Kansas Press, pp. 52–72.

Stone, C.N. (1989) *Regime Politics: Governing Atlanta, 1946–1988.* Lawrence: University of Kansas Press.

Stone, C.N. (1993) Urban regimes and the capacity to govern: a political economy approach. *Journal of Urban Affairs*, Vol. 15, pp. 1–28.

Stone, C.N. and Sanders, H.T. (eds.) (1987) *The Politics of Urban Development.* Lawrence: University Press of Kansas.

Warner, K. and Molotch, H.L. (1995) Power to build: how development persists despite local controls. *Urban Affairs Review*, Vol. 30, pp. 378–406.

ACKNOWLEDGEMENTS

The financial support of the National Science Foundation (Award No. SBR-9512033) is acknowledged. The present chapter is based on research conducted whilst the author was Assistant Professor in the Department of Earth Sciences at the University of California, Riverside. Thanks are due to anonymous residents and employees of the City of Moreno Valley for helping me to understand some of the issues which have influenced that city's growth. Keith Scurr drew the maps and John Garner produced black and white prints from my colour slides. The usual disclaimers apply.

Chapter 11

Understanding Suburbs as Historic Landscapes through Preservation

David L. Ames

The post-Second World War baby boom and the suburbanization that it fostered transformed twentieth-century society and created a new metropolitan landscape. But now, more than fifty years later, should we consider that landscape of sufficient historical significance to warrant preservation? Certainly, if the buildings and landscapes that are considered for preservation are those associated with nationally-significant events and embody important cultural values in their design and construction, then the post-Second World War landscape deserves preservation in some form. This is the landscape of the American Dream, of the single-family house on its own lot sited within the large-scale, self-contained subdivision with a curvilinear street pattern (Ames, 1995). As Richard Longstreth (1992, p. 219) has pointed out, 'never before has such a great segment of society been able to partake of this kind of environment, nor will it again in the fore-seeable future'. Yet, to consider preserving the suburban landscapes of the post-Second World War era, and even earlier ones, raises a number of questions about both the practice of historic preservation and the state of academic knowledge about the history of suburbanization needed to interpret their significance.

In the United States, such suburbs are now being considered for preservation. One criterion for the listing of a property on the National Register of Historic Places of the U.S. Department of Interior is that it be at least fifty years old. This criterion brings the suburban building boom of the late 1940s within the scope of the Register. Federally funded or licensed projects, such as transportation improvements, are required by law to consider the effects of the projects on all properties eligible for the National Register as historic landscapes. For this reason, and as a part of ongoing historic structures survey activities at the State and local levels, preservationists in State and local preservation offices and cultural resource consulting firms throughout the U. S. are being asked to evaluate the historic significance of suburban developments built after 1945 and to determine if they are eligible for the National Register.

The need to evaluate the post-Second World War suburbs and a growing interest by preservationists in older suburbs as historic resources (see, for example, Bishir and Earley, 1985) stimulated an interest at the National Register to consider suburbs more extensively and to develop guidelines for evaluating them. This chapter reports on my experience in researching and writing those guidelines in the form of a technical bulletin for the National Register of Historic Places of the United States for the evaluation of American suburbs as historic landscapes. The technical bulletin is intended to give U. S. historic preservationists guidelines for determining whether certain suburban areas meet the criteria for listing on the National Register of Historic Places. The origin of this work lies in a monograph I co-authored in 1992 with Susan Mulchahey Chase and Rebecca Siders for the Delaware State Historic Preservation Office, entitled *Suburbanization in the Vicinity of Wilmington, Delaware, 1880–1950: A Historic Context* (Chase *et al.*, 1992).

The demand that historic preservation makes on the scholarship of suburbanization is to provide the basis for interpreting the historic significance of the physical elements of the suburban landscape as a part of the built environment. As preservationists conduct research on suburban areas they are, in fact, undertaking the first phase of preservation; that of creating an archive of materials on historic suburbs. The guidelines in the technical bulletin for evaluating historic suburbs are to ensure that comparable documentation is collected and evaluated for each suburb studied. Such documentation should greatly increase our understanding of the richness and diversity of historic American suburbs. As the National Register makes nominations available, this information will be available to suburban scholars for their own research, thus extending our knowledge of the suburban phenomenon.

Parallels between Historic Preservation, Architectural History and the Suburban Academic Literature

The literature related to suburbanization comes from many disciplines and research traditions. Trying to develop a synthesis of the suburban literature that can serve as a context for evaluating what a particular suburb might represent on a historic continuum reveals points where the literature is biased, incomplete and, occasionally, wrongheaded. For example, the scale of suburbanization and the low-density form it took after the Second World War fostered the myth that it was the first extensive wave of suburbanization in North American urban history (Muller, 1981, p. 51). This impression about the suburbs was reinforced in the national consciousness by situation comedy television shows such as *Leave It to Beaver*, *Father Knows Best*, *the Brady Bunch*, and presented in numerous motion pictures. Indeed, suburbs are more often seen as a threat to historic resources than resources themselves.

The first serious scholarship on suburbanization focused on post-Second World War suburbs. Sociologists interpreted the large mass-produced subdivisions such as the Levittowns as being symptomatic of an American character moving from individualism to conformity. Political scientists worried about how the new suburban communities threatened the central city with their population and economic growth. Many planners and urbanists showered the post-war suburbs with criticism, focusing primarily on their uniformity and perceived monotony. The post-Second World War suburb has been one of the most condemned of American landscapes. Lewis Mumford, for example, scored the new suburbs as 'a low-grade uniform environment from which escape is impossible' (Mumford, 1961, p. 486). Indeed, by 1967, sociologist Herbert Gans felt compelled to open his now classic study *The Levittowners* with the declaration that 'this book is about a much maligned part of America, suburbia [which has] been blamed for many of the country's alleged and real ills from destroying farmland to emasculating husbands' (Gans, 1967, p. 5). Gans' study was one of the first to present a more balanced view in which he found the suburbs to be successful for allowing residents to attain a piece of the American Dream.

The post-Second World War period also signalled the decline of the central city. The public policy discussion was largely framed politically in terms of the central city – the old legal city – versus the new suburbs. Political scientists, geographers, and planners were concerned with how the expansion of the legal city had failed to keep pace with the functional metropolitan area as politically fragmented suburbs grew beyond the city. Again, it was viewed largely as a new development in metropolitan history, and suburbs were defined politically. Even in his recent book *The Suburbs*, sociologist J. John Palen specifically defines suburbs as 'incorporated or unincorporated spatial communities of moderate density that lie outside the central city but within the metropolitan area' (Palen, 1995, pp. 12–13).

Because it was largely ahistorical, research and commentary in the 1950s and early 1960s contributed to the myth that the post-Second World War suburbs were unique. The history of academic research on the suburbs is one of broadening the definition of the subject both historically and geographically. That expansion began in 1962 when Sam Bass Warner published *Streetcar Suburbs: The Process of Growth in Boston* (Warner, 1962). This book was seminal in conceptualizing suburban development as a historical process. Although dealing only with Boston, Warner's approach was comprehensive. He evaluated all new residential development from 1870 to 1900 and found 'one basic pattern organized the whole metropolis: people were segregated by income and mixed together with little regard to national origin' (Warner, 1962, p. 46). Warner articulated a basic model of suburban development in which advances in personal transportation – the streetcar and automobile – opened new land for suburban development while retaining its connection to the central city. He found that by 1900 Boston exhibited, on a smaller scale, the same two-part metropolitan structure of a poor inner city and outer middle-class suburbs thought to be 'new' in the 1950s and early 1960s. Warner's approach has been called the mass-transit model of suburbanization (Binford, 1985, p. 5).

In 1970, in a study of the residential structure of Midwestern cities, the geographer John S. Adams extended Warner's model and proposed that American cities and their suburbs were built-up during four intra-urban transport eras. They were the walking/horsecar era ending in the 1880s; the electric streetcar era from the 1880s through to the First World War; the recreational auto era from the 1920s to 1941; and the freeway era after the Second World War (Adams, 1970). In the early 1980s another geographer, Peter O. Muller, related these eras more fully to the suburbanization process (Muller, 1981), and they became recognized as the major phases in the mass transit model of surburbanization.

The first comprehensive historical treatment of the American suburb came with the publication of *Crabgrass Frontier: The Suburbanization of the United States*, by Kenneth T. Jackson (1985). He found that 'the process of suburbanization began between 1815 and 1835 and was well advanced by the advent of the civil war' (Jackson, 1985, p. 310). Jackson concluded that the invention in Chicago in the 1830s of the balloon-frame method of construction 'was as important as transit in making the private home available to middle income families and even those of marginal economic status' (Jackson, 1985, p. 125). Jackson established that suburbanization was a type of residential development deeply rooted in the historical process of American urban growth from the early nineteenth century.

Thus the scholarship on American suburbanization of searching for its origins and variations has provided a continual reinterpretation of the suburbanization process. For example, Harry Binford, in his book *The First Suburbs: Residential Communities in the Boston Periphery 1815–1860* (Binford, 1985), disconnects the origins of the residential suburb from mass transportation and commuter expansion and argues that 'in answer to the question of where the suburbs come from . . . the suburbanites created them, deliberately and self-consciously, as communities suiting their own goals and needs' (Binford, 1985, p. 2). Binford believes that the concept of the urban fringe – a model developed by geographers, economists, and sociologists concerned with city-country interaction – is more useful than the transit model in explaining the origins of suburbs.

John Stilgoe, a historian of landscapes, also believes that the urban fringe is the best explanatory model of suburban development. In his book *Borderland: Origins of the American Suburb, 1820–1940*, he starts his quest to explain the origin of the American suburb in the urban fringe, working toward the city from the outside – the 'borderland' (Stilgoe, 1988). He believes that the real link between the fringe and the city lies not in the transportation system but in the commuter and what it means to commute. He takes commute to 'mean to mitigate or to lessen and in my opinion the outer suburbs began and developed as a spatial means of grappling with and lessening the difficulty of urbanization and, especially, urbanization based on industrialization and corporate capitalism' (Stilgoe, 1988, p. 5). Stilgoe argues, in effect, that the need to live away from the city and in the urban fringes was so great that the 'Borderlanders' were willing to commute to the city using any transportation available. Binford (1985) and Stilgoe (1988) agree that suburbs represent consciously conceived and built communities that would exist in some form regardless of the transportation available.

A bias in the suburban research, stemming again from the post-Second World War experience, is that the suburbs have been largely thought of as middle class and above, as 'bourgeois Utopias' in Robert Fishman's terms (Fishman, 1985). As Richard Harris comments in his study of Toronto's working class suburbs, 'we have been given the impression that in the first half of this century . . . the social geography of the North American city can best be understood in terms of a counterpoint between inner-city poverty and suburban affluence' (Harris, 1996, p. 4). In contrast, Harris argues that, after the turn of the century, working-class suburbs became common. In confirmation, in a study of historic suburbs around Wilmington, Delaware, my co-authors and I found that in the first three decades of this century, developers aimed much of their advertising to households of modest means, addressing the 'working man' directly or noting that even people of 'narrow' income could own property (Chase *et al.*, 1992, p. 101). Hence the academic suburban literature to date has, for the most part, been studying a portion of the suburban social landscape.

Another limitation of the social science literature on the suburbs is that, ironically, for all of the association with the subdivision and single-family house, very little research has been conducted on the built environment of the suburbs. Larry Ford, a geographer, laments this, observing that most of the literature on American residential landscapes is more about housing than houses (Ford, 1994, p. 126). Conducted on the statistical, aggregate level, housing studies tell us little about the aesthetics of the urban landscape and the values involved in its creation, according to Ford. Studies that have addressed houses include Gwendolyn Wright's *Building the Dream* (1981), Clifford Clark's *The American Family House* (1986), and Alan Gowans' *The Comfortable House: North American Suburban Architecture 1890–1930* (1986). These studies tend to interpret the evolution of the American house as a reflection of changing family values. However, they do not systematically explore how the house evolves as part of that larger suburban landscape. An exception is *Making the Middle Landscape*, by Peter Rowe, an architect and urban designer (Rowe, 1991).

If the bias in social science research on the suburbs has been toward more recent middle-class suburbs, there are parallel issues in the practice of historic preservation and the literature of architectural history. Until recently, the orientation of both endeavours has been toward upper-class, high-style architecture. The relationship between architectural history and historic preservation has been a close one, as historic preservationists have relied on architectural historians for judgement about the significance of buildings. Although historic preservation has been accused of being too focused on the architecture of the élite, in part this has been a result of the method of scholarship of traditional architectural history and its parent field, art history. In this method, the quality of an artistic object is judged in comparison with the best of a genre. Thus, traditional architectural history tended to study architecture that could be considered high on the scale of academic style. Much did not even qualify as architecture. In 1970, the architectural historian Vincent Scully commented that, at one time, domestic architecture was not considered significant enough to warrant art-historical investigation (Scully, quoted by Gowans, 1986, p. i).

The architectural history that is most useful for understanding the significance of suburban landscapes is relatively recent and grows out of development of a field known as vernacular architecture, or the 'new' architectural history. Stimulated in part by the work of cultural geographer Fred B. Kniffen in an article 'Folk Housing: Key to Diffusion' (Kniffen, 1965), vernacular architecture emerged in the 1970s as a field devoted to the empirical study of everyday architecture. The study of vernacular architecture proceeds on the assumption that description is the first step in the study of a building and that one 'cannot proceed to interpretation without specifying how the object came to exist' (Upton and Vlach, 1986, p. xvii). Initially dealing primarily with rural agricultural buildings and landscape, the study of vernacular architecture now includes nearly all ordinary architecture. The art historian Gowans' book *The Comfortable House* (1986) represents the influence of the inclusive vernacular perspective on architectural history. These trends in broadening the definition of historic resources were also reflected at the National Register where, in the 1970s and 1980s, the definition of historic resources was expanded to include complexes of buildings, such as farms and industrial sites, and larger landscapes.

Consideration of the suburbs as historically significant faces issues within historic preservation. Historic preservation is, at its base, a popular grassroots movement; and to be successful it must nurture proactive community and political support. The passage of the 1966 National Historic Preservation Act (NHPA) was, in large part, a reaction to the toll of buildings that were being lost to the redevelopment of American cities through urban renewal, highway programmes, subsidized housing and other programmes. And, as Longstreth (1992, p. 213) points out, 'the impetus for protecting large segments of the past was also bolstered by a dislike for work of the present: shopping malls and commercial strips, new residential tracts . . . and the ever more ambitious roadways that served all of them'. Thus, in many ways, the post-Second World War suburbs, maligned as tacky and dull and held up by some as the archetype of poor planning, confront the traditional conception within the preservation community of what comprises a 'historically significant' property.

As increasing numbers of properties reflecting significant societal trends become old enough to provide the distance needed for historic evaluation, professional preservationists are charged to find ways to communicate their significance. An example of a great challenge will be the consideration for preservation of the urban renewal projects of the 1950s, which demolished vast sections of downtowns and helped stimulate support for the 1966 NHPA.

DEVELOPING AN HISTORIC CONTEXT FOR THE EVALUATION
OF HISTORIC SUBURBS FOR THE NATIONAL REGISTER OF
HISTORIC PLACES

Established by the 1966 NHPA, the National Register of Historic Places is intended to be 'the nation's inventory of historic places and repository of documentation on the variety of historic property types, significance, abundance, condition, ownership, needs and other information' (National Park Service (NPS), 1991, p. 1). To qualify for the National Register, a property – defined as objects, buildings, structures, sites or districts – must be historically significant; by representing 'a significant part of the history, architecture, archaeology, engineering or culture of an area, and [by exhibiting] the characteristics that make it a good representative of properties associated with that aspect of the past' (NPS, 1991, p. 7). Although called the 'National' Register of Historic Places, a property may be listed on the Register for significance at the local and State level as well as the national level.

Specifically, to be eligible for the National Register, a property must meet one of four criteria. It must either be associated with events or trends that have made a significant contribution to the broad patterns of our history; or it must have been associated with the lives of persons significant in our past; or it must, in terms of design and construction, embody the distinctive characteristics of a type, period or method of construction; or it must yield, or be likely to yield, information important in history or prehistory. However, with the exception of Federally-owned properties, listing on the National Register of Historic Places is honorific; it carries with it no obligation to preserve a property or penalties for not doing so. The listing process requires that property owners be notified and given the opportunity to object.

Hence, in one respect, the National Register Program is a research programme designed to be carried out by preservation offices of local and State governments to discover historically significant properties. A technical bulletin is thus the research design, the procedures for surveying and evaluating a particular type of resource – in this case American suburban landscapes. The research undertaken in evaluating the eligibility of suburban areas for the National Register can contribute a great deal to our understanding of suburbanization in the United States.

In 1983, the Secretary of the U.S. Department of Interior promulgated standards for surveying, evaluating and determining the eligibility of historic properties for the National Register of Historic Places (*Federal Register*, 1983). The standards define historic preservation planning as the process that organizes preservation activities: the identification, evaluation, registration, and treatment of historic properties in a logical sequence. The major innovation in the standards was the concept that historic resources should be initially identified deductively as the physical manifestations of broad 'historic contexts' that describe 'one or more aspects of the historic development of an area . . .' and describe 'the significant geographical patterns that individual historic properties represent'. The planning standard suggests that the properties associated with the historic context can be identified categories of properties called 'property types'. These are groupings of individual properties that link the ideas incorporated in the context with actual historic properties that illustrate those ideas. Thus the historic context is a predictive model in one sense.

After working with the new standards, in 1991, the National Register published a bulletin, *How to Apply the National Register Criteria for Evaluation* (NPS, 1991), which integrated the historic context approach to the evaluation of historic significance with the criteria of significance set out in the 1966 legislation. Accordingly, the significance of a property can be judged 'only when it is evaluated within its historic context' (NPS, 1991, p. 7). The bulletin also detailed the elements of a historic context for purposes of evaluating historical significance. Historic contexts are those patterns, themes, or trends in history by which a specific occupancy, property, or site is understood and its meaning (and ultimately its significance) within history or prehistory is determined. A historic context contains four major elements: (1) geographic zone, (2) a historic theme, (3) chronological periods and (4) known and expected property types.[1] In order to decide whether a property is significant within its historic context, the following must be determined:

- the facet of prehistory or history of the local area, State, or the nation that the property represents;
- whether that facet of prehistory or history is significant;
- whether it is a type of property that has relevance and importance in illustrating the historic context;
- how the property illustrates that history; and
- whether the property possesses the physical features necessary to convey the aspect of history or prehistory with which it is associated.

If a property being evaluated represents an important aspect of the area's history or prehistory *and* possesses the requisite quality of integrity, then it qualifies for the National Register.

The goal of the technical bulletin for evaluating historic suburban areas was to develop the framework of a national historic context for their evaluation. The bulletin will consist of three parts. The first part is a broad historic context for understanding the historical evolution of American suburbs and interpreting the historical significance of local ones. This is followed by instructions on how to undertake research on local suburbs and guidelines for determining whether such suburban areas meet the criteria of significance for listing on the National Register. In short, the context is an outline and synthesis of our current understanding of the evolution of American suburbs followed by a research design for exploring local suburbs in a way that relates them to the national experience and suburban literature.

Thus, from the suburban literature, it was possible to define the geographic zone of suburbanization, the historic themes reflected by suburbanization, the chronological periods of the evolution of suburban landscapes, and the major property types. The first step in evaluating suburbs is how to define them in physical terms.

DEFINING SUBURBS AS HISTORIC PHYSICAL PROPERTIES

In addition to the physical properties of buildings, structures, objects, sites, and districts, the National Register also recognizes designed historic landscapes. It defines these as 'a landscape that has significance as a design or work of art; was consciously designed and laid out by a master gardener, landscape architect, or horticulturalist to a design principle, or an owner or other amateur using a recognized style or tradition . . .' (Keller and Keller, undated, p. 2). Subdivisions and planned communities are listed as examples of historic districts and meet the definition of historic landscapes. (According to the National Register of Historic Places a 'district possesses a significant concentration, linkage, or continuity of sites, buildings, structures, or objects united historically or aesthetically by plan or physical development' (National Park Service, 1991, p. 6).)

The discipline of definition for the National Register is that historic properties must be defined clearly enough to be evaluated for their physical integrity. The National Register defines seven aspects of integrity, of which a property must retain at least four to meet the integrity criteria. They are location, design, setting, materials, workmanship, feeling, and association. Location, design, setting and feeling take on special meaning in defining suburbs.

Location is the place where the historic property was constructed or the place where the historic event occurred. Design is the combination of elements that create the form, plan, space, structure, and style of a property. Setting is the physical environment of a historic property. Feeling is a property's expression of the aesthetic or historic sense of a particular period of time.

For the purposes of the technical bulletin on suburban landscape, suburbanization is defined broadly as the process and product of predominantly residential land development on or near the edge of an existing city within daily commuting distance. The building block, the primary property type, of this residential landscape is the subdivision. This is defined as a unit of land that has been bought and, with some level of planning, subdivided into residential building lots and provided with facilities including transportation and basic utilities. The basic element of the subdivision, the second major suburban property type, is the single-family house on its own lot (or other low-density contrast housing in some cases). Together, the single-family house set in a subdivision has embodied the suburban ideal of living in an individual house in an approximation of a semi-rural, non-city setting providing the basic elements of community life with daily access to the city.

I believe that the literature supports such a generic physical definition of suburbs. Such a definition makes no *a priori* assumptions about the social and political attributes of suburbs as being defining characteristics. For example, it does not assume a traditional definition of suburbs as areas outside the political boundaries of the central city but considers these to be a type of suburb. In contrast, historical suburban development is defined by its locational relationship to the existing, built-up functional city, not to the legal city, and by the character of its landscape compared to that of the city. For example, many residential areas that were built as streetcar suburbs in the 1890s, or horsecar suburbs even earlier, have long since been incorporated into the legal central city. With the streetcars and their tracks now gone, and housing built at higher densities than is associated with suburbs today, these areas are not thought to have been suburbs originally.

At the same time, defining suburban areas exclusively in terms of their physical characteristics alone exposes a definition of modern residential development. What we have thought of as 'suburban' was actually a new form of homogeneous, lower density residential development that occurred first on the edges of eastern North American cities. Thus residential areas within many newer cities, that grew since the turn of the twentieth century especially in the Midwest and Western United States, exhibit residential landscape characteristics within the legal city that are 'suburban', such as single-family houses, homogeneous residential neighbourhoods, and curvilinear street patterns. In Los Angeles, which has been called the suburban metropolis, the single-family house in a subdivision is the building block of the entire city, which is the culmination of this process (Fishman, 1985, p. 155).

In terms of the origins of suburbs, a definition of suburbs based on their physical characteristics as a landscape may also help document the emergence of modern homogeneous residential development, as improvements in transportation allowed the separation of land uses in the American city beginning in the mid-nineteenth century.

As defined in physical terms, the definition of suburbs proposed in the bulletin makes no assumptions about the social class of suburban areas. This is important because of mounting evidence that suburbanization included working-class households from the outset and progressively cut across lines of social class and income from the wealthy to the working classes. Whereas suburbs of the well-to-do consisting of large single family houses in curvilinear developments established the suburban ideal, for middle- and working-class households the same aspirations were met in modest cottages and later in bungalows on small lots in gridded street patterns. The National Register evaluations of suburbs may yield much more information about the frequency and characteristics of working-class suburbs.

The geographical extent of suburbanization around cities has been defined by the limits of personal transportation in which one could commute daily to work in the city and within the suburban fringes. This is evidenced by transportation and physical development. The bulletin describes how the geographical limits of the suburbs expanded as new means of transportation made it possible for people to become more mobile.

HISTORIC THEMES AND CHRONOLOGICAL PERIODS OF SUBURBANIZATION

The historic context approach to evaluating historic significance marks a shift from finding the significance of properties as lying primarily in their association with events or persons external to them. Alternatively, it provides a framework for evaluating properties as the physical manifestation of significant societal processes and patterns of historical development. Consequently, in the past ten years or so, preservationists have increasingly shifted their basic unit of evaluation from individual structures to landscapes and historical districts. This orientation was well stated by the National Register in 1993 in a technical bulletin for the evaluation of rural landscapes. 'There has been a growing interest among preservationists in . . . understanding the forces that have shaped rural properties, interpreting their historical importance and planning for their protection . . .' (McClelland *et al.*, 1993, p. 1).

The bulletin on suburban landscapes is organized around four broad historic themes and trends that encompass the historic forces that created the historic suburban landscape (see also table 11.1):

• suburban and metropolitan demographic trends,
• the evolution of urban and metropolitan transportation systems,
• the evolution of subdivision design and suburban development practices, and
• the evolution of suburban housing and its financing.

Demographic trends document the approximate growth and extent of the suburban areas. The other three trends are specifically ordered to reflect the evolution of the suburban physical landscape from the largest geographical scale of being first ordered and organized by transportation, then, at an intermediate scale, the suburban building blocks of residential subdivisions being built, and finally, at the smallest scale, the construction of suburban housing. We believe that the transportation model, tying successive generations of suburbanization to advances in technologies of personal transportation, first proposed by Warner (1962) and expanded by Adams (1970) and Muller (1981), to be the 'best' process explanation of the geographical growth of suburbanization. This four-stage transportation model is used in the bulletin both to define transportation trends and as the basis for the chronological periods of suburbanization: (1) railroad and horsecar suburbs from the 1840s to the 1890s; (2) streetcar suburbs from 1888 to

Table 11.1. Chronological periods and historical trends used in the Technical Bulletin for the National Register of Historic Places on *Evaluating Suburbs as Historic Landscapes*.

What is a suburban historic landscape? An overview of the chronology of suburbanization in the United States

> Railroad and horsecar suburbs: 1840s–1890s
> Streetcar suburbs: 1888–1920s
> Early automobile suburbs: 1920s–1940s
> Freeway suburbs: 1940s–1960s

Major trends in the creation of historic American suburban areas

> *Transportation trends*
> Railroads, horsecars and streetcars: 1840s–1920s
> Early automobile: 1908–1940s
> Freeway period: 1940s–1960s

> *Trends in land development and subdivision design*
> Birth of the subdivision
> Subdivision property types
> > Rectilinear plats or subdivisions
> > Curvilinear subdivisions
> The development process
> > Types of developers
> > Financing suburban residential development
> Mass production: post-Second World War subdivision and zoning

> *Trends in suburban housing: 1850–1950*
> The evolution of the single-family suburban house
> > Stages in the evolution of the suburban house
> > Invention of the balloon frame as a suburban prerequisite
> The Victorian suburban villa and the homestead suburban temple house: 1860–1900
> > Adapting the villa to the suburbs
> > The homestead suburban temple house
> > Building the suburbs with pattern books
> The practical suburban house: the bungalow, foursquare and revival houses: 1900–1940
> > The open plan and bungalows
> > The American foursquare and revival houses
> > Mail order suburban housing
> Post-Second World War suburban houses: the Cape Cod, the ranch house and others, 1940s–1950s
> > Transforming the FHA minimal house to the Cape Cod
> > The suburban ranch house
> > Other post-Second World War suburban housing types

the 1920s; (3) early automobile suburbs from 1920s to 1945; and (4) freeway suburbs from 1945 to the 1960s.

A central idea communicated in the bulletin about transportation is how providing access made new land available for development and how, within each transportation period, a distinctive suburban landscape emerged with a unique combination of transportation, types of residential development, housing, and commercial landscapes. But specific transportation improvements were not the prerequisite for suburbanization: they simply helped households achieve their desires for a suburban location. The strength and persistence of the desire to suburbanize were reflected in trends in the residential development process and the evolution of the subdivision and suburban house. Suburban landscapes were built on the edges of small cities without streetcars, such as Fredericksburg, Virginia, in the late nineteenth and early twentieth centuries. This confirms the observations of Binford (1985) and Stilgoe (1988) that the urban fringe has long exhibited a suburban community coherence and character not dependent on transportation.

The second major trend by which suburbs should be evaluated, and perhaps the most important one, is how the building block of the suburbs – the subdivision and the suburban single-family house – evolved from the mid-1800s to mid-twentieth century. The evolution of the subdivision and single house is presented as two related trends: one for upper-income households and one for those of more modest means. As Mary Corbin Sies argues, it was in the planned, exclusive upper-class suburbs of the late nineteenth and early twentieth centuries that the American suburban ideal of shelter in a 'single-family house with a garden and plenty of open space in a locally controlled suburban community' became fully articulated as a value expressed as a landscape (Sies, 1997). Thus, while the curvilinear subdivision layout, the picturesque model, was the highest, most desirable form of residential development, it contained several features that could be achieved in simpler, higher density, less costly rectilinear subdivisions along streetcar lines. A subdivision of small lots set in a gridiron street pattern within walking distance of mass transit met the basic suburban criteria of uniform residential use of single-family houses on their own lots with separate access.

The suburban house evolved within the context of the subdivision as an element in creating a landscape in complete contrast to (and rejection of) that of the city. As a building, its evolution was reflected less in trends in architectural styles than in how changing house types and floor plans reflected changing concepts of the ideal family that the house was designed to support. This took place within the constant ideal of the suburban landscape as a semi-rural retreat from the city.

The bulletin also outlines the evolution of the suburban development process so that preservationists will understand the underlying continuity in suburbanization (one of the best and most comprehensive treatments of the suburban development process is Doucet and Weaver, 1991). This explains why, for example, the large curvilinear subdivisions of uniform houses built after the Second World War looked different from pre-war subdivisions that were much smaller and often architecturally quite diverse. The suburban land development process, as Anne Keating has written, 'consists of two distinct procedures: the initial subdivision and improvement of a tract of land, and the actual construction of buildings' (Keating, 1988, p. 124). From the 1870s until the 1920s, the two procedures were done by separate individuals or groups. Developers, or subdividers, acquired land, surveyed it, developed a plan, laid out building lots and roads, and improved the site with certain amenities and services (Chase, 1995, p. 119). The lots were sold to prospective owner-residents who contracted with a builder, or to speculators, or to builders who would buy a few parcels, building one or two houses at a time (Chase *et al.*, 1992, p. 90). It was after the Second World War, in the face of great demand and availability of construction credit and long-term financing, that the two steps in the development process were joined by single developers who built the prototypically, post-Second World War, larger scale, architecturally uniform subdivision that has become the icon of North American suburbanization.

While the bulletin should be judged on the quality of its synthesis of the scholarship on the North American suburbs, its purpose is to provide the basis for bringing historic suburbs into the realm of recognized historic landscapes and properties by the preservation community and by the general public.

Conclusion: The Gap between National Register Recognition and the Preservation or Conservation of Suburbs

Elsewhere in this volume, in the context of the U.K., Peter J. Larkham asks the questions 'why conserve?' and 'what to conserve in the suburban landscape?'. In answering those queries, he is able to draw upon a history of concern in the U.K. about suburban historic resources – 'a suburban-pro-conservation movement' – and the experience of a strong national system for the designation and control of conservation areas. Neither of these conditions exists in the U.S. Indeed, a primary purpose of the National Register Bulletin on historic suburban areas is to introduce to professional and lay preservationists the idea that suburban areas should be considered as historic landscapes.

Although the National Register of Historic Places in the U.S. was created as part of the 1966 NHPA and is a national policy, because of the constitutional separation of powers between Federal and State and local governments, actual listing on the National Register is largely honorific and carries no requirement for protection or conservation. (The only exception to this is when listed properties are owned by the Federal government or are being affected by Federally funded or licensed programmes.) In the U.S., only local government has the power to preserve or conserve historic properties acting through local preservation ordinances. Such ordinances must originate at the local level and, consequently, the jurisdictional pattern of preservation requirements in the U.S. is extraordinarily uneven – ranging from non-existent in many areas to fairly strong in a few areas.

But the National Register of Historic Places has enormous influence on the evaluation and designation of historic properties in the U.S., whether or not they are listed on the Register. This is because the criteria promulgated in the NHPA (listed earlier), and articulated in publications such as technical bulletins by the National Register, to evaluate the historic significance of properties have become widely accepted as the standards of preservation evaluation in the U.S. Also, many historic preservation efforts in the U.S. are initiated by local, grass-roots organizations such as historical societies, using the National Register criteria and bulletins to evaluate their local resources with the goal of convincing local governments to designate them officially as historic districts or properties.

Thus the challenge of preserving suburban areas as historic landscapes in the U.S. is perhaps more basic than in some other countries represented in this volume, such as the U.K. Here, the initial challenge is educational, establishing that they are of historic significance. This task faces stiff resistance both from many professional preservationists and from the public. There are at least two important reasons for this. One is the difficulty of many, numbering not a few preservationists, in accepting the recent past, including most of the twentieth century, as historically significant. The second is the prevalence of suburban sprawl, the rise of the new suburban critique it has stimulated, spearheaded by James Kunstler (1996) and others, including the President of the National Trust for Historic Preservation in the United States. So now in the 1990s, the American post-Second World War suburban landscape is experiencing its second round of condemnation. This both undermines an historic perspective on suburbanization and lends the word 'suburb' a pejorative implication. At the same time, there is a school of planning calling itself 'the New Urbanism', promoting remedies to the excesses of sprawl which, ironically, draw on planning principles from what many consider to be the high point of suburban planning and design from the turn of the twentieth century to the early 1930s. Grounded in Garden City concepts, their principles culminate with Clarence Perry and his 'Neighbourhood Unit', and Radburn, New Jersey, designed by Clarence Stein and Henry Wright as a suburban solution to urban congestion and the automobile. The 'New Urbanists' are, more accurately, 'New Suburbanists'.

But, as Richard Longstreth comments, 'the issue is not when something becomes "historic" but instead when adequate historical perspective can be gained on a particular phenomenon' (Longstreth, 1992). Historic perspective, and appreciation of historic suburbs, may come when several generations have known nothing but the suburbs. I teach a graduate course called 'The American Suburb'. My students, mostly in their early twenties, many third-generation suburbanites, seem to welcome a course which finds historic significance in the subdivisions of their origins. Many, commenting that they thought they were without a history, frequently move to documenting their home developments, and on holidays and weekends, conduct oral histories with parents and grandparents. The challenge in preserving historic suburbs may be less in convincing many younger people of their historic significance, than in giving them a framework for evaluating that significance.

NOTE

1. The remaining, less important, eight are criteria for evaluating existing or expected resources, distribution and potential distribution of property types, goals and priorities for the context, property types information needs and recent preservation activity, reference bibliography, method for involving general and professional public, and mechanism for updating the context.

REFERENCES

Adams, J.S. (1970) Residential structure of midwestern cities. *Annals of the Association of American Geographers*, Vol. 60, No. 1, pp. 37–62.

Ames, D.L. (1995) Interpreting post-World War II suburban landscapes as historic resources, in Slaton, D. and Schiffer, R.A. (eds.) *Preserving the Recent Past*. Washington, D.C.: Historic Preservation Education Foundation.

Binford, H. (1985) *The First Suburbs: Residential Communities on the Boston Periphery, 1815–1860*. Chicago: University of Chicago Press.

Bishir, C.W. and Earley, L.S. (1985) *Early Twentieth-Century Suburbs in North Carolina: Essays on History, Architecture and Planning*. Lillington, CC: Edwards Brothers for the Archives and Historic Preservation Section, North Carolina Department of Cultural Resources.

Chase, S.M. (1995) The Process of Suburbanization and the Use of Restrictive Deed Covenants as Private Zoning. Unpublished Ph.D. thesis, University of Delaware.

Chase, S.M., Ames, D.L. and Siders, R. (1992) *Suburbanization in the Vicinity of Wilmington, Delaware*. Newark, Delaware: Center for Historic Architecture and Engineering, University of Delaware.

Clark, C.E. (1986) *The American Family Home: 1800–1960*. Chapel Hill: University of North Carolina Press.

Doucet, M. and Weaver, J. (1991) *Housing the North American City*. Montreal and Kingston: McGill-Queen's University Press.

Federal Register (1983) Part IV: Department of the Interior, National Park Service, Archaeology and Historic Preservation: Secretary of the Interior Standards and Guidelines. *Federal Register*, Vol. 48, No. 190, September 29, pp. 44716–44742.

Fishman, R. (1985) *Bourgeois Utopias: The Rise and Fall of Suburbia*. New York: Basic Books.

Ford, L.R. (1994) *Cities and Buildings: Skyscrapers, Skid Rows and Suburbs*. Baltimore: Johns Hopkins University Press.

Gans, H.J. (1967) *The Levittowners: Ways of Life and Politics in a New Suburban Community*. New York: Pantheon.

Gowans, A. (1986) *The Comfortable House: North American Suburban Architecture, 1890–1930*. Cambridge, MA: M.I.T. Press.

Harris, R. (1996) *Unplanned Suburbs: Toronto's American Tragedy, 1900–1950.* Baltimore: Johns Hopkins University Press.

Jackson, K.T. (1985) *Crabgrass Frontier: The Suburbanization of America.* New York: Oxford University Press.

Keating, A.D. (1988) *Building Chicago: Suburban Development and the Creation of a Divided Metropolis.* Columbus, OH: Ohio State University.

Keller, T.J. and Keller, G.P. (undated) *How to Evaluate and Nominate Designed Historic Landscapes.* National Register Bulletin 18. Washington, D.C.: U.S. Department of Interior, National Park Service.

Kniffen, F. (1965) Folk housing. key to diffusion. *Annals of the Association of American Geographers*, Vol. 60, No. 5, pp. 549–577.

Kunstler, J.H. (1996) *Home From Nowhere.* New York: Simon and Schuster.

Longstreth, R. (1992) When the present becomes the past, in Lee, A. (ed.) *Past Meets Future: Saving America's Historic Environments.* Washington, D.C.: The Preservation Press.

McClelland, L.F., Keller, T., Keller, G.P. and Melnick, R.Z. (1993) *Guidelines for Evaluating and Documenting Rural Historic Landscapes.* National Register Bulletin no. 30. Washington, D.C.: U.S. Department of Interior, National Park Service.

Muller, P.O. (1981) *Contemporary Suburban America.* New York: Prentice-Hall.

Mumford, L. (1961) *The City in History: Its Origins, Its Transformation and Its Prospects.* New York: Harcourt Brace & World.

National Park Service (1991) *How to Apply the National Register Criteria for Evaluation.* National Register Bulletin 15. Washington, D.C.: U.S. Department of Interior, National Park Service.

Palen, J.J. (1995) *The Suburbs.* New York: McGraw-Hill.

Rowe, P.G. (1991) *Making the Middle Landscape.* Cambridge, MA: M.I.T. Press.

Sies, M.C. (1997) Paradise retained. An analysis of persistence in planned, exclusive suburbs 1880–1980. *Planning Perspectives*, Vol. 12, No. 2, pp. 165–192.

Stilgoe, J.R. (1988) *Borderland: Origins of the American Suburb, 1820–1939.* New Haven: Yale University Press.

Upton, D. and Vlach, J.M. (1986) *Common Places: Readings in Vernacular Architecture.* Athens, GA: University of Georgia Press.

Warner, S.B. (1962) *Streetcar Suburbs: The Process of Growth in Boston 1870–1900.* Boston: Boston University Press.

Wright, G. (1981) *Building the Dream: A Social History of Housing in America.* New York: Pantheon.

Chapter 12

Conservation and Management in UK Suburbs[1]

Peter J. Larkham

Why Conserve Suburbs?

Why conserve at all? This fundamental question has been repeatedly asked and addressed with respect to a wide range of cultural artefacts, not least of which are landscapes (Lowenthal and Binney, 1981). Amongst many such artefact groupings, what is viewed as 'significant' (i.e. worthy of collection or preservation) appears to be getting closer and closer to the present day. This is certainly true of buildings and landscape areas in the UK (Larkham, 1996*a*). What seems to be emerging is a view that the important issue is not what is retained, with concomitant problems of genuineness and/or originality, but the use(s) to which the past, and its intangible and tangible remnants, may be put (Lowenthal, 1985).

The suburban pro-conservation movement should be seen in the context of clear trends towards historicist styles for new dwellings at all socio-economic levels in many developed countries. It is unlikely that this is a conscious part of architectural post-modernism; developers state clearly that their designs are driven by customer demand. Thus in the UK the Redrow group has launched its 'Heritage Range', which includes

> the familiar thirties-style house – a popular classic, now just old enough to appeal to the nostalgic and not to look out of place as new. It comes complete with arched porchways and semi-circular bay windows, its exterior hinting at a certain inter-war cosiness but with rather more in the way of internal comfort. (Lennox, 1997)

In the USA, the neo-traditional layouts of many PUDs (Planned Urban Developments) offer overpoweringly traditional house designs in 'the tradition of upper-middle class attempts to mimic the villas, mansions and town houses of genuinely wealthy and socially established families' (Knox, 1992, p. 215 and figure 8.2).

The suburban sprawl, and particularly the extent of its speculative and municipal manifestations of the inter-war period, means that much of the UK's population live, or have lived, in the relatively low-density, expansive, areas of what Whitehand and Carr (this volume) term 'garden suburbs'. Many such

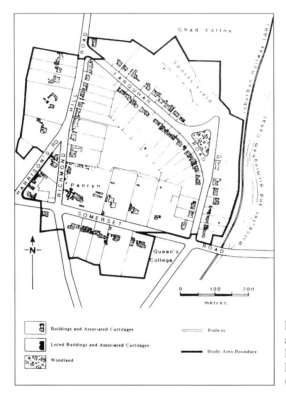

Figure 12.1. Changes to plot and street patterns in part of Edgbaston conservation area. Left, *c.* 1947. Right, *c.* 1990. (*Source*: Jones, 1991)

landscapes thus are part of the 'anonymous familiar' which might deserve recognition and retention (Meinig, 1979; Tarn, 1975). Indeed, this was explicitly recognized by the phrase 'the familiar and cherished local scene', which recurs in UK conservation guidance (Mynors, 1984). It is interesting that even the National Trust has recently, albeit amidst much debate, taken on two suburban properties: an Edwardian semi-detached villa in Worksop (Nottinghamshire) and Erno Goldfinger's own Modern house in London. It is inevitable, therefore, that some suburbs have been the focus of explicit preservation attempts or management proposals.

How to conserve? Suburban areas have raised many of the basic ethical dilemmas more familiar in other conservation debates but, perhaps owing to the relative newness and controversy of suburban conservation, lessons learned elsewhere have not always been applied here. Lowenthal, for example, gives an example of the 'originality' debate that pre-dates all official recognition. Some of the neo-Georgian houses in Hampstead Garden Suburb had open shutters, bolted to the walls, as an original decorative design feature. During the Second World War the residents of one house, in response to the threat of air raids, undid the original bolts, added hinges, and closed the shutters as a precaution against blast damage. 'After the war, the local preservation society insisted the hinges

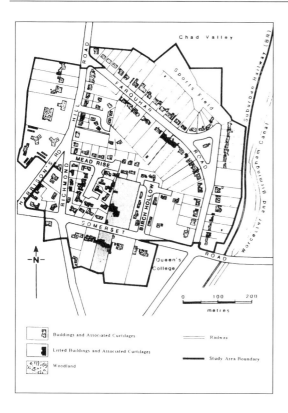

be removed and the shutters bolted back: they were authentically *fake* shutters' (Lowenthal, 1990, p. 16). The debates over 'character' and 'appearance' now common in town centres are less well articulated for suburbs where, in many cases, the key characteristics are regularity of layout, building form and style: so what differentiates one potentially conservation-worthy area from another? In some examples, 'originality' has been argued: i.e. freedom from later alterations and extensions, at least on the front elevation. Rear elevations, it seems, matter less and can more readily be altered.

What to conserve? There are different *types* of suburbs: the more exclusive, and usually earlier, suburban landscapes have been the subject of protection and management for much longer – in some cases, through legal restrictions on plots, building forms, styles and materials, and land uses, imposed prior to construction (e.g. Edgbaston, Birmingham: Jones, 1991). Indeed, there has long been interest in the landscapes of the élite and their origins and management – or conservation – from the many studies of country houses and their landscaped parks to residential urban élite landscapes (see Duncan and Duncan, 1984). But, even here, landscapes are considerably altered through continuous pressure for incremental change (figure 12.1). In a recent US study, Sies (1997) examines the 'persistence' of such planned, exclusive suburbs and their resistance to the 'normal' pattern of declining socio-economic status and physical condition. She suggests four key elements favouring such persistence over the past century; three of which relate to original design and layout, and the fourth is 'a communal consensus favouring persistence', an intangible factor.

> Suburbanites consistently articulated the value of their residential environment as a special place that met their needs for daily living and was worth spending their own effort and money to preserve. A crucial element of their satisfaction derived from the perception that they and their neighbors could control what happened within the borders of their community . . . The insistence on local control has a darker side, however. Residents of élite suburbs have invoked nearly all of the measures described [by Sies] to exclude from their communities persons they perceived to be different and to insulate themselves from the social and economic problems of the larger metropolis. (Sies, 1997, p. 186)

Middle- and working-class suburban dwellers have had less opportunity to exercise such control over their dwellings and their neighbours. Nevertheless, these suburbs were often planned and designed with similar care and attention to detail, often on the part of individual small speculative developers. Although built to similar bye-law and planning standards (e.g. the post-First World War Parker Morris standards), each estate could display considerable individual character. Yet it is only relatively recently that these suburbs have been deemed worthy of protection; and such efforts have often led to wide press coverage and expressions of surprise. When, in 1997, Birmingham City Council extended protection to 199 prefabricated American-designed and built wooden bungalows, developed for the Austin company's workers at Longbridge in 1917, it was featured in *The Times* (1997, p. 10). The same authority designated probably the first conserved area of 1930s speculative semi-detached houses in the UK a decade earlier (see below, and figure 12.2); this, too, featured in *The Times* (Franks, 1988) and caused much debate about 'debasing' the concept of conservation. Yet these areas are now quite acceptable for conservation purposes: the London Borough of Brent has designated no fewer than eight such inter-war areas between 1989 and 1995 (Box 12.1).

There has been some difficulty in justifying conservation of the more anonymous suburban landscapes, especially of 1930s speculative semi-detached housing. The London Borough of Harrow (1990*a*) has justified conservation of its West Towers area because of its outstanding quality of architectural detailing which has remained largely unaltered, and because it represents a 'significant group of buildings of a distinct physical identity and architectural cohesiveness'. These are contentious, although commonly-used, statements – at least in the context of inter-war (or even more recent) suburbs. There has been no such problem in justifying conservation of élite suburbs to professionals, press or public.

In one of the few works explicitly dealing with suburban conservation – itself little more than an historical commentary – Saunders (1981) notes several aspects pertinent to conservation in London's 'Metroland' suburbia. First, that the

Figure 12.2. School Road conservation area, Hall Green, Birmingham: developed during the 1930s and designated 1988 (*Photograph*: P.J. Larkham, 1996)

retention of earlier buildings and features during the phase of suburban development was 'fortuitous rather than conscious, demolition being regarded as simply wasteful rather than distasteful; but there was certainly some desire to retain beauty for its own sake' (Saunders, 1981, p. 166). This contrasts with today's explicit retention of such features in attempts to create place-identity and 'character'. However, in many areas, what was retained was not the original buildings (which were demolished as 'inconvenient') but the pre-urban cadaster of field and property boundaries, and the morphological frame of any existing streets, paths etc. This is also known in many other suburban layouts from the eighteenth century onwards.

Secondly, the post-war preservation movement, Saunders suggests, is driven by two conflicting views. One is the desire to preserve the pre-(sub)urban survivals, 'born of distaste for the drabness and uniformity of many suburbs'. He suggests that this is the most powerful motive, since (owing to similarities of plan type, building type, materials and styles) many suburbs are essentially place-less, i.e. not specific to any local vernacular. The other is the rise of a positive appreciation of the characteristics of suburbia, although Saunders' examples relate to the high-class distinctive suburbs of the late-Victorian and Edwardian period (increasingly subject to a wider architectural and aesthetic appreciation: cf Long, 1993), rather than to the middle-class semi-detached suburbia caricatured as 'By-pass Variegated' by Osbert Lancaster.

Box 12.1. Descriptions of 1930s conservation areas, Brent. (*Source*: London Borough of Brent, 1997, pp. 26–27)

SUBURBAN ESTATES BY RENOWNED INTER-WAR DEVELOPERS

Barn Hill
Designated in March 1990 and January 1993
Builders: Haymills

Mock-Tudor housing estate of 1926–29 on a steep hillside on which remnants survive of a landscape by Repton (1792). The street scenes, landscaping and views between buildings are especially important.

Design Guide and Article 4 Direction in force.[1]

Preston Park
Designated in January 1993
Builders: Clifford Sabey and F. & C. Costin

An attractive and pleasant planned residential suburb of 1927–37 where Sabey's cottage-style houses in narrow roads contrast against Costin's grander semis.

Mount Stewart
Designated in January 1993
Builders: F. & C. Costin

Part of the John Lyon Farm Estate developed by the Costins, using their pattern book of high-quality mock-Tudor designs. There is an extensive range of bay windows, leaded lights and brickwork and a high standard of joinery.

Design Guide and Article 4 Direction in force.

Northwick Circle
Designated in April 1989
Builders: F. & C. Costin

An excellent example of suburban town planning in mock-Tudor style, incorporating a focal point and radiating street pattern. Substantial gardens add to the open character.

Work on a Design Guide and Article 4 Direction to commence shortly.

Queens Walk
Designated in January 1990
Builder: C.W.B. Simmonds

An attractive street on the Kingsbury Hill estate of whitewashed detached and semi-detached houses dating from 1926.

continued

Sudbury Court
Designated in January 1990 and January 1993
Builders: Comben and Wakeling

This is one of the best mock-Tudor estates in the Borough. Dating from 1929–1935, the houses have a distinctive appearance with many fine features. Mature hedges, trees and shrubs are a significant feature of the street scenes of this garden suburb.

Design Guide and Article 4 Direction in force.

King Edward VII Conservation Area
Designated in July 1995
Builders: Comben and Wakeling

Earlier than Sudbury Court, this estate by James Comben and W.H. Wakeling in 1926–1929 was laid out adjoining King Edward VII Park. The street pattern, its landscaping and roundabouts provide an attractive setting of a suburban village character.

Lawns Court
Designated in July 1995
Architects: Welch, Cachemaille-Day and Lander

An estate of 50 flats built in the 'Moderne' style in 1932–1933. The juxtaposition of the buildings around a green and the mature landscaping provide an attractive setting for the buildings.

Leaflets giving descriptions and history have been prepared for each area.

Note

1. Details of the mechanisms of design guides and Article 4 Directions are given later in the text.

The rising tide of conservation visible in much of the developed world has thus reached the suburb as a development type. This is clear for suburbs of the inter-war period and earlier; but there are as yet only slight traces of conservation interests in later suburbs. The familiarity and wide spread of suburbs which might be subject to conservation, and the considerable investment which they represent, means that suburban conservation is now very much a contemporary issue. This chapter addresses the problems of whether, and to what extent, such quasi-legal designations actually do serve to protect these suburban areas, and what are the implications for the involvement of their residents.

THE SYSTEM OF PROTECTION: DEVELOPMENT CONTROL AND CONSERVATION

There has been a trend in the UK, where development rights were effectively nationalized in 1947, for the local planning authority (LPA) to seek to extend aesthetic control increasingly widely; often using mechanisms termed 'guidance' and 'advice' rather than compulsion. This trend ran against the view of the Conservative government (in power from 1979 to 1997) that LPAs should not 'interfere' in issues of aesthetics and design, except in specified areas of special character: this view is well expressed in Circulars 22/80 and 31/85 of the Department of the Environment (DoE, 1980, 1985). However, even the Conservative administration accepted that some areas were 'special' and, within these, a degree of aesthetic control was acceptable.

Various forms of design guidance are now common, many of which focus on topics such as the scale, nature and design of suburban dwelling extensions (Chapman and Larkham, 1992, figure 3). Planning policies to prevent the joining-together of groups of semi-detached houses to form terraces (known as 'terracization') – apparently argued more on aesthetic grounds than detriment to the amenity of neighbours – are becoming evident. The London Borough of Harrow, for example, has a policy for the largely semi-detached Pinnerwood Park conservation area (built 1932–1939; designated 1989) that 'proposals for infilling of the spaces between properties will normally be resisted' (London Borough of Harrow, 1990b, p. 55). This form of suburban management is now increasingly common across the country, even for quite ordinary residential neighbourhoods and building types.

However, there are 'special' areas where tighter controls exist. Conservation has become an accepted part of planning in most Western countries. In the UK, it takes two main forms. First, there is the placing of individual buildings of 'special architectural or historic interest' on a statutory list by the relevant Secretary of State: such 'listed buildings' are subject to tighter controls relating to alteration or demolition. Relatively few inter-war suburban houses are protected by listing; only a few key buildings by architects of national or international renown meet the stringent national criteria.

The second form of protection is the designation by the LPA of a conservation area, an area 'of special architectural or historical interest, the character or appearance of which it is desirable to preserve or enhance'. Over 10,000 such areas have been designated in the UK since 1967. It was not until the mid-1970s, and especially the early 1980s, that much attention was paid to residential areas. Typically, residential designations have been well-established areas, mainly of pre-Victorian date (although many such designations incidentally extend protection to much more modern inclusions: figure 12.3). However, by the early 1990s, 20 per cent of LPAs responding to the survey by Jones and Larkham (1993) had designated twentieth-century residential areas, including a small number first

Figure 12.3. Kirby Fields conservation area, Blaby, near Leicester. Area boundary of Victorian villa suburb shown dotted; 1970s and 1980s housing estates identified with bold line. (*Source*: amended from LPA designation map)

developed in the post-war period. It is evident that some LPAs have been seeking and designating modern areas of high townscape quality, presumably to prevent them from further architectural and aesthetic deterioration over time (Jones and Larkham, 1993, p. 60). However, working-class suburbs, including the great municipal estates of the inter-war period, are still significantly under-protected. Although still a relatively small proportion of the total, suburbs are becoming a higher proportion of the 200 or so areas designated each year. This broadening of the concept of conservation areas parallels the recent heated debates over the listing of inter-war, and particularly post-war, buildings.

But conservation areas are not preserved in aspic; development which preserves or enhances character or appearance, in the words of the Act, may be permitted. In particular, unlisted houses may readily be demolished and replaced notwithstanding the requirement that demolition consent be obtained for *any* building within a conservation area. Once more, *The Times* highlighted a case where an unlisted 1904 house in the style of Voysey, in a conservation area in Belsize Park, London, was faced with demolition. A battery of architectural historians and English Heritage argued that the building was 'a house of particular value' and that its loss would be serious in this 'unusually complete and hand-some street'. A planning inspector felt that, as the house was rendered in white, and the majority of its neighbours were of red brick, it was capable of being replaced by a new school building which would use hand-made bricks. The problem lies in the legal definition of a conservation area which – unlike the speech of the legislation's promoter, Duncan Sandys MP – uses 'conserve *or* enhance' rather than 'conserve *and* enhance' (Binney, 1994). In this case, despite the objections of local residents, the original building has been demolished. One local resident made a telling comment: 'A place is designated a conservation area because of its overall harmony and the more gaps there are, the harder it becomes to defend' (Françoise Findlay, Belsize Residents' Association, quoted in Binney, 1994).

This chapter focuses on complex and sometimes contradictory issues of management and conservation through examination of design guidance as a management tool, which may be applied to all forms of existing suburbs and may be used to shape the form and nature of new suburbs; and through studying management and change in designated conservation areas of quite different character.

THE SCALE AND NATURE OF CHANGE IN ENGLISH SUBURBIA

First, however, this chapter supplements that by Whitehand and Carr by discussing the nature and extent of change in UK suburbs. This is a necessary precursor to understanding the impact of any techniques of strategies of management.

Research in sample 25 ha 'mature residential areas' in the South-East and Midland regions of England by Whitehand and Larkham (1991*a*, 1991*b*) has shown that post-war suburban change is extensive. The pilot survey for this research, comparing current development patterns with large-scale 1950s plans, found that in some cases on the London fringe, over 50 per cent of the 25 ha study areas had undergone change. Even the smallest settlement examined, Gerrards Cross, contained continuous areas of several hectares in which few 1950s plots survived unmodified to the mid-1980s (Whitehand, 1988, figure 2). The amount of change is graphically represented in Jones' diagrams showing plots and dwellings in part of the conservation area in Edgbaston, Birmingham, in *c.* 1947 and 1990: the 'densification' is clearly shown in the plot subdivision, and new culs-de-sac (figure 12.1).

More detailed research in six such areas (three in each region; three of which were conservation areas) for the period 1960–1987 supported these preliminary findings. Although each area is sufficiently small that individual circumstances can markedly affect the pattern, it is clear that the residential urban landscape has undergone marked change in the study period. The extent of land subject to proposals for more intensive development or redevelopment does not vary much between the Midlands and South East, but there is a marked difference between regions in the density at which the new development has taken place. Whereas in the three South-East areas 770 dwellings were constructed, or under construction, during the study period, the comparable figure for the Midlands areas was only 195 dwellings (Whitehand *et al.*, 1992, p. 231).

It has been suggested that, during the course of attempts to develop or redevelop sites, it is common for several schemes to be put forward. The planning files generally contain data on dwelling type, density, access and whether existing buildings are to be demolished. It is thus possible to examine the relationship between applicants' apparent intentions and subsequent proposals and outcomes in the landscape. The amount of change between each scheme in a series in terms of these four variables can be assessed. A distinction can be drawn between schemes that are the same on all four variables (discounting minor differences in the line and width of roads) and those that are not. Such quantitative analysis of applications for the four residential areas of Amersham, Epsom, Gibbet Hill and Tettenhall shows significant differences between initial applications and actual developments in the two South-East regions, but little in the Midlands. If sites on which no development resulted are added, then only 25 per cent of sites in these two South-East areas underwent a development the same as that proposed in the initial application, compared with 65 per cent in the Midlands areas. Changes in density and building type tended to be the most important. On average, actual densities were lower than those initially applied for.

In terms of the urban landscape, outcomes on the ground can frequently be described as being inadvertent, almost unplanned, in that they often do not reflect the original intentions of developers, designers, or even the LPA. In some cases, even the first application was a modification of original intentions, sometimes as a result of discussions with the LPA. The LPAs themselves had clearly given little thought to the future of individual sites until stimulated by a planning application. The changing stance of LPAs during the development process is caused, in part, by this unpreparedness; in part, by changing attitudes of individual case officers (and the case officer often changed during a lengthy development saga); and, rarely, by the overturning of an officer's recommendation by the Planning Committee or at Appeal (Whitehand, 1989).

In many cases, the development process can be seen to be extremely lengthy. In the case of 151 sites where development was proposed in four of the 25 ha residential areas examined, the planning gestation period[2] varied greatly between areas but, nevertheless, had a mean of over 32 months (Whitehand and Larkham, 1991*a*; 1991*b*).

For the four areas, a total of 455 applications for new residential development were submitted, 174 in the two Midlands regions and 281 for the South-East regions. The approval rate for the Midlands was 67 per cent, and for the South East was 47 per cent (Whitehand and Larkham, 1991*b*, p. 59). The average site in the South-East regions attracted between three and four applications. The development process in these established residential areas is thus likely to be protracted, with decisions on individual applications taking longer than the DoE target of eight weeks, and in many cases with a whole series of applications being processed before development occurs. Indeed, the delay may be such that development occurs in conditions markedly different from those in which they were conceived; or the changing socio-economic conditions may themselves further postpone development (Whitehand and Larkham, 1991*a*).

THE MANAGEMENT OF SUBURBAN CHANGE

Legal Issues: Conservation Areas, Listing, Article 4 Directions

The designation of conservation areas and listed buildings occurs at different levels, and this introduces a tension between local and central government; and often between local communities and government at both levels. The conservation area is, almost without exception, a designation by the LPA. Generally welcomed by members of the public, but sometimes resisted by potential developers, the exact motives for many designations have been challenged (Jones and Larkham, 1993). 'Snob-zoning' and the alleged rise in property values have led local groups to demand wider, and more, designations, while LPA officers allegedly favour the increased control over design and demolition. Once designated, however, statute and case law provide the LPA with additional duties, the cost implications of which are rarely made explicit prior to designation.

The legal definition of a UK conservation area states that these areas are of special architectural or historic interest, the character or appearance of which should be preserved and enhanced (1990 Planning (Listed Buildings and Conservation Areas) Act. Local authorities must pay 'special attention to development issues in these areas. A series of high-profile court cases has tested the application of this legal wording. Since the landmark *Steinberg* case, for example, 'special' attention has explicitly to be given to every development in order to ensure that it preserves or enhances area character or appearance – and, since the *South Lakeland* case, at least does not actively damage those characteristics (Millichap, 1989).

Listed buildings are, however, listed by the Secretary of State. Although expert bodies such as English Heritage advise the Secretary of State, he/she is not bound to take that advice. Many buildings which local communities and LPAs would wish to see protected are refused that protection (see the Hall Green example below).

Although most forms of new buildings and alterations constitute 'development' and thus require planning permission, under the General Development Orders (GDOs) a range of (usually minor) developments are given automatic permission, and are referred to as 'permitted development'. However, in some circumstances, even these developments can be brought under control through a Direction under Article 4 of the GDO. Although a range of myths surrounds the use of these Article 4 Directions, conservation is clearly the largest single user (Larkham and Chapman, 1996). Until 1995, each Direction had to be confirmed by the Secretary of State: without such confirmation, which was often withheld, a Direction would last for only 6 months and then lapse. After a new General Permitted Development Order in 1995, LPAs could make some Directions, particularly relating to the external appearance of dwelling houses, without requiring the Secretary of State's express consent.

Such Article 4 Directions have been seen by planners as invaluable additional legal controls: one survey respondent stated that they were 'a vital tool for the proper planning control of conservation areas' (quoted in Larkham and Chapman, 1996, p. 14). Numerous Directions now exist for residential conservation areas, many having been put in place since the 1995 relaxation of the regulations. That for the Gidea Park conservation area, in the London Borough of Havering, is instructive. This area comprises a planned layout of properties constructed for a 1911 Exhibition and Competition and from a 1934 'Modern Homes' Competition and Exhibition. Designated in 1970, by the late 1980s the LPA was concerned about the increasing number of poorly-designed alterations and large extensions. Accordingly an Article 4 Direction was made, affording two additional levels of control over tightly-defined parts of the conservation area (Box 12.2).

The Nature and Extent of Suburban Design Guidance

The term 'design guide' is in general use, but no commonly-accepted definition has arisen save that adopted by Llewellyn-Davies *et al.* (1976): 'a design guide is a general set of design principles and standards required by the local authority and applying to a wide area and not just a particular site'. In a survey of LPA design guides in general, Chapman and Larkham (1992) found that house extensions formed the third most common subject for guidance (behind shop-fronts and building materials), with conservation areas being fifth of a total of 17 subject categories. That study identified some general issues with guidance. The time, effort and expense involved in the preparation, illustration and distribution represented significant resource input by LPAs. However there is a high level of repetition in similar guidance, both within and between LPAs; much guidance is extremely narrowly focused and evidently produced on an *ad hoc* or reactive basis; and target audiences are not always appreciated: material suitable for the general public, experienced architects/developers and the professional planning peer group being contained within the same publications (Chapman and Larkham, 1992, p. 23).

Box 12.2. Article 4 Direction for Gidea Park conservation area. (*Source*: London Borough of Havering, undated, p. 3)

Some relatively minor works do not normally require planning permission, but if widespread and carried out badly can have a cumulative and harmful effect on the environment ... Accordingly an Article 4 Direction has been made in the conservation area. It introduces two levels of control over permitted development.

CONTROL LEVEL ONE applies to all residential properties within the conservation area with the exception of properties fronting Eastern Avenue.

Planning permission is now required for

(a) the construction of dormer windows and roof alterations in roof slopes visible from a public highway
(b) the construction of a hardstanding for vehicles to the front and/or side of a house (including means of access to a highway).

CONTROL LEVEL TWO applies only to 1911 Competition/Exhibition housing groups, and later housing contributing to the group's identity.

Planning permission is now required for

(a) all enlargements, improvements and other alterations to a dwelling house (note: this includes dormers and roof alterations and other works such as window/door replacement, cladding and rendering)
(b) the construction of a hardstanding for vehicles to the front and/or side of a house
(c) the construction of a porch
(d) the construction of gates/fences/walls
(e) the formation of a means of access to a highway
(f) the painting of the exterior of a building (note: this does not affect maintenance or repainting in the same colour as existing).

Many LPA publications relating specifically to suburbs suffer from these problems and limitations. Many actually contain a mixture of such design guidance – often at a very detailed level – together with descriptions and analyses of area history, character and appearance; adopted planning standards and policies; and other educational material including definitions of relevant architectural terms. That for the Pinnerwood Park conservation area (London Borough of Harrow, 1990b) is a typical multi-function publication, in fact titled a 'policy statement' and containing numerous photographic and sketch illustrations, and some novel cartographic street surveys of key features. Its list of design-related policies is extensive (Box 12.3). It again shows the tensions regarding insistence on matching materials and finishes, but using subordinate designs; and the feeling that the

Box 12.3. Design-related policies for Pinnerwood Park. (*Source*: London Borough of Harrow, 1990*b*, pp. 55–56)

Policy 1   The Council will seek to ensure that all new development respects the character and layout of the area.

Policy 2   There will be a presumption against the demolition of buildings within the conservation area.

Policy 3   Proposals for new dwellings, and buildings other than those appropriate to, and used in association with, the existing dwelling, including the provision of new vehicular access, will normally be refused.

Policy 4   Proposals for infilling of the spaces between properties will normally be resisted.

Policy 5   Alterations which result in the loss of, or have a detrimental effect on, important features such as chimney[s] and roofscape[s] will be resisted.

Policy 6   Development which would result in the loss of, or damage to, significant garden trees will be resisted.

Policy 7   The bulk, height, position, size and detailed design of extensions should be sympathetic to the character and design of the existing buildings. Roof extensions, including the creation of mansard roofs, will not be acceptable, and the insertion of dormer windows and rooflights to the street and side elevations will be resisted.

Policy 8   The Council will encourage the retention of original design features, such as windows and doors, and where necessary will require the use of replica features in traditional materials in replacement and new works. Aluminium and uPVC replacement units will not normally be considered acceptable.

Policy 9   The painting of unpainted surfaces will not be acceptable.

Policy 10   In new works and replacement work, the Council will require that all materials, in particular brick and tile type and associated detailing, match the original building.

Policy 11   The Council will encourage the retention 'and use' of wicket fences, traditional gates, and close-boarded fences where possible, and will seek to control the hard surfacing of garden areas.

Policy 12   The Council will encourage statutory undertakers to retain traditional street furniture, for example post boxes, and reinstate appropriate furniture, such as telephone boxes, when the opportunity arises.

continued

Policy 13 The retention and reinstatement of grass verges will be encouraged.

Policy 14 Trees and shrub planting will be encouraged, particularly in the areas
identified in this document. Dead and diseased trees should be replaced
with appropriate species.

Policy 15 The trees and areas of woodland will be further protected by the creation
of additional Tree Preservation Orders where appropriate.

rear elevation is of lesser significance than front and side (figure 12.4). The desire
to control all aspects of development is taken to extreme in Havering's Gidea Park
conservation area. Here, regarding the 1911 and 1934 Competition and Exhibition
housing, the LPA will strongly resist rebuilding or demolition of houses:

> exceptions to this policy will generally only be favourably considered in the rare
> event of damage taking place requiring removal of a property on health or safety
> grounds. In such case the Council would expect a single replacement building of the
> same size and design as the original using renovated original materials or materials
> of the same colour and texture, and *in situ* structural components as far as possible.
> (London Borough of Havering, undated, p. 12)

The Brent policy in researching and promoting its residential design guides
(Box 12.4) is instructive in that it complies with the LPA's duty under the 1990
Planning (Listed Buildings and Conservation Areas) Act to prepare preservation
and enhancement schemes, and to bring these to the notice of residents. Even so,
this is still very much a traditional 'top-down' planning process.

Examination of design guidance reveals that there is a tension between the
desire of individuals to personalize their property, for a range of psychological
reasons, versus the evident desire on the part of LPAs to control and to impose
uniformity and conformity. The need for personalization is now increasingly
recognized in urban design approaches (e.g. Bentley *et al.*, 1985). This tension is
revealed in numerous small-scale conflicts of values and attitudes, including the
illustration of alterations deemed unsuitable by the now-defunct magazine
Traditional Homes as 'Mess of the Month'. Many LPA design guides, when
examined in detail, also reveal explicit guidance and policies designed to restrict
individual freedom of expression in urban built form, whether in the positioning,
design, architectural style, materials or even paint colour of new and altered
buildings (figure 12.5).

This actually reveals a tension unresolved in the under-developed aesthetic of
conservation:

• the suggestion that new construction (e.g. extensions and other alterations) be
physically distinct from the original, and be readily identifiable, so that the
historic identity and merit of the original remains clear. This appears to derive

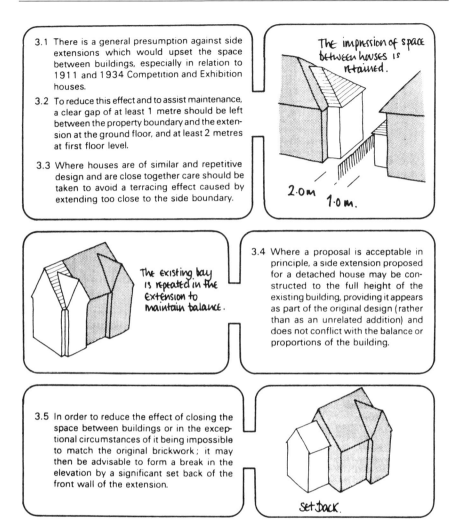

Figure 12.4. Example of local authority design guidance: implicit values and attitudes colouring advice on 'acceptability' of subordinate positioning of side extensions etc.

from SPAB guidelines, and may result in the new extensions being marginally set back, with a slightly different roofline, and using different materials (i.e. different brick colours); and

• the contrary position, clearly visible in many design guides, policy documents and in conditions attached to planning permissions (Larkham, 1996*b*, Appendix 3), that new work should match the existing structure in size, scale, details and materials. In many conservation areas, these policies mean that extensions are only visible through subtle differential weathering and traceable through planning files.

Box 12.4. Procedure for the preparation of residential conservation area design guides, Brent. (*Source:* London Borough of Brent, 1997, p. 27)

(1) Priority is given to those conservation areas under most immediate threat; particularly those from 'permitted development' rights.

(2) These areas are then surveyed in detail to find what features of each conservation area would most be missed and would need to be covered by an Article 4 Direction restricting 'permitted development' rights.

(3) These general principles of preservation are then embodied in a draft design guide for the area in question, which will also give guidance on the permissible designs of extensions to buildings and for consistent treatment to frontages to enhance the character of the area.

(4) A preliminary meeting is then held with the local residents' association for the area, detailing the key principles of the draft design guide and the areas which an Article 4 Direction may cover.

(5) Following this, all properties in the conservation area are leafleted, explaining how they can obtain an copy of the draft design guide. Also enclosed is a questionnaire asking them which controls they think the Council should exercise, e.g. whether they should control the replacement of windows, the painting of brickwork, etc. All residents will also be invited to a public meeting to be held during the consultation period . . .

(6) Following the results of the public meeting and the rest of the consultation process, a justification for the Direction, a finalised version of the design guide and Article 4 Direction are prepared and put to committee for approval.

(7) All properties within the conservation area are then leafleted on the effects of the additional controls. This practice is repeated every few years to ensure that all occupants are aware of these controls.

There is a further issue, which goes largely unremarked in planning policy, guidance and development control: and that is the lack of explicit recognition that

- area character and appearance may change markedly over time simply as a result of the weathering of raw new materials and the maturing of soft landscaping and planting schemes.

This was recognized in the earlier research by Whitehand and Larkham which focused deliberately on 'mature residential areas'. Examination of the growing body of local photographic history publications reveals the importance of such maturity to the originally harsh new suburban landscapes. Yet the choice of trees and shrubs is also subject to changing fashion and this, particularly applied to alien and fast-growing species such as the Leyland cypress (*x Cupressocyparis*

Figure 12.5. Example of local authority design guidance: the 'good' and 'bad' approach to controlling small-scale personalization (numbers refer to detailed textual guidance).

Figure 12.6. Impact of maturing planting on the suburban landscape (*Photograph*: P.J. Larkham, 1998)

leylandii) and the Chilean monkey-puzzle (*Araucaria araucana*), rapidly alters the character and appearance of areas (figure 12.6). The choice and planting of new species is hardly subject to control, a ready aspect of personalization. Virtually the only control is over the lopping or felling of trees with a Tree Preservation Order, or within a conservation area (which extends similar protection to trees).

Management in Residential Areas

Some findings from the earlier studies by Whitehand and Larkham, particularly the changes in schemes between original plans and actual development, are particularly relevant to the problem of management. The different roles of the agents active in the process, particularly applicant, architect and LPA, can be traced. For example, changes in the four residential study areas were closely associated with a change of applicant. Such changes were generally associated with the sale of the site, with planning permission, by an individual owner-occupier to a developer, or a conditional contract or option agreement between individual and developer, pending the acquisition of planning permission (Whitehand and Larkham, 1991*a*, p. 150).

For the same areas, the role of the LPA can be assessed by comparing the first application submitted with the first approval. In most cases, there was no change of applicant at this point. In the South-East areas, only one in two approved applications were the same as the original submission, with density being the most important single change. In contrast, for the two Midlands areas the figure was as high as seven out of eight. These facts suggest that LPA influence was much higher in the South East. However, much of the basis for this influence was not specified in formal plans. Indeed, none of the four LPAs had adopted Local Plans relating to the study areas by the end of the study period. In each area, the relevant formal plan for the greater part of the study period was a Town Map, in which primarily residential areas were differentiated only in terms of gross population densities calculated for areas much larger than the study area. More up-to-date documents existed for such matters as highways, parking and garden sizes; but most policies were non-statutory, sometimes difficult to access or even unwritten, in common with many other LPAs (Bruton and Nicholson, 1984). The majority of reasons given for refusing planning permission were site-specific, related to the circumstances of particular sites. Planning decisions were based, to a large extent, on the views of individual case officers. These views were strongly influenced by current practice within particular planning offices (Whitehand and Larkham, 1991*a*, p. 151).

It is clear from reviewing hundreds of planning files that there is little that could be described as 'management' of the urban landscape; nor, indeed, are there many developments that could justifiably be described as 'planned' outcomes (Whitehand, 1990*a*), since there is often considerable variation between original schemes and final development. Even within designated Conservation Areas, the effects of Local Plan documents have been quite small at the scale of the individual site (Whitehand and Larkham, 1991a). Yet these individual sites are the building-blocks of whole landscapes: the large-scale landscape change documented here suggests that policies are failing – where they even exist – because they are insufficiently site-specific.

In fact, if LPAs are judged by their actions in mature residential areas, then highway matters and development densities are almost inevitably seen as far higher priorities than the visual environment. The forms of developments, particularly their architectural styles, have tended to be afterthoughts, dealt with largely once battles over density and access have been concluded. Attempts by applicants to meet or overcome density and highway objections have often been at a cost to the urban landscape in terms of both the relationship between buildings and the survival of the mature trees and hedgerows so important in many residential Conservation Areas. As far as the urban landscape is concerned, there is a price to pay in lost cultural assets (Whitehand, 1990a; Whitehand et al., 1992).

The rather abstract concepts of townscape management and conservation are clearly replaced by that of profit on the part of developers, who often attempt to obtain different, more profitable, planning permissions once a site has been purchased (Whitehand and Larkham, 1991a, p. 152). On the part of the initiators, little overt thought is given to management, as development is often initiated by a change in the family life-cycle and consequent re-valuing of use values (Whitehand, 1990b). However, the likelihood of development occurring that is compatible with the surrounding area is greatest when private individuals undertake a small development in their garden, retaining either the original house or the new development for their own use: their vested interest in preserving amenity results in better development quality from many aspects. Likewise, local residents similarly consider amenity in general above principles of townscape management, as analysis of comments on various schemes shows (Larkham, 1990a). Lastly, LPAs clearly value administrative convenience above abstract management, as their reliance on easily-quantified density, parking and highway standards shows. Indeed, the dominant impression of the decision-making process leading to development (or non-development) is that it consists of a number of poorly co-ordinated activities in which expediency plays a major part (Whitehand, 1990a, p. 389).

MANAGEMENT IN SUBURBAN CONSERVATION AREAS

The management of suburban conservation areas commonly takes two forms: community-led and local authority-led. It is instructive to examine one case of each, particularly in the light of Sies' emphasis on the importance of local control in ensuring the retention of residential areas (Sies, 1997).

Local Authority-Led Management in Hall Green

Hall Green is a part of a large expanse of inter-war suburbia in south-east Birmingham. It is similar to its neighbouring areas of Acocks Green and Kings Heath. However, according to a local observer,

> what characterized the inter-war suburbanization of Hall Green was not only the great proportion of private housing but the quantity of green space remaining enclosed behind the new dwellings. Since 1945, however, further more intensive development has been a constant threat to this greenest of green suburbs. Large houses have been pulled down and replaced by groups of small townhouses or flats, and nurseries, sports grounds, unused areas behind gardens, and even long gardens themselves, have been targeted by developers. The fight to preserve Hall Green's character goes on unabated today. (Byrne, 1996, p. 8)

In short, the suburb itself is suffering from processes of intensification, as described elsewhere (Whitehand and Larkham, 1991*b*). But a small part of the area, School Road, has been designated as a conservation area.

School Road itself was constructed mainly by a single developer and consists of residential properties, a public house, a parade of shops and a group of almshouses. The houses have a distinct period character with bay windows and Tudor-style gables; there is also some Moderne-style detailing, such as 'sunburst' patterns in gates and doors, and a few curving bay windows (see figure 12.2). Although all of the housing is semi-detached, there are, according to Birmingham City Council (1992), four variations of size and design. The parade of shops is still at the centre of the community. The upper floors of these premises retain their mock-Tudor style, whilst the ground floors have modern fascia signs and advertisements.

The issues surrounding this designation even led to a feature article in *The Times*:

> Birmingham's aim is to wrap this arcadia in aspic by means of a conservation order, and all the signs are that it will manage to do so . . . If it does, then this may be the very first development of the period to be thus protected in this country. In practical terms it would mean that nothing in the designated area of about 150 homes could be added to or altered unless strictly in the style of the original . . . One immediate result of that would be to prevent any more of the bay windows disappearing as the softwood rots and the owners look for a cheaper replacement . . . School Road happens to be an excellent example of the genus, and the whole city has become so sensitive about conserving what is good that it is now doing so long before a desperate rearguard action is required. (Franks, 1988, p. 11)

The justification for designation, recalling that a conservation area must possess 'special' interest, is that this area is unusual in that it has remained largely unchanged since development: no infilling, few extensions or other alterations, and most buildings retain original period features.

The LPA has sought additional controls to retain this character:

although School Road has to a large extent retained its intrinsic character, some changes have taken place with the addition of storm porches, garages and the replacement of windows with metal or uPVC double glazing. Many of the shops have acquired large, garish and unsightly fascia signs. (Birmingham City Council, 1992, p. 1)

The LPA made an Article 4 Direction bringing under planning control various types of minor changes – e.g. replacing original steel-framed windows with uPVC – which are otherwise not controlled in the UK development control planning system. A six-month temporary Direction was made, while the Secretary of State was requested to make this a permanent Direction. However, approval was refused in December 1992 as the Secretary of State was 'not satisfied that a special case has been made for the withdrawal of permitted development rights' (Department of the Environment decision letter dated December 8, 1992). Consequently the Direction lapsed in May 1993.

No substantial explanation was given for the refusal, but the following points should be noted. First, the application for the Direction covered the whole of Hall Green Conservation Area, whereas the guidelines issued by the Department of the Environment state that the boundary of an area that is subject to such a Direction should be drawn selectively. Secondly, Hall Green contains a parade of shops. Advice given in government circulars on policy for conservation areas repeatedly emphasizes the need for local authorities to retain thriving commercial centres. It could be argued that, by placing a restrictive Direction on these premises, traders would be adversely financially affected. It is possible for the local authority to apply instead for an order controlling fascia signs and advertisements. Finally, the City Council did not mention any specific threat currently or potentially recognized.

The refusal of permission for this additional restriction on development within the conservation area rather dilutes the powers available to the LPA to effectively manage it, restraining development which might undermine the area's special interest. It is precisely these individually small-scale and usually uncontrolled changes which are seen to damage many conservation areas at present (English Historic Towns Forum, 1992).

However, the brick-built, flat-roofed Moderne-styled pub within the conservation area was the first building to be listed by the new Minister, Tony Banks, in mid-1997. Identified as a rare survival by CAMRA (the Campaign for Real Ale), the Three Magpies had been sold twice in the previous decade, and its new owners had applied for permission to knock the three original bars into one and make further alterations. English Heritage had twice recommended its listing to the previous Minister, Virginia Bottomley, but she had twice rejected this advice (Kennedy, 1997).

Hall Green, an area of middle-class semi-detached houses originally priced at about £700 (£65,000 in the mid-1990s) shows an example of continuity despite evident lack of control at the local, community, level. That continuity, particularly in the lack of changes to architectural details which contributes to the area's 'special' character, is largely a result of the persistence of original owners into the 1980s. However, as they die or move, incomers with greatly different require- ments and expectations have greatly increased the pressures for change. Central government has not supported the LPA in resisting these pressures.

Community-Led Management in Hampstead Garden Suburb

Hampstead Garden Suburb began to develop after the acquisition of 243 acres of land in March 1906. The best-known development here is by the Arts and Crafts architect Raymond Unwin, following Garden City principles and empowered by the 1906 Hampstead Garden Suburb Act. Further development took place in the inter-war period under the architect J.C.S. Soutar, but lacked the qualities of the earlier layouts and styles. A significant feature for the purposes of this chapter is that the Estate remained largely in single control throughout much of the post-war period, although there has been a complex interplay between charitable trusts and property companies. From the outset there have been formal residents' groups on the Estate which, by March 1911, had 1115 members; the Association continues today.

Economic pressures and changing ownership produced some neglect and decay, principally in the 1930s to 1950s.

> With new commercial landlords and virtually no planning controls, the appearance of the Suburb suffered. The evidence is still with us – odd and ugly dormers, plate glass windows, jarring colour schemes, box-like extensions, over-paved gardens, neglected back lands, mutilated trees and plastic fences. Mercifully, there are only a few new buildings as testimony to developers' expedience and '*laissez-faire*' landlords. (Lester, 1977, p. 45)

A special clause in the Leasehold Reform Act (1967) allowed new landlords to institute a Scheme of Management; although tenants were now able to purchase their property, this Scheme allowed stronger environmental management. The Suburb was designated as a conservation area in December 1968 and part was graded as an 'outstanding' conservation area (important for purposes of receiving governmental financial aid) in the mid-1970s.

The various residents' bodies and management trusts have been instrumental in securing the character of this suburb. Various buildings were Listed (i.e. given special protection) through the intervention of the architectural historian Sir Nikolaus Pevsner, a resident, in the early 1960s:

> I went to the then Senior Investigator at the Ministry of Housing and Local Government, Mr Garton, and could without effort persuade him that some listing ought to be done at once. To list the whole Suburb was out of the question – conservation areas did not then exist – and so one fine day in 1961 (I think it was 1961) Mr Garton and I wandered through the Suburb and marked for listing a limited number of outstanding houses strategically placed so that any likely

destructive move on the grand scale which was, so we thought, to be expected would find itself up against one of our listed buildings . . . (Pevsner, 1977, p. 4)

Few other residential areas can boast of such influential residents!

Then, in 1970, the New Hampstead Garden Suburb Trust Limited, with financial support from the recent purchaser of the Estate, commissioned the planning consultants Shankland Cox & Associates to carry out a conservation study of the area, which was published as a 146-page document in 1971 and formed the basis of negotiations with the LPA to form a local plan for the conservation area. It is unlikely that its own resources would have enabled the LPA to commission such eminent consultants to produce such a thorough study.

The study involved a character analysis of the area, an examination of then-current development pressures and the attitudes of residents, a series of short-term action recommendations, and brief long-term plans. Implementation of these proposals was discussed, and important factors here were seen to be a consultative procedure by the LPA, the management of property by landlords through restrictive covenants and the Scheme of Management, and the contribution of the residents and voluntary groups. However, the report stopped short of physical design specifications, although it discussed 'architectural design guidelines' at some length. It was not well received by the residents: after a public presentation, the Secretary of the Residents Association wrote 'regretting the bad manners of some who had attended the meeting, and criticizing strongly the shape of the Study in not distinguishing between immediate and long-term proposals, and in the use of planning shorthand or jargon (confusing to many people)' (quoted by Ikin, 1990, p. 134).

A last local initiative is the design study carried out in part of the Suburb by the Hampstead Garden Suburb Design Study Group, a group of local architects 'and others' in the mid-1970s. This is a well-illustrated and very detailed treatment of original design, maintenance and adaptation, having many of the characteristics of LPA-produced design guidance. Yet it conveys greater depth of knowledge and research than LPA resources usually permit; and, being produced by a local group – and published to mark the Queen's Silver Jubilee – it perhaps gains more immediacy and credibility than LPA publications, which may be seen as unduly interfering or constraining individual owners.

One of the long-standing problems of the Suburb has been its fragmented ownership (detailed by Ikin, 1990). It was concern over this which brought a Scheme of Management in 1974. The operation of such a Scheme, including the bringing-together of all covenants by c.1990, allowed a consistent local-level guidance for planning issues (Miller and Gray, 1992, chapter 10). Miller, an architect-planner and the longest-serving Director of the Hampstead Garden Suburb Trust, feels that 'a Scheme of Management, if professionally operated, provides a more comprehensive means of securing area conservation than does the local authority procedure under the planning acts, even with the benefit of full Article 4 Direction powers' (personal comm., 1996).

Many of the substantial houses in the wealthier part of the Suburb have long been listed, but it was not until late 1996 that, in one move, over 500 artisans' flats and cottages in the 'artisans' quarter' of the Suburb were listed. According to the then Minister, Lord Inglewood, these were 'arguably [the suburb's] most successful architecture' and where 'the chief interest of this social housing experiment lies'. But the original artisan community has long gone, and both one-bedroom flats and small cottages, in early 1997, commanded prices in excess of £200,000 (Baber, 1997).

This residential area is atypical in its national importance in twentieth-century planning and architectural history – which the Hall Green area certainly is not – and in the social and educational characteristics of its current residents. It is clear that the 'self-help' approach of locals and the management trusts have done much to secure the future of this area. It is also clear that some change must occur, but that its impact should be minimized; and design solutions and maintenance programmes to achieve these aims have been suggested. Hampstead is, therefore, a good example of community-level involvement and active townscape management, but is an atypical, wealthy and educated, élite community. Hall Green, however, is not; landholding is fragmented, no specific design guidance exists, no specific residents' group exists (the Hall Green residents' group covers a much wider geographical area), and tighter development controls have been refused at a national level. Conservation area designation alone does convey extra powers for the LPA, but these remain limited. Despite designation, the future for Hall Green as a managed conservation area is not promising.

Nevertheless, the general use of tools of aesthetic control such as design guidance and detailed Development Plan policies suggests that concern for managing the character and appearance of a wide range of suburban areas is now widespread. If such tools prove effective in influencing owners and designers, it is with them, rather than the specialized approach of conservation, that the future of English suburban form lies. However, the ability of LPAs to formulate effective guidance would be improved with a better knowledge of the nature and scale of changes in suburban areas.

It is clear that conservation is one aspect of wider townscape management, which requires the active co-operation of owners, designers, developers and LPAs together with explicit policies and guidance, and the political will and resources to enforce decisions where necessary.

CONCLUSION: CONSERVATION AND MANAGEMENT – OR MIS-MANAGEMENT

In the post-war period in the UK, further suburban growth has, to some extent, been curbed, particularly by the designation of green belts. Most recently there has been intense debate about sustainability, in particular the concept of the 'compact city' and its practicability. The tight constraints of green belts, in many places, has added to pressures for change to existing suburbs. The impact of sustainability – in its various forms – on suburban forms and life-styles is still to come. However, the story of changing suburbs has, in some respects, become more about changes to existing suburbs than about creating new suburbs: particularly adaptation to current fashions, including private cars, central heating and double-glazing; and intensive re-use of open spaces, gardens and, even, house sites. This is likely to be even more the case in the future. Increasingly the question is what to do with the legacy of buildings and layouts that have been inherited from past periods of suburban development.

Answers to this question can be given through concepts of urban landscape management. This chapter has sought to develop this concept using data from a series of research projects in urban morphology, planning, conservation and aesthetic control. The results of this investigation do not pretend to be typical or prescriptive, but they do shed light on a relatively little-regarded aspect of suburbia. The institutionalized UK planning system, wherein development rights have been nationalized and a process of planning applications has been in operation for half a century, is itself a system of management. This chapter has examined two facets of this: design guidance and conservation areas. In terms of what is happening to suburbs, particularly those to which society has attached special significance through conservation area designation, the picture is disappointing.

It is clear that, in practice, the operation of the UK's bureaucratic development control system is short-term and short-sighted. It is not equipped to consider urban landscape management nor large-scale urban design considerations: rather, it concentrates upon small-scale design issues. Many development proposals are amended by the system to mitigate the worst design proposals, but this tends to result in mediocrity rather than in the encouragement of good design (Larkham, 1995). Such amendments may also considerably prolong the development process.

The extensive nature of the process of change, particularly within those mature residential areas – and more recent suburbs – officially protected (to some degree) by conservation area status, is given little heed. Area character is rarely addressed thoroughly, in either historical or morphological terms, either before designation or in any regular review process. The amount of relatively small-scale change is rarely monitored (Larkham, 1990b). Without this appreciation of changing character, policy development remains weak and, often, insufficiently robust to withstand challenge at Appeal by a determined developer. Only in very recent years have there been any significant attempts to study area history, development, form, character and appearance on a systematic basis, and to use these data in the formulation of robust management policies ranging from area-wide to site-specific. Despite the well-developed bureaucratic development control system, and the conservation area system designed to protect the 10,000 or so designated areas, urban landscape management in England over the past three decades can largely be characterized as mis-management.

Despite recent official guidance (DoE/DNH, 1994; English Heritage, 1995), the UK system is still largely a 'top-down' system. There are significant tensions between local populations and government; and also between local government (the LPA) and central government. However, such tensions are inevitable given the desire to retain the 'special' nature of conservation designations versus what appears to be the major motivation of occupants, increased status and/or increased property value. And, as informed and wider public tastes change over time, there will be developments in the nature of what is felt appropriate to conserve. Birmingham led in conserving 1930s suburbia in the late 1980s; this is now generally accepted. Where next for suburban conservation?

Owing to the lack of a British tradition of living in central urban areas, suburbia is where the bulk of the population lives. From a range of surveys, the suburban ideal of individual houses and gardens in an arcadian setting with mature trees and planting remains the ideal for many people. We should follow the logic of our collective decision to protect certain of these suburban landscapes and develop the tools to do so effectively. These tools will almost certainly operate best at a very local level, as Sies (1997) argued with US examples. The complexity of current statutory regulation and coercion, and non-statutory local 'guidance', have clearly led to unresolved tensions and contradictions.

NOTES

1. This chapter is the definitive publication of ideas developed in joint publications with Jeremy Whitehand, Christine Carr and Terry Slater; I am grateful to them and to colleagues in the Urban Morphology Research Group for comments.

2. The 'planning gestation period' is defined as the time-lag between initial application and approval of the development that took place or, in cases where no scheme was implemented, the most recent planning decision.

REFERENCES

Baber, P. (1997) Credit where credit is due. *Planning Week*, January 9, p. 11.
Bentley, I., Alcock, A., Murrain, P., McGlynn, S. and Smith, G. (1985) *Responsive Environments: A Manual for Designers*. London: Architectural Press.
Binney, M. (1994) Des res, cons area: watch it come down. *The Times*, March 1, p. 18.
Birmingham City Council (1992) *Article 4 Direction: School Road Conservation Area, Hall Green: Reasons for the Making of the Direction*. Birmingham: Birmingham City Council (unpublished).
Brent, London Borough of (1997) *Brent Conservation Handbook*. London: London Borough of Brent.
Bruton, M. and Nicholson, D.J. (1984) The use of non-statutory local planning instruments in development control and Section 36 Appeals: Part 1. *Journal of Planning and Environment Law*, August, pp. 552–565.
Byrne, M. (1996) *Hall Green* [in the Archive Photographs series]. Stroud: Chalford.
Chapman, D.W. and Larkham, P.J. (1992) *Discovering the Art of Relationship: Urban*

Design, Aesthetic Control and Design Guidance. Research Paper no. 9. Birmingham: Faculty of the Built Environment, University of Central England.

Department of the Environment (1980) *Development Control: Policy and Practice*. Circular 22/80. London: HMSO.

Department of the Environment (1985) *Aesthetic Control*. Circular 31/85. London: HMSO.

Department of the Environment and Department of National Heritage (1994) *Planning and the Historic Environment*. Planning Policy Guidance Note 15. London: HMSO.

Duncan, J. and Duncan, N. (1984) A cultural analysis of urban residential landscapes in North America: the case of the anglophile élite, in Agnew, J., Mercer, T. and Sopher, D. (eds.) *The City in Cultural Context*. London: Allen and Unwin.

English Heritage (1995) *Conservation Area Practice*. Policy Note (second edition). London: English Heritage.

English Historic Towns Forum (1992) *Townscape in Trouble*. Bath: EHTF.

Franks, A. (1988) The street they froze in time. *The Times*, July 15, p. 11.

Harrow, London Borough of (1990*a*) *West Towers, Pinner, Conservation Area: Policy Statement*. London: Planning Division, London Borough of Harrow.

Harrow, London Borough of (1990*b*) *Pinnerwood Park Estate Conservation Area: Policy Statement*. London: Planning Division, London Borough of Harrow.

Havering, London Borough of (undated) *Gidea Park Conservation Area, Romford: Planning Policies and Design Guide*. London: London Borough of Havering.

Ikin, C.W. (1990) *Hampstead Garden Suburb: Dreams and Realities*. London: New Hampstead Garden Suburb Trust and Hampstead Garden Suburb Residents Association.

Jones, A.N. (1991) The Management of Residential Townscapes. Unpublished PhD thesis. Birmingham: School of Geography, University of Birmingham.

Jones, A.N. and Larkham, P.J. (1993) *The Character of Conservation Areas*. London: Royal Town Planning Institute.

Kennedy, M. (1997) Large, squat, brown and listed. *The Guardian*, June 2, p. 5.

Knox, P. (1992) The packaged landscapes of post-suburban America, in Whitehand, J.W.R. and Larkham, P.J. (eds.) *Urban Landscapes: International Perspectives*. London: Routledge, pp. 207–226.

Larkham, P.J. (1990*a*) Conservation and the management of historical townscapes, in Slater, T.R. (ed.) *The Built Form of Western Cities*. Leicester: Leicester University Press, pp. 349–369.

Larkham, P.J. (1990*b*) Development control information and planning research. *Local Government Studies*, Vol. 16, No. 2, pp. 1–7.

Larkham, P.J. (1995) Urban landscape management and mis-management in England, in Moudon, A.V. and Attoe, W. (eds.) *Urban Design: Reshaping Our Cities*. Seattle: University of Washington.

Larkham, P.J. (1996*a*) Designating conservation areas: patterns in time and space. *Journal of Urban Design*, Vol. 1, No. 3, pp. 315–327.

Larkham, P.J. (1996*b*) *Conservation and the City*. London: Routledge.

Larkham, P.J. and Chapman, D.W. (1996) Article 4 Directions and development control: planning myths, present uses and future possibilities. *Journal of Environmental Planning and Management*, Vol. 39, No. 1, pp. 5–19.

Lennox, M. (1997) Satisfying a growing demand for nostalgia. *Birmingham Post*, March 7, p. 27.

Lester, A.W. (1977) *Hampstead Garden Suburb: the Case and Appreciation of its Architectural Heritage*. London: Hampstead Garden Suburb Design Study Group.

Llewellyn-Davies, Weeks, Forestier-Walker and Bor (1976) *Design Guidance Survey*. London: Department of the Environment.

Long, H. (1993) *The Edwardian House*. Manchester: Manchester University Press.

Lowenthal, D. (1985) *The Past is a Foreign Country*. Cambridge: Cambridge University Press.

Lowenthal, D. (1990) Forging the past, in Jones, M. (ed.) *Fake? The Art of Deception*. London: British Museum Publications.

Lowenthal, D. and Binney, M. (eds.) (1981) *Our Past Before Us: Why do we Save it?* London: Temple Smith.

Meinig, D.W. (ed.) (1979) *The Interpretation of Ordinary Landscapes*. New York: Oxford University Press.

Miller, M. and Gray, A.S. (1992) *Hampstead Garden Suburb*. Chichester: Phillimore.

Millichap, D. (1989) Conservation areas and *Steinberg* – the Inspectorate's response. *Journal of Planning and Environment Law*, July, pp. 499–504.

Mynors, C. (1984) Conservation areas: protecting the familiar and cherished local scene. *Journal of Planning and Environment Law*, March, pp. 144–157; April, pp. 235–247.

Pevsner, N. (1977) Foreword, in Lester, A.W. (1977) *Hampstead Garden Suburb: the Case and Appreciation of its Architectural Heritage*. London: Hampstead Garden Suburb Design Study Group.

Saunders, M. (1981) Metroland: half-timbering and other souvenirs in the outer London suburbia, in Lowenthal, D. and Binney, M. (eds.) *Our Past Before Us: Why do we Save it?* London: Temple Smith.

Shankland Cox & Associates (1971) *Hampstead Garden Suburb: a Conservation Study*. London: Shankland Cox.

Sies, M.C. (1997) Paradise retained: an analysis of persistence in planned, exclusive suburbs, 1880–1980. *Planning Perspectives*, Vol. 12, pp. 165–191.

Tarn, J.N. (1975) The Derbyshire heritage: the conservation of ordinariness. *Town Planning Review*, Vol. 46, No. 4, pp. 451–465.

The Times (1997) The temporary wood village that put down roots. *The Times*, August 14, p. 10.

Whitehand, J.W.R. (1988) The changing urban landscape: the case of London's high-class residential fringe. *Geographical Journal*, Vol. 154, Part 3, pp. 351–366.

Whitehand, J.W.R. (1989) Development pressure, development control and suburban change: case studies in south-east England. *Town Planning Review*, Vol. 60, No. 4, pp. 403–421.

Whitehand, J.W.R. (1990*a*) Townscape management: ideal and reality, in Slater, T.R. (ed.) *The Built Form of Western Cities*. Leicester: Leicester University Press, pp. 370–393.

Whitehand, J.W.R. (1990*b*) Makers of the residential landscape: conflict and change in outer London. *Transactions of the Institute of British Geographers*, NS Vol. 15, No. 1, pp. 87–101.

Whitehand, J.W.R. and Larkham, P.J. (1991*a*) Suburban cramming and development control. *Journal of Property Research*, Vol. 8, No. 2, pp. 147–159.

Whitehand, J.W.R. and Larkham, P.J. (1991*b*) Housebuilding in the back garden: reshaping suburban townscapes in the Midlands and South East England. *Area*, Vol. 23, No. 1, pp. 57–65.

Whitehand, J.W.R., Larkham, P.J. and Jones, A.N. (1992) The changing suburban landscape in post-war England, in Whitehand, J.W.R. and Larkham, P.J. (eds) *Urban Landscapes: International Perspectives*. London: Routledge, pp. 227–265.

Index